The Diasporic Canon
American Anthologies of Contemporary Italian Poetry 1945-2015

LEGENDA

LEGENDA is the Modern Humanities Research Association's book imprint for new research in the Humanities. Founded in 1995 by Malcolm Bowie and others within the University of Oxford, Legenda has always been a collaborative publishing enterprise, directly governed by scholars. The Modern Humanities Research Association (MHRA) joined this collaboration in 1998, became half-owner in 2004, in partnership with Maney Publishing and then Routledge, and has since 2016 been sole owner. Titles range from medieval texts to contemporary cinema and form a widely comparative view of the modern humanities, including works on Arabic, Catalan, English, French, German, Greek, Italian, Portuguese, Russian, Spanish, and Yiddish literature. Editorial boards and committees of more than 60 leading academic specialists work in collaboration with bodies such as the Society for French Studies, the British Comparative Literature Association and the Association of Hispanists of Great Britain & Ireland.

The MHRA encourages and promotes advanced study and research in the field of the modern humanities, especially modern European languages and literature, including English, and also cinema. It aims to break down the barriers between scholars working in different disciplines and to maintain the unity of humanistic scholarship. The Association fulfils this purpose through the publication of journals, bibliographies, monographs, critical editions, and the MHRA Style Guide, and by making grants in support of research. Membership is open to all who work in the Humanities, whether independent or in a University post, and the participation of younger colleagues entering the field is especially welcomed.

ALSO PUBLISHED BY THE ASSOCIATION

Critical Texts
Tudor and Stuart Translations • *New Translations* • *European Translations*
MHRA Library of Medieval Welsh Literature

MHRA Bibliographies
Publications of the Modern Humanities Research Association

The Annual Bibliography of English Language & Literature
Austrian Studies
Modern Language Review
Portuguese Studies
The Slavonic and East European Review
Working Papers in the Humanities
The Yearbook of English Studies

www.mhra.org.uk
www.legendabooks.com

TRANSCRIPT

Transcript publishes books about all kinds of imagining across languages, media and cultures: translations and versions, inter-cultural and multi-lingual writing, illustrations and musical settings, adaptation for theatre, film, TV and new media, creative and critical responses. We are open to studies of any combination of languages and media, in any historical moments, and are keen to reach beyond Legenda's traditional focus on modern European languages to embrace anglophone and world cultures and the classics. We are interested in innovative critical approaches: we welcome not only the most rigorous scholarship and sharpest theory, but also modes of writing that stretch or cross the boundaries of those discourses.

www.legendabooks.com/series/transcript

TRANSCRIPT

1. *Adapting the Canon: Mediation, Visualization, Interpretation*, edited by Ann Lewis and Silke Arnold-de Simine
2. *Adapted Voices: Transpositions of Céline's Voyage au bout de la nuit and Queneau's Zazie dans le métro*, by Armelle Blin-Rolland
3. *Zola and the Art of Television: Adaptation, Recreation, Translation*, by Kate Griffiths
4. *Comparative Encounters between Artaud, Michaux and the Zhuangzi: Rationality, Cosmology and Ethics*, by Xiaofan Amy Li
5. *Minding Borders: Resilient Divisions in Literature, the Body and the Academy*, edited by Nicola Gardini, Adriana Jacobs, Ben Morgan, Mohamed-Salah Omri and Matthew Reynolds
6. *Memory Across Borders: Nabokov, Perec, Chamoiseau*, by Sara-Louise Cooper
7. *Erotic Literature in Adaptation and Translation*, edited by Johannes D. Kaminski
8. *Translating Petrarch's Poetry: L'Aura del Petrarca from the Quattrocento to the 21st Century*, edited by Carole Birkan-Berz, Guillaume Coatalen and Thomas Vuong
9. *Making Masud Khan: Psychoanalysis, Empire and Modernist Culture*, by Benjamin Poore
10. *Prismatic Translation*, edited by Matthew Reynolds
11. *The Patient, the Impostor and the Seducer: Medieval European Literature in Hebrew*, by Tovi Bibring
12. *Reading Dante and Proust by Analogy*, by Julia Caterina Hartley
13. *The First English Translations of Molière: Drama in Flux 1663-1732*, by Suzanne Jones
14. *After Clarice: Reading Lispector's Legacy in the Twenty-First Century*, edited by Adriana X. Jacobs and Claire Williams
15. *Uruguayan Theatre in Translation: Theory and Practice*, by Sophie Stevens
16. *Hamlet Translations: Prisms of Cultural Encounters across the Globe*, edited by Márta Minier and Lily Kahn
17. *The Foreign Connection: Writings on Poetry, Art and Translation*, by Jamie McKendrick
18. *Poetics, Performance and Politics in French and Italian Renaissance Comedy*, by Lucy Rayfield

The Diasporic Canon

American Anthologies of Contemporary Italian Poetry 1945–2015

❖

Marta Arnaldi

LEGENDA
Transcript 20
Modern Humanities Research Association
2022

Published by Legenda
an imprint of the Modern Humanities Research Association
Salisbury House, Station Road, Cambridge CB1 2LA

ISBN 978-1-78188-674-8

First published 2022

Copy-Editor: Dr Amanda Wrigley

CONTENTS

For Nicola Gardini

ACKNOWLEDGEMENTS

The research project from which this book originated was made possible by a Doctoral Award from the Arts and Humanities Research Council, an Oxford-Scatcherd European Scholarship, and a McHughen-Greschner bursary from Magdalen College, University of Oxford. To these funding bodies and benefactors, I remain deeply grateful.

I am indebted to my DPhil supervisor, Nicola Gardini, whose masterly writing and imaginative views have enriched my understanding of Italian origins, American culture, and academia; to my graduate college Magdalen; to my current colleges, St Anne's and The Queen's College; and to the Sub-Faculty of Italian at Oxford, especially to Simon Gilson, Francesca Southerdern, Giuseppe Stellardi, and Emanuela Tandello. To Martin McLaughlin, who has accompanied me on this journey from departure to destination, I owe an immense debt. With warmth and wisdom, he is to me more than a teacher and a mentor.

I am grateful to Magdalen College Library, Oxford, for generously funding the purchase of many of the poetry anthologies analysed in this monograph; the Taylor Institution Library at Oxford, with special thanks to Helen Buchanan and Clare Hills-Nova; New Directions Publishing, New York, in the person of Tynan Kogane; the Imperial War Museum, Duxford; the British Library, London; and the Beinecke Rare Book and Manuscript Library at Yale. A huge thank-you to Anne Chesher, Deputy Librarian at Magdalen College Library, for making the completion of this book possible; and to Tessa Shaw and Sarah Arkle at The Queen's College Library for helping me reproduce the visual poems examined here.

Special thanks to the people who read or discussed with me part or all of the manuscript and contributed in important ways to its diasporic design: Jacob Blakesley, Luigi Bonaffini, Charles Burdett, Peter Carravetta, Tyler Fisher, Charles Forsdick, Maria Antonietta Grignani, Peter Hainsworth, Gëzim Hajdari, Geraldine Hazbun, Daniela La Penna, Gianfranca Lavezzi, Chiara Marvaldi, Patrick McGuinness, Jaime McKendrick, Pietro Montorfani, Simon Park, Joseph Perricone, Martin Puchner, Matthew Reynolds, Stephen Romer, Catriona Seth, Beatrice Sica, Wes Williams, and Diego Zancani. A special thank-you to Reinier van Straten for helping me conceptualise, and believe in, this project, and for sharing with me the joy and challenges of living in translation.

I express my gratitude to the editors, artists, translators, and heirs who gave me permission to reproduce their (or their relatives') work: Diana Al-Hadid, Luigi Ballerini, Geoffrey Brock, Vittoria Contini, Jonathan Galassi, Thomas Harrison, Roberto Masnata, Maurizio Nannucci, Lamberto Pignotti, Thomas Powell, Sarenco, and Paul Vangelisti; and to Marzia D'Amico and Nicola Gardini for putting me in contact with some of these artists. To Nicola, I am especially grateful for allowing me to use his beautiful painting 'Two' as a moving cover image for this volume, and for helping me find paths, orbits, and destinations.

The book has benefitted greatly from the publishing skills of Graham Nelson, Legenda's managing editor; the thorough comments of anonymous peer reviewers; the meticulous copy-editing of Charlotte Wathey and Amanda Wrigley; the professional work of Anna J. Davies, who compiled the index; and the editorial sensitivity of Matthew Reynolds, General Editor of Legenda's Transcript series, where *The Diasporic Canon* has found a home. Thank you for the rigour and perceptivity with which you have treated my words.

Above all, and beyond words, I would like to thank my family and friends in Italy and England, in particular Diana and John, and my parents Chiara and Gianpiero. Without their love, this book would not be. 'Oxford, stupendo nome che, a quel tempo, per me apparteneva ancora alla Grande Storia del mondo. A quel tempo, neanche avrei osato segnarlo sul piccolo libro dei miei sogni, quel nome...' (Nicola Gardini).

M.A., Oxford, November 2020

NOTE ON CONVENTIONS

References to the primary sources of this study, i.e. English-language anthologies of contemporary Italian poetry published in the US between 1945 and 2015, are given in small capitals as a marker for the reader. These poetry anthologies are quoted by the surname of the editor and date of publication only, so: POGGIOLI 1948. A chronological list of these anthologies with full bibliographical details appears in Part 1 of the Appendix.

Quotations from primary sources are given in the English language, even in the case of the poems' titles and lines (which were originally written in Italian). This choice is coherent with the comparative perspective of this study as well as with the nature of its translated materials.

Translations, generally of prose and critical sources, are mine, unless otherwise stated.

The book includes a quadripartite Appendix providing information about the North American anthologies of contemporary Italian poetry published in the US and, where relevant, in Canada in the period examined (1945–2015); the structure and features of the anthologies analysed, including the most frequently anthologised poets; and the translators featuring in the anthologies. Part 4 of the Appendix presents a transcription and translation of Ennio Contini's letter to Ezra Pound, which is discussed in Chapter 5.

The Bibliography is divided into two parts: 'Primary Literature' and 'Secondary Literature'. The 'Primary Literature' section is intended as a list, in alphabetical order, of the creative works (poems, novels, etc.) and of the literary anthologies either quoted throughout the book or linked to this study. The 'Secondary Literature' section includes anthologies of Italian poetry and anthologies of American poetry published in their original languages. The Appendix, which focuses on North American poetry anthologies only, does not replace the function of the Bibliography. As a result, several works listed in the Appendix also appear in the Bibliography, but not vice versa. For example, Marguerite Caetani's *Anthology of New Italian Writers* (1950) is quoted in the Appendix in its shortest form (CAETANI 1950), but in the Bibliography it is referenced in the usual fashion: Caetani, Marguerite, ed, *An Anthology of New Italian Writers* (New York: New Directions, 1950). This duplication is intentional and reflects my attempt to be as rigorous as possible in the compilation of the lists of the works consulted.

INTRODUCTION

'Through the Fog of Another Alphabet'

> It's my skin listens, flayed to the twilight,
> searching for my voice through the fog
> of another alphabet.
>
> — GËZIM HAJDARI[1]

This book offers the first history of a national literary canon in another language and country. It investigates the ways in which contemporary Italian poetry was accommodated within the American literary and cultural system through the appearance of anthologies of varying importance and size.[2] It examines fifty English-language collections published in the US, from 1945 to the present, selected for their significance from a corpus of eighty-six titles, including journal publications in the form of complete issues and exhibition catalogues. These spatial and temporal boundaries have been set both for practical and theoretical reasons. Nearly seventy-five per cent of the anthologies published in English in the period considered were distributed by American publishers, whereas around twenty-five per cent were published in the UK. In addition, through the Marshall Plan, the end of the Second World War marked the beginning of a close relationship between Italy and the US on both a cultural and political level.[3] So far, critics have focused on the influence of American culture on Italian language and literature on the one hand, and, on the other, on the evolution of Italian American literature resulting from the Great Migration period, 1870–1924.[4] As yet there is no systematic study of the forms and impact of translated Italian poetry across the Atlantic in the twentieth and twenty-first centuries. It is this gap that this book aims to fill.

A poetry anthology is a 'prismatic', stratified entity.[5] Realised thanks to the collective efforts of editors, publishers, poets, and translators, the poetry collections analysed here were hidden within the pages of unknown journals, came out as special issues of literary reviews, took the form of exhibition catalogues, or stood out as institutional publications, particularly when promoted by established university presses. They could be monolingual (when the poems appeared in English translation only), bilingual (when the original was provided), trilingual (in the case of dialect anthologies), or multilingual, their poems being part of anthologies of European literature or else originally written in more than one language. As far as the content is concerned, they could be historical, when their temporal focus spans several decades; comprehensive, when they do not distinguish between male and female poets; single-sex, when they feature poetry by women only; or thematic, when they concentrate on specific currents, poetic schools, authors, or themes.[6] Structurally, they can be part of verse-only collections, include visual and concrete poems, or contribute to heterogeneous projects which encompass prose texts, essays, sketches, and paintings. This book analyses all these anthological modes, categories, and genres in order to evaluate the impact of various contemporaneous publications on the canon at large; but, owing to to their peculiar audience and characteristics, textbooks have not been considered.

Of the range of approaches offered by anthology studies as a discipline, this analysis is compiler-oriented.[7] Recent articles on the forms of the Italian canon in English have examined translational techniques and their sociocultural implications on the target literature, rather than on the editor's creative role.[8] By contrast, this study explores the potential of the anthologist as a writer, thus investigating the meanings, both transcultural and aesthetic, of his/her choices.[9] The evolution of a profoundly different canon from the domestic Italian one is a consequence, as well as proof, of these anthologies' institutional and artistic value. At the same time, the synergy among editors, poets, translators, and visual artists — who often happened to be the same individuals — provided the necessary fluidity to discuss the series of cultural transactions, historical anticipations of later developments in Italy, and paradoxes that characterised the transplantation of Italian lyric into the American context.

The idea of looking at the Italian poetic canon from a decentred perspective, i.e. outside Italy's national boundaries, was prompted by the intuition that literary canons have a horizontal as well as a vertical dimension. Through the medium of translation, they travel across space as well as through time, affecting the way we shape, respond to, and resist the society we live in. From this suprageographical perspective, international anthologies of poetry in translation prove to be 'the most enlightening and memorable [way] of transmitting culture [...] internationally' as they create 'a meaning and value greater than the sum of meanings and values of the individual items taken in isolation', or within their indigenous contexts.[10] Together with these poetic depositories, 'concepts of literature' and 'generic classifications' changed too, while 'the discrete principles underlying collections of all kinds of literature have become increasingly heterogeneous and flexible'.[11] Located at the intersection of translating and anthologising, these anthologies are not 'a mere subclass of anthologies of untranslated literature' but rather a compelling manifesto of today's mobility.[12]

This extraterritorial or, if one prefers, 'eccentric' standpoint found nourishment in works published both within and outside the field of Italian studies,[13] from the thought-provoking issue of the review *Nuova Corrente*, edited by Damiano Sinfonico and Stefano Verdino in 2014, to Homi Bhabha's and Jahan Ramazani's transnational theories.[14] This perspective, whilst being highly stimulating and innovative, demanded a considerable conceptual and historical effort, which presented me with a series of challenges: writing a history of the reception of Italian lyric in the US despite being an Italian(ist); unearthing and sifting massive amounts of material, often difficult to get hold of and consult; and developing a methodology that could encompass the variety and quantity of the primary sources.

In devising this theoretical framework, I found a pertinent paradigm in comparative critical studies, a discipline that 'constitutes itself through comparison (implicit or explicit) with other critical practices in other geographical and cultural locations'.[15] As Matthew Reynolds, Mohamed-Salah Omri, and Ben Morgan have put it, 'to write comparative criticism is [...] to be aware of yourself as participating in the construction of one among many possible literary and cultural worlds'; it is an act of critical diversity.[16] Especially when focusing on anthologies of translated poetry (a plural, multiactor object by definition), any critical act 'needs to be aware of itself as selecting some texts among many possible others; as adopting some tactics rather than others, in order to represent those texts in one language (or some languages) rather than others'.[17] The term 'comparative' is all the more important here in that two nations (the US and Italy), two literary traditions (the American and the Italian), and multiple languages (English, Italian, and many dialects from the Italian peninsula) are at stake, as well as texts of different genre (poetry and criticism) and nature (poetic and visual). The comparative lens is therefore not just 'a way of talking about a shared cultural or aesthetic encounter which has happened somewhere else', and which has been enabled by translation.[18] Comparative research is 'itself a means of encounter', or, to be specific, 'a truly interdisciplinary [and polyglossic] intellectual space, in which different and sometimes incompatible critical languages [the Italian and the American, but also, as an intermediary between the two, the French] meet in order to disagree and misunderstand as much as to converge, and in which the disagreements and misunderstanding can be recognized as having value'.[19]

In line with this critical agenda, the present study will provide a comparative account of the paradoxes and misunderstandings that have characterised the movements of poetic texts from Italy to the US, alongside the blending of, and resistance to, critical approaches both domestic and foreign. Through a kaleidoscopic reading, the volume will contrast theories of the avant-garde, feminism, modern philology, social linguistics, and race as they have been assimilated and used in the Italian and American contexts, and in the imaginary diasporic space where both countries, and literatures, coexist. This variety of perspectives will be applied to the anthologised poems in a similarly kaleidoscopic way, i.e. to segments of poems rather than to whole texts, and from a hybrid and constantly changing double lens, the Italian and the American. Such a method, based on a 'diasporic' reinterpretation of close reading, does justice to the inherent mobility of these texts as well as to their 'scattered' cultural existence.

This comparative critical analysis has been specially inspired by Emily Apter's concept of a 'translation zone', that is a 'broad intellectual topography that is neither the property of a single nation, nor an amorphous condition associated with postnationalism, but rather a zone of critical engagement that connects the "l" and the "n" of transLation and transNation'. Apter continues by saying that the use of the term 'zone' as 'theoretical mainstay' was suggested to her by Guillaume Apollinaire's 1912 poem 'Zone', which 'defined a psychogeographical territory identified with the Paris periphery where bohemia, migrants, and marginals converge'.[20] As we will see, Apter's configuration of a translation zone is not dissimilar to Bhabha's notion of a 'third space', another spatial construct designed to capture the moment of cultural production in the life, or as the life, of marginalised populations, including artists, migrants, and women.

Apter's paradigm has the merit of encapsulating a series of issues that are of utmost importance for this study: the relation between language and nation; the prominence of space in processes of canon formation; the role of translation in literary history; the (ethical) function of minorities in the shaping of literary taste; and the necessity to replace 'the old center-periphery model with a world system comprised of multiple linguistic singularities or interlocking small worlds, each a locus of poetic opacity'.[21] Apter's translation zone advocates a programme of comparative literature and, by extension, criticism, which, by using 'translation as a fulcrum', seeks to 'be the name of language worlds characterized by linguistic multiplicity and phantom inter-nations'.[22] As it endorses Apter's radical programme, this book outlines the blurred, opaque, and linguistically-blended borders of a poetic inter-nation (Italian translated lyric in the US), one that is only apparently steady and/or well-defined; a nation that can be seen comparatively through Hajdari's 'fog of another alphabet'.

The theoretical and practical obstacles encountered at the beginning of this research project turned out to be its own points of innovation and strength. The ever-changing, multiperspectival field of comparative criticism provided a home to diasporic meanderings outside the more obvious territories of Italian studies, Italian American studies, and American studies. What this book offers is not a history of expatriate Italian, American and/or Italian American poets, translators, and editors operating in the US, nor a simple stylistic and rhetorical analysis of contemporary Italian lyric in English translation. Rather, it scrutinises a unique literary object, that is a body of poetry that includes both and neither of the above. It is my hope that the book will carve out a translational zone of contact across, and beyond, these disciplines.

By positioning this work within the constellation of comparative criticism, I have applied to the poetic corpus a variety of perspectives from anthology studies, translation studies, and diaspora studies. These three areas combined have formed a gravitational field whereby distinctive elements exist both independently of and in attraction to one another. I shall consider these rules of multiple attraction first in reference to anthology studies and translation studies, and second with respect to diaspora studies vis-à-vis the other two fields.

It would be impossible to examine the evolution of a poetic canon in translation without considering translation's 'active role' in the transmission/migration of culture, including language, literature, and the nation.[23] In a continuous and instantaneous way, translations create literary worlds that, in the context of the analysis and interpretation of literary canons, demand a shifting of the focus from the past to the present. As Bhabha has put it, 'in the production of the nation as narration there is a split between the continuist, accumulative temporality of the pedagogical [i.e. the canon as diachronic entity], and the repetitious, recursive strategy of the performative', which presents the canon as a spatial construct.[24]

Translation scholar Anthony Pym has suggested something similar when he remarks that 'translation histories are deceptively diachronic'.[25] Pym argues 'for a mode of historical diachrony based on the primacy of intercultural synchrony. [...] No other historical approach can properly grasp the importance of translation' in shaping 'foreign' taxonomies.[26]

Paradoxically, the spatial horizon of the anthology of poetry in translation provides the 'appropriate time-frame for representing those residual and emergent meaning and practices [such as avant-garde, women's and dialect poetry, located] in the margins of the contemporary experience of society'.[27] Even though the nexus between translation and margins is hardly new, its implications are becoming more and more urgent in literature as well as in society. This study takes these implications as a priority by committing itself to revisiting Gilles Deleuze and Félix Guattari's influential idea of minor literature as experiment, politics, and deterritorialisation in the light of translation's experimental, political, and deterritorialised agenda.[28]

The crossover of translating and anthologising sought here endorses a vision of translated literature as a coherent system within, rather than a passive and arbitrary expression of, what Itamar Even-Zohar has called the 'literary polysystem'.[29] Even-Zohar has rightly observed that histories of translated literature are 'seldom incorporated into the historical account' of national literatures 'in any coherent way'.[30] According to him, translated literature is not only integral to any literary polysystem, but is also 'a most active system within it', one that negotiates between conservative and innovative forces.[31] The history of Italian translated lyric in the US is punctuated by anthological examples that confirm this line. The new, one could say, reaches the old in translation.

Even-Zohar's comprehensive understanding of translation has the effect of problematising the allegedly fixed, peripheral position of translated works. As shown in this study, Italian poetic texts transplanted into the US and translated into English can be in turn, and/or at once, central and peripheral, depending on the literary polysystem(s) under scrutiny. For instance, women poets have been long excluded from the Italian literary canon and, to a certain extent, still are; yet, the fact that these poets have been consistently anthologised and translated in the US does not automatically position them at the centre of the American poetic scene. As a consequence, translations can be, but not always are, a subsystem of the receiving or target literature, a finding that both validates and resists Gideon Toury's idea that translations are 'facts of the target culture'.[32] The need for a contextual (or, to use Toury's word, 'descriptive') study of translations has also been put forward by a branch of translation studies known as the sociology of literary translation. Within this field, sociology (or sociologies) of poetry translation 'considers the study of poetry translation as social acts' by employing a variety of sociological concepts and tools, including statistical methods.[33] Even though this volume does not engage with these views directly, it accounts for the historical, societal, and economic impact of poetry on the evolution and exportation of culture; it turns carefully selected anthological data into a meaningful story, rather than presenting itself as an exhaustive quantitative survey.

This book's theoretical constellation gravitates around the unifying concept of diaspora, which is the planet around which the anthological and translational pivot. With its multiple valences — national, transnational, and postnational — the term 'diaspora', literally meaning 'a scattering of seeds' in Ancient Greek, offers a space to think about 'the discordant movements of modernity'.[34] Although it is classically used to connote the trauma of forced migration, in particular the exoduses of the Jews and the Armenians, diaspora has attained new epistemological, political, and identitarian resonances, applied as it is to different cultures and contexts, and across a number of fields.[35] As they acknowledge the possibilities of diaspora, contemporary scholars are still divided into two groups: those who use the term in a strict sense, thus distinguishing between migrants, exiles, expatriates, and refugees; and those who use it in a far-reaching and multiperspectival manner, as a metaphor.[36] I align myself with the latter. I believe that 'diaspora is best approached not as a social entity that can be measured [against specific temporal and/or spatial settings] but as an idea that helps explain the world migration creates'.[37] As a result, the focus of this study is not on the types and processes of Italian migration to the US, or, occasionally, of American migration to Italy and/or Europe, but on 'the connections [these] migrants form[ed] abroad and the kinds of culture they produce[d]'.[38]

Thanks to this analytical flexibility, I shall use the terms 'exile', 'nomadism', 'migration', 'erraticness', and 'expatriation' as mutable yet distinctive variants of 'diaspora', which will work as an umbrella term. I have privileged diaspora over the bidirectional idea of exile because the former conveys the sense of fluidity, or 'liquidity' (Zygmunt Bauman's term), that is peculiar to contemporary society.[39] The exilic subjectivity emphasises forms of reconnection with the origins by moving on a double-arrowed straight line between the poles of homeland and host-land. Diaspora, conversely, transcends this linear model to reveal the 'multifaceted, [synchronous and diagonal] patterns of interaction' that characterise the migrants' in-between condition.[40]

This understanding of diaspora as connectivity, hybridity, and interstitiality is routes-oriented rather than roots-oriented.[41] It tries to do justice to the complexities, and paradoxes, of this canon's trajectories, at once labyrinthine and unexpected. This notion of diasporicity has allowed me to trace Italian poetry's journey from Italy to the US, and back, whilst following its steps and/or detours through England, Japan, Russia, and France. This comparative critical approach to concepts and experiences of diaspora foregrounds a supranational reading of critical terms (feminism), cultural phenomena (the avant-garde), and translation categories (domestication and foreignisation) that have hitherto been considered in opposition to one another, despite being diasporically linked. Most importantly, this approach combines a subject-oriented focus (the diasporic editor, translator, and/or poet) with an historically collective perspective (migration in the global age), thus bridging the gap between poetry and cultural studies, literature and sociology.[42]

These advantages notwithstanding, I am acutely aware of the danger of extending the meaning of diaspora too far, thus risking a critical platitude. Although it is true that poetry and exile have been linked since the beginnings of Western literature

(Homer), not all (Italian) poets can be considered diasporic. By the same token, it would be unhelpful to apply the diasporic paradigm to any international canon just because translation is the most visible form in which words migrate. Stefano Luconi addressed a series of reasons why diaspora is not a viable category to describe Italian emigration to the US. Although his critique is convincing in its own terms, it springs from a different definition of diaspora. In an essay published in 2013, Luconi asserted that migrants need to comply with three paramount criteria in order to qualify for diasporic status: dispersion, homeland orientation, and connection to the motherland.[43] He rightly claimed that Italian migrants, specifically those going to the US, pursued forms of repatriation, assimilation, and detachment from the homeland that do not fit with such a definition of the diasporic. The idea of diaspora endorsed in this book, however, is based on the reverse premise; inspired by Bhabha's intuition of the 'third-place', it captures precisely the migrant's oscillations between resistance and assimilation, metamorphosis and melancholia, rather than focusing on backward movements, and forms of return. In this theoretical system, there is no contradiction between the contrasting feelings of foreignness and belonging that have problematised the reception of Italian lyric in the US. This literary tradition is neither Italian nor American; instead, it exists in the liminal space where two worlds negotiated, exchanged, and transformed their cultural and literary values.

In the light of these considerations, I call this transplanted canon diasporic: first, because it was created by expatriates, migrants, and political refugees; second, because it promoted peripheral groups — namely avant-garde, women, and dialect poets — who have been diasporically moved away from literary centres; and third, because it constructed a hybrid culture, half-American and half-Italian, that expressed itself through different forms of translation (bilingual, trilingual, multilingual, and visual).

The five parts which make up this volume reflect this metaphorical conception of diaspora, both structurally and thematically. They explore the potential of deviance, marginality, eccentricity and distortion as successful trends in the export of Italian poetry to America; they provide a picture of its progression and tendencies, rather than focussing on specific editors, poets and/or translators. Parts I–IV map different stages, at times actual turning points, in the shaping of this diasporic model. Special attention is paid to this canon's American roots and influences, especially Ezra Pound, as well as to its Italian imprint, a double vision that is essential to the understanding of this diasporic narrative as a whole. Parts I and II analyse in turn the emergence and evolution of an avant-garde poetic line, which is the oldest and most enduring strand. Parts III and IV describe the making of a female and dialect thread respectively as the result of the eruption of gendered, ethnic, and transnational perspectives. Part V tackles the issue of translation itself by bringing together these seemingly scattered discourses; it looks at the ways in which the diasporic canon, conceived as a unit of avant-garde, feminine, and dialect poetry, was shaped by an ethically-oriented, 'foreignizing' translatorly practice.[44] Diasporic motifs are explored throughout as they emerge from the anthologised texts: travel, migration, estrangement, mourning, multilingualism, but also metaliterature, religion, and anatomy.

The result of this diasporic analysis is a composite volume where each part works as a free-standing unit whilst also contributing to a larger overarching narrative. Within this structure, a comparative analysis is undertaken of diachronically successive publications and intertwined cultural moments. Emphasis will be placed on the role of the publishing houses (from New Directions and Chelsea Editions to the Canadian exception of Legas) as well as on the competing influences of contemporary poets and critics from the US and Italy. In the spirit of pluralism that characterises comparative criticism, this study does not adopt any specific theoretical standpoint; yet, because of its critical nomadism, it is greatly indebted to, and infused with, thoughts and works by a number of scholars. I would like to acknowledge here not only Apter, Even-Zohar, Pym, and Kevin Kenny, who helped me both set and transcend the boundaries of this study, but also Bhabha, Reynolds, Marjorie Perloff, Julia Kristeva, and Lawrence Venuti, with whom I engage in the methodological introductions at the beginning of each chapter: diaspora and avant-garde, diaspora and women, diaspora and dialect, and diaspora and translation.

The book concludes with a four-part Appendix which provides the reader, I hope, with a powerful instrument of analysis, comparison, and consultation. Thanks to its multilayered structure, the Appendix complements and completes the data supplied by the thirteen tables and eleven figures found in the main text. Part 1 registers, in chronological order, all the anthologies of contemporary Italian poetry that, to my knowledge, have been published in the US from 1945 to 2015, including those that I did not examine in this study (with some mention of later anthologies up to 2018). Following the book's criteria, the anthologies listed include mixed collections of poetry and prose as well as historical selections that, in some cases, start as early as the Middle Ages. Even though, in this kind of inventory, failure to achieve an all-inclusive list is inevitable, all efforts have been done to present a comprehensive catalogue.

Part 2 is divided into three sections offering: (i) an overview of the content (selection of poets) and features (volume or journal publication, monolingual or bilingual etc.) of the analysed anthologies; (ii) a list of the poets present in each anthology as well as an indication of the number of poems per poet; and (iii) a series of tables registering the frequency of the most anthologised poets. Frequency has been calculated as the number of appearances across the anthologies analysed (occurrences) accompanied by a percentage value.

Part 3 has a similar threefold structure which provides: (i) a full list of the translators featured in each anthology alongside the name the poets translated by each translator; (ii) a series of tables summarising information about the most anthologised poets and their translators; and (iii) a series of tables registering the most popular translators used across the anthologies as well as the names of the poets translated.[45] Part 4 of the Appendix presents a transcription and translation of Ennio Contini's letter to Pound, which is discussed in Chapter 5. The autograph letter, signed by Contini, is kept at the Beneicke Rare Book and Manuscript Library, Yale University.

In addition to having a strong theoretical and textual focus, this study has required extensive archival research. In the effort to assess all the anthologies published in the period 1945–2015, as well as the relevant material associated with them (letters, interviews, diaries, and connected publications), Robin Healey's *Twentieth-Century Italian Literature in English Translation: An Annotated Bibliography, 1929–1997* (1998) proved to be an invaluable resource.[46] This text does not however cover the publications of the last twenty years; moreover, certain anthologies, such as Peter Miller's 1958 selection for *Folio*, are not registered in it. To assist archival research, I contacted, and in some cases worked in close collaboration with, publishing houses, libraries, and museums around the world: New Directions Publishing, New York; the Houghton Library at Harvard; the Beinecke Rare Book and Manuscript Library at Yale; the British Library in London; the Imperial War Museum in Duxford, UK; and the Taylor Institution Library at Oxford. This allowed me not only to retrieve very rare anthologies, Renato Poggioli's 1947 collection for the review *Voices* being an example (Duxford), but also to gain access to special collections, such as Nat Scammacca's *Antigruppo* materials (Oxford). Much work remains to be done, and new anthological projects, either abandoned or aborted, are yet to be discovered. It is my hope that this study can help us set foot in this intriguing, uncharted territory of literary history.

As it speaks to the contemporary migration crisis, this book's diasporic angle is motivated by contingent historical circumstances; at the same time, it reacts and responds to the transnational turn taken by the humanities in the past twenty years[47] (and, more recently, Italian studies) by offering a poetry-centred perspective.[48] Thanks to its transdisciplinary and comparative focus, it will make a contribution to the fields of Italian, American, and Italian American studies, as well as to the disciplines of anthology studies, translation studies, and diaspora studies. It will also provide a model for future diasporic investigations by foregrounding the importance of poetry in the understanding of contemporary phenomena of dislocation and displacement. As art critic John Berger pointed out in *Ways of Seeing*, we see from the present, as 'the past is never there waiting to be discovered, to be recognized for exactly what it is'.[49] Yet, at the same time, the diasporic perspective is justified by reasons that are inherent in this canon's own idiosyncrasies, composition, and structure. Diaspora is not only a vessel or a lens; it is also the buried alphabet, or unsequenced DNA, of which this poetic matter is made. Diaspora is the language that was waiting to be deciphered.

I would like to conclude by reiterating some of the practical pieces of information given in the 'Note on Conventions' with which the book has opened. References to the anthologies, both Italian and American, are given in small capitals as a marker for the reader (e.g., POGGIOLI 1948). Translations, generally of prose and critical sources, are mine, unless otherwise stated. By contrast, quotations from the American primary sources are given in English, even in the case of the poems' titles and lines. This choice is coherent with the comparative perspective of this study as well as with the very nature of its translated materials. It is justified by, and conforms to, the diasporic outlook of the volume.

I should also stress that every effort has been made to trace copyright holders to ensure that the visual poems reproduced here are correctly acknowledged and used by permission of their creators. In the event of any errors or omissions, the record will be corrected in any subsequent edition of the book.

Notes to the Introduction

1. Gëzim Hajdari, 'It's My Skin Sings Out, Flayed to the Twilight', in *Stigmata*, trans. by Cristina Viti (Bristol: Shearsman Books, 2016), p. 55.
2. I use the adjective 'American' throughout to refer to the United States.
3. 'Proclaimed by US Secretary of State George Marshall at Harvard University on 5 June 1947, the Marshall Plan was the largest and most successful program of foreign assistance ever undertaken by the US government. [...] Between 1948 and 1951, Congress authorized more than $13 billion for the European Recovery Program', which included Italy. See Thomas Alan Schwartz, 'Marshall Plan', in *The Oxford Companion to International Relations*, ed. by Joel Krieger (Oxford: Oxford University Press, 2014) <https://www.oxfordreference.com/view/10.1093/acref/9780199738878.001.0001/acref-9780199738878> [accessed 20 July 2021].
4. To give just a few examples: *Italy and the USA: Cultural Change Through Language and Narrative*, ed. by Guido Bonsaver, Alessandro Carlucci, and Matthew Reza (Oxford: Legenda, 2019); Martino Marazzi, *Little America: gli Stati Uniti e gli scrittori italiani del Novecento* (Milan: Marcos y Marcos, 1997); Barbara Alfano, *The Mirage of America in Contemporary Italian Literature and Film* (Toronto: University of Toronto Press, 2013); and the seminal 2014 anthology *Italoamericana: The Literature of the Great Migration, 1880–1943*, ed. by Francesco Durante and others (New York: Fordham University Press, 2014).
5. The adjective 'prismatic' has been used by Matthew Reynolds with reference to translation. According to Reynolds, it is important 'to see translation, not as fundamentally a single act involving one source-text in one language, and one translation-text in one another language, which just happens to occur again and again, but rather as paradigmatically generating multiple texts' and, therefore, as a potentially unlimited generative force. From this perspective, 'translation's dominant metaphor would change: it would no longer be a "channel" between one language and another but rather a "prism"'. 'Introduction', in *Prismatic Translation*, ed. by Matthew Reynolds (Oxford: Legenda, 2019), pp. 1–18 (pp. 2–3).
6. I borrow the distinction between comprehensive and single-sex anthologies from Rebecca West, 'Who's In, Who's Out? A Feminist and "Queering" Perspective on Modern Italian Lyric Anthology Formation in Italy and the United States (1970–2005)', in *Dentro/fuori, sopra/sotto: critica femminista e canone letterario negli studi di italianistica*, ed. by Alessia Ronchetti and Maria Serena Sapegno (Ravenna: Longo, 2007), pp. 26–37. In the Appendix, I have marked 'single-sex' anthologies as a subgroup of the 'thematic' collections (see Appendix 2.1).
7. Ton Naaijkens, 'The World of World Poetry: Anthologies of Translated Poetry as a Subject of Study', *Neophilologus*, 90 (2006), 509–20.
8. Daniela Caselli, 'Value and Authority in Anthologies of Italian Poetry in English (1956–1992)', in *Twentieth-Century Poetic Translation: Literary Cultures in Italian and English*, ed. by Daniela Caselli and Daniela La Penna (London: Continuum, 2008), pp. 55–67; and Massimo Bacigalupo, 'Il Novecento nelle antologie in lingua inglese', in *Visti da fuori: la poesia italiana oggi in Europa*, ed. by Damiano Sinfonico and Stefano Verdino, special issue of *Nuova Corrente*, 153 (2014), 71–77.
9. See André Lefevere, *Translation, Rewriting, and the Manipulation of Literary Frame* (London: Routledge, 1992); and *Creative Constraints: Translation and Authorship*, ed. by Rita Wilson and Leah Gerber (Clayton: Monash University Publishing, 2012).
10. Armin Paul Frank, 'Anthologies of Translation', in *Routledge Encyclopaedia of Translation Studies*, ed. by Mona Baker and Gabriela Saldanha (London & New York: Routledge, 1998), pp. 13–16 (p. 13).
11. Harald Kittel, 'International Anthologies of Literature in Translation: An Introduction to Incipient Research', in *International Anthologies of Literature in Translation*, ed. by Harald Kittel (Berlin: Erich Schmidt, 1995), pp. ix–xxvii (p. x).

12. Ibid., p. xv.
13. I use the term 'eccentric' in a geometrical sense in order to capture the innovative and subversive potential of works that were published far from Italy's geographical and literary centre.
14. See *Visti da fuori*, ed. by Sinfonico and Verdino; Homi Bhabha, *The Location of Culture* (London: Routledge, 1994); and Jahan Ramazani, *A Transnational Poetics* (Chicago & London: University of Chicago Press, 2009).
15. Matthew Reynolds, Mohamed-Salah Omri and Ben Morgan, 'Guest Editors' Introduction', in *Comparative Criticism: Histories and Methods*, special issue of *Comparative Critical Studies*, 12 (2015), 147–59 (p. 148).
16. Ibid.
17. Ibid.
18. Ibid., p. 158.
19. Ibid., pp. 158, 148.
20. Emily Apter, *The Translation Zone: A New Comparative Literature* (Princeton, NJ: Princeton University Press, 2006), p. 5.
21. Ibid., p. 245.
22. Ibid., pp. 243, 244–45.
23. Antony Pym, *Translation and Text Transfer: An Essay on the Principles of Cross-cultural Communication* (New York: Peter Lang, 1992), p. 154.
24. Bhabha, *The Location of Culture*, p. 209.
25. Pym, *Translation and Text Transfer*, p. 152.
26. Ibid., p. 154.
27. Bhabha, *The Location of Culture*, pp. 212–13.
28. Gilles Deleuze and Félix Guattari, *Kafka: pour une littérature mineure* (Paris: Minuit, 1975).
29. 'Polysystem' theory conceives of literature 'not as an isolated activity in society, regulated by laws exclusively (and inherently) different from all the rest of the human activities, but as an integral — often central and very powerful — factor among the latter'. Itamar Even-Zohar, 'Polysystem Studies', *Poetics Today*, 11 (1990), 1–268 (p. 2).
30. Ibid., p. 45.
31. Ibid., p. 46.
32. Gideon Toury, *Descriptive Translation Studies, and Beyond* (Amsterdam: Benjamin, 1995), p. 23. Toury understands the 'descriptive' as loosely 'contextual'. He believes that 'what constitutes the subject matter of a proper discipline of Translation Studies is (observable or reconstructable) facts of real life rather than merely speculative entities resulting from preconceived hypotheses and theoretical models. It is therefore empirical by its very nature and should be worked out accordingly' (p. 2).
33. Jacob Blakesley, 'Introduction', in *Sociologies of Poetry Translation: Emerging Perspectives*, ed. by Jacob Blakesley (London: Bloomsbury Academic, 2018), pp. 1–20 (p. 2). Franco Moretti's 'distant' approach, one based on an abstract, scientific and transgeographical analysis of literature, has proved to be crucial to the development of this field. See Franco Moretti, *Graphs, Maps, Trees: Abstract Models for a Literary History* (London: Verso, 2005); and, by the same author, *Distant Reading* (London: Verso, 2013).
34. Jana Evans Braziel and Anita Mannur, 'Nation, Migration, Globalization: Points of Contention and Diaspora Studies', in *Theorizing Diaspora: A Reader*, ed. by Jana Evans Braziel and Anita Mannur (Oxford: Blackwell, 2003), pp. 1–22 (p. 3).
35. See Braziel and Mannur, 'Nation, Migration, Globalization'.
36. Françoise Král, *Critical Identities in Contemporary Anglophone Diasporic Literature* (Basingstoke: Palgrave Macmillan, 2009), p. 12.
37. Kevin Kenny, *Diaspora: A Very Short Introduction* (Oxford: Oxford University Press, 2013), p. 1.
38. Ibid., p. 12.
39. Zygmunt Bauman, *Liquid Modernity* (Cambridge: Polity Press, 2000).
40. Kenny, *Diaspora*, p. 108.
41. Ibid.
42. *Poetry after Cultural Studies*, ed. by Heidi Bean and Mike Chasar (Iowa City: University of Iowa Press, 2011).

43. Stefano Luconi, 'Italian Migration and Diasporic Approaches: Historical Phenomena and Scholarly Interpretations', in *The Cultures of Italian Migration: Diverse Trajectories and Discrete Perspectives*, ed. by Graziella Parati and Anthony Julian Tamburri (Lanham, MD: Fairleigh Dickinson University Press, 2013), pp. 153–68 (p. 123).
44. Lawrence Venuti, *The Translator's Invisibility: A History of Translation* (London: Routledge, 1995).
45. Despite being a vital piece of information, the names of the translators have often been difficult to retrieve. I would like to thank the staff of the Bodleian Library at the University of Oxford and Nayt Rundquist, Managing Editor at New Rivers Press, for their help in the final stages of this search.
46. Robin Healey, *Twentieth-Century Italian Literature in English Translation: An Annotated Bibliography, 1929–1997* (Toronto: University of Toronto Press, 1998). In 2019, after the completion of this book, Healey published a new edition of his bibliography, this time including translations of Italian literature into English up until 2016: Robin Healey, *Italian Literature Since 1900 in English Translation: An Annotated Bibliography, 1929–2016* (Toronto: University of Toronto Press, 2019). Quotations in this book refer to the 1998 edition.
47. Ramazani, *A Transnational Poetics*; and Paul Jay, *Global Matters: The Transnational Turn in Literary Studies* (Ithaca, NY: Cornell University Press, 2010).
48. Emma Bond, 'Towards a Trans-national Turn in Italian Studies?', *Italian Studies*, 69 (2014), 415–24.
49. John Berger, *Ways of Seeing* (London: Penguin, 1972), p. 11.

PART I

❖

Diasporic Avant-gardes

CHAPTER 1

Diaspora and the Avant-garde: A Transnational Trajectory

Decentring the Avant-garde

Recent directions in avant-garde studies have insisted on the need to 'rethink the master narratives of the avant-garde', in terms of 'cross-language, cross-nation, cross-ethnic contacts and confrontations'.[1] This 'topographical turn', as it has been described, has resulted in a totally renewed conception of the avant-garde as a discipline. Understood as a deterritorialised phenomenon circulating beyond its national boundaries, the avant-garde expresses some kind of resistance to a presupposed centre. This tension between centre and peripheries often consisted in a 'revolt against practices, institutions and traditions that are seen to be at the core of the hegemonic culture'.[2] The avant-garde is in itself a diasporic reality, in that the ways in which experimental poetics and cultural displacement intersected throughout the twentieth century, and beyond, are essentially avant-garde.

The first systematic attempt to theorise the link between diaspora and the avant-garde was carried out by Carry Noland and Barrett Watten in the seminal volume which makes the title of this chapter. Published in 2011, *Diasporic Avant-gardes: Experimental Poetics and Cultural Displacement* gives a sense of the 'intimacy and foreignness' that characterises the bond between avant-garde and diasporic poets, both from the viewpoint of their formal strategies and social backgrounds.[3] Noland and Watten suggested that the interaction between avant-garde and diasporic communities operate on a number of levels: philosophical, political, and cultural.

From a philosophical angle, experimental poetics and experiences of displacement share an 'ethics of ontology', i.e. a mode of interpreting the world that can be understood through the lens of Edmund Husserl's phenomenology of existence. On the one hand, the subject loses his/her psychic unity, split as s/he is between different practices and/or countries; this 'schizomorphic' state is constitutional to Italian 1960s neo-avant-gardists, also known as Gruppo 63. On the other hand, the same subject becomes the object of a 'constant interrogation of being', through which all meanings, possibilities, and expectations are deferred.[4] The poetic self renounces his/her centrality in order to allow the other (subjects, languages, or objects) to come forth and exist. Alongside this ethical element (i.e. the receptiveness for, and projection onto, the diverse), this ontological conception of the avant-garde has a modernising, restorative meaning. When reflecting on the neo-avant-gardists' programme of self-reduction, John Picchione pointed out that 'the Novissimi [another name for the group] do not proclaim the death of the subject or the disappearance of the self'; rather, they put forward 'a strategy generated by the urgency to revisit the world anew and to unfold, through innovative linguistic modes, new possibilities of existence'.[5] These avant-garde modalities of self-suspension and, in some cases, self-effacement are comparable to what Bhabha called the diasporic, 'unhomely' condition.[6]

The avant-garde's emphasis on, and sometimes obsession with, the other often took the shape of an 'ambiguous engagement' with the margins, be they women, natives, colonised populations, or immigrants.[7] This does not come as a surprise if we consider that, historically, the avant-garde's obsession with otherness coincided both with the processes of decolonisation and the development of new forms of transnationalism. A major interpreter of postmodernity, Paul Gilroy disclosed the correlations between diaspora and the rise of avant-garde practices across the Black Atlantic, which resulted from the juxtaposition of African, American, Caribbean, and British experiences.[8] Not only did postcolonialism (and modernity at large) produce new models of hybrid, aesthetic representations, but it also determined patterns of artistic mobility. Noland and Watten pointed out the role played by 'East European, Caribbean, African American and African writers in shaping the intellectual and artistic life of early twentieth-century Europe'.[9] Whereas 'voluntary exile was key to the development of modernism', diaspora is defined as the very motor of the avant-garde, postmodernist revolution.[10]

This decentred, occasionally postcolonial, gaze discloses the avant-garde's subversive elements on the one hand, and justifies its intercultural significations on the other. Working in synergy, the political and cultural dimensions are operative in any avant-garde practice that challenges the subject's, as well as society's, hegemonic position. Diaspora and the avant-garde often share 'a project of cultural transformation' and 'critique of imperialism (racial, social, aesthetic)' that bring together their politically aesthetic, and aesthetically political, orders.[11] Although the avant-garde's political intentions have been frequently related to 'a notion of bourgeois culture and tradition, which the avant-garde attempts to overthrow', its subversive gestures extend to a form of 'institutional critique that we see as the driving force of the avant-garde project' across the world.[12] This understanding of the avant-garde is particularly meaningful if we consider that some of the leading lights of avant-garde literature, such as Pound and Filippo Tommaso Marinetti, were problematically involved with fascism.

In order to describe the militant essence of the avant-garde, contemporary critics adopted different, diasporic perspectives, from Per Bäckström and Benedikt Hjartarson's centre-periphery approach to Noland and Watten's sociological interpretations. As the latter put it, the avant-garde is more than 'a purely formal phenomenon'; it is also a 'social formation, a way of imagining and forming community through specific and historically conditioned modes of composition, reproduction, performance, and distribution'.[13] As a result, the avant-garde is not uniquely understood in terms of its transnational activities, but also in terms of its diasporic 'networks' (Western centres of the avant-garde) and 'rhizomes' (non-hierarchical, radiating points).[14] Throughout the twentieth century, communities of artists from different countries came together in the publication of journals, anthologies, and manifestoes as well as in the organisation of conferences, exhibitions, and film screenings, as this chapter will document.

If militancy is a precondition for the avant-garde's subversive nucleus, cultural hybridity is one of its most important manifestations. Conceived as a diasporic reality, the avant-garde generated 'new forms of identity and new understanding of alterity' that led to expressions of 'cultural syncretism'.[15] The contact between two or more cultures and/or communities shapes a frictional, in-between zone, from where the 'articulation of cultural difference' springs.[16] According to Bhabha, this spatial and temporal dimension, which is both ultrahistorical and transgeographical, is proper to marginal groups insofar as it portrays their interstitial condition. Without dealing directly with avant-garde instances, Bhabha remarked that 'the borderline work of culture demands an encounter with "newness" that is not part of the continuum of past and present'; rather, 'it creates a sense of the new as an insurgent act of cultural translation'. 'Such art,' Bhabha continues, 'renews the past, refiguring it as a contingent in-between space, that innovates and interrupts the performance of the present'.[17] Whereas national canons are often relegated to the past, the Italian, transnational canon analysed in this book sprang from the contemporaneous transmigration of both texts and people. If we apply Bhabha's theory to our object of investigation, we may argue that diaspora and the avant-garde provided the narrative of contingency, transculturalism, and revolt that shaped the history of Italian poetry in America.

Before moving onto the analysis of the ways in which the American avant-garde appropriated its Italian ramifications, it is interesting to notice how the experience of postwar America was described as 'a massive stage of cultural exchange, mimicry, incorporation, and denial'.[18] Charged with specific, diasporic meanings, postwar avant-gardes in the US — including Black Mountain poetry (1950–56), Greenwich Village (1950–63), the Black Arts Movement (1962–70), and the L=A=N=G=U=A=G=E poets of New York and San Francisco (1979–89) — embodied not only the dream of 'a progressive alternative culture' and the 'consumer's lust for novelty', but also this country's multicultural identity.[19] In this scenario, the Italian avant-garde, as proposed by its diasporic editors, was treated as an instance of contemporary militant writing, rather than as an exotic importation. American anthologists appraised Italian experimentalism in a manner that revealed their decentred (marginal) and decentring (revolutionary) position within the receiving culture. As diasporic individuals, they endorsed the avant-garde's political discourses, thus inscribing the history of the Italian translated canon in the circles of transnational dissidence. At the same time, as American citizens, they destabilised the cultural system in the United States by 'developing affiliations with marginal linguistic and cultural values'.[20]

The 'Twin Impulse': Tradition and the Avant-garde in Italy and the US

The avant-garde is a protean, mobile, and all-encompassing entity. Strictly intertwined with the development of 'western modernity, capitalist culture, and the global impact of both, the avant-garde is perhaps the most important and influential concept in the history of modern culture'.[21] Although it was conceived as a military word, coined in France at the time of the French Revolution (1789–94), the term 'avant-garde' soon started to be applied to the artistic and cultural fields in order to signal an idea of newness, up-to-dateness, and rupture with the past. Yet, the avant-garde's sense of novelty does not come without ambiguities as avant-garde practices were often perceived as a contradiction in terms: first, because what is thought to be new in a specific spatiotemporal context is already anterior with respect to the present; and second, because the avant-garde offers itself as an alternative canon against the same traditional set of values that it itself refuses. Therefore, despite embodying a sense of deviation from the norm, the avant-garde continually, and paradoxically, calls for a rethinking of conventions.

Any discussion on the facets of the term 'avant-garde' entails an exploration of its competing tradition(s). Just as there cannot be avant-garde without a feeling of the literary past, there cannot be tradition without an understanding of contemporaneity. For Seth Lerer the term 'tradition' holds an active, revolutionary meaning. Rather than a synonym for 'conservatorism, preservation, or unthinking reverence', it refers to the continuous process through which the past becomes present and the present becomes future. 'To work with tradition,' Lerer adds, 'is to make anew, not just to curate'.[22] In this sense, tradition and the avant-garde are not mere opposites, but magnetic poles that mutually attract and superimpose on each other.

Moreover, any discussion on tradition and the avant-garde cannot overlook the issue of canonicity. Coming from the Latin *traditio*, meaning 'handing down, a surrendering, and a delivery from one group to the other', the term tradition 'shows that behind the word and its own history there lies a sense of power and control, of passing on but also giving up' that we commonly associate with the notion of the canon.[23] As this chapter will establish, different ideas on the avant-garde involve different ideas on the canon, and vice versa.

In the course of the twentieth century, diverse conceptions of tradition and the avant-garde informed both Italian and American criticism. European by birth (its first artistic applications dating back to the first decades of the last century), the avant-garde became a distinctive feature of American culture. As Roy Pearce put it, 'the "Americanness" of American poetry is, quite simply, its compulsive "modernism" — or, with some poets in the twentieth century, its compulsive "traditionalism", which is, ironically enough, a form of "modernism"'.[24] This twin impulse, as Pearce called it, derives from the peculiar role ('at once pioneering and avant-garde') of American literature against other national traditions; yet, at the same time, it can also be read as a template for contemporary art at large.[25]

The Italian situation is the opposite. Much like the US, Italy has a comparatively young political identity; its literary history, though, is many centuries-long, highly distinctive and crystallised. The Italian nation is not just the product of political manoeuvres and revolutions; it was born first and foremost out of the efforts of its literary intelligentsia, the idea of a unified country being advocated already by Dante in the Middle Ages. Whereas the search for innovation is a hallmark of American letters, Italian literature is infused with a sense of admiration for, if not devotion to, its literary roots.

Predictably, such differences between Italy and the US determined an almost antithetical conceptualisation of the avant-garde as a cultural construction. Whilst the Italian avant-garde expressed two separate, historical moments (futurism in the first two decades of the twentieth century and the so-called neo-avant-garde in the 1960s), American avant-gardes of various forms crosscut US literature persistently. If we exclude the time of radical innovation which coincided with the preworld war period, there have been five major avant-garde movements that concerned American poetry since 1945: Black Mountain College; the New York School of poets; the Black Arts Movement; the L=A=N=G=U=A=G=E poets of New York and San Francisco; and the Beats, whose geopoetical ramifications include Greenwich Village, San Francisco, and the Pacific Northwest (especially Washington and Oregon). Although the Italian neo-avant-garde found a correspondent in the L=A=N=G=U=A=G=E poetry of the 1960s and 1970s (both in chronological and aesthetic terms), its role within the Italian poetic canon is by no means comparable to that of its American counterpart. L=A=N=G=U=A=G=E poetry was not simply an expression of the shimmering experimentations of the American literary scene; it was also the vertex of a counterhegemonic, poetic canon started by Walt Whitman and Emily Dickinson in the nineteenth century, and continued by William Carlos Williams and Pound. By defending a poetry governed by 'theoretical conception', 'exquisite or grotesque fragments', and 'impressions partly visual, partly metrical', these experimental writers gave shape to the American avant-garde tradition as we know it today.[26]

Conversely, the Italian literary canon does not place a similar emphasis on innovation. Although, in twentieth-century Italy, the tension between the old and the new played a key role in authors such as Giuseppe Ungaretti, the question of canonicity has relied more heavily on modern (Eugenio Montale) and ancient (Petrarch) models on the one hand, and on the function of poetic generations and schools on the other. As a result, whilst the avant-garde is an ongoing phase in American poetry — representing a continuous form of resistance to a more formalist, classicising way of writing — in Italy it is limited to the experience of the futurists and the neo-avant-gardists, and to their problematic reception.[27]

Interestingly enough, futurism and the neo-avant-garde, two interrelated yet distinctive phenomena, shared a similar critical destiny in Italy. Both dismissed as inferior with respect to the standards of the literary tradition, these movements have been criticised respectively for their fascist implications and intellectualism. As Cinzia Sartini Blum noted, the juxtaposition between fascism and futurism provoked 'facile condemnations of the movement, leading to an all too hasty dismissal of its historical significance'.[28] In the introduction to the first edition of *I*

Novissimi's anthology (1961), poet and editor Alfredo Giuliani pointed out that the reasons for the neo-avant-garde's marginalisation is to be found in Italian critics' scepticism towards the new. 'In Italy,' Giuliani observed, 'whenever a writer wants to be contemporary he must take on social immaturity, political parochialism, makeshift improvisations and anxieties that claim to be solutions, and a perpetual mixture of anarchism and legalism'.[29] At the other end of the spectrum, avant-garde poetry in the US triggered a critical debate that resulted in a true anthological battle (see Chapter 5), a sign of the recognition that experimentalism has been given across the Atlantic as a cultural and societal phenomenon.

Since the diasporic canon is a product of the hybridisation between Italian and American culture, it is possible to identify points of contact, as well as differences, between these two traditions. The features shared by Italian and American avant-garde poetry in the second half of the century happened to be supremely transnational, being also embraced by other avant-garde practitioners across the world. Among these connections are: the ambition to create alternative traditions, or to unearth hidden ones; a solid philosophical core, both phenomenological and existentialist; a strong commitment to literary and art theory; the antiacademic stance; a sense of community; and the political dimension.

The subject's diasporic postures deprived him/her of his/her secular roots, replaced by the recovery of the avant-garde's prehistoric tradition, one that precedes, and therefore transcends, its national memory. In an attempt to glimpse its own auroral state, the transnational avant-garde traced both transhistorical and transgeographical associations that worked as a catalyst for the passage of poems and ideas on the one hand, and challenged received views on identity and tradition on the other. Beyond the differences and similarities that capture the Italian and the American comprehension of the avant-garde experience, there lies the necessity to overcome any fixed hermeneutic model, in order to embrace the richness of diaspora as a critical tool.

Notes to Chapter 1

1. Carrie Noland and Barrett Watten, 'Introduction', in *Diasporic Avant-gardes: Experimental Poetics and Cultural Displacement*, ed. by Carrie Noland and Barrett Watten (Basingstoke: Palgrave Macmillan, 2011), pp. 1–32 (pp. 4, 15).
2. Per Bäckström and Benedikt Hjartarson, 'Rethinking the Topography of the International Avant-garde: Introduction', in *Decentring the Avant-garde*, ed. by Per Bäckström and Benedikt Hjartarson, Avant-garde Critical Studies 30 (Leiden: Brill, 2014), pp. 7–32 (p. 14).
3. Noland and Watten, 'Introduction', p. 1.
4. Ibid., p. 10.
5. John Picchione, *The New Avant-garde in Italy: Theoretical Debate and Poetic Practices* (Toronto: University of Toronto Press, 2004), p. 16.
6. See Bhabha, *The Location of Culture*.
7. Bäckström and Hjartarson, 'Rethinking the Topography of the International Avant-garde', p. 16.
8. See Paul Gilroy, *The Black Atlantic: Modernity and Double Consciousness* (Cambridge, MA: Harvard University Press, 1993).
9. Noland and Watten, 'Introduction', pp. 3–4.

10. Ibid., p. 4.
11. Bäckström and Hjartarson, 'Rethinking the Topography of the International Avant-garde', p. 13.
12. Ibid.
13. Noland and Watten, 'Introduction', p. 4.
14. Bäckström and Hjartarson, 'Rethinking the Topography of the International Avant-garde', p. 163.
15. Noland and Watten, 'Introduction', p. 12.
16. Bhabha, *The Location of Culture*, p. 2. See also Mary Louise Pratt, 'Arts of the Contact Zone', *Profession* (1991), 33–40.
17. Bhabha, *The Location of Culture*, p. 10.
18. Noland and Watten, 'Introduction', p. 12.
19. Robert von Hallberg, 'Avant-Gardes', in *The Cambridge History of American Literature*, ed. by Sacvan Bercovitch, 8 vols (Cambridge: Cambridge University Press, 1994–2005), VIII, 83–122 (p. 83).
20. Venuti, *The Translator's Invisibility*, p. 125.
21. David Cottington, *The Avant-garde: A Very Short Introduction* (Oxford: Oxford University Press, 2013), p. 1.
22. Seth Lerer, *Tradition: A Feeling for the Literary Past* (Oxford: Oxford University Press, 2016), pp. viii–ix.
23. Ibid., pp. 1–2.
24. Roy Pearce, *The Continuity of American Poetry* (Princeton, NJ: Princeton University Press, 1961), p. 5.
25. Ibid., p. 9.
26. Marjorie Perloff, *The Poetics of Indeterminacy: Rimbaud to Cage* (Princeton, NJ: Princeton University Press, 1985), p. viii.
27. See, for instance, Gilberto Finzi, *Poesia in Italia: Montale, Novissimi, postnovissimi, 1959–1978* (Milan: Mursia, 1979).
28. Cited in Willard Bohn, *The Other Futurism: Futurist Activity in Venice, Padua and Verona* (Toronto: University of Toronto Press, 2004), p. 4.
29. Giuliani 1995, p. 38.

CHAPTER 2

❖

A Diasporic Ancestor: Ezra Pound

If the diasporic canon draws its models from both the Italian and the American traditions, it is not fortuitous that its progenitor happened to be an American expatriate in Italy: the 'poetic revolutionary' Pound, whose critical and poetic interests anticipated the features of the diasporic tradition, determined its developments, and shaped it from afar. Like many editors analysed here, Pound was a rebel and political prisoner, a mediator between Europe and the US, and a transnational avant-gardist; at the same time, he was an anthologist, a translator, and the explorer of alternative literary traditions. His name is inextricably bound to questions of canonicity, transnationalism, exile, and the avant-garde in ways that are illuminating for the literary historian today. On the one hand, Pound was the main representative of the American sidestream canon, both multicultural and avant-garde, which contrasted with the literary tradition embodied by Eliot and the New Critics. Pound's family tree goes, 'by way of Williams, to Black Mountains, the Objectivists, and the Confessional Poets', reaching out to the L=A=N=G=U=A=G=E poets, Louis Zukofsky, and Charles Olson.[1] As well as being a powerful symbolic presence within the American context, Pound was the initiator of the Italian diasporic tradition analysed here. In this chapter, I shall show how and why Pound epitomised in himself, by means of his subversive programme, the paradoxes and eccentricities of the Italian poetic diaspora.

Among the 'modernist expatriates' who moved to the old continent (among whom Williams and Marianne Moore), Pound is the one for whom Italy represented a literary territory at once canonical and revolutionary. The land of Dante and Guido Cavalcanti, but also of Marinetti and Umberto Boccioni, Italy provided him with an ideal mixture of classicism and experimentation. He recognised in the Italian medieval poets and the troubadours the origins of Western literature, and drew from futurism the idea of a diasporic avant-garde.

Perloff illuminated the linkage between Pound and futurism. In *The Futurist Moment* — a title that repeats an expression taken from Poggioli's *Teoria dell'arte d'avanguardia* [Theory of the Avant-garde] (1962) — she disclosed a series of decisive points: (i) that Italian futurism had a major influence on Pound's transnational poetics (Pound creating 'vorticism' a year after the first futurist exhibition in London); (ii) that the spirit of futurism informed all the posterior avant-gardes; and

(iii) that the futurists' world, which could be 'traversed without a passport', is an intuitive image for contemporary diasporas.[2]

Pound's connections to Italy, however, are far from straightforward. His Italian period was haunted by his adherence to fascism and arrest for political treachery. An outcast and exile, Pound composed the *Pisan Cantos* (1948) in captivity, as if they were the elegy by 'the last American living the tragedy of Europe'.[3] His Italian exile (1924–45) was then followed by thirteen years of reclusion at St. Elizabeth's psychiatric hospital in the US. After being released, Pound returned to Italy in 1958, where he would die. His biography shows that his attraction towards Italy was clearly more than an artistic infatuation. It was also the utopian cultivation of *mussolinismo* as a myth and the tragic ending of this pursuit. Half-ideal and half-cursed, Italy represented the in-between place where a series of opposites combined: past and future, East and West, the other and the alike. Thanks to its contradictions and cultural complexities, it encapsulated the quintessence of the diasporic.

Beyond biographical reasons, there is a specific, historical fact that makes Pound the hidden ancestor of the Italian canon in America. This event is the encounter in Rapallo, near Genoa, with the publisher-to-be James Laughlin. It was 1933. Laughlin, then a student at Harvard, had sought Pound for career advice in a moment of lack of motivation. Pound directed Laughlin towards a career in publishing and, following Pound's suggestion, the young American started his own annual journal *New Directions in Prose and Poetry* (1936). This event is paramount because Laughlin would become the publisher of both Poggioli and Marguerite Caetani a decade later. The meeting between Laughlin and Pound brought a crucial change not only to the history of American publishing (New Directions being one of the most innovative publishing houses in the US), but also to the ways of exporting Italian lyric. Pound became Laughlin's mentor and Laughlin became Pound's publisher, as well as the promoter of the first diasporic anthologists. The history of anthologisation of contemporary Italian poetry in the US had begun in a small Ligurian town, not in New York, thus performing a paradoxical, geographical reversal.

The reasons that allow us to rethink Pound's impact on the diasporic tradition are manifold. Pound was a reference point not only for Laughlin, but also for other protagonists of the diasporic network. It is sufficient to mention here two important contributors: the American poet and translator Charles Guenther, who put together three anthologies of Italian verse in the years 1959–61 (Guenther and Sellin 1959, Guenther 1959, and Guenther 1961); and the Italian poet Contini, who introduced the editor Alfredo De Palchi to the poetic world when they were both detained in prison on the island of Procida (see Chapter 5). Pound met both Guenther and Contini, and corresponded with them. He also agreed to publish some Italian translations of his *Cantos* in one of Contini's collections of verse, *L'alleluja* (1952), a further sign of his operative role in forging this tradition.[4]

Another aspect that should not be overlooked is Pound's conception of the anthology as a multicultural and multilayered object. The author of four seminal anthologies, from *Des imagistes* (1914) to *Confucius to Cummings* (1964), Pound conceived of the anthology as 'a laboratory for readers'. He believed that the anthology offers a scientific insight into the world of literature, because for him the 'proper METHOD for studying poetry and good letters is the method of contemporary biologists, that is careful first-hand examination of the matter, and continual COMPARISON of one "slide" or specimen with another'.[5] Like a museum curator, 'the anthologist can pick works written in different places and times, by authors who did not know each other, to make wholly new connections of subject and style'.[6] As Peter Howarth pointed out, Pound's anthology is in fact a 'vortex', as it crystallises his desire to 'see creation, collaboration and circulation as part of one seamless cultural totality'.[7] Pound's idea of the anthologist as a transnational author certainly appealed to the expatriate editors who were forging a canon in translation.

Similarly, Pound believed that the task of the anthologist, the writer, and the translator overlapped in their communal attempt to shape literary history and taste. For him, there seems to be no fundamental distinction between translation and original composition, to the point that his own poetics has been defined as a poetics of translation.[8] As early as 1901, Pound began his comparative examination of European literature and, in 1915, he defined 'his Goethean conception of world literature as involving a criticism of excellence "based on world-poetry"'.[9] Pound's translations from the Chinese are particularly famous, but his corpus comprehends a surprisingly large number of translations from thirteen languages, four of which are non-European.[10] In all his works, Pound treated translation as a 'not historical, but contemporary or timeless' activity; like Poggioli, he thought that translation is the realm of the avant-garde inasmuch as it captures the contemporary and rejects traditional logics (see Chapter 3).[11]

A further element of Pound's poetics that is peculiar to the diasporic vision is his antiacademic stance. American poets always had an ambivalent attitude towards universities, 'the most important sites of reception, evaluation, and increasingly production of modern poetry'.[12] As the founder of the 'Ezuversity', a competing alternative to academia, Pound represents the most critical moment in the relationship of poetry to higher education. Pound's 'lectures' were conducted both in person and via letters and essays; they were then translated into the life of the Black Mountain College after the Second World War, and continue today in the numerous creative writing workshops and poet-theorist professions that exist in America. Laughlin was one of Pound's first pupils, as were Cid Corman and Guenther, which testifies to the genealogical link between these critics.

On a stylistic level, Pound provided the diasporic editors with tools from various genres and disciplines, such as prose-writing, music, and the visual arts. The Italian diasporic canon differs from the domestic one also for its avant-garde, visual elements, a trait that derives directly from Pound himself. Imagism, as Pound defined it in his 1913 essay 'A Few Don'ts by an Imagist', focuses on 'the direct treatment of the "thing", whether subjective or objective' by using 'absolutely no word that does not contribute to the presentation'.[13] Pound's understanding of the poem as a sharp, unique image (something that is also valid for Eliot's 'objective correlative') travelled on to postwar Italy, where it found an equivalence in the poetics of the neo-avant-gardists. It is not accidental that the diasporic canon put to the fore these experimental poets at a time when they were neglected in Italy.

There is a final aspect of Pound's poetics that can be defined as diasporic: his conviction that poetry and theory are strictly intertwined. Parts I and II of this book show how the poetry of diaspora found its initial, theoretical input in transnational theories of the avant-garde. By drawing comparisons with contemporary American criticism, Parts III and IV will clarify the links between diaspora, gender, and ethnic theories instead. Whereas in Italy the dialogue between cultural studies and literary historiography has always been problematic, American critics confronted the role of theory early on, despite the resistance by some of them (one name above all, Harold Bloom).[14] If not the inventor, certainly the discoverer of the correlations between art and theory, Pound coined a term for this reciprocity, *logopoeia*, which he described as 'the dance of the intellect among words' (also the title of one of Perloff's major works).[15]

The Italian diasporic tradition, whose embryonic phases date back to the encounter between Laughlin and Pound in the late 1930s, manifested all of its peculiar features from its beginnings. Militant, transnational, avant-garde, and displaced, it extended to the fields of theory and translation in order to offer new ways of looking at the arts both within and without academia. As Hugh Kenner pointed out in his ground-breaking study, we live in 'the Pound era'.[16] Pound provided 'a box of tools, as abundant for this generation as those Spenser provided for the Elizabethans, and a man that is not influenced in this sense of trying to use at least some of those tools, is simply not living in his own century'.[17] Similarly, within her revisionist history of twentieth-century poetics, Perloff argued that Pound is, 'in the English-speaking world, the pivotal figure in the transformation of the romantic (and modernistic) lyric into what we now think of as postmodern poetry'.[18] Navigating Pound's legacy, the diasporic editors used Pound's set of instruments and poetic influence to both differentiate and assimilate their paths to that of the 'counteranthologist' they most admired. The diasporic canon took its starting point from the least canonical of all American writers; perhaps not such a contradiction after all.

Notes to Chapter 2

1. Marjorie Perloff, *Poetic License: Essays on Modernist and Postmodernist Lyric* (Evanston, IL: Northwestern University Press, 1990), p. 121.
2. Marjorie Perloff, *The Futurist Moment: Avant-garde, Avant Guerre, and the Language of Rupture* (Chicago: University of Chicago Press, 1986), p. xxxvii. See Renato Poggioli, *Teoria dell'arte d'avanguardia* (Bologna: Il mulino, 1962).
3. Ira B. Nadel, 'Introduction: Understanding Pound', in *The Cambridge Companion to Ezra Pound*, ed. by Ira B. Nadel (Cambridge: Cambridge University Press, 1999), pp. 1–21 (p. 13).
4. Ennio Contini, *L'alleluja: poesie di Ennio Contini e la prima decade dei 'Cantos' di Ezra Pound tradotti da Mary de Rachewiltz* (Rome: Siciliana, 1952).
5. Nadel, 'Introduction', p. 11.
6. Peter Howarth, *The Cambridge Introduction to Modernist Poetry* (Cambridge: Cambridge University Press, 2012), p. 44.
7. Ibid., p. 45.
8. Andrés Claro, 'Ezra Pound's Poetics of Translation: Principles, Performances, Implications' (unpublished doctoral thesis, University of Oxford, 2004–05).
9. Nadel, 'Introduction', p. 204.

10. See *Ezra Pound: Translations*, ed. by Hugh Kenner (New York: New Directions, 1953); and Michael Alexander, 'Ezra Pound as Translator', *Translation and Literature*, 6 (1997), 23–30.
11. Ming Xie, 'Pound as Translator', in *The Cambridge Companion to Ezra Pound*, ed. by Nadel, pp. 204–23 (p. 210).
12. Stephen Fredman, *A Concise Companion to Twentieth-Century American Poetry* (Malden, MA: Blackwell, 2005), p. 5.
13. Cited in Nadel, 'Introduction', p. 2
14. Harold Bloom, *The Western Canon: The Books and School of the Ages* (New York & London: Harcourt Brace, 1994).
15. *Literary Essays of Ezra Pound*, ed. and with an introduction by T. S. Eliot (New York: New Directions, 1954), p. 25. See Marjorie Perloff, *The Dance of the Intellect: Studies in the Poetry of the Pound Tradition* (Cambridge: Cambridge University Press, 1985).
16. Hugh Kenner, *The Pound Era* (London: Faber & Faber, 1952).
17. Eric Mottram, 'Conversation with Basil Bunting on the Occasion of his 75th Birthday, 1975', *Poetry Information*, 19 (1978), 3–10 (p. 3).
18. Perloff, *The Dance of the Intellect*, p. 181.

CHAPTER 3

Renato Poggioli: The Beginnings of the Italian Diasporic Canon in America

Whereas the prehistory of the Italian diasporic canon started with the figure of Pound, its history, commencing in post-1945 America, began with another exile, the Florence-born, antifascist Poggioli. Upon his arrival in America, Poggioli began to compile the first postwar anthologies of Italian poetry published in the US, an expression not only of his interest in comparative literature, but also of the close ties between the two countries after the Second World War. Since these anthologies are the product of both the 'trauma of exile' and the positive effects of 'geographical and emotional displacement', Poggioli is responsible for inscribing the reception of Italian letters in the English language into the diasporic domain.[1] As Edward Said put it, 'a beginning not only creates but is its own method because it has intention'.[2] With this in mind, I shall explore here the methodological and creational objectives that justified the origins of this anthological history, and its global destinations.

From Alienation to Exile: Poggioli's *Theory of the Avant-garde*

In order to understand Poggioli's foundational role in the making of the Italian diasporic tradition, it is paramount to clarify his vision of the avant-garde as a transhistorical and transnational phenomenon. According to Ernesto Livorni, Poggioli's interest in the avant-garde had a diasporic cause, derived as it was from his 'privileged position of exile away from his own Italian culture as well as from his adopted one' (Poggioli lived in the Soviet Union for six years before moving to the US).[3]

The accomplished expression of a project aimed to foster a transnational literary spirit, Poggioli's *Teoria dell'arte d'avanguardia* (1962) rooted itself in the diaspora of European intellectuals across the world. Poggioli's notion of the avant-garde is in itself diasporic, not only because it diverges from that cultivated by fellow Italian critics, but also because it was profoundly influenced by his nomadic, academic life. In his foreword to the volume, Poggioli acknowledged that the experience of migration changed his approach to literary studies and, in particular, his understanding of the avant-garde as a supranational entity. He observed that:

> lo sperimentalismo dell'arte d'avanguardia si manifesta non solo in profondità, dentro i limiti d'un'arte determinata, ma anche in estensione, nel tentativo d'allargare i confini di quell'arte o d'invadere il territorio d'un'altra, a vantaggio dell'una o d'ambedue.
>
> [The experimental aspect of avant-garde art is manifested not only in depth, within the limits of a given art form, but also in breadth, in the attempts to enlarge the frontiers of that form or to invade other territories, to the advantage of one or both of the arts.][4]

Poggioli went even further by claiming that 'la critica giusta' [proper criticism] should facilitate the idea and the experience of a tradition that is dynamic and alive, instead of trying to introduce the canons of a dead tradition into the sphere of the avant-garde.[5]

Poggioli pointed out that tradition itself is to be understood not as a museum, but as an *atelier*, as a continuous process of formation, the constant creation of new values, and the melting pot of new experiences. This horizontal conception of tradition, which informed his anthological project, matched with his diasporic idea of the avant-garde as an idiosyncratic manifestation.

The fortune of the term 'avant-garde' is paradoxical precisely because of its geography: despite originating in France, it flourished in the Anglo-American context. As a result of this cultural dislocation (perhaps a sign of the avant-garde's inner diasporicity), Anglo-American avant-gardism is less theoretical and more intuitive than its European counterpart. At the same time, Anglophone artists and/or critics have tended to confound the problem of the avant-garde with that of contemporaneity at large.[6]

Poggioli argued that there is no substantial difference between the avant-garde and modern art in its contingent manifestations. In order to demonstrate this, he read the history of contemporary literature in an anachronistic way, specifically in the light of the various forms of experimentalism that have characterised Western culture since romanticism. For Poggioli, romanticism is potentially what the avant-garde is actually, in the sense that the avant-garde fulfilled the potential of romanticism. As romantic artists reacted against classicism in the name of the new, the avant-gardists looked for a reconnection with their ancestors, and a sense of renewal. Such rejection of the past took different shades in different literary traditions (*antipassatismo*); in Italy, however, it never became programmatic as this country's reverence for the ancients resulted in forms of cultural closure.[7] This sense of chronological suspension allows us to conceive of the avant-garde as a suprapolitical entity, if we consider Pound's fascist connection on the one hand, and Poggioli's resolute antifascism on the other.

In depicting the avant-garde's transhistorical features, Poggioli is aware of the risks of turning this movement into a *passe-partout* that encapsulates the spirit of transgression that is proper to every time. In the concluding pages of *Teoria*, Poggioli specified that both modernity and the avant-garde entered their endemic, chronic state in a manner that is peculiar to the contemporary world.[8] As Poggioli posited it, 'il genio artistico moderno è essenzialmente avanguardistico' [the modern artistic genius is quintessentially avant-garde]; or, to use another of Poggioli's definitions, 'l'avanguardia è legge di natura dell'arte contemporanea e moderna' [the avant-garde is the natural law of modern and contemporary art].[9] Our age witnessed the 'happy transition' from an avant-garde in the narrow sense to an avant-garde in the broad sense, a passage that profoundly affected our common perception of the diasporic.[10]

So far, I have discussed Poggioli's transformative idea of the avant-garde as a reality that manipulates old values on the one hand and creates new ones on the other; yet, there is a second aspect of his theorisation that needs to be addressed: the nexus between avant-garde and alienation. Poggioli offered a blurred definition of the two, as if they were both a constitutional part of modernity; the state of alienation, he argued, has become the default condition of the artist rather than an extreme one.[11] By the term 'alienation', Poggioli referred to a psychological, economic, societal, and cultural state that is by no means limited to the political condition.

This idea of alienation connects with both diaspora and the avant-garde. For Poggioli, the artist is a rebel. If alienation is the content of contemporary art, the avant-garde is its form. The writer's social protest manifests itself in stylistic terms, because what we experience as 'alienation from society' is 'alienation from tradition', too.[12] Likewise, Poggioli drew a parallel between the concept of alienation and the literature of exile as they are both characterised by an absence of freedom. He explained that the avant-garde only develops without the pressure of social and/or political forces, which is among the reasons why it prospered in the American democratic system.[13]

On the crucial point of freedom, Poggioli's ideas of alienation, exile, and the avant-garde intersect. If the artist is alienated from his/her society, then s/he becomes an exile, either in psychological and/or physical terms; the art s/he produces can only be the fruit of his/her struggle for, or recovery of, freedom. Inasmuch as the avant-garde can be seen as a panmodern entity, that is one that describes contemporaneity both in its transhistorical and supranational aspects, diaspora is thus understood as an extension of the modern artist's alienated, and alienating, state.

'Rebuilding the House of Man': Exile, Reconstruction, and the Ethical Imperative

Poggioli's appreciation of the avant-garde echoed the interest in experimentation that animated the poetry and the visual arts of postwar America. His encounter with the American literary and artistic dimensions, however, overcame the boundaries of high culture by extending to the fringes of American migrant society. Poggioli's scholarly profile does not extinguish his multifaceted identity, which is also shaped by his experience as a political refugee. Most of Poggioli's critical production, both in Italian and English, is a metaliterary meditation on the theme of exile: from his 1933 article on 'Gli esiliati della cultura' [The Cultural Exiles] to his piece on the 'Italian Literature of Exile' (1941); and from his inaugural essay in the journal *Inventario* to his 1946 'Letter to Italy'.[14]

Poggioli's postwar anthologies represent a case of diasporic literature that has hitherto remained unexplored. Published in the US in the 1940s, the anthologies Poggioli 1947a, Poggioli 1947b, and Poggioli 1948 emphasise the nexus between literature and exile in a way that is possibly unique in his exilic production. Whereas in his previous works Poggioli discussed the theme of exile through the example of writers who actually experienced it (Emilio Lussu, Ignazio Silone, Guglielmo Ferrero, Giuseppe Antonio Borgese, and the Russian symbolists), his poetry anthologies investigated the topic from a personal angle, that is the editor's perspective. These anthologies offer also a sight of the contemporary Italian scene from the vantage point of a compatriot but through an extraterritorial perspective.

The theme of exile sprang naturally from the events of Poggioli's biography. Leaving Europe in 1938, he was one of the European intellectuals who escaped persecution in the 1930s, participating in 'one of the greatest scholarly migrations' in history.[15] Just as for the majority of academics who left their countries in the years preceding the Second World War (Erich Auerbach, Leo Spitzer, René Wellek...), so for Poggioli the US represented both a land of exile and freedom. After leaving Poland in 1938, where he had been appointed lecturer in Italian at Warsaw, Poggioli declined a position in Slavonic studies at Florence, an unequivocal sign of his discontent with Benito Mussolini's regime. Poggioli's American exile began in New England, first at Smith College (1938–39), then at Brown (1939–46) and Harvard (1947–63). Without ever cutting the visceral cord with his motherland, Poggioli would never return permanently to Italy. Poggioli's decision to leave his motherland was a personal one; yet, existing research provides evidence of the risk of physical harm that the refugee scholar had to face despite his freedom of movement.[16]

Once in the US, Poggioli engaged in antifascist political activities, some of which took place in and around the Pioneer Valley. As remarked by Charles Killinger, Poggioli's campaign is to be read 'in the context of the Italian exilic community of which he was part' and not as an isolated experience.[17] Joining other targets of the fascist authorities, among whom were Gaetano Salvemini and Lionello Venturi, Poggioli founded the Mazzini Society with the aim of opposing all forms of dictatorship. Killinger reported that, 'from its origin in 1939 through his induction into the US Army [1943–45], Poggioli remained an activist in this group, one of the most vital antifascist organisations outside Italy'.[18] Emblematically, the group embraced the name *fuoriusciti*, literally meaning 'gone out', a title that was originally applied to them by the fascists.

These details of Poggioli's militancy allow us to include him in the cadres of the so-called Italian immigrant radical culture. In the US, Italian radicalism is a form of political resistance that has informed the history of the Italian American left since the late nineteenth century. In her ground-breaking study on the culture of these migrants, Marcella Bencivenni dug into the origins of their 'radical milieu'. 'The heart of this movement,' she argues, 'was a transnational generation of social rebels or *sovversivi* — as they were collectively called in Italian — that included anarchists, socialists, syndicalists, and, after World War I, antifascist and communist refugees', among whom we can count Poggioli.[19] The group displayed a diasporic identity not only because it was formed by expatriates, but also because it was the 'product of a reciprocal interaction between Old World experiences and New World developments'.[20]

If we look at the features of Italian American radicalism, there are at least three reasons why Poggioli may be considered one of its representatives: (i) its position of marginality; (ii) its broad definition of the political; and (iii) its ethical dimension. Bencivenni distinguished the leaders of the Italian American communities into two groups: the *prominenti* and the *sovversivi*. Whereas the former had the political and social power, the latter 'functioned as the real strategists and spokesmen of the *colonie italiane*', by offering an 'alternative political leadership' which was 'at odds with the traditional beliefs of the majority of Italian immigrants' and the American capitalists alike.[21] The *sovversivi*'s 'militant vanguardism' was at the core not only of their 'commitment to the humanist principle of liberty, equality, and social justice', but also of their experimentalism.[22] Being artists, writers, and editors as well as political organisers, these *sovversivi* bridged the gap between politics and culture, acknowledging 'the importance of the cultural terrain as a site of struggle'.[23]

Poetry, in particular, appears to be 'the richest, oldest, and most interesting expression of Italian immigrant literary radicalism'.[24] The radical press abounded in verse, often written in the *sovversivi*'s original dialects, an indicator of the popularity enjoyed by social poets such as Arturo Giovannitti, Virgilia D'Andrea, and Antonino Crivello within these migrant communities.[25]

Although Bencivenni's analysis concentrates on the period 1890–1940, her definition of *sovversivo* can be applied to Poggioli as his 'literary choices seamlessly flow into the realm of political activism'.[26] Poggioli happened to operate in one of the most uncertain moments of twentieth-century history, which proved to be fertile for the development of a diasporic poetics. In a memorable and much cited passage of his essay 'Cultural Criticism and Society' of 1951, German philosopher Theodor Adorno claimed that 'to write poetry after Auschwitz is barbaric'.[27] The horror of the Holocaust, together with the deaths caused by what is considered the most destructive global conflict in human history, put into question the function of culture and, more specifically, the credibility of literature. As a result, in Italy as in the rest of Europe, the war produced socially engaged writers who could no longer ignore the events of history. In his essay 'The Italian Success Story', Poggioli pointed out that 'the ordeal of war, even when not creating new poets, has changed the old ones', as 'lyrical inspiration has rejected the temptation of narcissism forever'. Poggioli went on to say that 'the new writers do not utter lamentations even about the ruins of the present, since they do not look for glory but for life'.[28] Elsewhere, he declared that the separation between literature and social affairs is an unacceptable one, since poetry is first and foremost a word pronounced on political matters.[29]

Driven by the same ideas of transformation that informed his avant-garde vision, Poggioli's anthological project had an ethical, rather than a purely aesthetical, scope. His poetry anthologies are the product of the climate of experimentation and political radicalism that had its roots in the ideology of the *sovversivi*. It is no accident that Poggioli's writing of the *Theory* is closely intertwined with the composition of his anthological works, both theoretically and chronologically.

The epistolary exchange with Italian author and translator Cesare Pavese informs us that the process of compilation of Poggioli's monograph had already started in 1947, that is during the years when his anthologies were published.[30]

I argue that Poggioli's anthologies are part of the ideological constellation that link them to some of his concomitant projects, such as the literary journals *Inventario* and *Biblioteca Contemporanea*, which he directed as an exile in the US. What these contemporaneous activities have in common is the desire to reconstruct the Italian nation by means of culture. Whilst Poggioli's anthologies offer a vivid representation of this literature of reconstruction (examples of which will follow in this chapter), the most telling occurrence of Poggioli's poetics is perhaps contained in his essay 'Non programma ma premio' [Not a Programme but a Prize]. Placed at the beginning of the first issue of *Inventario* (1946–63), the following lines embody Poggioli's spirit of renovation:

> Ma ora, mentre una civiltà muore ed un'altra sta forse nascendo, l'intelligenza ha dinanzi a sé una nobile e grande funzione. Questa funzione è quella di guidare l'anima europea, e nel nostro caso italiana, in un lungo e necessario esame di coscienza. [...] Europa ed Italia debbono rimettere in ordine o ricostruire le loro case da sé, non solo le case degli uomini, ma anche la Casa dell'uomo. La nostra rivista vuol partecipare, modestamente ma seriamente, a questa opera di ricostruzione.[31]
>
> [But now, while a civilisation is dying and another one is perhaps coming into being, the intelligentsia has a noble and important task, i.e. that of leading the European soul, and in our case the Italian soul, through a long and necessary process of self-examination. [...] Europe and Italy must tidy up and rebuild their own houses by themselves, not only the houses of men, but also the House of man. Our journal intends to take part in this reconstructive endeavour, with both modesty and seriousness.]

The idea of rebuilding the 'house of man' (Italy's spiritual and cultural dwelling) is as much an emanation of Poggioli's exilic perspective as the articulation of the intellectual's ethical tasks. As Bencivenni points out, the collective values of the Italian immigrant community were, from the outset, essentially ethical.[32] At the end of the Second World War, a similar sense of ending, and of new beginning, was equally perceived in Europe, where 'the sheer scale of physical devastation of the continent was such that a return to the past seemed impossible', whilst 'some kind of radical departure' was necessary.[33] The urgency to establish new parameters of thought, combined with the desire to 'reconceptualise history through specific generic experiments', is an aspect of the so-called 'culture of reconstruction'.[34] With specific reference to the poetry of Pier Paolo Pasolini, Attilio Bertolucci, and Mario Luzi (Poggioli anthologised this last), this ethical attitude has been defined in terms of 'poiesis of history', that is the process by which the poet brings to the fore 'issues of poetic *hereditas* within the context of a twentieth-century historical consciousness'.[35]

Despite being understudied, this moralising energy played a fundamental role in the shaping of the Italian canon in the US. With its biblical resonances, this idea of spiritual reconstruction triggered the religious thread that constitutes one of the major semantic areas of the Italian diasporic tradition. Although Poggioli's selection hints at questions of poetic mysticism without turning it into a main theme, Italian religious poets had an important role in future twentieth-century American anthologies. Religion (understood as culture's sacred heart), ethics, politics, and the avant-garde go hand in hand in Poggioli's poetic cosmos. As expressed by Borgese, who, in Poggioli's words, 'trovò nelle vie dell'esilio una seconda patria, un'altra lingua e una nuova cultura' [found in the ways of exile a second homeland, another language and a new culture], there was a time for rebuilding by opening oneself up to the possibilities of the diverse.[36] The following section will describe how Poggioli's poetry anthologies grew out of this desire for renovation, combined with the ideas of experimentation and cultural radicalism that he internalised during his exilic years.

From Pound to Poggioli through Laughlin: New Directions and the Meanings of 'Active Tradition'

Although the journal *Inventario* has long been considered Poggioli's privileged channel for intercultural communication, his poetry anthologies played an equally fundamental role in the circulation of his transnational credo. He thought that the exposure to a foreign culture would save Italy from the risk of isolation and self-implosion. In a letter of 16 March 1947 to the then-editor and translator for Einaudi, Pavese, Poggioli stated, 'Quello che voglio continuare a fare è un lavoro di diffusione della letteratura italiana in America. [...] Intendo anche lavorare un poco nel campo della presentazione in Italia di buone cose americane' [What I intend to do is to keep disseminating Italian literature in America. [...] I also intend to work a bit more in order to present good American things to Italy].[37] At the same time, Poggioli embarked on a series of projects that aimed to eradicate 'the customary literary individualism and aesthetic narcissism of the Italian writer'.[38] His cultural mission was therefore twofold: to transplant Italian literature to the US on the one hand, and to introduce American authors to Italy on the other. Just like *Inventario* and *Biblioteca Contemporanea*, his anthologies helped the exchange of literary works between Italy and the US.

Poggioli's perspectives on the origins of comparative literature, which he believed was 'born out of the historic circumstances of exile', allow us to appreciate the restorative function of translation.[39] Existing in a land of 'in-between-ness', that is between two different languages and cultures, Poggioli's anthologies provide an example of poetic rebirth grounded in literature's own capability of self-transformation. In the introduction to his *New Directions in Prose and Poetry* anthology, Poggioli linked the avant-garde to issues of translation, canonicity, and historicity. First, he asserted that experimental writing and translated poetry share an avant-garde core; and second, he put forward the idea that the Italian canon should be expanded in a direction that embraced experimental as well as traditional authors. In line with the definitions provided in his *Teoria dell'arte d'avanguardia*, Poggioli claimed that 'avant-garde literature is not, as is commonly believed, something outside tradition'.[40] Rather, 'because it aims at reform or revolution, it is more conscious of the value of tradition than conventional literature, which is usually regarded as traditional *par excellence*'. In the same introduction, he went further by saying that 'for a writer or reader of avant-garde literature there is nothing more disorienting or disturbing than the experimental writing of another environment'; this form of disturbance, however, is a positive one, as it offers 'a splendid pretext and an effective stimulus for further experimentation'.[41]

Poggioli called these forms of crosscultural explorations 'active tradition'. According to him, literature can be investigated on at least two levels: nationally and diachronically, i.e. as a part of a country's literary heritage ('passive tradition'); and internationally and synchronically, that is, within a broader, multinational context ('active tradition'). In this manner, Poggioli justified the translation and anthologisation of the contemporary Italian poets presented in his latest work. Despite 'belong[ing] to a literary culture known to all civilized world in its remote past', they are part of an artistic world that is 'completely unknown in its active tradition, in the forms and beliefs of its present poetic ideal'.[42] From a diasporic angle, Poggioli's understanding of literature as an idiosyncratic, multinational affair testifies to his exilic conception of literary canons.

Poggioli's attempt to spread Italian literature among an English-speaking audience found support in the activity of the American publisher Laughlin. Poggioli's shaping force in the creation of an American awareness of contemporary Italian poetry would have been less effective if he had not been able to count on the concomitant efforts of one of the most prominent American publishers. The founder and director of New Directions, Laughlin published Poggioli's 1948 anthology in a series named *New Directions in Prose and Poetry*, a yearly anthology of American and non-American writers usually belonging to the avant-garde movements (the tenth issue, where the anthology appeared, also contained poems from France and Peru). The sense of a close collaboration between Poggioli and Laughlin is corroborated by their intention to realise a further collection of poems for New Directions entitled *Italian Poets of Today* (due in 1949). Poggioli mentioned the manuscript of this anthology in a letter to Pavese dated 4 January 1949:

> Sto per dare all'editore il manoscritto della mia antologia *Italian Poets of Today*. L'editore è James Laughlin, *New Directions*. Il traduttore è William Weaver. Pubblicheremo il testo a fronte, ed una mia lunga introduzione. I poeti d'Einaudi sono naturalmente Saba e Montale.[43]
>
> [I am in the process of submitting to the publisher the manuscript of my anthology *Italian Poets of Today*. The publisher is James Laughlin, *New Directions*. The translator is William Weaver. The anthology will be bilingual and there will feature a long introduction of mine. The obvious poets published by Einaudi will be Saba and Montale.]

This poetry collection, of which I have found no trace, remained an aborted project that nonetheless testifies to the intense co-operation between the two intellectuals in the postwar years.

Laughlin and Poggioli shared the conviction that literature works as an agent of social change and cultural transformation. 'In those days,' Laughlin recalled in 1992, 'publishing was as much a social contract as a money contract. I came along in the Depression, when publishers were having a hard time. I had a sense of mission — I thought I was saving the world'.[44] In his prefaces to the first (1936) and second (1937) issues of *New Directions in Prose and Poetry*, Laughlin maintained that the aim of experimental literature is to transform society in that avant-garde writing has always worked as 'catalyst' for societal changes.[45] Although by 1946 'New Directions came to be known as a firm whose writers were avant-garde but not political forces', Laughlin's ideas on poetry, politics, and activism would steer his publishing policy throughout.[46]

Laughlin was the bridge between Pound and Poggioli, the US and Italy. Without his trip to Rapallo, when he looked for Pound's mentorship, New Directions would not have existed nor, with it, the formulation of an avant-garde, diasporic way of looking at the Italian poetic production. In Laughlin's opening essay to Poggioli 1948, the publisher's statements resonate profoundly with Poggioli's own declarations. Laughlin illustrated the idea according to which Italy and the US could benefit from a mutual, cultural exposure in the years following the Second World War: Italy by exporting its own literary tradition, a safe way of restoration through transformation; and the US by sharpening its literary taste through contact with the illustrious Italian inheritance. These words could be Poggioli's; except that, as often happens in diasporic contexts, the focus shifted, Laughlin's intention being primarily that of nurturing American culture rather than restoring literature in Poggioli's home country.

Shaping the Poetry of Exile: Poggioli's Anthologies 1947–48

This overview of Poggioli's theoretical thought, seen in the light of the historical events of his time, provides us with the necessary tools to appreciate his contribution as an anthologist in the 1940s. Poggioli's selection was indeed the product of a series of concurrent circumstances: the availability of translators and/or translations; the preparatory work done for *Inventario*; his reviews that appeared in *Italica* in 1948; and his personal preference for certain poets and themes. Most importantly, however, his anthologies were a hotbed for diasporic tropes. Far from being three separate works, these collections can be read as a single book of poems that was assembled in a two-year period (1947–48) and around specific themes. The idea of a comprehensive volume, or, as it has been defined, of a 'poetic autobiography', is justified by the presence of a series of threads that crisscross the anthologies from one year to the next: alienation and migrancy; the forms of the avant-garde; an interest in interdisciplinarity, namely the encounter between poetry and the visual arts; and the evolution of a historical and mystical thread.[47] Table 3.1 offers a snapshot of Poggioli's poetic selections; each poet is followed by his/her translator (please note that only surnames are given in the tables throughout this book). At this point, all poets and translators are male. The table highlights, in bold, the poets recurring in more than one anthology. The order of appearance is that which one finds in the anthologies.

TABLE 3.1. Renato Poggioli's poetic corpus with a list of translators.

POGGIOLI 1947A	POGGIOLI 1947B	POGGIOLI 1948
Campana, trans. by Ramsey	**Saba**, trans. Clapp	**Ungaretti**, trans. by Weaver
Saba, trans. by Clapp	**Palazzeschi**, trans. Clapp	**Montale**, trans. by English
Palazzeschi, trans. by Clapp	**Ungaretti**, trans. by Conley	**Luzi**, trans. by Weaver
Ungaretti, trans. by Weaver	**Montale**, trans. by English [with the exception of 'The Customs-House', tr. by Weaver]	Giglio, trans. by Weaver
Montale, trans. by English	**De Libero**, trans. by Clapp	—
Quasimodo, trans. by Weaver	De Pisis, trans. by Clapp	—
De Libero, trans. by Clapp	**Luzi**, trans. by Ramsey	—
—	Monterosso, trans. by English	—

To our surprise, apart from Montale, whose fortune abroad is well known, it is the Alexandria-born poet Ungaretti who is present in each of the three collections. According to Venuti, at the centre of the Italian poetic canon in English lies Montale, 'flanked by many other Italian poets who exhibit a stylistic affinity'. At the margins 'are the successive waves of experimentalism that swept through Italian poetry in the post-World II period'.[48] Although Venuti is right in assessing that Montale is amongst the most translated twentieth-century poet in English — second only to Pasolini according to the data collected in this study (see Appendix 2.3) — Ungaretti (third place) and Salvatore Quasimodo (second place shared with Montale) have also proved to be extremely popular, with the former representing an important exilic case for diasporic editors.[49] Poggioli defined Ungaretti as 'the leading Italian poet of today', whereas Luigi Ballerini, one of the continuators of Poggioli's avant-garde line, saw him as a poet 'to whom a long tradition of experimental Italian poetry can be traced back'.[50] Evidently, despite his adherence to fascism (Mussolini wrote a preface to Ungaretti's *Il porto sepolto* in 1923), Ungaretti appealed to the radical anthologists almost as strongly as Montale, whose profile is less cosmopolitan. As a result, if Montale is the most canonical poet in Italy (a record that is reflected by the many monographic translations of his poetry), Ungaretti is his American double.

From a diasporic perspective, the overall predominance of Pasolini across the translated corpus examined here does not contradict the Ungaretti model pioneered by Poggioli; rather, it confirms it. First appearing in GUENTHER AND SELLIN 1959, Pasolini has been a constant avant-garde and multilingual presence, featuring in highly innovative collections, from those edited by De Palchi and Corman in the 1960s to Luigi Bonaffini's anthologies of Italian dialect poetry in the late 1990s and early 2000s. Similarly, most of the other poets anthologised by Poggioli had a fortunate reception in the American transplanted canon, with Luzi and Umberto

Saba appearing fifteen times across the corpus, Aldo Palazzeschi twelve, Dino Campana ten, and Libero De Libero seven.[51]

As revealed by Table 3.1, an important aspect of Poggioli's diasporic poetics is the emphasis on both canonical and lesser-known authors. Poggioli's anthologies juxtapose the names of Montale and Filippo De Pisis (a poet-painter), or of Ungaretti and Tommaso Giglio (a poet-journalist and translator), while a minor poet such as De Libero occurs twice ('minor' refers here and elsewhere to a poet's degree of popularity and not to the quality of his/her output). Since Poggioli's selection is numerically limited (only eleven poets scattered throughout three volumes), single appearances are not necessarily a sign of disinterest and/or inferiority. On the contrary, in POGGIOLI 1947A, the leading position of an experimental poet such as Campana testifies to the editor's admiration for the 'forerunner of contemporary Italian lyrical modernism'.[52]

Another element to consider is that, whereas POGGIOLI 1948 is a poetry-only anthology, POGGIOLI 1947A and POGGIOLI 1947B present a mixture of prose, both creative and critical, and verse. The diasporic anthology is a site for experimentations, especially within the anthological genre. In addition to Poggioli's essay on 'Italian Literature Between Two Wars', a valuable introduction to the anthology as a whole, POGGIOLI 1947A includes pieces by Italo Svevo, Federigo Tozzi, Emilio Cecchi, Elio Vittorini, Gianna Manzini, Ferrero, as well as a small selection of texts by foreign authors, poets, and critics (Samuel Putnam, Vivienne Koch, Norman Macleod, Donald Weeks, and Maurice Lindsay). Similarly, POGGIOLI 1947B, an Italian-French issue of the review *Voices*, features, among others, poems by Paul Éluard, Henri Michaux, and Pierre-Jean Jouve, alongside articles and reviews, some of which centred on the issue of canonicity. See, for instance, 'A Great Tradition and a Minor One' by Walter Adams.[53]

Translation occupied an important portion of Poggioli's activity, from his translation of Alexander Blok in 1933 to his versions of Novalis in 1960; he believed in the creativity and autonomy of the translator 'as a producer of literary culture'.[54] In his famous essay on translation, entitled 'The Added Artificer', Poggioli went even further by saying that 'even the choice of the text to translate is a creative act led by a preference' or by what Poggioli himself called an 'elective affinity'.[55] Nonetheless, Poggioli did not translate the poets he anthologised. His conception of the anthology as a multifaceted, collective endeavour also emerges from his decision to employ several translators (see Table 3.1).

The idea of the poet-editor and/or poet-translator, launched by Poggioli, would have a certain appeal to future diasporic editors. His anthologies provided a suitable model for later generations, as today's anthologies still oscillate between pure poetry and mixed selections, English-only and multilingual volumes.

Poggioli's anthologies are pioneering also in regard to their themes. They offer an opportunity to analyse *in vitro* the embryonic phases of the Italian diasporic tradition. With Poggioli, diaspora became the narrative force that triggered the transportation of Italian poetry to America. Diaspora provided the critic with the possibility of looking at literature without any linguistic, cultural, or ideological boundaries, as a way of mediation between different countries and times. Poggioli turned his exile into a compelling metaphor to describe the paradoxical meanderings of memory and imagination, 'separation and desire, perspective and witness, alienation and new being'.[56] A truly diasporic product, his anthologies bear the traces of this constant attempt at reconciling opposites. Even Poggioli's diasporic condition is in itself contradictory. Whereas it fell at first into the category of 'forced exile', it became in time 'a voluntary condition', the aesthetic value that underpinned the complexity of his 'poetic autobiography' from his early years right through to his late works.[57]

Mattia Acetoso provided the first systematic attempt to link Poggioli's criticism to the exilic dimension. In an essay published in 2013, 'Renato Poggioli's Intellectual Project and the Psychology of Exile', Acetoso identified three key ideas that characterise Poggioli's 'psychology of exile': (i) that exile is not only the physical expression of a geopolitical rupture, but also the representation of a spiritual, psychological situation; (ii) that exile is both a creative instrument and an intellectual, almost utopian, project; and (iii) the belief, informing all Poggioli's works, that exile is 'the opportunity for the establishment of a new culture of letters'.[58] As Acetoso has pointed out, for Poggioli 'exile represents a loss, but it also corresponds to the imaginative process that attempts to compensate for that loss'. He adds that 'exile is to be understood as a privileged space from which to observe one's own culture and build a project of moral reconstruction for it'; or, to use another of his images, that exile is the 'opportunity to reverse the logical sequence of loss, in a process that negotiates crucial issues such as language and the looming idea of a return'.[59]

My analysis, which adopts a diasporic approach, owes much to Acetoso's study. Yet, it also distinguishes itself on at least two levels: first, it deals with Poggioli's exilic works rather than with his preexilic ones (the anthologies were actually composed during the time of Poggioli's expatriation); and second, it understands diaspora as a fluid rather than a binary model. Drawing on Michael Seidel's *Exile and the Narrative Imagination*, Acetoso defended the idea that exile is 'an opportunity to turn absence and distance into a compensatory creative process'.[60] 'The task for the exile,' Seidel said, 'is to transform the figure of rupture back into a "figure of connection"'.[61] According to this interpretation, Poggioli's anthologies can be read as his ideal return home, since a physical homecoming proved to be impossible in the end. Yet, Poggioli's anthological work opened the way to a complex understanding of the experience of diaspora, which is not necessarily a double-edged entity. As his anthologies show, diaspora is a liminal space resulting from 'the multiplication of contact zones and the broad spectrum of [migratory] situations', something that has 'forced theorists to [...] increasingly pay attention to [new categories, such as] hybridity', interstitiality, and fluctuation.[62]

This idea of diaspora is helpful not just to understand Poggioli's exilic trajectory as an editor, but also to examine the themes narrativised across the collections. The emphasis on certain motifs gave the anthologist the space to create his own nomadic narrative whilst also providing a response to the dilemma of canonisation. Poggioli tells us a story of travel and migration: from his own exile, that is the exile of the narrator, to Campana's mystical wandering towards the dreamy shore of Montevideo (Poggioli 1947a); and from Palazzeschi's interior journey through the cities of memory and imagination (Poggioli 1947a and Poggioli 1947b) to Quasimodo's literary exile, lamenting poetry's silence after the tragedy of war.

Apart from the selection of poems, certain figures must have appealed to the editor as an embodiment of the so-called literature of *destierro*, 'exile' in Spanish; Saba, Triestine by birth, half-Catholic and half-Jewish, is in this sense an ideal representative (see Poggioli 1947a and Poggioli 1947b).[63]

A further instance of Poggioli's exploration of the theme of exile is the inclusion of De Libero's poetry, which is a nostalgic and commemorative recollection of his rural homeland, Ciociaria.[64] Libero's poems, also translated by Frederick Mortimer Clapp, belong to the collection *Il libro del forestiero* [The Book of the Foreigner] (1945), a title that directly recalls the exilic condition. Similarly, Francesco Monterosso's civil poetry is a testament of love for his treacherous country: 'Soldier, go in. Father and mother lost, | Even the cat is gone'.[65] This sense of abandonment, conveyed by a coarse yet melancholic vocabulary, is an important aspect of Monterosso's radical verse.

The most telling example of the 'thousand ramifications' of the 'psychological and aesthetic nature' of exile is offered by the presence of the germinal parts of Ungaretti's *La terra promessa* [The Promised Land]. At the time Poggioli put together his anthology for *New Directions in Prose and Poetry*, *La terra promessa* was still part of a 'work in progress' that Ungaretti started in 1935 and would publish with Mondadori in 1950. The series of twelve choruses anthologised by Poggioli for the American journal appeared for the first time in *Inventario*.[66] It is not uncommon that literary works were published in translation before, or immediately after, their publication in the original language; a powerful evidence of literature's transnational circuits.

Like *Il dolore* [Sorrow] (1947), *La terra promessa* belongs to the so-called second season of Ungaretti's career, which started with the poet's recovery of tradition and the use of ancient metres, rhythms, and myths, a practice that is already evident in *Il sentimento del tempo* [The Feeling of Time] (1933). It is interesting to notice how Ungaretti's return to tradition is a humble, rather than a triumphant, one. Imbued with the pathos of a spiritual quest, it is interlaced with one of the greatest crises of history and his life (at the time of the Nazi occupation in Rome, Ungaretti lost his son). Although signs of the mystical were already present in his *Allegria di naufragi* [Joy of Shipwrecks] (1915–42), it is only with his latest works that this theme becomes crucial. It goes without saying that a title such as *La terra promessa* is rich in religious as well as diasporic resonances. This is the land that God promised to Abraham and his descendants; the Jews, repeatedly exiled from their home country, have been longing for the fulfilment of this promise for centuries. Similarly, at the time of the Romans, Aeneas looked for the land, Italy, indicated to him by the gods. Future diasporic editors, amongst whom Sergio Pacifici and Ballerini, have emblematically chosen Ungaretti's title for their anthologies in translation (Pacifici 1957 and Ballerini 1999).

As an editor, Poggioli was certainly attracted by the idea of a poetry that has both spiritual and material implications. As shown by Ungaretti's example, exile and reconstruction are historical, psychological, and ethical forces that closely cooperated in defining the Italian diasporic poetics. In a seemingly contradictory way, the second edition of Ungaretti's *Il porto sepolto* [The Buried Harbour], which constitutes the oldest nucleus of *Allegria*, was published by Stamperia Apuana, La Spezia, in 1923, with a preface by Mussolini. This fact, however, is not at odds with Poggioli's ideology of subversion. By no means did Poggioli engage with Ungaretti's fascist beliefs at the time of this publication; rather, Poggioli and his diasporic successors put forward Ungaretti's profile as an exilic avant-gardist, one that was aesthetically radical to the point of being often perceived as 'foreign' by Italian intellectuals.

From a diasporic standpoint, Ungaretti's lines, in William Weaver's translation, stage the alienation of the lyrical subject in a quite compelling manner. Through the inclusion of Dido's lament against time and space, we can interpret the heroine's experience of loss as a powerful image for the poet's sense of estrangement. Here are some instances:

> I cry and my heart is afire without peace
> Since the time when I have become only
> A thing in ruins and abandoned.
> [...]
> We were transported by anxiety, along sleep
> Toward what other, elsewhere?[67]

Both the poet's and the editor's exilic states (banished, departed, outcast) will take different forms throughout the history of the diasporic tradition; yet, the origins of this deracination are to be identified in Poggioli's early collections.

In addition to the theme of wandering and exile, and in constant dialogue with it, the anthologies display an indirect yet continuing meditation on history and war. This is evident not only in the texts that clearly deal with the memory and/or heritage of the conflict (see Quasimodo's and Montale's poems, translated by Weaver and Maurice English respectively), but also in Poggioli's decision to feature recent poetry inspired by experiences of mourning and loss. For instance, Poggioli 1947b features poems from Ungaretti's *Il dolore*, translated by Weaver and published in Italian in the same year; besides, 1947 is the year in which Luzi's *Quaderno gotico* [Gothic Notebook] appeared (see Poggioli 1947a, also translated by Weaver), a collection that Poggioli would review in *Books Abroad* the following year. Again, the concern for poetry's destiny after the Second World War is combined with a certain taste for biblical, apocalyptic tones: from Ungaretti's human utopia (the 'City of Man') to Montale's depiction of Hitler as a 'an infernal messenger'; and from Luzi's image of love as a spiritual conflict between earth and heavens to Giglio's adaptation of the language of the Bible to the desolation of contemporary man.

There is a final aspect of Poggioli's selection that remains to be addressed: its diasporically avant-garde nature. I have already discussed how his theorisation of the avant-garde is chronologically intertwined with his exilic writing. Yet, the reasons to believe that his anthologies are directly informed by his avant-garde studies and, more specifically, by his idea of 'active tradition' go beyond a shared temporal framework.

The introductions to his anthologies stage the dialectics between tradition and innovation in a slightly different manner. Whereas both the introductions to his 1947 anthologies provide a historical representation of twentieth-century poetry, the opening essay of POGGIOLI 1948 focuses on the challenges of creating a new poetic tradition. This is due to the fact that, with its penchant for experimentalism, *New Directions in Prose and Poetry* appeared to be Poggioli's ideal forum for a scholarly discussion on tradition and canonicity. In his unconventional portrayal of postwar Italian poetry, poets like Ungaretti, Montale, Luzi, and Giglio are linked to one another through a paradoxically interchiastic relationship: Montale with Luzi and Giglio with Ungaretti, but also vice versa. For Poggioli, contemporary Italian poetry experienced a division between content and form, which was visible, for instance, in the poetry of Luzi and Giglio: whereas the former represented the 'super-world' of Ungaretti through the 'strident style' of Montale, the latter depicted a mechanical universe by adopting a language of illuminations and revelations that echoed Ungaretti's works. Poggioli added that 'a further paradox is that Luzi seems more "poetic" than the "prosaic" Montale; Giglio, more "prosaic" than the "poetic" Ungaretti'.[68] These cryptic ways through which artists interacted represent one of the major obstacles to canon formation as the defining features of one poet were used paradoxically to characterise another.

The 1947 publications show not only similarities, but also points of variation. For example, POGGIOLI 1947A includes Quasimodo's poetry, whereas POGGIOLI 1947B features poems by De Pisis, Luzi, and Monterosso. This difference is indicative of the fact that the anthologies pursued two distinctive purposes: POGGIOLI 1947A proposed a canon of modern Italian literature that dates back to the poetry of Giovanni Pascoli, Giosuè Carducci, and Gabriele D'Annunzio (and that was completed by the presence both of Quasimodo and prose writers), whereas POGGIOLI 1947B explored the emerging 'voices' of postwar Italy, both within and outside its national boundaries. It is worth noticing that the only copy of POGGIOLI 1947B available in England is kept at the Imperial War Museum in Duxford, an obvious sign of the complex connections between poetry and war.

Poggioli's diasporic approach to the avant-garde explains some of his selection criteria: the presence of figures that could embody the intersection between poetry and the visual arts, such as the painter De Pisis (POGGIOLI 1947B); the inclusion of Monterosso's popular song as a 'historical and psychological document' of Resistance Italy (POGGIOLI 1947B); the connection between Campana and modernism (POGGIOLI 1947A); and the incorporation of Ungaretti's and Montale's poetry into the avant-garde and modernist streams (POGGIOLI 1948). The idea that these two major poets are the Italian representatives of the modernist revolution proved to be a long-lasting one. Poggioli argued that 'Ungaretti [...] performed with great originality a function within Italian poetry similar to that of Apollinaire or Valéry in French poetry, while Montale has more than once been defined as a kind of Italian T. S. Eliot'.[69] More than sixty years later, poet-editor Geoffrey Brock distinguished between an Italian and American modernist tradition, the former concerned with tone and rhetoric, and the latter with form.[70]

A final proof of the deep influences of the American literary environment on Poggioli's selection is his preference for long, narrative poems. The number of lines per poem increased considerably from the 1947 anthologies to that of 1948. Reproducing the contemporary American taste for narrative poetry, POGGIOLI 1948 includes excerpts not only from Ungaretti's *The Promised Land*, but also from Montale's *The Hitler Spring*, Giglio's *Themes for a Symphony*, and Luzi's *Gothic Notebook*. In particular, the latter is a collection of fourteen poems of more than two hundred lines in total, whose inclusion certainly represents an interesting anthological case. Poggioli's decision to anthologise narrative poems is a nonconformist one, considering the dominant hermetic trend in postwar Italy. By contrast, the long poem was a vibrant poetic form in twentieth-century American literature. Its representatives, who frequently were avant-garde poets themselves, ranged from Robert Frost and T. S. Eliot to Williams and Pound.[71]

Notes to Chapter 3

1. Charles Killinger, 'Renato Poggioli and Antifascism in the United States', in *Renato Poggioli: An Intellectual Biography*, ed. by Roberto Ludovico, Lino Pertile, and Massimo Riva (Florence: Olschki, 2013), pp. 39–57 (p. 43).
2. Edward Said, *Beginnings: Intention and Method* (Baltimore, MD: Johns Hopkins University Press, 1975), p. xiii.
3. Ernesto Livorni, 'Renato Poggioli's *Theory of the Avant-garde* and its Legacy', in *Renato Poggioli*, ed. by Ludovico, Pertile, and Riva, pp. 179–96 (p. 180).
4. Poggioli, *Teoria dell'arte d'avanguardia*, p. 153; *The Theory of the Avant-garde*, trans. by Gerald Fitzgerald (Cambridge, MA: Harvard University Press, 1965), p. 133.
5. Poggioli, *Teoria dell'arte d'avanguardia*, p. 181.
6. See ibid., p. 21.
7. See ibid., p. 67.
8. See ibid., p. 249.
9. Ibid., pp. 250–51.
10. Ibid., p. 245.
11. Ibid., p. 148.
12. Ibid.
13. Ibid., p. 112.
14. Renato Poggioli, 'Gli esiliati della cultura', *Solaria*, 1 (1933), 45–54; 'Italian Literature of Exile', *Decision*, 1 (1941), 40–43; 'Non programma ma premio', *Inventario*, 1 (1946), 1–6 (repr. in *Il secolo dei manifesti: programmi delle riviste del Novecento*, ed. by Giuseppe Lupo and Giuseppe Langella (Turin: N. Aragno, 2006), pp. 340–47); and 'Letter to Italy', *Briarcliff Quarterly*, 11 (1946), 209–11.
15. Giorgio Carnevale and Stefania Pastore, 'Omaggio a John Tedeschi', in *Intellettuali in esilio: dall'Inquisizione romana al fascismo*, ed. by John Tedeschi, Giorgio Caravale, and Stefania Pastore (Rome: Storia e Letteratura, 2012), pp. vii–xiv (p. viii).
16. Killinger, 'Renato Poggioli and Antifascism in the United States', p. 42.
17. Ibid., p. 39.
18. Ibid.
19. Marcella Bencivenni, *Italian Immigrant Radical Culture: The Idealism of the Sovversivi in the United States, 1890–1940* (New York: New York University Press, 2011), p. 2.
20. Ibid., p. 14.

21. Ibid., p. 38.
22. Ibid., p. 3.
23. Ibid.
24. Ibid., p. 138.
25. See ibid., pp. 138–53.
26. Roberto Ludovico, 'Introduction', in *Renato Poggioli*, ed. by Ludovico, Pertile, and Riva, pp. ix–xvii (p. xvi).
27. Theodor Adorno, 'Cultural Criticism and Society', in *Prisms*, trans. by Samuel and Sherry Weber (Cambridge, MA: MIT Press, 1967), pp. 17–34 (p. 34).
28. Renato Poggioli, 'The Italian Success Story', in *The Spirit of the Letter: Essays in European Literature* (Cambridge, MA: Harvard University Press, 1953), pp. 199–221 (pp. 214, 219).
29. Poggioli 1947a, p. 344.
30. *A 'Meeting of Minds': carteggio 1947–1950. Cesare Pavese, Renato Poggioli*, ed. by Silvia Savioli (Alessandria: L'orso, 2010), p. 41.
31. Poggioli, 'Non programma ma premio, p. 342.
32. See Bencivenni, *Italian Immigrant Radical Culture*, p. 44.
33. Nicholas Hewitt, *The Culture of Reconstruction: European Literature, Thought and Film, 1945–50* (Basingstoke: Palgrave Macmillan, 1989), pp. 1–2.
34. Ibid.
35. Keala Jewell, *The Poiesis of History: Experimenting with Genre in Post-war Italy* (Ithaca, NY: Cornell University Press, 1992), p. 4.
36. See Poggioli, 'Gli esiliati della cultura', pp. 45–54; and Antonio Borgese, *Tempo di edificare* (Milan: Treves, 1923).
37. Cited in *'A Meeting of Minds'*, ed. by Savioli, p. 40.
38. Poggioli 1947a, p. 227.
39. Anna Botta, 'Renato Poggioli and the Byzantine Origins of Comparative Literature', in *Renato Poggioli*, ed. by Ludovico, Pertile, and Riva, pp. 145–61 (p. 149).
40. Poggioli 1948, p. 310.
41. Ibid.
42. Ibid.
43. *'A Meeting of Minds'*, ed. by Savioli, p. 72.
44. Cited in Greg Barnhisel, *James Laughlin, New Directions, and the Remaking of Ezra Pound* (Amherst: University of Massachusetts Press, 2005), p. 62.
45. Ibid., p. 63.
46. Ibid., p. 202.
47. Mattia Acetoso, 'Renato Poggioli's Intellectual Project and the Psychology of Exile', in *Renato Poggioli*, ed. by Ludovico, Pertile, and Riva, pp. 125–43 (p. 127).
48. Venuti, *The Translator's Invisibility*, p. 239.
49. Pasolini is the most represented poet in the anthologies examined in this book (19 presences out of 50 anthologies, which corresponds to 38 per cent of the anthologies). Montale and Quasimodo appear 18 times out of 50 (36 per cent), immediately followed by Ungaretti who features 17 times out of 50 (34 per cent); for a list of the most anthologised poets, see Appendix 2.3.
50. Caselli, 'Value and Authority in Anthologies of Italian Poetry in English (1956–1992)', p. 65.
51. See Appendix 2.3.
52. Poggioli 1947a, p. 229.
53. Poggioli 1947b, pp. 49–51.
54. Rita Wilson and Leah Gerber, 'Introduction', in *Creative Constraints*, ed. by Wilson and Gerber, pp. ix–xv (p. ix).
55. Renato Poggioli, 'The Added Artificer', in *The Spirit of the Letter*, pp. 355–66 (p. 359).
56. Michael Seidel, *Exile and the Narrative Imagination* (New Haven, CT: Yale University Press, 1986), p. x.
57. Acetoso, 'Renato Poggioli's Intellectual Project and the Psychology of Exile', p. 127.
58. Ibid., p. 142.
59. Ibid.

60. Seidel, *Exile and the Narrative Imagination*, p. 128.
61. Ibid.
62. Král, *Critical Identities in Contemporary Anglophone Diasporic Literature*, p. 2.
63. For a definition of the literature of *destierro* see Poggioli, 'Italian Literature of Exile'.
64. Libero De Libero, 'Cicada' and 'Return to Patrica', trans. by Frederick Mortimer Clapp, in POGGIOLI 1947A, pp. 275–76.
65. Francesco Monterosso, 'Song of the Patriot of the Marches', trans. by Maurice English, in POGGIOLI 1947B, pp. 21–22.
66. See *Inventario*, 3–4 (1946–47).
67. Giuseppe Ungaretti, 'The Promised Land', trans. by William Weaver, in POGGIOLI 1948, p. 315.
68. POGGIOLI 1948, p. 311.
69. Ibid., p. 310.
70. BROCK 2012, p. XXX.
71. See Christopher MacGowan, *Twentieth-Century American Poetry* (Oxford: Blackwell, 2004), pp. 287–93.

CHAPTER 4

❖

The Hidden Anthologist: Marguerite Caetani's Exilic Patronage

The experience of exile linked Poggioli's anthological enterprise with that of Caetani. Both editors operated in the aftermath of the Second World War, sharing their views on avant-garde literature and diaspora alongside a similar concern for the cultural reconstruction of Italy. Yet, despite a common uneasiness with the fascist regime, their militancy is profoundly different. In this chapter I shall analyse how Caetani both continued and supplemented Poggioli's radical line by accentuating some of its traits on the one hand, and introducing new ones on the other.

The Garden of Exile: Death and Rebirth in Caetani's Arcadia

Although Caetani does not fit the category of the exile as obviously as Poggioli, her life-long dedication to the artistic world displays the features of an aesthetic isolation. At a first glance, Caetani's exile was more aesthetic than political. Taking refuge in the realm of poetry and nature, she lived most of her life in a form of intellectual seclusion, her contacts being limited to interactions with writers and artists. Caetani's isolation stemmed from her attitude towards the arts, which she considered as a separate realm from history and society. For Caetani, poetry is in itself a kind of transcendence, a mode of opposition against the 'foreground, the factual daily record' as well as the image of some remote, ideal world.[1] Yet, despite Caetani's efforts at self-effacement, her selection of poets remains a militant work which testifies to the political nature of the anthology as a genre. A patroness and a princess, Caetani nuanced the profile of the exile anthologist on a number of levels. First, she is neither a political refugee nor was she obliged to leave her country. The reasons why she spent most of her life abroad (first in France and then in Italy) were as much biographical as related to her cosmopolitan urge. Second, Caetani never theorised on the category of exile, leaving no written documents whatsoever on her critical conceptions. Her role as a critic and editor can be appreciated through the consideration of her cultural patronage, which we deduce from the intense correspondence that she had with poets and artists both from North America and Europe.

The product of the editor's escape to the realm of poetry and the countryside, Caetani's *Anthology of New Italian Writers* (CAETANI 1950) was conceived against the background of a garden near Rome, Ninfa. The image of the garden epitomises Caetani's ideas on literature and criticism, while also conveying the contradictory mixture that characterised her personality: multiculturalism and openness on the one hand, and separation and seclusion on the other. Caetani reached Ninfa after two decades spent in France, where she had arrived from Connecticut as a twenty-two-year-old woman. Paris is fundamental to understanding both the genesis of Caetani's anthology and the conditions of her aesthetic exile. In Versailles, Caetani founded the literary journal *Commerce* (1924–32), which marked the beginning of her life-long dedication to literature. Additionally, Paris is the city where she met her future husband, the composer Prince Roffredo Caetani, the heir of a notable Italian family. Plunged into the dynamism of the modernist capital, Marguerite animated a multicultural, artistic community whose international spirit was to underlay her anthological project in Italy ten years later.

If Caetani's withdrawal into the world of literature had already begun in Paris, it is only in Rome that her position as an émigrée and an outsider — out of history and of the conventions of literary circles — became more evident. The Caetanis moved from Paris to Rome in 1932, the year in which Marguerite was forced to cease *Commerce* for financial reasons. Whilst she decided to keep a flat in Paris, she never returned to America, which we may read as an intentional act of separation from her native country. At the same time, while becoming better and better acquainted with Europe, she never renounced her American citizenship. In particular, she regarded Italy as a land both of origins and exile: a motherland, because she recognised in Italy the archetypal image of poetry, 'a mindset, an abstraction of notions, a way of being — at its best the beloved Mother of Western civilization'; and a land of exile, because, once there, she never returned home.[2]

Caetani's aesthetic exile was also a psychological one, as it was not without suffering and grief. We know that Caetani was a victim of the fascist dictatorship (as was Poggioli), although she tried not to engage with contemporary politics. During the Second World War, she lost her only son while he was fighting in Albania for a regime that he, and she, detested. The loss of Camillo also meant the end of the Caetani dynasty since his sister Lelia (a painter and keen horticulturalist like her mother) remained childless. In the 1940s, the property of Ninfa was used to shelter both partisans and evacuated civilians, becoming Caetani's tacit act of resistance against Mussolini. As Helen Barolini pointed out, 'the decade of her life when she lived in a fascist society so alien to her heritage and so devastating in her personal life is when one can sympathize more deeply with the dilemma of her divided loyalties'.[3]

In the fascist years, Caetani experienced the ambiguous situation of living in an adopted land (Italy) that was enemy to her country of birth (the US). The war profoundly exacerbated Caetani's sense of estrangement in a country that seemed to have lost its artistic freedom and humanistic values. Whereas the earliest American visitors to Italy were attracted by the splendour of its past, Caetani found a nation that was worn out by war.[4] Italy, Caetani's long-dreamt-of Arcadia, was a nation that was yet to be built.

The difficulty of the historical situation, however, did little to lessen Caetani's faith in the arts. In the cultural revival that followed the Liberation, she found the path towards a personal return to life. To recover from a tragedy that was both private and historical, Caetani engaged in a second editorial project that aimed at rebuilding Italian society by means of culture. In a letter that Caetani sent to her sister Katherine, she expressed her longing for 'some light and air and a bit of phantasy' in Italian literature, because the 'dry-as-dust existing publications which were all politics, criticism, and history' monopolised the postwar literary scene.[5] Caetani's new programme, which we can summarise in three points, continued the transnational line of *Commerce*, but addressed the specificities of the Italian situation: 'raise Italy in world opinion from the ignominy of the fascist period, to showcase Italian writers who had been silenced during the regime, and to do so in an international review'.[6]

The princess found the ideal conditions to fulfil her cultural mission at Ninfa. In the aftermath of the war, the garden became a stimulating environment where artists and scholars from across different disciplines and countries gathered with diplomats and ordinary people. Just as the garden of Ninfa flourished in the ruins of time and war, Caetani realised that Italian letters too could have a chance to rise from the ashes of the fascist dictatorship. Similarly, her personal wounds were eased by the garden's healing power. At Ninfa, a place of both encounters and isolation, the private and the historical intermingled to the point of fusion.

The garden is a compelling metaphor to describe both the negative and beneficial aspects of the diasporic condition. Imbued with desires for renovation and internationalism, Caetani conceived here not only the idea of a new literary periodical, *Botteghe Oscure* (1948–60), but also the plan for her English-language anthology. These editorial operations are all the more intertwined as all the poets included in the 1950 anthology had already made an appearance in the first five issues of the review.[7]

Botteghe Oscure's goal was twofold and echoed Poggioli's ideas closely: on the one hand, it wanted to give young Italian writers a chance to reach an international audience; and, on the other, it aimed to introduce them to the foreign authors who had been inaccessible to the Italians during the years of fascist censorship.[8] It is worth observing that the earliest issues of the review hosted mainly Italian authors (the opening issue with Italian writers exclusively), whereas the presence of foreign voices grew from the second issue onwards.[9] The dominance of Italian writers in the late 1940s reveals Caetani's urgency to reestablish the country's literary reputation in the postwar years.

The striking similarities between Poggioli and Caetani suggest that the two editors exchanged letters and/or information at the time of the anthologies' compilation. However, the only evidence we have of a link between the two is the presence of annotated copies of Caetani's *Botteghe Oscure* in Poggioli's private library.[10] The idea of a common project is also supported by the fact that Laughlin, who shared similar views on literature and translation, published both. Their connections with Laughlin tied the transplantation of contemporary Italian poetry into the American system to the avant-garde dimension. Moreover, the geography of these projects by Laughlin, Poggioli, and Caetani (from Italy to America, and back), as well as their engagement in the postwar period, illuminates the philanthropic motivation of their work, which was not directly intended for academia. Both Poggioli's and Caetani's anthologies are political responses to the crisis of the postwar years as well as adaptations to the changes that it involved, and imposed.

Beyond Reticence: Caetani's *Anthology of New Italian Writers*

Caetani's *Anthology of New Italian Writers* was first printed in Rome by the Istituto Grafico Tiberino and, later in the same year, appeared both in Britain (John Lehmann's publications) and in the US (New Directions). If in Italy the anthology went almost unnoticed, in America it elicited contradictory opinions amongst the critics. For instance, whereas Thomas Bergin criticised the poetry selection, Oscar De Liso praised it as being innovative and 'first rate'.[11] Caetani's further efforts to export Italian writers across the Atlantic is revealed by the fact that, later in the 1950s, she asked Farrar Straus (the then distributor of *Botteghe Oscure* in America) to publish a second anthology of Italian literature in English. The project could not be fulfilled because of a misunderstanding between the editor and the publishing house; yet, it testifies to Caetani's dedication to the dissemination of Italian poetry abroad.[12]

Caetani's anthology presents an alternation of poetry and prose, a feature that already characterised *Botteghe Oscure*. Just as the review was issued without a specific ideological programme, the anthology contained texts without introductions and/or commentaries, with the apparatus limited to a series of bio-bibliographical notes on the authors at the end. The anthology broke the pattern of poetry and theory inaugurated by Poggioli and testified to Caetani's poetics of self-effacement. A further instance of her reticence is the omission of the editor's name. The absence of editorial matter, however, should not be interpreted as a lack of critical engagement: not only is the selection of poets and poems thoughtfully supervised, but also the decision to employ a single translator (the young yet proficient Weaver) demonstrates Caetani's rigorous programme.

Although the anthology displays a well-defined structure, Caetani's editorial criteria are difficult to define. This sense of self-effacement is palpable not only in the anthologist's decision to include unknown poets, a clearly avant-garde trait, but also in her role as a female editor. She was the first woman to compile an anthology of contemporary Italian verse in English. Even if she did not include any female voices, Caetani would pave the way for the anthologisation of women poets by providing the precedent of a female, diasporic editorship. Her volume anticipated those to be published in Italy, where the first anthology compiled by a woman came out in 1960.[13]

A further element that supports Caetani's poetics of self-effacement is the fact that she was an American philanthropist with no specialism in Italian literature. Some of her choices are likely to have been suggested by Giorgio Bassani, not only

Caetani's closest collaborator in the laboratory of *Botteghe Oscure*, but also the editor of the journal's Italian section. Although it is hard to establish the extent to which Bassani influenced the selection, the correspondence between the two testifies to Marguerite's invisible yet decisive role. Whereas Bassani tended to exclude avant-garde poets, Caetani was 'alla ricerca continua di quello che percepisce come voce nuova, in tutti i paesi e in tutte le lingue' [continously in search of what she perceived as new in any country and language].[14] Caetani's selection was based on the age and popularity of a poet rather than on specific stylistic and/or linguistic features: the younger and more unknown a writer was, the greater his/her chance of inclusion. Besides, Caetani's literary taste was strongly influenced by her American heritage. Her preference for introspective atmospheres, such as those evoked by the German-American poet Theodore Roethke, deeply affected her choices. Caetani 1950 stands out as a typically diasporic case as it placed itself between different countries and value systems.

Caetani's conception of the avant-garde, as emerges from her selection, resonates with Poggioli's theories. If we accept Poggioli's definition of the avant-garde as a synonym for contemporary literature, we may be able to link Caetani's preference for the work of young artists to Poggioli's critical ideas. For Caetani, an American who witnessed the rise of modernism in Paris, the essence of contemporary literature was experimental. In an interview with Eugene Walter in 1958, she affirmed that European writers were reluctant to experiment with language, whereas 'from America comes work that appears to be more lively, more varied, more original than what is produced in Europe'.[15] Her criticism of the immobility of European letters was enhanced further by her praise of the freshness of American works.

Caetani's literary taste, though, was not unidirectional. The result of various contaminations, it was built on contradictory forces, from the classicism of the Italian tradition to the manifold expressions of American experimentalism. With reference to *Botteghe Oscure*'s poetry contributions, critic Massimiliano Tortora divided Caetani's poets into three main groups: the poets of the 'linea sabiana' [Saba's line] writing prose-like poems (Caproni, Bertolucci); the experimental poets, who began within the Officina group (Francesco Leonetti, Pasolini, Roversi); and the modern classicists, i.e. poets that were able to combine traditional forms with contemporary, factual, and domestic themes.[16] Considering that hermeticism was the predominant poetic trend in 1940s Italy, Caetani's poetics reflected American, rather than Italian, literary expectations. Her selection was dictated by her preference for domestic, existential themes, which found a correspondence in her favourite American poets: Roethke, Williams, Moore, Lowell, Hayden Carruth, and E.E. Cummings, to name but a few.[17]

The range of Caetani's poems (twenty) finds its coherence in a solid narrative frame, in which the flux of memory, landscape, history, and private life intersect. Whereas the prose section deals with more engaged pieces of writing (such as Gugliemo Petroni's *The House is Moving*), the poems allude to the epic of ordinary life. This low-toned epic punctuates the entire collection, from its representations of memory (Bassani's 'In Memoriam') to the often-violated idyll of childhood and nature (Bertolucci's 'The Indian Hut'); and from the theme of marriage and friendship (Fortini) to the cities of Bassani (Ferrara) and Caproni (Genoa).

Caproni's 'The Funicular', translated by Weaver, stands out as a case of a contemporary poem that echoes classical motifs and structures. Against the background of a misty, intangible Genoa, an unmythical Proserpina makes her last apparition: a modern goddess who washes doorways and 'befogged glasses' in slippers. In the context of postwar Italy, Caetani's employment of epic models proved to be a crucial choice. Already adopted by Poggioli and expressed through his preference for narrative poetry, the 'modern epic verse' is another of Pound's inventions. Pound 'sincerely feared that unless poetry could successfully challenge the novel in the breadths of its representational powers, it might become as irrelevant and out-of-date as "the art of dancing in armour"'.[18] Pound's *Cantos* are a shining example of modern epic, the fragmentary cosmos where myth and history collide.

Apart from the search for a Poundian epic, a further thread that weaves through Caetani's collection is the transience of nature, which is often conveyed in religious tones (Rinaldi's 'Prayer') or through the use of biblical images (Roversi's 'Rachel'). The anthology also gives space to the metaliterary theme explored in the form of the mysterious yet indissoluble bond between language and life. Future collections will emphasise the centrality of metaliterature as a diasporic trope. In 1950, avoiding war was not a canonical choice. Focusing on the themes of everyday life (with the exception of Gatto's 'Novel 1917'), the semantics of Caetani's anthology reproduces a fundamental trait of her personality, that is a problematic understanding of the relation between poetry and history. If the formula 'poiesis of history' synthesises Poggioli's anthological work, Caetani's anthology seems to propose a 'poiesis of everyday life'.

Caetani's poetics of self-effacement was neither a form of cultural and/or economical superiority, nor of political indifference. Rather, it was the rhetorical artifice that enabled her to create a truly avant-garde, militant anthology. Whereas Poggioli's activity as an antifascist was explicit, Caetani's contribution to Italy's reconstruction remained as shadowy as she was, especially if we take into consideration the laceration of her diasporic identity. It is precisely through her commitment to the remaking of the nation that she was able to transform the ivory tower of her isolation into a political deed. The princess's isolation was redeemed by her avant-garde attempt to make the obscure visible, and the silent heard.

* * * * *

In her retrospective journey to the sources of literature and life, Caetani transformed Ninfa from the garden of archetypal symbols into a space of poetic rebirth, a process that finds its parallel in the dialectics between diaspora and artistic creativity. Neither Poggioli nor Caetani returned home. However, both of them used the power of the exilic imagination to go back, mythically and metaphorically, to their common motherland, poetry. Exile provided them with the tool of foresight, vision, and imagination, in a world that was going towards the tensions of the Cold War; poetry, on the other hand, was the space for the anthologist's recompense, reconnection, and homecoming. Travelling back from America to Italy (Poggioli), and vice versa (Caetani), the boundaries between nations and languages were ultimately able to blur.

Notes to Chapter 4

1. Helen Barolini, *Their Other Side: Six American Women and the Lure of Italy* (New York: Fordham University Press, 2006), p. 204.
2. Barolini, *Their Other Side*, p. xix.
3. Ibid., p. 205.
4. See Van Wyck Brooks, *The Dream of Arcadia: American Writers and Artists in Italy, 1760–1915* (London: Dent, 1958).
5. Cited in Barolini, *Their Other Side*, p. 211.
6. Ibid.
7. The poets included in CAETANI 1950 had appeared in issues of *Botteghe Oscure* as follows: Giorgio Bassani, issues 1 and 5; Bertolucci, 1 and 4; Giorgio Caproni, 3; Franco Fortini, 4; Alfonso Gatto, 3; Antonio Rinaldi, 1; and Roberto Roversi, 4. William Weaver was the translator of them all.
8. John Brown, 'Guiding the Commerce of Ideas', *Books Abroad*, 47.2 (1973), 307–11 (p. 309).
9. See Stefania Valli, *La rivista 'Botteghe Oscure' e Marguerite Caetani: la corrispondenza con gli autori italiani, 1948–1960* (Rome: L'Erma di Bretschneider, 1999), p. 61.
10. Dante Della Terza, *Da Vienna a Baltimora: la diaspora degli intellettuali europei negli Stati Uniti d'America* (Rome: Editori Riuniti, 1987), p. 174.
11. Cited in Lorenzo Salvagni, 'In the Garden of Letters: Marguerite Caetani and the International Literary Review *Botteghe Oscure*' (unpublished doctoral thesis, University of North Carolina at Chapel Hill, 2013), p. 148.
12. Barolini, *Their Other Side*, p. 220.
13. *Poeti del Novecento italiani e stranieri*, ed. by Elena Croce (Turin: Einaudi, 1960).
14. Valli, *La rivista 'Botteghe Oscure' e Marguerite Caetani*, p. xi.
15. Cited in Salvagni, 'In the Garden of Letters', p. 100.
16. Tortora's division is cited in Salvagni, 'In the Garden of Letters', p. 104.
17. Barolini, *Their Other Side*, p. 215.
18. Michael André Bernstein, *The Tale of the Tribe: Ezra Pound and the Modern Verse Epic* (Princeton, NJ: Princeton University Press, 1980), p. 20.

PART II

❖

The Avant-garde and its Diasporic Legacies

CHAPTER 5

Roaring Sixties: Alfredo De Palchi, or the Editor *Révolté*

Caetani's anthology was followed by a period of silence which was broken by a handful of poetry collections. Whereas we witnessed the publication of four anthologies of Italian poetry in translation between 1947 and 1950, in the 1950s the majority of translations from the Italian concentrated on prose and, partially, music. Despite the scarcity of poetry volumes, the 1950s and 1960s represented an important incubator for the evolution of the diasporic tradition, especially thanks to the development of a strongly biographical practice. The model anticipated by Pound, theorised by Poggioli, and embraced by Caetani was put to test and then reinforced, as revealed by the hesitation between canonical and avant-garde authors.

This chapter will describe the persistence of diasporically avant-garde modes in the process of transplantation of Italian poetry in the US by documenting moments of stasis and acceleration. Special attention will be paid to the figure of De Palchi, whose anthologies occupied, almost entirely, the 1960s literary scene.

The 'Battle of the Anthologies': Tradition and Experimentation in the 1950s and Beyond

Poggioli and Caetani inscribed the American history of Italian poetry in the name of the exilic avant-garde. After their anthologies, the American press promoted various forms of poetic experimentation, from Miller's 1958 selection for *Folio* (MILLER 1958) to Corman's avant-garde versions for the *Origin* review (CORMAN 1963). Yet, despite the legacy of these forerunners, a conservative trend was to develop together with the dominant, experimental vocation.

The classicist line began in the United States with Pacifici's collection (PACIFICI 1957), whereas in England it had already been introduced by Carlo Dionisotti's literal translations in 1952.[1] After Pacifici's attempt to anthologise well-established figures (see Ungaretti, Saba, Quasimodo, and Montale), space was made for establishing this Italian quartet, who were presented in historical anthologies, sometimes illustrated (DE LUCA AND GIULIANO 1966; DE' LUCCHI 1967; REBAY 1969). Historical collections were less popular in the US than in England, where anthologies of this kind were produced by institutional presses in the same period: *The Oxford Book of Italian Verse* (1952), edited and revised by Dionisotti, and the *Penguin Book of Italian Verse* (1958), compiled by George Kay.

In the US, the attention towards Italian canonical poets was less a critical inversion than a response to the American literary debate. In the 1950s and 1960s, divergent attitudes towards the Italian poetic tradition resulted from a controversy between two literary groups: the formalists on the one hand, and the avant-gardists on the other. This ideological conflict, also known as the 'battle of the anthologies', followed the publication of two almost contemporaneous anthologies: Donald Allen's *The New American Poetry: 1945–1960*, which fostered a multiethnic and stylistically diverse reading of literature; and *New Poets of England and America* (1962), edited by Donald Hall and Robert Pack, which promoted a more formal tradition of works.[2] In particular, Allen focused on the emergence of the postwar American avant-gardes (Black Mountain College, the New York School, and the Beat Generation) claiming that these literary groups were already established in terms of public, press, and tradition.[3] This conflictual stance in American literary criticism translated into a decade of heterogeneous directions for the anthologists of Italian verse. While Italian poetry's dual mainstay, both traditional and experimental, was at once identified and unearthed, American editors engaged with its Poundian heritage either by following or opposing it.

Fighting for a space in this literary arena, anticanonical anthologies, generally hosted by small, avant-garde journals, won over traditional ones. The most important example of this kind is offered by the three consecutive issues of the *Literary Review* (1959–60) edited and translated by Eric Sellin and Charles Guenther (Sellin 1959, Guenther and Sellin 1959, Guenther 1959). Guenther was a poet-translator as well as a friend and admirer of Pound. In 1961, he published his own selection of Italian poems with Inferno Press, San Francisco; however, with the exception of Diego Valeri, none of the poets anthologised in the volume are new compared to the dense selection of writers prepared for the magazine (see Appendix 2.2). In the *Literary Review*, the editors presented for the first time to the American audience important poets such as Pasolini, Vittorio Sereni, Camillo Sbarbaro, and Maria Luisa Spaziani, the latter being, as well as little-known, a woman (see Chapter 9). At the same time, some names were inherited from Poggioli's and Caetani's anthologies, both the obvious ones (Quasimodo, Ungaretti, and Montale) and the less so (De Libero, Luzi, Bertolucci, and Gatto). By contrast, other authors made a once-only appearance, justified by the anthologies' avant-garde profile: Ugo Fasolo, Luigi Fiorentino, and Enrico Fracassi.

The agonistic background of the 1960s ignited a special interest in Italian and, more broadly, European literature, with the effect of raising the number of literary translations, also in the form of poetry anthologies. For the single year 1960, Healey's annotated bibliography of Italian literature in English translation lists fifteen novels, two poetry collections, and four theatrical pieces. Published two years after *Life Studies* (1959), Lowell's *Imitations* of Montale put Italian and American poetry directly into dialogue, blurring the boundaries between translation and creative writing. Concurrently, the American poet Stanley Burnshaw decided to anthologise Italian poems without translating them; on the other hand, he provided detailed commentaries on the foreign texts. His transnational book of poems,

The Poem Itself (Burnshaw 1960), was reprinted three times in seven years, scoring an extraordinary record in the history of poetry publishing.

In fiction, a shift towards historical and/or politically engaged writing is visible in the publication of works by Silone (*Fontamara*), Vittorini (*Erica e i suoi fratelli*, *La garibaldina*), Carlo Cassola (*Fausto e Anna*), and Primo Levi (*Se questo è un uomo*). The reinforcement of political motives is not unexpected, given the profusion of historical novels published in the previous years. Nonetheless, it was only in the 1960s that the emphasis on militant literature became a primary trait also in poetry anthologies in translation. This is noticeable in the series of collections published by De Palchi between 1961 and 1966. By turning political activism into a form of personal protest, he pushed the radical side of the Italian diasporic canon to its extreme consequences. Whereas the 1950s were a time of ideological oscillation, with editors exploring opposing anthological possibilities, the 1960s were dominated by this single, diasporic anthologist who consolidated Italian avant-gardism in the US.

The Birth of the Poet-editor: De Palchi's Biographical Approach

Among the advocates of the experimental line, De Palchi stands out for introducing a strong biographical approach. The editor of four collections of poetry (prepared in collaboration with his first wife Sonia Raiziss), De Palchi was an all-round artist for whom the nexus between poetry and life is tangible. Although it would be impossible to understand Poggioli's and Caetani's anthologies without taking into account the events of their life, it is only with De Palchi that biography became an integral part of critical discourse.

In order to highlight the existential nature of De Palchi's production, his biographer Luigi Fontanella linked the editor's life to that of other outcasts of Western literature, such as Campana, François Villon, Charles Baudelaire, and the Italian American writer Giose Rimanelli.[4] Critics have also stressed De Palchi's cosmopolitanism, the spiritual materialism, or visceral mysticism, of his poetry as well as its protean, exilic forms.[5] No matter which perspective we choose to approach De Palchi's diasporic poetics, it is possible to identify three main episodes and/or traits that determined his literary conceptions: (i) a nomadic vein, which took him to the US in 1956, aged thirty; (ii) six years of torture and incarceration, first by the fascists and then by the partisans (1945–51); and (iii) the meeting with the poet Contini in Procida prison in 1946. These experiences resurface in De Palchi's life and work in a manner that is both compulsive and subterranean.

The drama of incarceration immediately connected De Palchi's destiny to that of his diasporic predecessor, Pound. It is not coincidental that Contini, also a political prisoner at the time of De Palchi's imprisonment, published with Pound a collection of poems that includes the first ten *Cantos* in Italian translation (*L'alleluja*, 1952). A letter written by Contini to Pound on Christmas Day 1958 is conserved at the Yale Beinecke Rare Books and Manuscript Library, a precious piece of evidence of Pound's importance for Italian outsiders (for a transcription of this letter see the Appendix 4). The encounter with Contini was fundamental for the artistic development of the young De Palchi, who at the time was only eighteen. A poet forgotten by both publishers and critics, Contini showed De Palchi the redeeming power of poetry, especially through the example of French symbolism. Prison thus turned into a 'coming-of-age experience', providing De Palchi with the 'stoic energy to resist, to react, [...] to grow, and, last but not least, to write his poetry as a real homme révolté'.[6] Inspired by these and other idiosyncrasies, De Palchi's activity began under the sign of anticonformism: 'I didn't follow the standard canons,' De Palchi declared, 'I didn't know them, and if I did I would have dismissed them anyway. [...] I am a group of one'.[7]

The combination of imprisonment and exile made De Palchi's poetry radical. There is a striking correspondence between De Palchi's experience and that of the Italian immigrants who fled to the US in the late nineteenth and early twentieth centuries. Much like De Palchi, Giovannitti, whom Bencivenni defined as 'a poet and prophet of labor', transformed 'his cell into a study room, feeding his mind with masterpieces of great writers'.[8] Similarly, anarchist poetess D'Andrea, who escaped Mussolini's persecution, wrote her verse while being held in prison. Whereas most Italian American radical poets 'tended primarily to talk of general social and political conditions rather than individual experiences, D'Andrea's poems fused the personal and the political'.[9] In both D'Andrea and De Palchi, 'themes of revolutionary change and social inequality intermix with [the poets'] inner feelings, while pessimism about [their] political time is softened by the awareness of the power of love and the beauty of life'.[10] These characteristics of De Palchi's poetics, which resonate with the *sovversivi*'s rebellious programme, are fundamental to appreciate his anthological enterprise.

After his liberation in 1951, De Palchi moved to France and Spain before settling in the US, where he would live for the rest of his life. His arrival in New York marked the beginning of De Palchi's second life in an environment that was more congenial to his subversive vein. Here, however, he was unable to integrate into American literary society, becoming an outsider also within his host community. In an attempt to capture the essence of De Palchi's isolation, Fontanella introduced the idea of a double exile: 'the first from [his] literary patria, which no longer recognized [him]'; and the second 'from the new "patria", which [he] experienced, in a manner of speaking, only transversally, and that therefore could easily ghettoize [him]'.[11] Unlike the refugee Poggioli, De Palchi was not an academic and therefore was less exposed to cultural contaminations. De Palchi's position is 'more transgressive, and, above all, more antiacademic than any other contemporary Italian writer in America'.[12] His initial and second exile helped 'to produce that familiar feeling [...] of belonging neither here nor there, yet also, paradoxically, [...] the sense of belonging any place, real or imaginary, whatever it may be'.[13]

De Palchi's editorial line continued Poggioli's diasporic project inasmuch as both men left Italy in a time of tyranny and political turmoil. Yet, simultaneously, it also complicates it, inaugurating a new trend in the history of Italian poetry's anthologisation. Being a poet himself (or, as he has been defined, an 'antipoet'),

De Palchi's profile as an anthologist is no longer distinguishable from his activity as a poet and translator. Poggioli already believed in the all-round image of the artist as a poet, translator, and critic; nonetheless, his anthologies did not include his poetry and/or his translations. By contrast, De Palchi's convergence of tasks and purposes, which we may call 'autobiographical', had important consequences both for the selective process and for his targeted readership. This is the origin of a new mode of transplanting Italian poetry in American soil, which became the norm from the 1960s onwards. At the time of De Palchi's contributions, numerous professors were poets and/or translators themselves, also working in the publishing industry (Laughlin, Corman, Guenther). In America, this tradition was not new: in the nineteenth century, the poet William Cullen Bryant was also the editor of the *New York Evening Post*. In addition to De Palchi, influential poet-editors of the diasporic line include Fontanella and Ballerini, whose work I shall analyse in Chapters 6 and 7.

The Practice of the Avant-garde in De Palchi's Anthologies

With De Palchi's collections, the life of the anthologist turned into a matter of critical debate. Given the complexities of De Palchi's profile, this biographical turn explains some of the paradoxes that emerge from the editor's contradictory choices, from the coexistence of well-established and unknown writers to the emphasis on the mystical (see De Palchi's preference for poet David Maria Turoldo, who was ordained a priest). In fact, there is perhaps no more paradoxical figure than De Palchi in the history of the Italian diasporic tradition. While assiduously working for the translation and circulation of his native literature across the Atlantic, he refused all connections with Italy. He attacked the Italian avant-garde of the 1960s, preferring instead its American forms (Pound) and historical foundations (Tristan Tzara).

Although Caetani's selection was already inclusive of the youngest poets, it is only with De Palchi that Poggioli's theory of the avant-garde finds its first, practical application. This is visible both from a publishing perspective, i.e. the place of his anthologies' publication, and from a poetic one, that is on the basis of his selection criteria. All of De Palchi's anthologies, except for one, were issued by *Chelsea*, an experimental journal founded by a group of American artists based in New York City.

All the collections (De Palchi 1961, De Palchi 1962, De Palchi 1966a, and De Palchi 1966b) were compiled in collaboration with Sonia Raiziss; in addition, the 1961 and 1962 issues saw the collaboration of Ursule Molinaro, a French-born visual artist and novelist, and Venable Herndon, an American screen writer.

The 1960s proved to be a crucial turning point in the publishing field. Two years after its 1958 launch, Raiziss and De Palchi took on the editorship of *Chelsea*, promoting international as well as crosscultural writers: a meaningful choice at a time of canon revisionism. From this moment on, Italian poetry would be accommodated either by small, experimental publishers (*Chelsea*, *Folio*, Inferno Press) or by major university presses (Berkeley and Fairleigh Dickinson), losing the privileged, commercial position that it enjoyed in the aftermath of the Second World War. Yet, although this was a different environment from the one in which

Poggioli operated ten years earlier, when the publisher New Directions fulfilled the role of both avant-garde flag and established firm, Laughlin's inspirational values were confirmed.

Poggioli and De Palchi were concerned with the transmission of innovative verse alongside the recognition of a moral and/or political ethics. There cannot be avant-garde poetry without freedom; at the same time, it is only through the experience of persecution and exile that the best avant-garde literature is created, translated, and received from one country to the other. More specifically, there are two ideas that link De Palchi's avant-gardism with Poggioli's theorisation: the conviction that canons are politically charged; and the belief that the up-to-dateness of the avant-garde lies in its spirit of alienation and, therefore, expatriation. This dynamic view, which places De Palchi among the supporters of a transnational idea of the avant-garde, justifies some of the ambiguities at work in his editorship.

As far as selection criteria are concerned, it is possible to identify three main trends. De Palchi was simultaneously concerned with (i) anticanonical figures, namely avant-garde, southern, and young poets; (ii) political authors such as soldiers and prisoners or, more generally, militant writers; and (iii) transnationalism. Poets such as Bartolo Cattafi, Rocco Scotellaro, and Nanni Balestrini belong to the first and second category, whereas the issue of internationalism comes to the fore in Campana, Sereni, Giorgio Orelli and Nelo Risi either because of their biographies or themes. It is worth noting that, from De Palchi 1962 onwards, Pasolini becomes a ubiquitous presence in the Italian canon transplanted in the US, one that epitomises characteristics of the three categories. De Palchi can also be credited with popularising Luzi and Risi in America, both poets appearing fifteen times each throughout the whole corpus.

Table 5.1 provides a snapshot of De Palchi's selections in the anthologies examined. Authors with two or three occurrences are marked in italics and bold respectively. Three Italian poets (Risi, Sereni, and Gatto) and two Italian American poets (Gregory Corso and Lawrence Ferlinghetti) appear in a special issue of *Chelsea* dedicated to 'Plays and Political Poetry' (1960), a further sign of De Palchi's militant aspirations.

Table 5.1. Alfredo De Palchi's poetic corpus with a list of translators.

De Palchi 1961	De Palchi 1962	De Palchi 1966a	De Palchi 1966b
Quasimodo Trans. by M. and A. Viscusi, and by Molinaro	*Luzi* Trans. by Guenther	**Sereni** Trans. by Raiziss	Saba Trans. by Nims, Lawner, Stefanile
Sereni Trans. by Molinaro	*Orelli* Trans. by Lawner	*Risi* Trans. by Corman and Herndon	Cardarelli Trans. by Raiziss and De Palchi
Risi Trans. by Raiziss and De Palchi	**Turoldo** Trans. by Margo and Anthony Viscusi	**Pasolini** Trans. by Gardner	Campana Trans. by Nims, Raiziss and De Palchi

Sinisgalli Trans. by Raiziss and De Palchi	Cimatti Trans. by William Weaver	Zanzotto Trans. by Raiziss	Ungaretti Trans. by Raiziss and De Palchi, Nims, Mandelbaum, Weaver
Cattafi Trans. by Cambon	*Erba* Trans. by Lynne Lawner	Balestrini Trans. by Salomon	Montale Trans. by Lowell, Brandeis, Raiziss and De Palchi, Nims
Scotellaro Trans. by Bergin	**Pasolini** Trans. by Lynne Lawner	Acutis Trans. by Hathaway	*Quasimodo* Trans. by Mandelbaum, Garrett, Guenther
Turoldo Trans. by M. and A. Viscusi	—	Fortini Trans. by Guenther	Pavese Trans. by di Giovanni
Gatto Trans. by Cambon	—	Ceserano Trans. by Stefanile	*Sinisgalli* Trans. by Raiziss and De Palchi, Weaver
De Palchi Trans. by Raiziss	—	**Cattafi** Trans. by White	*Luzi* Trans. by Sellin, Guenther
—	—	Della Corte Trans. by Raiziss	**Sereni** Trans. by Raiziss and Cambon, Raiziss, Sellin
—	—	Sanguineti Trans. by Hathaway	**Turoldo** Trans. by M. and A. Viscusi
—	—	Pagliarani Trans. by Wright	**Pasolini** Trans. by Lawner, Wright
—	—	Pignotti Trans. by Guest and La Bianca	**Cattafi** Trans. by Cambon, Raiziss
—	—	—	*Scotellaro* Trans. by Weaver, Bergin, Guenther
—	—	—	*Erba* Trans. by Fitzgerald, Lawner
—	—	—	*Orelli* Trans. by Lawner
—	—	—	Piccolo Trans. by Raiziss and De Palchi

Although the anthologies may be read transversally as a single book of poetry, each collection features specific aims. Accompanied by a dossier of visual poetry and a sample of avant-garde prose (narrative, theatrical, and essayistic), De Palchi 1966a is the most experimental of all the anthologies. In the foreword to the volume, Glauco Cambon, also a poet and critic who migrated to the US, announced that the 'present all-Italian issue of *Chelsea* has to do' with the 'iconoclastic writers' that constituted the 'most controversial movements' of postwar Italy. 'The editors,' he continued, 'did not intend their selection as a normative anthology, but merely as representative of certain radical trends in modern Italian literature, as well as of other, less extreme, ones'.[14]

This is the first time that the Italian neo-avant-garde is granted a predominant position within an American anthology. Italian poetry is exposed here to a kind of Husserlian, philosophical mode that expresses itself through the writer's sense of alienation both from society and language. These poets' phenomenological orientation 'proposes the suspension of all pre-constituted ideologies' that prevent 'access to a pre-conceptual experience of the world', including the centrality of the subject.[15] Although adapted to the advancement of continental philosophy, the neo-avant-gardists' reduction of the lyrical 'I' is in fact an inflection of Poggioli's quest for the auroral meanings of contemporary literature, which he placed in the suspended territories of diasporic poetry.

De Palchi 1966a treats the visual arts as an integral part of the avant-garde's creative expressions. These poets' subversive writings are both an extension of the Anglophone modernist revolution (Edoardo Sanguineti, for instance, pushed 'Pound's polyglot and elliptical epic' to an extreme), and an exploration of poetry's visual possibilities.[16] Sixteen Italian artists are associated with thirteen artworks, three of which are the fruit of collaboration: Antonio Porta and Romano Racazzi, Giuliani and Toti Scjaolja, and Adriano Spatola and Giuseppe Landini. Balestrini and Lamberto Pignotti are also anthologised as poets, which allows a sense of fluidity between art and texts.

Themes of alienation, revolt, and war resonate throughout the anthology, finding specific correspondences between images and words. Pignotti's defence of the 'dolce avanguardia', a remedy against the strains of modern life, finds its counter-voice in his prosaic verse:

> There is no history.
> [...]
> And this faith is in itself a form of protest against the anonymity of the results of mass production in a *technological civilization:*
> [...]
> What is left then?[17]

In the same collection, traces of Husserl's phenomenology, especially the focus on inanimate objects and the suspension of the lyrical I, punctuate a complex, interpersonal discourse: '(but let me speak) ... a loss of man ... another strophe' (Balestrini); 'and they were talking, in the dark (and I, in bed, reading a novel of Sollers)' (Sanguineti); 'you should try to understand what I am | but maybe not | looking with downcast eyes | *un regard de soie*' (Sergio Acutis).[18] The link between poetry, philosophy, and the visual arts, as it appeared in De Palchi 1966a, will constitute an essential trait in future, anthological works prioritising avant-garde verse.

De Palchi 1961 and De Palchi 1962 are also mixed volumes focusing on different genres; however, their heterogeneity is limited to the written word, as they do not include any visual representation. By way of compensation, they feature authors from different countries, rather than concentrating on the Italian case. This cultural and linguistic mix has the effect of internationalising Italian poetry in a way that had never been pursued before. Nine Italian poets open the poetic section of De Palchi 1961, followed by important names such as Williams, Blaise Cendrars, Vladimir Mayakovsky, and Boris Pasternak. Similarly, the Italian poets featured in De Palchi 1962 are part of a longer list including Oliver Wendell Holmes, Raymond Queneau, and André Breton. De Palchi's transnational selection cannot be fully appreciated without taking into account the numerous formal and semantic connections among poets of different nationalities. For instance, 'The Destruction of Cathedrals' by New York poet Daisy Aldan ('I am weary of visiting cathedrals. | Let me make a pilgrimage to the trembling cathedral of my own spirit') echoes Luciano Erba's condemnation of the devastations of war: 'I wish there weren't any Tartarean tortures | on the banks of Adda on a holiday'.[19] The theme of reconstruction, something that dates back to Poggioli's efforts to rebuild the house of man, is revisited by the editor De Palchi in the light of society's new priorities.

At the other end of the spectrum, De Palchi 1966b stands out as the anthologist's most canonising endeavour. The third section of Willis Barnstone's anthology of European verse — preceded by French, German, and Greek poetry on the one hand and followed by Russian and Spanish poetry on the other — this collection provides a selection of seventeen Italian poets representing Italy's 'wild weather after World War II'.[20] As in the previous anthologies, the emphasis is on radicalism, transnationalism, and the avant-garde. Campana's 'vagabond mania', which expressed itself through an 'aberrant life', madness, and imprisonment, 'set him apart in Italian poetry'.[21] Similarly, the abundance of southern and/or politically engaged poets, such as Cattafi, Pasolini, and Lucio Piccolo, is more a poetic manifesto of the 'economically and socially dispossessed' than a form of ethnic and/or linguistic exploration.[22]

Although the themes of this anthology align with those of the first three, De Palchi 1966b includes Italy's most famous poets, a decision that supposedly disrupts the editor's experimental line. Yet, these major poets are not presented according to Italian critical conventions; rather, they stand in opposition to any preconceived discourse, in a way that makes them consonant with the anthologist's avant-garde beliefs. De Palchi appreciated all poets for their transgressive potential, even the most canonical ones. Ungaretti, who is claimed to be 'among the first and foremost in the European vanguard', is the single author in whom 'the revolution against all Italianate decorums' resides.[23] Montale, who is responsible for giving a 'personal accent' to poetry, is anthologised for his long, narrative verse, rather than for his hermetic pursuits.[24] Vincenzo Cardarelli, who 'launched the avant-garde of La Ronda' (to my knowledge no critic had defined La Ronda as an avant-garde movement before), is said to be considered 'the antecedent of certain present-day realists in Italy'.[25] De Palchi is testing here the limits of Italian criticism, while reinforcing Ungaretti's leading role within the Italian diasporic canon.

De Palchi's adherence to the avant-garde is not a straightforward one. His poetry selection is experimental, but it also shows a form of loyalty towards certain forms that are based on precise, poetic traditions (French, American, and Italian). In a truly American sense, De Palchi defied tradition by engaging with it. His contrasting poetics is at work, for instance, in the anthologisation of Quasimodo's 'White Rivermouth'.[26] This poem, translated by Molinaro, represents a typically diasporic case as it appeared first in French translation and then in the original, a reversal that is not uncommon in the history of literary translations. Despite Quasimodo's highly literary language, 'White Rivermouth' is rich in nominal sentences that elicit a sense of fragmentation on the one hand, and challenge our understanding of the poet's overall poetics on the other:

Evil also the snow;
a wearier silence
the falling of ripe leaves.[27]

Quasimodo's erudite verse is transfigured into a developmental, tentative syntax. Similarly, De Palchi compared Ungaretti's brevity of words and sentences to the Imagists' technique, and Andrea Zanzotto's cosmic world to Thomas Hardy's romantic writing.[28] De Palchi's avant-gardism reflects a series of transgeographical and transhistorical stratifications; it is the ongoing, interdisciplinary remaking through which he maintained a subversively interacting dialogue with a supranational literary history.

Exile and the Mystical: De Palchi's Individual Canon

Besides the communal horizon of the avant-garde, the theme of exile intersects De Palchi's anthologies. With its multiple inflections (biographical, political, and transnational), exile springs from poems which exhibit a sense of existential anguish and isolation, often compared to silence and death:

What paste
what gelatine
what crumbling clay
and how much spittle
to cement the incommunicable.[29]

Sometimes, more overtly, the poet's diasporic condition is expressed through images of geographical and cultural displacement: 'There are caravans walking on forever' and 'One always sails from Greenwich | from the zero marked on every map';[30] 'Tomorrow is sea and desert'.[31]

Exile often takes the form of an expropriation of the poet's body. Once humans are alienated from themselves and their similes, exile affects the matter, the landscape, and even God, in a universal contagion. The poet, the objects, nature, and all the living are united both in their solitude and suffering: 'The whole world is my unburied body';[32] 'Suddenly my veins | turned black, a mysterious being | danced in me';[33] 'The streets are lacerated wounds';[34] and 'I watched life on life perform | vivisection'.[35] The boundaries between the poet and the editor have been blurred in the representation of the overarching themes of compassion, anatomy, and alienation.

In this diasporic history of Italian avant-gardism, what strikes us most is the profound consonance, both aesthetic and linguistic, between the verse of De Palchi and Turoldo, a poet-priest whose production has been relegated to the fringes of the Italian domestic canon. Despite his minor status in Italy, however, Turoldo is an important presence in the American anthologies of the 1960s and 1970s, overall featuring in eight out of fifty anthologies (see Appendix 2.3). First anthologised by De Palchi, who included Turoldo's poems in three anthologies out of four, Turoldo then features in six other collections: BRADSHAW 1964, BRADSHAW 1971, MILLER, O'NEAL, AND McDONNELL 1970, LIND 1974, MARCHIONE 1974 and FELDMAN AND SWANN 1979. Vittoria Bradshaw's 1971 anthology dedicates a section to mystical poets, whereas Margherita Marchione's work, edited by a nun and scholar, intermixes poetry and religion without being thematically constrained.

Most of these anthologies, however, are avant-garde-oriented rather than focused on religion. American anthologists were looking for the marginal and the new, no matter what kind. Turoldo appealed to De Palchi first and foremost for his exilic, militant profile. Born in Coderno, a small village in the border region of Friuli near Udine, Turoldo was associated with the Italian antifascist movement of the Resistance, as he edited the clandestine review *L'Uomo* from his convent in Milan. As Antonio D'Elia put it, Turoldo's poetry is that of an eternal pilgrim who 'moves, as he passes by, the schemes of history'; the pilgrim's wanderings are the expression of a sensorial gnosis that explores reality in a visceral manner.[36] This explains why Turoldo's poems are imbued with metaphors of destruction, regeneration, and travel, a series of motifs that echoes Poggioli's image of the house. In this semantic system, Christ himself is said to be the poet's 'sweetest ruin'.[37]

Turoldo's language reflects the importance granted to sensorial life. All the senses constitute the contemplative as well as the physical dimension of his poetry. Sight, particularly, is explored through the examination of the effects of light on the poet's external and internal world:

> Then I shall hear again
> the sweetness of morning bells
> that awakened such melancholy in me
> at every encounter with the light.[38]

> These hands stretched out
> to fabulous spaces set with stars
> [...]
> The earth is all a wound.[39]

Similarly, desire and abstinence, innocence and guilt shape the poet's exilic status, suspended between the secular and the religious:

> But when I pass from death into life,
> I already know I shall have to agree with you, O Lord.
> [...]
> it was You I smelled in my flesh,
> You hidden in every desire.[40]

The voluptuous pity of testing
what it was to kill;
[...]
I didn't kill
to be alone
[...]
I didn't kill
from envy of God.[41]

De Palchi's interest in a marginally religious poet like Turoldo is an alarm bell for the literary historian. It offers a compelling example of the ways in which the process of anthologisation of Italian avant-garde poetry went hand in hand with the development of certain motifs. De Palchi's focus on the outcasts of Italian literature took the form of an 'individual canon', as he himself defined it, that is a canon that is the fruit of the intellectual's battle for originality and spontaneity, against those who built 'the cemeteries of poetry' and criticism.[42] By being private and unrepeatable, this canon is the extension of the editor's life as well as a rejection of what he perceived as mediocrity. De Palchi deprived Italian poets of their national, most obvious identity, in order to reread them in the light of new political, societal, and aesthetic purposes.

After its closure in 2007, the life of *Chelsea* magazine continued with Chelsea Editions, the publishing house for which De Palchi served as an editor until the end of his life. According to its online mission statement, Chelsea Editions is a non-profit organisation that was created with the purpose of offering 'an outlet for Italian poetry, neglected by the large presses and by most of the small ones as well'.[43] Founded with a cosmopolitan orientation, Chelsea Editions became one of the most important platforms for the dissemination of avant-garde poetry from Italy. De Palchi's commitment to the spreading of Italian poetry abroad, alongside the rich intertextuality of his poetry, put him at the margins of, rather than beyond, Italian literary expectations. In this respect, De Palchi's critical process truly endorses the diasporic paradigm: while opening up to the influences of foreign literatures of all ages, it gives voice to the neglected and the persecuted.

Notes to Chapter 5

1. *The Oxford Book of Italian Verse: XIIIth Century-XIXth Century. Chosen by St. John Lucas. Second Edition Revised with XXth Century Supplement*, ed. by Carlo Dionisotti (Oxford: Clarendon Press, 1952).
2. *The New American Poetry, 1945–1960*, ed. by Donald Allen (New York: Grove Press, 1960); *New Poets of England and America*, ed. by Donald Hall and Robert Pack (Cleveland, OH: Meridian Books, 1962).
3. Donald Allen, 'Preface', in *The New American Poetry, 1945–1960*, ed. by Allen, p. xi.
4. Luigi Fontanella, *Migrating Words: Italian Writers in the United States* (New York: Bordighera Press, 2012).
5. *Scritti sulla poesia di Alfredo De Palchi: con inediti dell'autore,* ed. by Roberto Bertoldo, Barbara Carle, and Luigi Fontanella (Turin: Ebenon, 2000).
6. Fontanella, *Migrating Words*, p. 171.
7. Louis Bourgeois, 'The Scorpion's Dark Dance: An Interview with Alfredo De Palchi', *Rain*

Taxi, 15 (2010) <http://www.alfredodepalchi.com/interviste/The%20Scorpion's%20Dark%20Dance.pdf> [accessed 12 October 2020].
8. Bencivenni, *Italian Immigrant Radical Culture*, p. 174.
9. Ibid., p. 148.
10. Ibid.
11. Fontanella, *Migrating Words*, p. 207.
12. Ibid., pp. 207–08.
13. Ibid.
14. De Palchi 1966a, p. 5.
15. Picchione, *The New Avant-garde in Italy*, p. 15.
16. Glauco Cambon, 'Foreword', in De Palchi 1966a, pp. 3–6 (p. 4).
17. Lamberto Pignotti, 'A Form of Protest Against the Anonimity of Mass Production in a Technological Civilization', trans. by Barbara Guest and Nicola La Bianca, in De Palchi 1966a, p. 151. Pignotti's visual poem 'La dolce avanguardia' is included in De Palchi 1966a, p. 184 (see Chapter 20).
18. Nanni Balestrini, from *Hanging Stone*, trans. by I. L. Salomon, in De Palchi 1966a, p. 130; Edoardo Sanguineti, 'Hell's Purgatory', trans. by Baxter Hathaway, in De Palchi 1966a, p. 131; Sergio Acutis, 'Catalepton 6', trans. by Baxter Hathaway, in De Palchi 1966a, p. 135.
19. Daisy Aldan, 'The Destruction of Cathedrals', in De Palchi 1962, pp. 44–45; Luciano Erba, 'Super Flumina', trans. by Lynne Lawner, in De Palchi 1962, p. 85.
20. De Palchi 1966b, p. 269.
21. Ibid., p. 285.
22. Ibid., p. 355.
23. Ibid., p. 272.
24. Ibid., p. 298.
25. Ibid., p. 284.
26. Salvatore Quasimodo, 'White Rivermouth', trans. by Ursule Molinaro, in De Palchi 1961, pp. 8–9.
27. Ibid., p. 9.
28. See De Palchi 1966b, p. 289, and De Palchi 1966a, p. 79.
29. Nelo Risi, 'On the River I Watch', trans. by Sonia Raiziss and Alfredo De Palchi, in De Palchi 1961, p. 13.
30. Bartolo Cattafi, 'The Agave' and 'Sailing from Greenwich', trans. by Glauco Cambon, in De Palchi 1961, pp. 16–17.
31. Vittorio Sereni, 'An Italian in Greece', trans. by Sonia Raiziss and Glauco Cambon, in De Palchi 1966b, p. 333.
32. Pier Paolo Pasolini, from *The Beautiful Flags*, trans. by Charles Wright, in De Palchi 1966b, p. 347.
33. David Maria Turoldo, 'The Secret of Cain, trans. by Margo and Anthony Viscusi, in De Palchi 1966b, p. 342.
34. Rocco Scoltellaro, 'The Adige Roars', trans. by Thomas Bergin, in De Palchi 1961, p. 18.
35. Alfredo De Palchi, 'Black Glasses', trans. by Sonia Raiziss, in De Palchi 1961, p. 23.
36. Antonio D'Elia, *La peregrinatio poetica di David Maria Turoldo* (Florence: Olschki, 2012), pp. 127–30.
37. Ibid., pp. 127–30.
38. David Maria Turoldo, 'Love and Death', trans. by Margo and Anthony Viscusi, in De Palchi 1961, p. 19.
39. David Maria Turoldo, 'These Hands', trans. by Margo and Anthony Viscusi, in De Palchi 1962, p. 92.
40. David Maria Turoldo, 'Love and Death', trans. by Margo and Anthony Viscusi, in De Palchi 1961, p. 19.
41. Turoldo, 'The Secret of Cain', in De Palchi 1966B, p. 341.
42. See Roberto Bertoldo, 'Intervista ad Alfredo De Palchi' (2012) <http://www.alfredodepalchi.com/interviste/int_de%20Palchi.html> [accessed 28 September 2018].

43. Chelsea Editions, 'Mission Statement' <http://www.chelseaeditionsbooks.org/About.htm> [accessed 28 September 2018].

CHAPTER 6

Displacing Futurism: Editors and Poets in 1970s and 1980s America

De Palchi's 1960s anthologies reveal the transformations undergone by the diasporic avant-garde by enacting its contradictory patterns. From the 1970s onwards, this thread of the translated Italian canon grew rapidly, either by taking the form of a reappraisal of the futurist movement or by promoting the poetry of the Italian neo-avant-garde. These two threads were both chronologically and critically intertwined: not only because the latter represented a development of the former, but also because they could not exist in isolation. This chapter analyses the role played by futurist anthologies in the canonisation of avant-garde, diasporic poets in the 1970s and 1980s; these anthologies had a major impact on the contemporaneous activity of Ballerini, whose work is crucial to the understanding of the circulation of Italian avant-garde poetry today (see Chapter 7).

The cultural and theoretical legacy of Italian futurism in American culture has been widely documented.[1] After Perloff revealed the connections between Pound and the futurists, there is no doubt that the latter had an important influence on the American literary imagination. Yet, despite the fact that much work has been done on futurism's transnational dimensions, its contribution to the reception of Italian lyric in the US has remained unexplored.

The rediscovery of futurism in the 1970s and 1980s worked as a catalyst for the appropriation of visual and concrete poetry from Italy. De Palchi 1962, which represents the first systematic attempt to canonise Italian neo-avant-gardists, came out in the same year as Joshua Taylor's catalogue *Futurism*, based on a contemporaneous exhibition at the Museum of Modern Art, New York. In his foreword to the volume, Taylor argued that 'the sympathy between certain futurist procedures and current endeavours [was] largely responsible for the growing interest in this movement'.[2] In the eyes of the Americans, Italy's most renowned art form, which continued in the form of Italian neo-avant-gardism, became a synonym for contemporary Italian poetry all together in the centennial year of Italian unification (1861–1961).

It is possible to appreciate the impact of futurist poetry on the formation of the Italian diasporic canon by considering two sets of publications: (i) the proliferation of thematic anthologies (Group A) and single author collections (Group B) that celebrated the revival of futurist poetics and/or its evolution in the forms of Italian neo-avant-gardism; and (ii) the consistently increasing presence of neo-avant-garde poets in general volumes, if we understand the neo-avant-garde as a development of futurism (Group C). Table 6.1 lists the most significant publications in these areas in the years 1970–89. Due to the interdisciplinary nature of the avant-garde, the works given here blur the boundaries of poetry, philosophy, criticism, and the visual arts, also extending to genres such as letter- and cookery-writing. Under Group C, I have indicated the poets who are classifiable as neo-avant-garde or experimental. Despite falling out of the spatial and temporal framework considered here, VITIELLO 1992 and Porta's Canadian collection (*Passenger*, 1986) are included for their relevance as anthologies of experimental verse (I have signalled them with an asterisk).[3]

TABLE 6.1. Experimental poetry anthologies 1970–89

Group A Thematic Anthologies	Group B Single Author Collections (in translation)	Group C Comprehensive Anthologies
KIRBY 1971	De Palchi, *Sessions with My Analyst: Poems* (1970).	BRADSHAW 1971: Giuliani, Balestrini, Pagliarani, Porta, Sanguineti, Vivaldi, Costa.
APOLLONIO 1973	Marinetti, *Selected Writing* (1972); *Stung by Salt and Water* (1987); *The Futurist Cookbook* (1989).	JUDGE AND DRAGOSEI 1974: Matti, Pagliarani, Risi, Sanguineti.
BALLERINI 1973	Spatola, *Majakovskiiiiiij* (1975); *Various Devices* (1978).	TUSIANI 1974: Marinetti
BALLERINI 1978	Sandri, *From K to S. Ark of the Asymmetric* (1976).	FELDMAN AND SWANN 1979: Balestrini, Ballerini, De Palchi, Finzi, Giuliani, Niccolai, Pagliarani, Porta, Risi, Sandri, Sanguineti, Spatola, Vivaldi.
STEFANILE 1980	Porta, *As If It Were a Rhythm* (1978); *Passenger: Selected Poems* (1986)*; *Kisses from Another Dream* (1987).	SMITH 1981: Giuliani, Marmori, Pignotti, Rosselli, Sanguineti, Balestrini, Porta, Spatola.
SPATOLA AND VANGELISTI 1982	Niccolai, *Harry's Bar e altre poesie* (1981).	—
HARRISON 1983	Ballerini, *Che figurato muore* (1988).	—
VANGELISTI 1989	—	—
VITIELLO 1992*	—	—

This process of canonisation occurred thanks to the concurrent efforts of a group of poet-editors, who sometimes operated as translators. In these years, the profile of the American editor changed profoundly, incorporating poets from Italy (Spatola) as well as American critics (Bradshaw, Thomas Harrison, Lawrence Smith). The image of the editor as an Italian migrant survived in the work of anthologists such as Ballerini and Paolo Valesio; yet, from this moment onwards, it is the Italian lyric subject (avant-garde, female, etc.), more than the figure of the editor, that is definable as diasporic. Therefore, the anthologies published in this period mark the shift from a biographically embodied exile to aesthetic forms of expatriation which can be either philosophical or visual. Through a revisitation of Poggioli's stances, experimental poetry from Italy was inflected in visual, philosophical, and transnational ways that inhabited diasporicity in a new manner.

In Italy, the 1960s and 1970s were dominated by a series of meetings of the literary avant-garde (Palermo, 1963; Florence, 1963; La Spezia, 1966; Fano, 1967), within which the Gruppo 63 and Gruppo 70 were formed. The *Novissimi* anthology, edited by Giuliani in 1961, is the first, important literary manifesto of Italian neo-avant-gardism, featuring Balestrini, Porta, Sanguineti, Elio Pagliarani, and Giuliani himself. *I Novissimi* (translated into English only in 1995, Giuliani 1995) does not contain any visual poems; however, it is in response to the poetics forged by *I Novissimi* that Italian visual poets produced their work (Spatola, Pignotti, Giovanna Sandri, Giulia Niccolai, Martino Oberto). Conversely, the bond between poetry and image became almost a convention in American anthologies of this period. Feldman and Swann 1979 and Spatola and Vangelisti 1982, a comprehensive and a thematic anthology, present thirty-three and ten visual works respectively, the majority of which deal with metaliterary motifs. Sarenco's 'Homage to Poetry' depicts poetry as contemporary man's last worshipped god (see Chapter 20).

In addition to incorporating the visual arts, American anthologies became the stage for a truly philosophical endeavour. This is particularly visible in Ballerini 1978 and Harrison 1983, two volumes that concentrated on neo-avant-garde poetry's existentialist aspects, thus developing what De Palchi had started. These collections treated the philosophy of Martin Heidegger and Friedrich Nietzsche as a theoretical framework within which to pursue 'considerations of [Italian] poetry in terms of ontology and reference'.[4] According to Harrison, 'poetry begins to search for language' in a way that became more and more self-referential.[5] This metaliterary vision entrusted poetry with the power of telling itself in the very process of looking for its own motivations and meanings; as this line by Raffaele Perrotta puts it, 'metalanguage is still language. With all that this entails. | Let language be such'.[6] By exploring Heidegger's idea that language is a spatial entity, Italian ontological poems are 'pithy and enigmatic declarations spoken as if from "elsewhere", from a beyond of which the poet receives some glimmer'.[7] Such philosophical poems are intrinsically diasporic, as they reproduce the subject's sense of displacement:

> To Call being what is dislocated in
> *and*
> *is* but that for which there is a being.[8]

A further aspect of Italian neo-avant-garde poetry is the juxtaposition of philosophical and philological modes: 'Philosophy: Philology: | intrepid couple; finally joined'.[9] For the *Novissimi*, philology was a form of archaeology that enabled them to reconnect with the project of the historical avant-gardes (futurism, Dadaism, surrealism). These poets' efforts to recover their distant roots, both spatially (Anglo-American poetry) and temporally (Italian poetry of the *stilnovo*) was also philological. BALLERINI 1978 intersected these coordinates by opening with a dedication to the thirteenth-century poet Cavalcanti, admired by Pound.

Both anthologies embody an extreme attempt to canonise the neo-avant-garde in the US as a result of the reappropriations of futurism in the 1970s. Their conceptually difficult poetry, at times multilingual and discursive, seems at odds with the exilic canon analysed here. Yet, rather than contrasting, or separating from, the anthologies of the Italian diaspora, they are an expression of the American editors' programme which privileged experimental verse. BALLERINI 1978 and HARRISON 1983 were both conceived within diasporic frameworks and circles of people. The former is an issue of the *Chelsea* review, directed by De Palchi and Raiziss, whereas Harrison contributed to Ballerini's 1992 anthology, *Shearsmen of Sorts*, with an essay entitled 'The Lyric and the Antilyric'.[10]

Table 6.2 shows to what extent BALLERINI 1978 and HARRISON 1983 reinforced the canon of avant-garde poetry launched by De Palchi, and continued by Ruth Feldman and Brian Swann, and Spatola and Paul Vangelisti. While reoffering some of the avant-gardists encountered before (Villa, Porta, Giuliani), they also introduced new names (Rubina Giorgi, Alfredo Di Legge, Raffaele Perrotta).

TABLE 6.2. A comparison of the poetic canons of BALLERINI 1978 and HARRISON 1983, with a list of translators.

BALLERINI 1978	HARRISON 1983
Villa Trans. by Milazzo and Pauluzzi	Cagnone [all poets translated by Harrison]
Diacono Trans. by Ballerini and Milazzo	Giuliani
Cagnone Trans. by Salamone	Garelli
Giorgi Trans. by Verzani and Milazzo	Zanzotto
Di Legge Trans. by Ballerini and Milazzo	Chiappelli
Perrotta Trans. by Scanlon	Lumelli
—	Ballerini
—	Vattimo
—	Perrotta
—	Porta

In Italy, a couple of futurist anthologies were produced, a sign of the renewed interest in the movement.[11] The Italian canon, though, less permeable to experimentation, did not accommodate futurist and neo-avant-garde poetry as widely as did the American one. An historical anthology published by Garzanti, in two volumes of more than five hundred pages, each featured poems by Giuliani and Cesare Vivaldi exclusively, without even including Marinetti.[12] American collections, by contrast, registered an important number of experimental poets, who occupied a considerable portion of the anthologies as a whole (Table 6.1, Group C).

The comparison between the Italian and the American situation is further complicated by the transnational implications of the neo-avant-garde movement. Among its poets, those who were more directly affected by, and/or involved with, American culture are Spatola, Niccolai, and Ballerini for reasons that are biographical as much as aesthetic. However, the most compelling case of transnational neo-avant-gardism is perhaps offered by poet Scammacca. A Sicilian American always travelling between the old and the new continents, Scammacca founded in southern Italy the experimental movement Antigruppo (1966). This literary group polemicised against Gruppo 63 and Italian hermeticism; at the same time, it imitated the spirit of the Beat Generation, and of Ferlinghetti in particular, with whom Scammacca was in contact. As emerges from Scammacca's manifesto, 'Analisi Antigruppo', these poets had a radical, anticonventional stance towards the dominant poetics of their time, overtly condemning the neo-avant-garde's formalism. Scammacca's works — a poetry collection (*Bye Bye America*) and his manifesto — were translated into English in 1986 and 1985 respectively. Scammacca, however, does not appear in any of the thematic or comprehensive anthologies of this period. Rather than being associated with the dissemination of Italian experimental poetry abroad, the activity of the Antigruppo is surprisingly linked to that of dialect poetry, especially from Sicily (see Part IV). This fact sheds new light on the protean legacy of futurism, which extended its scope to regional literatures, and it also outlines the predominance of neo-avant-gardist views in shaping the Italian diasporic canon in the USA.

Notes to Chapter 6

1. 'A Century of Futurism, 1909–2009', ed. by Federico Luisetti and Luca Somigli, *Annali di Italianistica*, 27 (2009), 1–138.
2. Joshua Taylor, *Futurism* (New York: Museum of Modern Art, 1961), p. 7.
3. Antonio Porta, *Passenger: Selected Poems, 1958–79*, trans. by Pasquale Verdicchio (Toronto: Guernica, 1986).
4. HARRISON 1983, p. 15.
5. Ibid., p. 15.
6. Raffaele Perrotta, 'Poetics', trans. by Thomas Harrison, in HARRISON 1983, p. 239.
7. HARRISON 1983, p. 42.
8. Martino Oberto, from *Anaphilosophia*, trans. by Rosa Maria Salamone, in BALLERINI 1978, p. 87.
9. Raffaele Perrotta, 'Poetics', trans. by Thomas Harrison, in HARRISON 1983, p. 239.
10. Thomas Harrison, 'The Lyric and the Antilyric', in BALLERINI 1992, pp. 109–30.
11. *Poesia futurista italiana*, ed. by Ruggero Jacobbi (Parma: Guanda, 1968); *Poesia visiva in Italia, 1962–1974*, ed. by Luciano Caruso (Catanzaro: Studio d'Arte il Meridione, 1974).

12. *Poesia italiana: il Novecento*, ed. by Piero Gelli and Gina Lagorio (Milan: Garzanti, 1980).

CHAPTER 7

Dispersive Subjectivities: Luigi Ballerini's 'Research Anthologies'

Emeritus professor of Italian at UCLA, as well as a poet and a translator, Ballerini is responsible for bringing the Italian diasporic avant-garde into the new millennium. I place Ballerini both at the conclusion and at the acme of this tale of transplantation for reasons that are not exclusively chronological. His criticism explores patterns of diasporicity which, because of their complexity, has both shaken and redefined the diasporic paradigm.

Ballerini's anthological activity encompasses four decades of Italian and American literary history. He is the editor of ten anthologies of poetry in translation: four Italian anthologies of American poetry and five American anthologies of Italian verse (Ballerini 1973, Ballerini 1978, Ballerini 1991, Ballerini 1999, and Ballerini 2017).[1] Although the span of this latter group surpasses the temporal and spatial boundaries of this study, it is nevertheless worth consideration in a chapter entirely dedicated to its editor. In Chapter 6, I discussed the link between Ballerini's 1970s anthologies and the revival of futurism. The present chapter analyses further Ballerini's activity by describing the ways in which diaspora and the avant-garde are complexly, and sometimes paradoxically, interpolated across all his anthological production.

Like Poggioli and De Palchi, Ballerini is an Italian who migrated to the US. His diasporic poetics draws on Poggioli's emphasis on the visual arts, De Palchi's creative approach (Ballerini is also a poet-editor and a translator), and the thematic anthologists' aesthetic modes. More so than those of his predecessors, Ballerini's collections are built upon the Poundian principle whereby poetry and criticism are deeply interwoven (*logopoeia*). Ballerini discussed this concept in the introduction to his 2017 anthology, in which he used Francesco Muzzioli's definition of 'research poetry' in order to encapsulate the self-enquiring nature of experimental writing; however, this idea is at work in all the anthologies that he compiled.[2]

With the exclusion of *The Promised Land* (Ballerini 1999), which contains texts only, Ballerini's collections perfect Poggioli's hybrid, anthological genre combining primary sources and secondary criticism. Poetic manifestos, essays, installations, and paintings are neither less significant nor less creative than the very poems they accompany. This is not the first time that Italian poetry is presented to the American audience by means of a strong critical component. The majority of the journal publications analysed here present a combination of essays and verse; Ballerini, however, has the merit of giving the genre its first, institutionalised form.

So far, Ballerini's anthologies have represented the most methodologically consistent contribution towards the spread of Italian avant-garde poetry in the English-speaking world. Their attempt to make experimental poetry canonical is particularly visible from the 1990s onwards, when BALLERINI 1999 aimed to 'revisit the territory of earlier expeditions, to provide a more comprehensive and less provisional geography'.[3] Almost ten years later, BALLERINI 2017 carried on the canonising programme of that 1999 anthology: on the one hand, it enlarged the dialogue with other anthologies, both Italian and American; and, on the other, it nourished Ballerini's encyclopaedic aspiration to document Italian poetry from its medieval origins to the present day. The so-called 'Da Ponte Italian Poetry Project' comprises five anthologies, four of which are co-edited by Ballerini and a member of his team. Over two thousand pages long, BALLERINI 2017 is the series's penultimate volume showcasing Italian poetry after 1956. Like Poggioli, Ballerini places Ungaretti, rather than Montale, at the beginning of the modern Italian tradition, further evidence of his ambition to shake its conventional foundations.

The number of poets regularly increased after Ballerini's second anthology: seven names in BALLERINI 1978, then twenty-two (BALLERINI 1992), thirty (BALLERINI 1999), and forty-one (BALLERINI 2017). Recurring poets are Spatola, Oberto, Balestrini, Pagliarani, Giuliani, Emilio Villa, Nanni Cagnone, and Corrado Costa, a true parade of Italian avant-gardists. Popular translators are Vangelisti, Richard Milazzo, Beppe Cavatorta, David Jacobson, as well as Ballerini himself. BALLERINI 1999 is the most varied volume, as it gives ample space to both dialect poets (Franco Loi, Mauro Marè, and Raffaello Baldini, who opens the book) and women (Sandri, Niccolai, Sebastiana Comand, Biancamaria Frabotta, Milli Graffi, Rossana Ombres, Amelia Rosselli). On the basis of its selection, BALLERINI 1999 perfectly encapsulates the three forms of the diasporic described in this book. Conceived as the catalogue of an exhibition, BALLERINI 1973 holds a special place. His first anthology amounts to fifty-five visual poets in total: twenty-one for the period 1912–40 and thirty-four for the period 1941–72. In the true spirit of transnationalism, the volume opens with the work of Guillaume Apollinaire; Giacomo Balla, Umberto Boccioni, Carlo Carrà, Fortunato Depero, Ardengo Soffici, and Marinetti follow, accompanied by a large group of other experimentalists. Whereas the first half of the anthology is inherently futurist (there are eleven works by Marinetti alone), the second half puts forward some of the most recognisable neo-avant-gardists, such as Niccolai, Sandri, Spatola, and Villa. The comparative analysis of Ballerini's anthologies shows that their selection criteria are consistent. Inspired by the principle of 'interchangeability of the arts', these collections variously juxtapose poems, 'paintings, collage, sculpture, drawings, graphics and books, both commercial and unique handmade copies'; here and there, we can even encounter musical scores.[4] Thanks to Ballerini, this anthological mode, on the threshold between criticism and the creative arts, became a convention without losing its offbeat character.

Table 7.1 offers a snapshot of Ballerini's most anthologised poets (first column); each row gives each poet's frequency, marked with an asterisk, across his five anthologies. The first five rows display poets that are typically experimental; rows six and seven focus on experimental women writers; and the last three rows register, from the 1990s onwards, the introduction of more canonical poets, including multilingual writer Amelia Rosselli. Ballerini's canon resembles none of his colleagues' back in Italy. Rather than anthologising Luzi, Erba, or Caproni (although these names appear in some of the collections), Ballerini gives more credit to Spatola and Villa, the latter being a constant presence throughout. Balestrini and Pagliarani, two important neo-avant-gardists whose names I have not included, return in Ballerini 1999 and Ballerini 2017, after their first appearance in De Palchi 1966a.

Table 7.1. List of frequently anthologised poets in Luigi Ballerini's poetry anthologies

	Ballerini 1973	Ballerini 1978	Ballerini 1992	Ballerini 1999	Ballerini 2017
Cagnone	—	★	★	★	—
Oberto	★	★	—	—	★
Spatola	★	—	★	★	★
Villa	★	★	★	★	★
Pignotti	★	—	—	—	★
Comand	—	—	★	★	—
Niccolai	★	—	—	★	★
Zanzotto	—	—	★	★	★
Rosselli	—	—	★	★	★
Pasolini	—	—	—	—	★

Besides a few shared names (it is worth adding Lorenzo Calogero and Cattafi), a point of convergence between De Palchi and Ballerini is the inclusion of the poet-editor. Both De Palchi and Ballerini anthologised themselves, thus pushing the boundaries between poetry and criticism. Ballerini explored this pattern further by anthologising Spatola four times out of five. It was to Spatola, co-editor of *Italian Poetry, 1960–1980: From Neo to Post-avant-garde* (Spatola and Vangelisti 1982), that Ballerini dedicated two of his collections (Ballerini 1992 and Ballerini 2017), the former opening with a touching, tragic-comic letter to his dead friend. Pictures of the dedicatees and dedicatory poems are not a mere apparatus, but an integral part of Ballerini's anthologies. Suffice it to mention Wallace Stevens' 'The Man with the Blue Guitar', which both opens Ballerini 1992 and gives it its title, *Shearsmen of Sorts*.

I consider Ballerini's avant-garde anthologies diasporic in the light of both their selection criteria and structure. The sets of data analysed here reveal that Ballerini rewrote the history of contemporary Italian poetry in a manner that takes into consideration the influence of American literary culture. This is evident from his appropriation of Pound's concept of *logopoeia* to his emphasis on the pictorial. Ballerini's diasporic approach, though, also extends to the poetic postures and themes of his authors. His avant-garde poets use a displaced narrative voice challenging the frontiers of language and the possibilities of telling. Their verse is essentially metalinguistic in that it questions its own existence in a self-referential way ('research poetry').

Metaliterature is one of diasporic poetry's most common themes; yet, in Ballerini it emerges obsessively. Critic and anthologist Harrison defined the horizontal, interstitial space inhabited by Ballerini's avant-garde poets as 'antilyric'. Speaking about Cesare Viviani (for whom 'è la terza persona che salva' [the third person saves us]), and therefore moving away from the lyrical 'I', Harrison observed, in his essay 'The Lyric and the Antilyric' in Ballerini 1992, that antilyric poetry changed 'the space, the force, the physiognomy, the movement of the subject'. In this essay, the antilyrical 'I' is said to live and perceive itself in a new manner. 'The shattering of the monadic, egocentric lyric,' Harrison specified, 'occurs under the aegis of a new economy of subjective expression', called *smarrimento*. Meaning both disorientation and loss, *smarrimento* inspired a kind of poetry that, by embracing a decentred perspective, calls upon the poets' 'immanent and dispersed' gaze.[5] In line with Harrison, and by borrowing Remo Bodei's expression, we can say that Ballerini explored the diasporic possibilities elicited by avant-garde poets' 'aleatory being' both along the axis of language and that of loss.[6] Thus, the progressive marginalisation of the lyrical subject goes hand in hand with the dominance of exilic themes (estrangement, mourning, melancholia) and metadiscursive tones.

The poetry of both Biagio Cepollaro and Comand embodies all the threads of this multiperspectival, diasporic narrative. Among the promoters of Gruppo 93, Cepollaro experimented with language (dialect, neologisms, theatre, religion, the visual arts) both in 'In Cézanne's Studio' and 'Toulouse Lautrec'. A few poems later, Cepollaro's twisted words assume the form of a posthumous elegy, partaking in the subject's sense of bewilderment:

it aint rejoicin if the guy forgets
and notta word
nottan answer
ring slowly around.[7]

On the other hand, Comand questions the status of metaliterary poetry by bringing to the fore the theme of aphasia:

The silence shelled
petals of stone
nude out of breath
the most beautiful flesh
is born out of death.[8]

Comand's images of loss and displacement are equally compelling: 'the image is already here, of that which is missing'; 'when what surrounds will turn back in on me | and I'll no longer come away from nothing'; 'I didn't have the courage | to pretend I was never home'; 'what's lost is not | someone who was here'.[9]

Rosselli's poetry offers the most eloquent application of Ballerini's approach, at once avant-garde and diasporic. A refugee and orphan, Rosselli's 'development as a writer [was] marred by suffering, exile, and disability'.[10] Her poems combine metaliterary and autobiographical traits in a complex way, as they primarily tell the story of 'their own making'.[11] Rosselli's poetic voice, 'désancré de l'origine' [disanchored from the origin] (Michel de Certeau), inhabits multiple linguistic spaces as if it were haunted by an uncontrollable, centrifugal sense of vertigo:

> But it has grown dark
> in my evanescent heart
> undisciplined master
> of poetry.[12]

The examples of this diasporic mode, half-metaliterary and half-elegiac, could be multiplied: from Edoardo Cacciatore's image of memory as 'the widow of a tramp' to Frabotta's lines 'at the border of a promised land'.[13] Other occurrences include these lines by Luzi:

> human tongue
> burnt in my pages,
> entirely, secularly.[14]

Sandri's poem 'among | of' is a striking manifesto of diasporic in-between-ness from its very title.[15] As the next chapters will reveal, this mode became a constant in the reception of Italian lyric abroad.

* * * * *

Both the origins and the development of the Italian diasporic canon followed a path of crosscultural fertilisation that simultaneously challenged and enriched the reception of avant-garde lyric as a transnational phenomenon. There does seem to be a diasporic, transhistorical line that drew together the rise of the European avant-gardes at the beginning of the century, their influence on the American literary world, and the revival of futurist modes in the late twentieth century. Italian avant-garde poetry in translation, one of the fruits of this conjunction, reached the other side of the globe, with the Australian-based Frederick May including six *Novissimi* out of twenty-two poets in his 1970 anthology.[16] At the same time, it also permeated the American domestic canon if we consider that the Italian poets represented in the second volume of the University of California book of modern and postmodern poetry, *Poems for the Millennium* (1998) [Rothenberg and Joris 1998], are Campana, Montale and Ungaretti, followed by six futurists: Carrà, Depero, Marinetti, Palazzeschi, Paolo Buzzi, and Francesco Cangiullo.

If Poggioli's *Teoria dell'arte d'avanguardia* was a point of departure for diasporic editors throughout, Ballerini's expression 'the legacy of the new' crystallises the directions and meanings of the avant-garde thread from its beginnings up to now. By justifying a new way of looking at the time-honoured Italian tradition, avant-garde anthologists placed it in the centre of foreign American territory through an act of critical self-displacement.

Notes to Chapter 7

1. The four anthologies of American poetry are: *La rosa disabitata: poesia trascendentale americana, 1960–1980*, ed. by Luigi Ballerini and Richard Milazzo (Milan: Feltrinelli, 1981); *Nuova poesia americana: Los Angeles*, ed. by Luigi Ballerini and Paul Vangelisti (Milan: Mondadori, 2005); *Nuova poesia americana: San Francisco*, ed. by Luigi Ballerini and Paul Vangelisti (Milan: Mondadori, 2006); *Perché New York?*, ed. by Luigi Ballerini and Federica Santini (Piacenza: Scritture, 2007).
2. BALLERINI 2017, p. 8.
3. BALLERINI 1999, p. 15.
4. BALLERINI 1973, pp. 3, 8.
5. Harrison, 'The Lyric and the Antilyric', in BALLERINI 1992, pp. 109–30 (p. 113).
6. Remo Bodei, '"In the Schism of Telling": A Guided Tour of Some Themes in Contemporary Italian Poetry', in BALLERINI 1992, pp. 55–72 (p. 56).
7. Biagio Cepollaro, 'Requiem in C', trans. by Michael Moore, in BALLERINI 1992, p. 517.
8. Sebastiana Comand, 'But in What Tongue to Have an Echo', trans. by Paul Vangelisti, in BALLERINI 1992, p. 531.
9. Sebastiana Comand, 'Of the Shadows that Eats Us Alive', trans. by Paul Vangelisti, in BALLERINI 1992, pp. 525, 523, 519.
10. Lucia Re, 'Amelia Rosselli: A Life of Poetry', in Amelia Rosselli, *War Variations*, trans. by Lucia Re and Paul Vangelisti (Los Angeles: Otis Books, 2016), pp. 5–26 (p. 5).
11. BALLERINI 1992, pp.140–41.
12. Amelia Rosselli, from *Appunti sparsi e dispersi* [Scattered and Lost Notes], trans. by Lucia Re and Paul Vangelisti, in BALLERINI 1992, p. 373.
13. Edoardo Cacciatore, 'Campo di fiori', trans. by David Jacobson, in BALLERINI 1999, p. 93; Biancamaria Frabotta, 'Heloise', trans. by Keala Jewell and Paul Vangelisti, in BALLERINI 1999, p. 199.
14. Mario Luzi, from *Naming*, trans. by Stephen Sartarelli, in BALLERINI 1999, p. 295.
15. Giovanna Sandri, 'among/of', trans. by Jeremy Parzen, in BALLERINI 1999, p. 437. It is worth mentioning that a similar selection of poems by Cacciatore and Luzi (to name but two examples) was present in BALLERINI 1992, proof of Ballerini's programme of canon formation.
16. *Modern Italian Poetry: Selections with English Parallel*, compiled by Vanni Scheiwiller, ed. by Frederick May (Sidney: South Head Press, 1970).

PART III

❖

Gendering Diaspora

CHAPTER 8

'Sujets en procès': Women and Diaspora

From Virginia Woolf's famous statement that 'as a woman I have no country' to Bhabha's equation of migrant women with 'margins', exile has been built into the female condition.[1] Among this vast array of perspectives, Kristeva's position stands out not only for its coherence (almost an oath of fidelity to the cause of exile), but also for its applicability. Although exile has always been at the forefront of her studies, Kristeva has integrated her reflections on the deterritorialised subject within a broader theoretical spectrum. Not only has she envisaged the imbrication between language and the self, nation and the individual, women and melancholia, but she has also investigated the religious sphere, the avant-garde, and the mechanisms of artistic creation. She has explored the kaleidoscopic nature of diaspora with its diversity of nuances and shapes (mystical, experimental, psychological...), just as Pound did, in his own way, fifty years earlier.

A double citizen of Bulgaria and France as well as an exile herself, Kristeva sprinkles her philosophical and linguistic works with images of dislocation. Two exilic configurations, in particular, capture the link between women and migration in a compelling way: the encounter with the foreign that is common to people of all cultures and ages, and the idea of the 'sujet en procès' [subject in process]. Discussed at various stages throughout her career, these concepts have foregrounded Kristeva's understanding of subjectivity as a mobile system. We are not 'discrete beings learning to act independently and autonomously', nor are we fixed identities unable to transform.[2] Rather than 'a model of the self that is stable and unified, Kristeva offers us one of the self that is always in process and heterogeneous'.[3] In 'Le temps des femmes' [The Time of Women], an essay published in 1979, Kristeva emphasised 'the *multiplicity* of female expressions and preoccupations so as not to homogenise "woman", while at the same time insisting on the necessary recognition of sexual difference'.[4] A similar idea of fluidity emerges from her 1988 study on the notion of foreignness, where she defended the imperative of:

> Ne pas chercher à fixer, à choisifier l'étrangeté de l'étranger. Juste la toucher, l'effleurer, sans lui donner de structure définitive. Simplement en esquisser le mouvement perpetuel [...]. Etrangeté à peine effleurée et qui, déjà, s'éloigne.[5]
>
> [Let us not seek to solidify, to turn the otherness of the foreigner into a thing.

> Let us merely touch it, brush by it, without giving it a permanent structure. Simply sketching out its perpetual motion [...]. An otherness barely touched upon and that already moves away.][6]

Kristeva inscribed women into the exilic trajectory of migrants through the theorisation of the symbolic (historical, linear, and male) and the semiotic (eternal, cyclical, and female) orders. The symbolic and the semiotic indicate 'a dimension of language as well as a stage in the child's psycho-sexual development'; referring to two different psychic registers, these terms have acquired gendered connotations, with the 'semiotic signifying the feminine/maternal and the symbolic representing the masculine/paternal'.[7] No living being, however, is 'immune from semiotic disruptions'; as it does in avant-garde poetry, the semiotic is the more 'unconsciously driven [...] mode of signifying' that 'disrupts the more orderly, symbolic effort at communication'.[8] Thus, the distinction between the symbolic and semiotic realms offers us two distinctive ways of analysing literary texts. At a semiotic-genotext level, we experience 'the motility between the words' and their 'potentially disruptive [and diasporic] meaning'; at a symbolic-phenotext level, conversely, we perceive texts as plain, structured, and 'mappable piece[s] of communication'.[9] Nowhere is this dual aspect of texts more manifest than in the work of exilic, avant-garde, and/or women writers.

Just like the diasporic anthologists analysed in this volume, Kristeva insisted on the interchangeability among different categories of exiles: women and avant-garde artists, avant-garde and migrant authors, women and migrants, and so on and so forth. In her 1977 essay entitled 'Un nouveau type d'intellectuel: le dissident' [A New Type of Intellectual: The Dissident], she distinguished three groups of exiles opposing different kinds of authority: the intellectual versus the political establishment; the psychoanalyst who fights against religion; and the experimental writer whose voice undermines linguistic conventions.[10] In addition to these three groups, she discussed the 'subversive potential' of women who are 'trapped within the frontiers of [their] body and even of [their] species, and consequently always feel *exiled* both by the general clichés that make up a common consensus and by the very powers of generalization intrinsic to language'.[11] Women's eccentric condition therefore results in double, triple, or multiple forms of exile: from themselves, from society, from history, and, ultimately, from all kinds of established order. 'How can one avoid sinking into the mire of common sense,' Kristeva asked, 'if not by becoming a stranger to one's own country, language, sex and identity? Writing is impossible without some kind of exile'.[12]

It is worth noticing that women poets tend to be prolific translators, a fact that both determines and exacerbates their exilic condition. This is the case not only for Italian female poets, but for women authors in general. This trend invites us to reappraise translation as a form of literary canon including those marginalised authors who found no space in literature's traditional institutions. In particular, women's privileged attachment to, and experience of, translation has had a decisive effect on the shaping of female Western canons in cultures other than the national. Whereas men have inhabited time and the canon they created in order to become

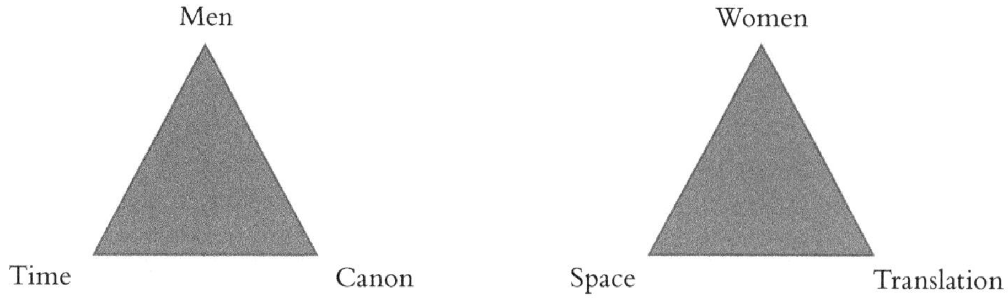

Fig. 8.1. Two contrasting models of literary existence

immortal, women have occupied space and conducted a transient life; they existed in trans-lation. As shown in Figure 8.1 (above), men and women have so far displayed different triangulations of literary existence.

Kristeva's theories migrated from France to the US at a crucial time in the history of Italian poetry's anthologisation (see Chapter 10). Although they had the merit of conceptualising the American avant-garde in a coherent system of values, they reproposed the diasporic beliefs of Poggioli and his successors from a feminist standpoint. At the same time, women editors and poets added a further, fundamental dimension to the diasporic matrix, something that was already palpable in Caetani's therapeutic editorship from the garden of Ninfa. Female writing, especially in translation, began to treat the diasporic status as one of melancholy. Feelings of loss are embedded in both women's and migrants' lives, as they both negotiate objects, spaces, and meanings that are reinvented, retrieved, or that have perished. This is evident in the editors' selections, which, especially from the 1990s onwards, concentrated on experiences of mourning, recollection, and grief, a pattern that was to become programmatic in anthologies of dialect poetry (see Part IV). It is not accidental that Kristeva's meditation on depression and the feminine, poignantly developed in *Soleil noir: dépression et mélancholie* [Black Sun: Depression and Melancholia] (1987), matured together with her exile theories, while also nourishing the evolution of diasporic perspectives in the anthological genre.[13]

Kristeva's multilayered thought, imbued with elements of linguistics, politics, and psychoanalysis, found a synthesis in her understanding of American civilisation. Kristeva conceived of the US as a European-looking, avant-garde country, where '"aesthetic" experiments are more frequent and more varied' than on the Old Continent. By defining the research of Americans as non-verbal, focused as it is on 'gesture, colour and sound' rather than on words, she has presented the Europeans with a less analytical and more spontaneous way of practicing the arts.[14] At the same time, she describes the US as a country of losses, one that presupposes the 'draining of marginalized European personalities onto an American exile', also known as 'the grafting of the European avant-garde on to the United States' both in the run-up to and in the aftermath of the Second World War.[15] These migrants' elegiac art, which constituted American art *tout court*, shaped the American sense of time, heterogeneous and unlinear, resulting from the 'conjunction of several temporalities' and histories (Jewish, English, French, Italian, African, Indian...).[16]

By exploring women's inner, interpersonal, and geographical borders, Kristeva outlines a system of correspondences between the subject and the nation that has proven to be profoundly inspirational for diasporic poets, editors, and critics; see, for instance, her 1998 interview with Philippe Petit, emblematically entitled *Contre la dépression nationale* [Against National Depression].[17] In particular, her reflections on American migration allow her to combine a firmly feminist approach with a deep investigation of the melancholic mind. Although the nexus between women and (the Irish, Chinese, Indian...) diaspora has been widely investigated so far, the forms in which Italian women's diasporic conditions influenced a transnational, and translational, interpretation of the Italian canon are yet to be explored. It is this gap that Chapters 9 to 11 aim to fill.

Notes to Chapter 8

1. Virginia Woolf, *Three Guineas* (Oxford: Blackwell, 1938), p. 99; Bhabha, *The Location of Culture*, p. 291.
2. Noëlle McAfee, *Julia Kristeva* (New York: Routledge, 2004), p. 39.
3. Ibid.
4. *The Kristeva Reader*, ed. by Toril Moi (Oxford: Blackwell, 1986), p. 187. Kristeva's essay was originally published as 'Le Temps des femmes' in *33/34: Cahiers de Recherche de Sciences des Textes et Documents*, 5 (1979), 5–19. The essay was translated into English by Alice Jardine and Harry Blake as 'Women's Time', *Signs*, 7 (1981), 13–35.
5. Julia Kristeva, *Etrangers à nous-mêmes* (Paris: Fayard, 1988), p. 11.
6. Julia Kristeva, *Strangers to Ourselves*, trans. by Leon S. Roudiez (New York: Columbia University Press, 1991), p. 3.
7. Brigit Schippers, *Julia Kristeva and Feminist Thought* (Edinburgh: Edinburgh University Press, 2011), p. 28.
8. McAfee, *Julia Kristeva*, p. 39.
9. Ibid., p. 25.
10. Julia Kristeva, 'Un nouveau type d'intellectuel: le dissident', *Tel Quel*, 74 (1977), 3–8; 'A New Type of Intellectual: The Dissident', in *The Kristeva Reader*, ed. by Moi, pp. 292–300.
11. Kristeva, 'A New Type of Intellectual', p. 298.
12. Ibid.
13. See my own investigation of the relation between women's poetry, depression and exile, 'Transnational Melancholia: Depression and Exile in Italian Women's Poetry from the Early-Modern to the Contemporary', in *Women in Transition: Crossing Boundaries, Crossing Borders*, ed. by Maria-José Blanco and Claire Williams (London: Routledge, 2021), pp. 133–48.
14. Julia Kristeva, 'Why the United States?', in *The Kristeva Reader*, ed. by Moi, pp. 272–91 (p. 275).
15. Ibid., p. 276.
16. Ibid.
17. Julia Kristeva, *Contre la dépression nationale: entretien avec Philippe Petit* (Paris: Textuel, 1998).

CHAPTER 9

Mainstream and Avant-garde: Italian Women Poets in America

This chapter investigates the emergence of contemporary Italian women's poetry in the US as part of the American avant-garde stream. It will discuss the appearance of Italian women poets in comprehensive anthologies that were published from the late 1950s to the 1970s, both in journals and volumes (Guenther and Sellin 1959, Corman 1963, Bradshaw 1971, and Feldman and Swann 1979). Treated as an instance of minor literature, first confessional and then avant-garde, Italian female poetry intermingled with the complex mosaic of voices that coloured the poetic landscape of postwar America, thus contributing to a literary phenomenon known as pluralism.[1] While registering forms of assimilation and hybridity, American editors considered women poets' oscillations between the margins and the mainstream canon as an expression of their (still) ungendered, radical poetics.

1950s-1960s: The Influence of Confessional Poetry and Pluralism

The first single-sex anthology of female Italian poets was published in the mid-1980s, yet American anthologies had been incorporating women since the late 1950s, when Spaziani made her first appearance in a special issue of *The Literary Review* (Guenther and Sellin 1959). Long before the irruption of gendered perspectives into the debate on canonicity, American editors treated the feminine as an extension of the avant-garde. Women were therefore compared to other liminal figures, such as homosexual and dialect writers; forced to confront the American situation, torn between traditional and innovative forces, they became an important stronghold for experimental positions. These anthologists' attempt to bring together female and male authors is particularly significant if we consider that contemporaneous, and even later, anthologies from Italy had little to no place for women.[2]

The focus on the diverse was crucial in the America of the 1960s, when the discussion on canon formation became so exacerbated as to break out into the so-called 'battle of the anthologies' (see Chapter 5). This is already visible in the generous selection of Spaziani's poems in Guenther and Sellin 1959, which collected a series of texts that had been previously transmitted on the Italian radio by anonymous broadcasters. Spaziani, who was then thirty-five, was presented by the editors Guenther and Sellin as 'one of the most complex and interesting personalities among our young poets'.[3] The anthologists commented on Spaziani's 'learned and reflective' art showing the poet's original contribution to hermeticism, one of Italy's mainstream movements; in this way, they integrated a female voice into the postwar Italian scenario, something that was yet to happen in Italy. A further way in which this collection worked towards the anthologisation of lesser-known poets is by juxtaposing unknown and well-established figures. Reiterating a pattern that was already at work both in Poggioli and Caetani, GUENTHER AND SELLIN 1959 foregrounded a heterogeneous selection where Spaziani's verse surfaces from a collage of different voices, from Caproni and Sereni, to De Libero and Scotellaro. At the same time, the presence of English translations from her poetry collection *Il gong* [The Gong] was a progressive editorial choice insofar as Spaziani's original was still to be published in Italy (Mondadori would publish *Il gong* in 1962).

As well as avant-garde, GUENTHER AND SELLIN 1959 described Spaziani's poetry as confessional. Transposed into, and read within, the American context, its themes resonate with those of the confessional poets who were interested in psychological verse and personal poetry on once-taboo subjects: sex, self-analysis, and illness. As critic Ramazani put it, 'women, gay and lesbian, and "ethnic" American poets — previously impeded from naming their experiences in their own literary voices — thus turned so-called personal or confessional poetry into a tool of collective self-definition and liberation'.[4] A few years later, De Palchi's biographical approach, based on the editor's experience as a prisoner, can also be interpreted as an expression of confessional poetics (Chapter 5).

In Guenther and Sellin's selection, Spaziani's confessional mode surfaces in her nocturnal lines as well as in the depiction of the Parisian cityscape, almost an extension of the poet's feelings; Spaziani's 'emotive matter', the editors observe, seems to 'overflow in the landscape and become a completely visible, animated substance'.[5] Thus, memory, the constellations, travel, and death shape the poet's intimate, quasi-mythological writing:

> In the deep
> necropolis of clay the silent Patriarchs
> inscribes the millenniums with a dagger
> on the young moon.
> The Negro rumbas shake at night
> the declining refugee of Verlaine.[6]

Concurrently, her constant dialogue with nature results in an empathic representation of the inanimate life:

> A mulberry tree
> moaned in tossing, so high
> that its cry sometimes awoke me.[7]

From an Italian standpoint, considering a poet like Spaziani confessional is an extravagant move that questions the received idea that all postwar Italian verse is a mere appendix of the hermetic season. Yet, at the same time, it unearths an important point of contact between Italy and the US in the development of female literature's transnational elements. The editors' unconventional, forward-looking way of reading Spaziani's poetry is therefore diasporic inasmuch as it combines the Italian hermetic with the American confessional perspective. Involved in an affair with Montale, who drew upon this relationship with her in creating the character of 'la Volpe' in *La bufera e altro* [The Storm and Other Things], Spaziani acquired at this stage an authentic, international profile that was based on the merits of her own poetry rather than on her personal and/or fictionalised life.

In the 1960s, the reception of Italian women's poetry was still influenced by confessional interpretations, but it also opened up to a more general, pluralistic dimension. Pluralism is the American habit of bringing together poetry 'from different generations, aesthetics, ethnicities and nationalities', a definition that Ramazani interpolated with that of the avant-garde.[8] Although this procedure was already at work in previous anthologies (namely in those of Poggioli and Caetani), it was only in the new decade that it became part of a more established programme. This is particularly evident in Corman 1963, which placed side by side not only female (Margherita Guidacci) and lesser-known male writers (Giuliano Gramigna), but also Risi's neo-avant-garde texts, Montale's historic mode (*La bufera e altro*), and Alberico Sala's and Emilio Tadini's verse, inspired by the visual arts. As his predecessors had done, Corman anthologised Guidacci as a confessional writer; yet, at the same time, he emphasised her contribution to the complex Italian literary panorama. Although stanzas 1–6 of *La sabbia e l'angelo* [The Sand and The Angel] (1946) represent the incipit of what can be read as Guidacci's most personal work, the focus on content is more an instance of Corman's pluralistic approach than a statement of Guidacci's poetics (which indeed valued form greatly). A poet and translator himself, Corman was a member of the Black Mountain College, the 'first American academic institution to cultivate avant-garde activity in the arts and to produce its own avant-garde movement'.[9] Corman's involvement with the avant-garde naturally informed various levels of his anthological endeavour, from the adoption of a pluralistic insight to the promotion of transnational perspectives. These latter are exemplified by the editor's attempt to set up an innovative way of circulating Italian poetry outside its linguistic and national boundaries. Corman published his selection in the literary magazine *Origin*, whose second series was based in Kyoto, Japan; on request, he would send free copies of the journal to individuals and libraries across the world, creating an international channel for the dissemination of Italian poetry.

Corman's collection is one example of the hotbed of anthologies associated with these years. Others include De Palchi's editorial contribution to the avant-garde stream (see Chapter 5), and the interpolation of southern and dialect poetry in the anthologies described in Chapter 13. Different anthological directions contributed to the definition of the Italian diasporic poetics, a cultural hybrid which intersected the Italian with the American mode. Suffice it to say that Golino 1962, published by the University of California Press, retained the Italian critical categories (*crepuscolarismo*, hermeticism etc.), while also pairing Pasolini and Guidacci, its single woman poet, under the common label of 'New Trends', a clear homage to female writing's experimental dimension. Pluralistic fusions of this kind did not occur in the UK, where most of the publications were oriented towards traditional writers.[10]

1970s: Towards the Avant-garde Turn

At the beginning of the 1970s, confessional and pluralistic views were still at the core of BRADSHAW 1971, a survey of postwar Italy; however, women's tendency towards confessional verse was now combined with an engagement with history and society. The 1970s saw a radical transformation in the perception of poetic reality that proved to be no longer based on the evidence of exclusively personal experiences. Female artists voiced a peculiar form of protest against societal constraints, embracing the mystical-religious experience as a form of political and/or ideological revolt. In contemporary poetry's evolution 'from pure silence to impure dialogue' (the title of BRADSHAW 1971), women exploited their marginal condition in order to approach the themes of war and social reformation.[11] Bradshaw's 'poetics of impurity' lies not only in the juxtaposition of diverse artistic expressions, but also in the prioritisation of poetry's multiple dimensions (religion, politics, and society). The neorealist poetry of Pavese and Scotellaro is presented together with the prayer-like style of Guidacci and Alda Merini; likewise, the 'private lyricism' of Cristina Campo and Biagia Marniti coexists with the experimentalism of the neo-avant-gardists (Giuliani, Porta, and Balestrini). Although Bradshaw, a woman herself, published this collection in 1971 at a time when feminism had already made its irruption into American criticism and academia, women poets were still not part of the dominant critical discourse. Yet, as Bradshaw's selection suggests, they were already offering an original response to the impasse of hermetic solipsism. Whereas several male writers adopted a neorealist perspective (Pavese, Scotellaro, Luciano Morandini), women discussed society's transformations by means of intimacy and religion, thus contributing to the shaping of the diasporic, religious thread: 'If you want, man, to leave your imprint, you should scratch the sand, | [...] As you yourself are sand, you are the death which after you still lingers'.[12] These lines by Guidacci are reminiscent of one of the most popular biblical verses, 'Remember, man, you are dust and to dust you will return' (Genesis 3:19).

Even ten years after the 1968 revolution, the question of genre was still avoided by American editors; nonetheless, an important twist in the anthologisation of Italian poetry had taken place. In 1979 Feldman and Swann published an anthology of contemporary Italian poetry whose central focus was to introduce the work of young, experimental writers. This anthology represented a novelty insofar as it assumed the marginal as a unifying paradigm to describe the contemporary poetic situation. Young, homosexual, dialect, folk, experimental, transnational, women, and feminist poets were selected as a sample of the spirit of the age: the 'absolutely out' that, in Cambon's introductory words, embodied the anthology's 'thrill of discovery'.[13] Out of seventy-seven anthologised poets, thirteen were neo-avant-gardists (often experimenting with the visual arts), ten had lived in, or had come from, a country other than Italy, and twelve were women; Pasolini and Vivaldi are anthologised in their dialects, a further proof of this volume's pluralistic structure (see Chapter 14). As the editors stated in their foreword, some of these poets were little known for the most innovative aspects of their production, an example being Pasolini's experimentation with the dialect of Friuli; others, such as Stanislao Nievo, Federico Hinderman, and Renato Gorgoni, were still little-known in Italy itself. Female poets do not constitute a category of their own, but share some common traits with the male authors. For example, Niccolai is associated with the Italian neo-avant-garde, or Gruppo 63, whose representatives in this anthology are Vivaldi and Balestrini; similarly, Sandri's visual experiments find a poetic equivalent in Spatola's concrete texts. New themes surface, such as travel and motherhood; mainly expressed in narrative form, they revitalised Poggioli's and Caetani's interest in the genre. This is palpable throughout the anthology, from Dacia Maraini's and Elsa Morante's long poems to Elizabeth Ferrero's poetic maps (see the poem 'Geography'). Feldman and Swann reproposed the poetry of Spaziani and Guidacci, but this time inscribed within a broader, transnational context; Spaziani's 'Journey in the Orient', for instance, transposes women's itinerant dimension into a postmodern return home: 'Samarkand is the past, but so long past | that I find it sometimes in the doorway of my house'.[14]

Eccentricity and poetic diversity are the inspiring forces not only of Feldman and Swann 1979, but also of other American publications of this period.[15] However, as noticeable from the comparison between the Italian and the American literary scenes, both the notion and the experience of the avant-garde differed substantially from one country to the other. I already discussed how the avant-garde is a synonym for innovative poetry in the US, whereas in Italy it is mainly associated with the spread of futurism and its afterlives (see Chapter 6). Between the 1960s and the 1970s, the critical distance between these two homonymous yet distinctive concepts expanded to the point of defining two separate realities. On the one hand, the development of new experimental schools of poetry both in Italy (Gruppo 63) and in the US (L=A=N=G=U=A=G=E poets); and, on the other, the anthologisation of peripheral groups, especially in America. This dichotomy, however, did not prevent the Italian and the American avant-garde from standing in a position of mutual influence. Just like the reception of Italian women's poetry in the US was filtered by the spread of American pluralism, the American avant-garde experience had European, and especially French, roots. Perloff outlined the trajectory of this transatlantic connection in her seminal work *The Poetics of Indeterminacy: Rimbaud to Cage* (1981); here she claims that the origins of American postmodernist innovations lie in the European avant-garde movements.

To complicate the picture, Feldman and Swann 1979 blurred the avant-garde's indistinct contours even further. While reflecting the fluid nature of American experimentalism, their selection was greatly influenced by the recent Gruppo 63 experience. Many Italian neo-avant-gardists migrated to the US, including women (Niccolai), where they contributed to the making of the Italian diasporic canon described in this book. The case of the poet and academic Ballerini offers a typical example of this trend; as Feldman and Swann acknowledged, Ballerini worked as a mediator between the editors and the poets, also supplying the artwork that embellishes the volume.[16] His art selection is partly taken from the catalogue of the exhibition that Ballerini himself presented at the Finch College Museum, New York, in 1973 (see Chapter 7). Sandri and Niccolai are among the female visual artists who are anthologised both by Ballerini and by Feldman and Swann; in addition, their 1979 anthology contains examples of Sandri's artefacts as well as an abstract representation by Patricia Vicinelli. The link between the visual arts and avant-garde poetry is a significant one not only because it can be traced as far back as Poggioli, but also because it characterises contemporary American poetry more widely, from Pound and Cummings to the poets of the New York School.[17]

The nexus between, and assimilation of, the avant-garde and Italian women's poetry is therefore paradoxical. Female poets in Italy were showing critical distance from, if not perplexity towards, the principles of Gruppo 63; Niccolai rejected the neo-avant-garde idea of impersonality, whereas Rosselli resolutely denied her affinity with the group. Yet, by a strange twist of fate, they reached the American public through the same medium they contested and/or refused. This was possible because, between the 1950s and 1970s, Italian women's poetry in the US underwent subtle but continuous transformations. From the early association with confessional poetry to the avant-garde turn, it engaged with various American currents, thus becoming a new, diasporic entity. In such a complex landscape, pluralism allowed American anthologists to overcome the conundrum of incompatible literary classifications: the inconsistency of posthermetic labels on the one hand, and the incongruities between two different conceptions of the avant-garde on the other. Recasting the polymorphic nature of the American avant-garde, this first set of anthologies paved the way for the feminist revolution that was about to come.

Notes to Chapter 9

1. See Franco Dean, 'Pluralism and Postmodernism: The Histories and Geographies of Ethnic American Literature', in *The Cambridge Companion to Postmodern American Fiction*, ed. by Paula Geyh (New York: Cambridge University Press, 2017), pp. 112–30. For a discussion on Italian women and race see Chapter 13.
2. *Lirici nuovi*, ed. by Luciano Anceschi (Milan: Mursia, 1964); *Poesia del Novecento*, ed. by Edoardo Sanguineti (Turin: Einaudi, 1969); *Antologia della poesia italiana*, ed. by Cesare Segre and Carlo Ossola (Turin: Einaudi, 1999).
3. Guenther and Sellin 1959, p. 150.
4. Jahan Ramazani, 'Introduction', in *The Norton Anthology of Modern and Contemporary Poetry*, ed. by Jahan Ramazani, Richard Ellmann, and Robert O'Clair, 2 vols (New York & London: Norton, 2003), II, xliii–lxvii (pp. xiii–xiv).
5. Guenther and Sellin 1959, p. 151.
6. Maria Luisa Spaziani, 'March in Rue Mouffetard', trans. by Eric Sellin and Charles Guenther, in Guenther and Sellin 1959, p. 154.
7. Maria Luisa Spaziani, 'I Remember a Season', trans. by Eric Sellin and Charles Guenther, in Guenther and Sellin 1959, p. 151.
8. *The Norton Anthology of Modern and Contemporary Poetry*, ed. by Ramazani, Ellmann and O'Clair, II, xliii.
9. Fredman, *A Concise Companion to Twentieth-Century American Poetry*, p. 60.
10. For example, *An Italian Quartet: Saba, Ungaretti, Montale, Quasimodo*, ed. by Robin Fulton (London: London Magazine Edition, 1966).

11. Bradshaw 1971, p. xv.
12. Margherita Guidacci, 'The Sand and the Angel', trans. by Vittoria Bradshaw, in Bradshaw 1971, p. 207.
13. See Glauco Cambon, 'Introduction', in Feldman and Swann 1979, pp. 9–12.
14. Maria Luisa Spaziani, 'Journey to the Orient', trans. by Ruth Feldman, in Feldman and Swann 1979, p. 212.
15. *The Actualist Anthology*, ed. by Morty Sklar and Darrell Gray (Iowa City, IA: The Spirit that Moves Us Press, 1977); *The Antaeus Anthology*, ed. by Daniel Halpern (New York: Bantam Dell, 1986).
16. Feldman and Swann 1979, p. 5.
17. See *Words into Pictures: E. E. Cummings' Art Across Borders*, ed. by Jiří Flajšar and Zénó Vernyik (Newcastle upon Tyne: Cambridge Scholars, 2007).

CHAPTER 10

❖

The Defiant Muse: The Horizon(s) of Theory

This chapter is dedicated to the analysis of *The Defiant Muse: Italian Feminist Poems from the Middle Ages to the Present*, a single-sex anthology published by Beverly Allen, Muriel Kittel, and Keala Jane Jewell in 1986 (ALLEN 1986). This anthology represents a turning point in the discussion on women and canonicity as it marks the emergence of gender studies in the making of diasporic poetics. By discussing the importance of contemporary French theorists, especially Kristeva, in the dissemination of feminist thought in America, I shall argue that American editors used feminism as a broad category to foster the reappraisal of the diverse.

1980s: The Dissemination of French Feminist Theories in the US

American anthologies began to give Italian women poets a separate critical space in the 1980s. Their main purpose was still to include poets that tended to be excluded from the dominant canon; yet, in conjunction with the development of so-called 'second-wave feminism', that is feminism in its activist phase, a new interest in femininity arose.[1] In 1986 the Feminist Press, New York, published four volumes of the series *The Defiant Muse*, a set of anthologies of feminist poetry in various languages: Spanish, German, French, Italian, Dutch and Flemish, Hebrew, and Vietnamese. As Florence Howe (a co-founder of the publishing house) explained, the aim of this editorial enterprise was to promote not only women's poetry, but specifically feminist verse, something that had never been done before. This particular focus had two distinctive goals: to appreciate the feminist essence of women's writing; and to introduce to the American public poets who were still unknown in their home countries.[2] Although Howe was primarily concerned with feminist topics, it is interesting to observe how the causes of feminism intermingled with the American penchant for marginal authors. It is not accidental that 1986 was also the year of publication of HALLER 1986, the first anthology of Italian dialect poetry in the English language (see Chapter 15).

The Italian issue of the series, which was co-edited by a trio of American women scholars (Allen, Kittel, and Jewell) is both a militant publication and a treatise on postmodern aesthetics. In her introduction to the volume, Allen discusses the theoretical issues at stake: the innate link between the feminine and the same act of writing alongside the complex relationship between minor and mainstream literature.[3] The anthology has the historicising purpose of showcasing more than fifty feminist poets from the Middle Ages to the present; simultaneously, it opens up to other genres and styles, such as folk literature and dialect verse. This is justified by the fact that, in Italy, 'feminist poetry is not the only literary production to have been marginalized by the traditional canon'; as the editor points out, 'a rich body of dialect literature has also existed since the beginning of the Italian language, giving a perspective from which the aulic works are revealed as an option, an opting for the aulic'.[4]

Some contemporary Italian women poets appeared in the English language for the first time, such as Liana Catri and Ida Vallerugo, the latter also being known for her writing in dialect; others had long been relegated to the oral tradition, such as the anonymous composers of popular songs from the early twentieth century. Resulting in a mosaic of distinctive yet consonant voices, Allen's historical account was based in fact on a postmodern narrative that employed a deconstructed, female gaze: courtly and working-class women, poets from both the north and the south of Italy, politics and poetics, social revolt and religion, everything is tied by the common thread of femininity.

Tatiana Crivelli pointed out the close relationship between feminism and post-modernism, arguing that the former had a pioneering role in the dissemination of deconstructionist theories in the US.[5] Between the 1970s and 1980s, the translation of French linguistic, philosophical, and psychoanalytical works — either by men (Jacques Derrida) or women (Kristeva, Hélène Cixous, and Luce Irigaray) — had enormous impact on the evolution of American literary theories. The feminist review *Signs* hosted several translations, from Cixous's 'The Laugh of the Medusa' (1976) to Kristeva's 'Women's Time' (1981), while Cornell University Press, New York, published Irigaray's most famous monographs (*Speculum of the Other Woman* and *This Sex Which Is Not Mine*) in two separate editions that came out in 1985.[6] At the same time, a special issue of *Yale French Studies* examined the interactions between French and American feminisms, fostering a pluralistic understanding of their complementary nature.[7] As Colette Gaudin observed in the review's introduction, the transplantation of the French feminists to the US laid bare an unwritten history of complexities and discontinuities; feminism, 'far from bringing to literary criticism the assurance of a unified ideology, introduce[ed], on the contrary, a different deconstructive twist into existing critical approaches'.[8]

By using feminism as a tool to deconstruct the relation between language and identity, nation and translation, *The Defiant Muse* silently engaged with these works. This was the first time that a poetry anthology projected onto the territory of literary history its theoretical foundations. Allen reread the Italian feminist tradition in a deconstructed way that implied the mediation of contemporary French thinkers and their philosophical concepts. From Cixous's texts Allen drew the idea of *écriture féminine*, i.e. the belief that the female body is a source of literary inspiration:

> Write yourself. Your body must be heard. [...] Because this is the invention of a new *insurgent* writing which, when the moment of her liberation has come,

> will allow her to carry out the indispensable ruptures and transformations in her history.[9]

Concurrently, Allen's recognition of women's writing as an 'empowering feminist act' echoed Irigaray's studies on women's societal and cultural exclusion, whereas Kristeva's theories underlie the poems dealing with psychoanalytic issues, from motherhood to sex, and from power to desire.[10]

Kristeva's exilic thought represented in fact the ideal counterpart to Allen's anthological programme in that Kristeva's philosophy embodied the editor's penchant for dislocated writers; similarly, in the decades following Allen's seminal publication, Kristeva's representation of women as *sujets en procès* had significant consequences for the history of the anthologisation of Italian female poets. From Allen's tradition of marginality to twenty-first-century adaptations of the idea of female 'mobility', Italian women poets in America have been read through the lens of contemporary (and specifically French) feminist theories. In other words, Kristeva's interpretation of feminism, only conceivable within the realm of the semiotic, had a crucial role in the defence of the communality of all subjects who inhabit marginal(ised) positions. Allen herself declared that the concept of gender is appropriate to determine marginality at large, as otherness enables the production of alternative ways of discourse.[11] By proposing the model of a new 'literary archaeology', *The Defiant Muse* fostered the (re)discovery of 'texts by men as well as women who by virtue of their sexuality, ethnicity, regionality, so-called race, or the simple fact that they write in dialect, are nudged away from positions of centrality'.[12] Allen's gendered perspective incorporated the pluralistic positions of her predecessors; yet, at the same time, it engaged with the contemporaneous feminist debate, which by this time was moving away from its early political demands to embrace linguistic, psychological, and poetic stances.

The Defiant Muse between Italy and the US: Genealogy and Themes

This encounter between literary theory and historiography produced the first canon of Italian women poets in English. Whereas Italian anthologies were displaying a 'reshuffling of poets from room to room in the canonical house of Italian poetry', Allen's proposal suggested an actual, deconstructed tour of the house itself.[13] This comparison with Italy had both a cultural and genealogic meaning: cultural because it read the connection between Italy and the US from a feminist perspective; and genealogic because it reassessed the contribution of Italian feminism to the creation of a deconstructed canon in the US. In the opening note to *The Defiant Muse*, the editors acknowledged their debt to two Italian critics who had just published their own single-sex anthologies: Frabotta and Laura Di Nola.[14] Frabotta's 1976 anthology was translated into English by Corrado Federici for Guernica in 2002, a daring act of transhistorical translation (Frabotta 2002). The reasons for, and significance of, this editorial choice have remained undiscussed by critics; although an analysis of these motivations falls outside the remit of this book, it is nonetheless needed as it may open important and unexpected paths of enquiry within, and beyond, the history of translation and (feminist) literary canons.

The poets of Frabotta's selection were reiterated by Allen, with the exception of five: Anna Maria Ortese, Vera Gherarducci, Iole Tognelli, Gilda Musa, and Antonella Carosella; at the same time, some of Allen's most original choices, such as Marianna Fiore, Marta Fabiani, and Gabriella Sica, stemmed directly from Di Nola's volume.[15] This lineage is significant not only because it underlines the intertextual nature of the anthology as a genre, but also because it sheds light onto the cultural synergies between Italy and America in the 1970s and 1980s. In particular, the ways in which female poetry was anthologised in Italy illuminate profound divergences between the two countries. Frabotta's introduction to *Donne in poesia* touches on the question of women's identity and its aesthetic representation rather than insisting on the anthologisation of minor groups. Even Di Nola's *Poesia femminista italiana* proves to be subject-focused despite a militant, self-defining title. In other words, Frabotta's and Di Nola's captivated tone leaves no space for a broad-breadth project à la Allen; their militant work is more an act of accusation of Italy's patriarchal society than an attempt to revise the Italian canon:

> Solo [...] vivendo dei rapporti da soggetto, la donna potrà iniziare a esistere [...] e scrollarsi di dosso furiosamente, come fanno gran parte delle autrici in questa raccolta, secoli di incrostazioni nel tempo di un grido, è già rivoluzionario.[16]
>
> [Women will begin to exist only when they will be able to relate to their own self and to others as subjects. [...] What most of the authors collected here have been doing so far is already revolutionary: furiously shaking off centuries of encrustation in the short time of a cry.]

Conversely, Allen's deconstructionist approach resonates with a particular trend of American literary studies that privileged feminist perspectives. *The Defiant Muse* belongs to a vaster critical constellation for which feminism is a pretext to dive into broader, postmodern analyses. Some of these works are likely to have influenced Allen's anthology directly; I think, for instance, of Howe and Bass's anthology of feminist American verse, which distinguished itself for engaging with a spectrum of different traditions: Jewish poetry, transnational poetry, and the avant-garde.[17] Other anthologies aligned with Allen's feminist vision by focusing on the intersections between language and sexuality.[18] Poet and academic Alicia Suskin Ostriker enucleated this specific bond in a seminal work that is emblematically entitled *Stealing the Language* (1986). This study, which came out in the same year of Allen's publication, unified under the common discourse of language the thematic flourishing of American women's poetry in the postwar years: 'the quest for identity and the obstacle of the divided self, the centrality of the body, the release of forbidden anger, the imperative of intimacy, and the rewriting of mythology'.[19]

Allen's selection presented a similar level of thematic conceptualisation, especially in its contemporary section. This is not surprising considering that, out of fifty-two anthologised poets, thirty-four wrote in the twentieth century and twenty-nine were alive at the time of the anthology's publication. The scarcity of poets from the Middle Ages and the Renaissance was dictated by the limited availability of texts in translation; their presence, however, is a guarantee of the consistency of women's writing throughout the centuries. In particular, on Renaissance Italian women writers, there has been a significant increase in the number of publications from the 1990s onwards.[20] The modern and contemporary selection begins with the so-called Decadents (Vittoria Aganoor Pompili, Annie Vivanti, Ada Negri) and continues with the poetry of Amelia Guglielminetti and Sibilla Aleramo. Some names, such as those of Spaziani, Guidacci, and Niccolai, resurface from the comprehensive FELDMAN AND SWANN 1979; however, Allen put forward a new generation of poets. The most remarkable entry is that of Rosselli, who, despite a relatively late appearance, was destined to become the most canonical woman poet both in Italy and abroad. Other important introductions are Mariella Bettarini and Frabotta, arguably the two major representatives of the Italian feminist movement. Allen anthologised some of their most militant poems, thus accommodating in the repertoire of contemporary Italian poetry the topics of the new social and political agenda.

Allen's selective criteria reflect her engagement with theory. If the early anthologies underlined women's bent for confessional verse, spiritual and private life are only some of the aspects emerging from her collection. Likewise, Feldman and Swann's interest in the 'absolutely out' had given the way to a complex representation of the feminist experience. As Allen observed, twentieth-century female poetry in Italy saw a 'remarkable expansion of themes' due to the participation of women in international intellectual affairs.[21] These feminists' portrayal of power, language, and sex can be read as an expression of the dissemination of psychoanalytic theories in the 1970s and 1980s. This is evident in Bettarini's Oedipal configurations, Rosselli's multilingual identity, as well as in the treatment of hetero- and homosexual love in works by Frabotta and Vivian Lamarque.

Allen continuously stressed the 'inextricable links between theme and style so important to contemporary feminist consciousness'.[22] There is no such a thing as a feminist subject without a feminist, and therefore deconstructed, use of language. Different poets expressed this association of content and words in distinctive ways: Maraini asserted that the 'sophistication | of form is something that goes with power';[23] Amalia Guglielminetti established a new poetic status based on the humbleness of everyday speech, 'I did not want to sing, I wanted to speak';[24] Antonia Pozzi, by contrast, enabled language to release the pain of the poet's 'prisoner words'.[25]

Metaliterary reflections crisscross the anthology from the beginning to the end. Often concealed behind the most militant poems, they echo from Patrizia Cavalli's 'sterile' poetry — 'I have no seed to scatter through the world'[26] — to Fabiani's domestic epiphanies:

> The poetess has paragraphs of words
> threads she unravels as phrases
> unusual comparisons
> among the gleams
> of a kitchen stove.[27]

This link between womanliness and literary creation is particularly significant as it is at the core of the most important feminist publications of the period (see, for instance, Kristeva's *Revolution in Poetic Language*, which was translated in 1984).

The theme of self-reflection played a quintessential role in the construction of the feminist 'I'. According to Allen, 'the poem, like the feminist, perhaps, makes subjectivity problematic as it represents or as it works to avoid representing it'.[28] This element of self-awareness is already at work in the poems from the Renaissance (see Vittoria Colonna's 'I write only to relieve my inner grief'), but it is especially visible in modern and contemporary texts. If we exclude Vivanti, who defined her femininity in terms of geographical displacement — 'What is my fatherland? Mama is German, | Papa is Italian, I was born in England' — Allen's poets convey their experience of alienation through the comparison with the other, i.e. with men.[29] From this perspective, feminist subjectivity is defined in a Derridean way, that is as the result of a subtraction (or a *différence*): the female 'I' is what the male 'I' is not.[30] Practically speaking, female poets redeem their subordination by means of a feminist reading of both private life and society. Anna Malfaiera defined herself and, by extension, her female peers on the basis of a fierce opposition between men and women; her slogan-like poem staged one of the harshest feminist battles — the right to accept, or to refuse, motherhood: 'Men are irrational weak and vile. | Into this world I refuse to bring a child'.[31] Similarly, the destinies of the two genders are kept separate in Catri's 'The Spiral Staircase', a:

phallic forest of myths
in permanent effective service
where man is tree
female the shade
born at his feet.[32]

Conversely, in Armanda Guiducci, the feminist polemic is mitigated by a sense of mystery before the diversity of creation and the reality of love:

Different from me entirely: male, foreign,
different flash, different heart, different mind,
and yet my own body in extension,
my voice that doubles itself and continues me:
[...]
my necessary opposite, a cruel marvel
it is to love you: to enjoy two lives
in this one, to have double death.[33]

The meditation on language and love is also at the core of Rosselli's poems. Allen presented Rosselli's split self by anthologising one of the texts that she originally wrote in English. In 'On Fatherisch Men', the poet employs an archaic Shakespearean language to set the myth of the primordial father who is both an ancestor and a lover:

Have thee not recognized I bee
a Devilish Maiden, pulling at Thy flucid Beard? Yet
I do Love thee, and beg thee be
a True Father. Mine is Gone
into the Grave.[34]

Here Rosselli seems to blur the most traumatic events of her life with feminist issues: the murder of her father, the dreaming vision of a masculine genealogy, and the painful reality of sex as loss. Located on the border between different nations, traditions, and mythologies, Rosselli's language embodies the instability of the female, diasporic subject as described by Kristeva: a fluctuating identity inhabiting at times the symbolic and the semiotic.

Kristeva's influence on Allen's selection extends to the treatment of biological and/or civil relationships. Catri and Maraini compare their mothers to fellow animals and sisters representing at the same time life's non-sense and the redemptive power of literature:

All right mother
give birth to me please.
[...]
I want to sing so strongly
that the song could break my heart
and go on living
without me.[35]

Likewise, Rosanna Guerrini turns the poetic language into an act of contrition that expresses her ineptitude both as a woman and mother:

You will do he will do you will do
You will be he will be you will be.
[...]
I'd do that too,
but my lips are sewn shut
only my arms move.[36]

Among the traditional institutions, marriage is by far the most opposed. The housewife's lament was already a leitmotif in popular songs at the turn of the twentieth century, when familial life was described as deception, 'downfall', and misfortune, a curse from which it was impossible to escape: 'We go to our downfall | as soon as we're brides'; 'Dirindina the discontented, | papa has fun and mama's tormented'.[37] On a similar note, Loretta Merenda's 'Local News' deals with marriage as an experience of duplicity and incredulity:

What do you want me to say
about your marriage
[...]
We looked on from the outside
like the profane.[38]

It is worth noticing how a similar range of expressions substantiates the feminist polemic from the dialect of the Venetian silk-spinners to the power-imbued language of the 1980s, a sign of the postmodern hybridisation between low culture and high culture, present and past.

Apart from metaliterature, the body is also a connecting thread in Allen's anthology. With its nerves, limbs, and fluids, anatomy is a way to access both the poet's inner being and the external world. This is particularly evident in Niccolai's 'GN is happy', a neo-avant-garde sequence of funambulist images in which the female lyrical 'I', the male central figure ('lui'), the dedicatee (Isabella), Othello and Desdemona, Tom Jones, and many others, including goats and snakes, exchange roles and body parts:

> THE MARE BECOMES THE MONKEY
> and the back becomes the mouth that bites the back
> I AM ALSO A CAMEL. Wouldn't you like that?
> [...]
> I have never understood that Othello and Desdemona were
> the same person.[39]

This poem treats the theme of desire in a way that involves both physicality and imagination; for instance, the concluding lines contain an allusion to sex hidden in the metaphor of the alternation between day and night, light and darkness:

> We live at night and make the dawn
> we do this lovely well-thought work
> which is the making of the dawn. What's done is dawn
> AND DURING THE DAY WE MAKE THE REST OF OUR BODIES.
> Each of us wants to give a shape to our own desires.[40]

The idea of the woman's body as giver of life is at the forefront of the poems by Guidacci and Guiducci. Both authors link the body to visions of decadence and the passing of time, rather than focusing on the experience of pleasure. Guidacci transforms the body of a middle-aged woman into a senescent tree, transfiguring the most classical of metamorphoses into nostalgia:

> It may be the last
> Time I have a baby at my breast, for the years
> Press on to parch
> My lymph.[41]

Conversely, Guiducci's words express the struggles of both woman- and motherhood in a disenchanted, polemic language:

> I have made days, children,
> fed bodies and minutes with love,
> spilled out milk from breasts and pitchers
> over the mornings' insistent thresholds.
> [...]
> What great labor to create for oneself a body
> [...]
> And now that I possess one,
> [...]
> now the body is mature grows old dies.[42]

Despite the common focus on the body's biological circles, Guidacci and Guiducci inflect the anatomical theme in a variety of ways. The former sees in her motherly body a sign of the infinite, the possibility of going beyond her own corporeal limits:

> I feel
> Within me the sweet surge of milk rising
> To my breast: tenderness

That spontaneously fills my every fiber
Dilates my borders.[43]

Then immediately after:

My body is the instrument of a miracle
As it already was in giving life. My breast
Is the fabled hill, rivers
Of plenty are flowing in a golden
Age.[44]

This religious imagery is totally absent in Guiducci's 'Song of the Hammer', which can be read as a lament against men's indifference in the discovery of women's diversity:

I have split myself open like a pomegranate
over my aborted and unborn children.
I have tried
to transform an encounter into permanence,
to encompass in man
his diversity.
But how what I encompassed
has now turned against me.[45]

In Livia Candiani the bodily imagery intermingles with other thematic configurations, such as the poet's self-portrait, the logics of power and the expression of rage. 'The Death of Poetry', the title of one of Candiani's poems, is described in a post-Barthesian way, both as the death of the author and her resurrection.[46] Candiani's militancy responds here to her broader metahistorical vision:

my bier opened
my death
stopped traveling
and I have emerged
from a larger and heavier
new placenta
the historic placenta
and have begun to scream
with the redness of my rage.[47]

Anger is also at the core of Silvia Batisti's poem 'This Rage', which problematises the relationships between the human, especially female, body, and the progress of science:

But he is mistaken who thinks
that space is limited to consciousness,
and the body — used as a guinea pig by the genes —
only an object, with simple vegetative
functions; man is combustible
material that burns with honor
in any old piazza.[48]

* * * * *

As shown here, there has been a pattern of anthologisation in the US that made both Italian and American women's poetry canonical on the basis of a shared semantics. Not only did women's poetry prove to be an extension of marginal literature, but it also introduced into the American national canon topics that had long remained unexplored. Allen's poets dealt with all the themes that Ostriker listed to define female poetry in America: the reality of women's divided self, the language of the body alongside the correspondences between sexuality and poetics. However, Allen did not engage with an important aspect of female poetry as presented by Ostriker: its relation to myth. For women poets, myth is a source of cultural and linguistic reappropriation, a process that Ostriker called 'revisionist mythmaking'.[49] Although Italian poetry offered significant examples in this respect, it was only in the new millennium that American anthologists started to acknowledge Italian women's revisionist practices. Except from this delay, Allen's selection was in tune with the current trends of American criticism, which, by this time, was appropriating the French feminist dimensions. By overcoming its national setting, Italian women's poetry migrated to the liminal space reserved for marginal, supranational identities.

Notes to Chapter 10

1. Margaret Walters, *Feminism: A Very Short Introduction* (Oxford: Oxford University Press, 2005).
2. Florence Howe, 'Publisher's Preface', in Allen 1986, p. vii.
3. Beverley Allen, 'Introduction', in Allen 1986, pp. xv–xxi.
4. Ibid., p. xv. See also *Revisioning Italy: National Identity and Global Culture*, ed. by Beverly Allen and Mary J. Russo (Minneapolis: University of Minnesota Press, 1997).
5. See Mary Poovey, 'Feminism and Deconstruction', *Feminist Studies*, 14 (1988), 51–65, and Tatiana Crivelli, 'L'eccezione che non fa la regola: riflessioni sul rapporto tra scrittura femminile e canone', in *Dentro/fuori, sopra/sotto*, ed. by Ronchetti and Sapegno, pp. 39–52.
6. Hélène Cixous, 'The Laugh of the Medusa', trans. by Paula Cohen and Keith Cohen, *Signs*, 4 (1976), 875–93; Kristeva, 'Women's Time'; Luce Irigaray, *Speculum of the Other Woman*, trans. by Gillian C. Gill (Ithaca, NY: Cornell University Press, 1985); *This Sex Which Is Not Mine*, trans. by Catherine Porter and Carolyn Burker (Ithaca, NY: Cornell University Press, 1985).
7. *Feminist Readings: French Texts/American Contexts*, ed. by Colette Gaudin and others, special issue of *Yale French Studies*, 62 (1981).
8. Ibid., p. 13.
9. Cixous, 'The Laugh of the Medusa', p. 880.
10. Allen 1986, p. xv. See Luce Irigaray, *Ethique de la différence sexuelle* (Paris: Minuit, 1984).
11. Beverly Allen, 'From One Closet to Another? Feminism, Literary Archaeology, and the Canon', in *Italian Women Writers from the Renaissance to the Present: Revising the Canon*, ed. and with an introduction by Maria Ornella Marotti (University Park: Pennsylvania State University Press, 1996), pp. 25–36 (p. 33).
12. Ibid., p. 31.
13. Lucia Re, '(De)Constructing the Canon: The Agon of the Anthologies in the Scene of Modern Italian Poetry', *MLR*, 87 (1992), 585–603 (p. 602).
14. *Donne in poesia: antologia della poesia femminile in Italia dal dopoguerra a oggi*, ed. by Biancamaria Frabotta (Rome: Savelli, 1976); *Poesia femminista italiana*, ed. by Laura Di Nola (Rome: Savelli, 1978).
15. Allen 1986, p. viii.
16. *Poesia femminista italiana*, ed. by Di Nola, p. 12.
17. *No More Masks! An Anthology of Poems by Women*, ed. by Florence Howe and Ellen Bass (Garden City, NY: Anchor Press, 1973).

18. *I Hear My Sisters Saying: Poems by Twentieth-Century Women*, ed. by Carol Konek and Dorothy Walters (New York: Crowell, 1976); *New Poets, Women: An Anthology*, ed. by Terry Wetherby (Milbrae, CA: Les Femmes Publishing, 1976).
19. Alicia Suskin Ostriker, *Stealing the Language: The Emergence of Women's Poets in America* (Boston, MA: Beacon Press, 1986), inside cover.
20. See the following anthologies: *Women Poets of the Italian Renaissance: Courtly Ladies and Courtesans*, ed. by Laura Anna Stortoni and Mary Prentice Lilie (New York: Italica Press, 1997); *Lyric Poetry by Women of the Italian Renaissance*, ed. by Virginia Cox (Baltimore, MD: John Hopkins University Press, 2009).
21. ALLEN 1986, p. xx.
22. Ibid.
23. Dacia Maraini, 'Poems by Women', trans. by Muriel Kittel, in ALLEN 1986, p. 97.
24. Amalia Guglielminetti, 'My Voice', trans. by Muriel Kittel, in ALLEN 1986, p. 49.
25. Antonia Pozzi, 'The Closing Door', trans. by Muriel Kittel, in ALLEN 1986, p. 57.
26. Patrizia Cavalli, 'I Have No Seed to Scatter through the World', trans. by Muriel Kittel, in ALLEN 1986, p. 119.
27. Marta Fabiani, 'The Poetess', trans. by Muriel Kittel, in ALLEN 1986, p. 133.
28. ALLEN 1986, p. xvi.
29. Annie Vivanti, 'Ego', trans. by Muriel Kittel, in ALLEN 1986, p. 41.
30. Poovey, 'Feminism and Deconstruction', p. 53. See also Jacques Derrida, 'La Différence', in *Marges de la philosophie* (Paris: Minuit, 1960), pp. 1–29.
31. Anna Malfaiera, 'I Can No Longer Laugh with Real Joy', trans. by Muriel Kittel, in ALLEN 1986, p. 73.
32. Liana Catri, 'The Spiral Staircase', trans. by Muriel Kittel, in ALLEN 1986, p. 75.
33. Armanda Guiducci, 'Man', trans. by Muriel Kittel, in ALLEN 1986, p. 63.
34. Amelia Rosselli, 'On Fatherish Men', in ALLEN 1986, p. 79. The poem was originally written in English.
35. Franca Maria Catri, 'Sister Mother', trans. by Muriel Kittel, in ALLEN 1986, p. 85.
36. Rosanna Guerrini, 'To My Children', trans. by Muriel Kittel, in ALLEN 1986, pp. 93–95.
37. Anonymous Popular Songs, 'The Housewife's Lament' and 'The Discontented Woman', both trans. by Muriel Kittel, in ALLEN 1986, pp. 51, 53.
38. Loretta Merenda, 'Local News', trans. by Muriel Kittel, in ALLEN 1986, p. 125.
39. Giulia Niccolai, 'GN IS HAPPY', trans. by Beverly Allen, in ALLEN 1986, p. 91.
40. Ibid.
41. Margherita Guidacci, 'Many Times November Has Come', trans. by Muriel Kittel, ALLEN 1986, p. 63.
42. Armanda Guiducci, 'Song of the Hammer', trans. by Muriel Kittel, ALLEN 1986, p. 67.
43. Guidacci, 'Many Times November Has Come', p. 61.
44. Ibid., pp. 61–63.
45. Guiducci, 'Song of the Hammer', p. 67.
46. The title of Livia Candiani's poem 'The Death of Poetry' reminds us of Roland Barthes, 'The Death of the Author', in *Image, Music, Text*, ed. and trans. by Stephen Heath (New York: Hill & Wang, 1977), pp. 142–48 (first published as 'La Mort de l'auteur', *Manteia*, 5 (1968), 12–17).
47. Livia Candiani, 'The Death of Poetry', trans. by Muriel Kittel, ALLEN 1986, pp. 131–33.
48. Silvia Batisti, 'This Rage', trans. by Muriel Kittel, ALLEN 1986, p. 125.
49. Ostriker, *Stealing the Language*, p. 210.

CHAPTER 11

Contemporary Italian Women Poets and the Transnational Paradigm

1990s-2000s: Transnational Feminism

Ten years after the publication of *The Defiant Muse*, American editors proved to be even more interested in the poetry of peripheral groups, namely dialect poets and women. Just as 1986 saw the contemporaneous publication of Hermann Haller's dialect anthology and Allen's volume, so new female and dialect collections came out almost simultaneously in the late 1990s and early 2000s. In this decade, the publishers Legas and Italica, both of which are based in North America, published three anthologies of dialect poetry (Bonaffini 1997, Bonaffini 1999, and Bonaffini 2001) and an anthology of, and by, women, *Contemporary Italian Women Poets* (Blum and Trubowitz 2001), the latter constituting a reference point for any study on Italian female writing. Such patterns of publication are not merely coincidental, but reveal an important turning point in the reception of Italian poetry that coincided with the consolidation of transnational perspectives.[1] In this chapter, I shall analyse Blum and Trubowitz 2001 as a paradigm of the shift from feminist poetry to transnational literature that occurred at the dawn of the twenty-first century. Although postmodernist aspirations were already at work in Allen 1986, Blum and Trubowitz 2001 marked the beginning of a new way of considering female writers, as transnational subjects and figures of mobility. I shall use Blum's definition of women writers as 'figures of subjectivity in progress' to foreground the idea of an itinerant, diasporic canon.[2] Recasting Kristeva's idea of the *sujet en progrès*, Blum considered the metaphor of the journey in feminine literature as a way of enacting 'the moral and epistemological predicament of a decentred, fragmented subject'; in this poetically transformative journey, the double movement 'toward (self-) discovery and expanded relationship with the world' actualises the interplay between individual lives and global values that characterises the postmodern condition.[3]

The perception of women as representatives of different nationalities, ethnicities, and cultures testifies to this anthology's engagement with 'third-wave feminism', whose beginnings are marked in the early 1990s.[4] Fostering a transnational interpretation of gender and sexuality, this late development of feminist thought proved to be even more diversified than the one that took place in the 1960s. Third-wave feminism fostered not only the realisation of poetry anthologies in the main foreign languages, but also the dissemination of foreign criticism exploring queer and feminist topics.[5] In the US, this tension between tradition and multiculturalism exploded in the so-called 'canon war', which transposed into a global setting the controversy between formalism and the avant-garde. Starting in 1994 with the publication of Bloom's *The Western Canon*, this theoretical confrontation brought to the fore the same issues that were already at stake during the battle of the anthologies thirty years before. Multiculturalism worked as a means of ideological continuity between the 1960s and the 1990s; it also revealed that these resonances started with, and went far beyond, the interest in marginalised authors.

At the end of the century, Italian critics turned towards the poetry of minorities; these voices, however, remained confined to countercurrent publications that did not alter the traditionalist attitude of Italian academia. Among these isolated works, it is worth mentioning Vittoriano Esposito's second volume of his series entitled *L'altro Novecento nella poesia italiana* (1997), entirely dedicated to women.[6] In the same period, Alberto Asor Rosa presented his anticonventional stance in a famous study focusing on the hidden aspects of Italian literature: 'Non credo in una critica letteraria custode dell'istituzione. Credo in una critica letteraria che sia una pervicace esplorazione di confini' [I do not believe that literary criticism should be the keeper of tradition. Rather, it should be a courageous exploration of borders].[7] Given the idiosyncratic positions of both Italy and America, Blum and Trubowitz's proposal proves to be programmatic on a number of levels. First, it anthologises a restricted number of contemporary women poets, both famous and unknown; and second, it carries forward the project of a diasporic canon whose first signs are visible in the anthologies of the postwar years. The acknowledgement of Anglo-American influences, as well as the choice of bilingual texts, speaks for Blum and Trubowitz's transnationalism; at the same time, the anthology's diasporic meaning lies in the sense of displacement that the poems share. Whilst ALLEN 1986 was a transhistorical report of feminist poetry, BLUM AND TRUBOVITZ 2001 fostered a transgeographical reading of the national literary tradition. In the introduction to the latter anthology, women Italian poets are juxtaposed with major Anglo-American writers, both male and female, among whom Dickinson, Whitman, and Sylvia Plath. Moreover, the editors point out that the dissemination of Anglo-American culture in Italy is the product of translations by female authors; to support this idea, a list of translations appears at the end of each poet's biography. Some poets acquire a transterritorial dimension for engaging directly with the American literary production: this is the case of Luciana Frezza, who paradoxically compares her 'controlled manner of expression to methods of writing and living practiced by the Beat generation' in the US; similarly, Ombres, Jolanda Insana, and Piera Oppezzo, among many others, endorsed the form of the long American poem rather than using posthermetic solutions.[8]

This explains why Blum and Trubowitz presented their anthology as the point of arrival of a process of anthologisation that privileged a fluid idea of poetic history. Opening both to transnational literature and women, this model proved to be a successful one in the US, not only through the publication of single-sex selections, but also thanks to women's growing presence in the comprehensive anthologies that had been published in the previous ten years. In 2012, Brock selected eight women among twenty-two poets who were born after the 1930s (BROCK 2012); since the whole anthology includes ten women in total, this choice reveals the dramatic increase in female poets in the second half of the twentieth century. Similarly, MONTORFANI 2014 extended to transnational figures and women transcending the boundaries of the Italian literary tradition.[9]

In Italy, conversely, women's poetry remained isolated from mainstream currents; in a single-sex anthology published in 2002, editors Maria Pia Ammirati and Ornella Palumbo offered a 'catalogue of the existent' that nonetheless did not touch the discourse on women and canonicity:

> L'antologia è di per sé un paradosso. [...] È stato anche questo il motivo che ci ha spinte a dare un panorama il quanto più ampio possibile che potesse scavalcare l'antologico e farsi catalogo dell'esistente.
>
> [The anthology is in itself a paradox. [...] This is the reason that pushed us to offer the widest possible overview, one that could transcend the anthological form in order to become a catalogue of the existent].[10]

Although in the last decade there has been an increase in Italian anthologies dealing with the work of marginal figures, especially migrants and female writers, no attempt has been made to relate this poetry to the dominant male tradition. Conversely, BLUM AND TRUBOWITZ 2001 displayed a well-defined project of canon revision; with its twenty-five poets in translation, it transnationalised Italian women's poetry while historicising it.

Classicising the Diasporic Canon

BLUM AND TRUBOWITZ 2001's transnational approach is not at odds with its attempt to anthologise, and therefore centralise, Italian lyric. That there is no contrast between canonical (centripetal) and diasporic (centrifugal) forces is primarily evident in the anthologists' ambition to make the transnational traditional; or, in other words, to place the literature away from, and of, the margins, at the centre. The editors looked at Italian literary production from the outside, proposing a national, gendered canon that was also open to its extraterritorial dimensions. An interesting modality in which the anthologists revised, and displaced, the Italian tradition is through the destabilisation of stereotyped taxonomies. In the anthology's introduction, a division in poetic decades takes the place of more popular classifications in poetic schools and/or generations of poets; concurrently, the representation of women poets both within and outside the Italian canon challenges conventional dichotomies, such as the opposition between traditional verse and feminist poetry.[11] Although the editors are aware of the difficulties of associating Italian women's poetry with any form of poetic experimentation, they detect in its vitality a sign of the enduring influence of the avant-garde.[12] Once more, the term 'avant-garde' is employed in a Poundian way and not as a restrictive definition of linguistic innovation. Thus, Blum and Trubowitz's dual strategy serves their diasporic programme: it dislocates long-established conventions on the one hand, and it incorporates female poets into the territory of literary history on the other.

This is the first time that a single-sex anthology offers a precise account of the degree of women's participation in mainstream poetic movements. The twenty-five anthologised poets are presented over the course of three main historical periods, from the crisis of hermeticism to the most recent developments. Most of the names were already anthologised in English, such as Guidacci, Spaziani, Niccolai, and Insana; yet, a considerable number of poets are introduced for the first time: Gherarducci, Campo, Elena Clementelli, Gabriella Leto, Anna Cascella, Luciana Notari, and Rosita Copioli. Most of these newly-introduced poets are modern languages scholars who published on Anglo-American literature and translated from English. Campo translated into Italian John Donne, Dickinson, Williams and Pound, while Cascella reviewed British and American literature for RAI, the national public broadcasting company of Italy. These editorial choices testify not only to the erudite source of Italian poetry, but also to the editors' ambition to offer a transcultural interpretation of it. As for the other poets, they had already appeared either in ALLEN 1986 or in Catherine O'Brien's *Italian Women Poets*, or in both of them.[13] Although published in Ireland, and therefore beyond my field of enquiry, O'Brien's anthology cannot be left out of this analysis insofar as it is the second single-sex anthology of Italian women poets published in English.

Blum and Trubowitz combined the approaches of Allen and O'Brien. While the former recognised in the feminist protest the common thread of women's poetry across time, the latter avoided questions of historical genealogy, focusing instead on the individual achievement of eleven contemporary poets. O'Brien moved forward in time the beginnings of contemporary Italian female poetry by anthologising works by post-1945 authors only (with the exception of Pozzi who died in 1938). Bringing together these two different anthological traditions, Blum and Trubowitz illustrated 'both a survey of marginalized body of work and an analysis of women's deliberate divergences from established poetic histories'.[14] This method allows the editors to construct an inclusive canon that does justice to female writing without running the risk of homologising it. It is precisely by including women authors from different generations and regions, both unknown and internationally acclaimed, that Blum and Trubowitz absorbed the lesson of the avant-garde. Despite a variety of genres and motivations, the diasporic canon developed and changed in accordance with its historical shifts and cultural evolution.

Table 11.1 offers a comparative reading of the three anthologies by registering the frequency of common poets, arranged in alphabetical order; the presence of each writer is marked with an asterisk. For reasons of temporal coherence, I reproduce the contemporary section of ALLEN 1986 only, i.e. its twenty and twenty-first century authors.

TABLE 11.1. A comparative analysis of ALLEN 1986, O'BRIEN, *Italian Women Poets*, and BLUM AND TRUBOWITZ 2001 on the basis of frequently anthologised poets

	ALLEN 1986	O'Brien, *Italian Women Poets*	BLUM AND TRUBOWITZ 2001
Bettarini	★		★
Cavalli	★		★
Frabotta	★	★	★
Guidacci	★	★	★
Guiducci	★		★
Insana	★	★	★
Lamarque	★	★	★
Maraini	★		★
Menicanti		★	★
Merini		★	★
Niccolai	★		★
Ombres	★		★
Opezzo	★		★
Pozzi	★	★	
Rosselli	★	★	★
Sica	★		★
Spaziani	★	★	★
Valduga		★	★

Six poets are common to the three anthologies (Frabotta, Guidacci, Insana, Lamarque, Rosselli, and Spaziani), whereas a series of poets migrated from ALLEN 1986 to BLUM AND TRUBOWITZ 2001 without being included by O'Brien: Bettarini, Cavalli, Guidacci, Maraini, Niccolai, Ombres, Opezzo, and Sica. Conversely, O'Brien, introduced Menicanti, Merini, and Patrizia Valduga, the former resurfacing in BLUM AND TRUBOWITZ 2001. Only Pozzi is shared between ALLEN 1986 and O'Brien. There are also poets who are new to BLUM AND TRUBOWITZ 2001, such as Campo, Clementelli, and Copioli, thus testifying to the editors' effort to both enlarge and stabilise the canon. Translations are by editors Muriel Kittel, unless otherwise stated (ALLEN 1986), O'Brien (*Italian Women Poets*), and Blum and Trubowitz (BLUM AND TRUBOWITZ 2001).

It is interesting to observe how the selection of specific poems resulted in a totally different interpretation of the same author; to mention but one example, Allen concentrated on Bettarini's feminist poetry, whereas Blum and Trubowitz challenged the largely political reading of her work by including poems on motherhood and metaliterature.

Blum and Trubowitz 2001's introduction lists the general issues at stake, a technique that recalls Allen's and Ostriker's semantic configurations:

> The quest for identity and self-representation; the interwoven experiences of loving and writing; the tense and often painful connections between textuality, sexuality, power, and intimacy; metaphysical reflections on everyday life; and the trauma that can result from daily experience, including the extreme challenge of living with physical and mental illness.[15]

At the same time, these themes incorporate prefeminist motifs, such as the presence of religious and/or biographical sketches (see Poggioli 1948; Bradshaw 1971; Marchione 1974).

The multilayered concept of diaspora as presented in this study proves to be a useful tool to describe female poets' displacement, both literal and metaphorical. All the poems anthologised here deal with migrancy as a way of being part of the globalised world; as Blum pointed out in her study on women's displacement in contemporary Italian literature, female writing internalises the cultural importance of migration so much so that the latter has become 'a trope for feminist thinking/writing'.[16] Poet Frabotta coined the term *viandanza* (the title of two essays and a poetry collection of hers) to draw the connection among the feminine, wayfaring, and hospitality.[17] 'It was precisely the oscillation between nostalgia and transformation,' she wrote, 'that [...] gave "wayfaring" a somewhat special polysemy and room to welcome variegated yet compatible meanings: from the impossible female *nostos* [...] into the maternal womb, to that which, persisting and remaining in the womb of maternal language, is called poetry'.[18] Frabotta conceives the wayfarer's course as 'a continuous return to a new departure'; his/her journey is 'not to be understood in the name of "an authenticity that refers back to the closed circle of the self, repossession and belonging", but rather in a spirit of "humbleness" and the "precariousness of fleeting hospitality"'.[19] This sense of fluidity and hospitality, which is crucial to diasporic poetics, also characterises Clementelli's verse as it echoes the inner mobility of time and space:

> Subterranean geography,
> vast currents,
> against the surface where my present is guest.[20]

In order to interpret Blum and Trubowitz's selection in the light of women poets' displaced condition, I would like to propose a diasporic model that draws together the anthology's different themes (see Figure 11.1). Pole A embodies the multiform expressions of the lyrical 'I', from the search for identity to the exploration of the body; B indicates the poet's relational nature in her journey towards the other, who can be a lover, a parental figure, or society; C refers to the time of history in which women live and from which they are excluded; and D explores female poetry's activity of 'revisionist mythmaking' as a way of transcending both temporal and societal boundaries. This model makes use of Kristeva's conceptual framework in that poles C and D are a projection of Kristeva's distinction between the symbolic and the semiotic orders.[21] According to Kristeva's model of signification, the male-symbolic order represents the linear time of history, whereas the female-semiotic order is the time of nature and eternity. In particular, between A and B, and C and D there is biunivocal correspondence, which means that the journey's directions from and towards the four points are flexible; the poet can 'migrate' from the self to the other, and from time to myth, but also vice versa.

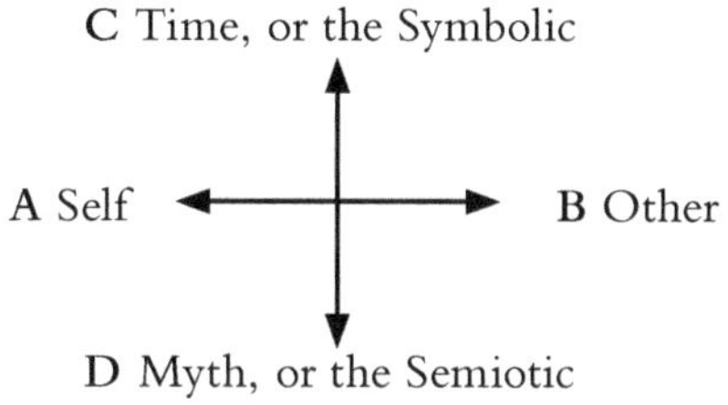

FIG. 11.1. Diasporic modality in BLUM AND TRUBOWITZ 2001

Blum and Trubowitz did not employ feminism as a key concept to define contemporary female poetry in Italy, yet the emphasis on women's diaspora(s), both physical and symbolic, resonates with the ideas of third-wave feminists. This is evident in the subject's oscillations between the self and the other as well as in women's attempts to define culture by means of a radical revisionism. The Italian title of one of Guiducci's poems, 'Parto', which can be interpreted both as 'departing' [I leave] and 'giving birth', can be an example of feminist, diasporic poetry. The poem activates various levels of meaning showing that life is a form of diaspora not only from one space to another, but also from the maternal body to the child's body:

> Darkness broke into life, and I knew
> (as water knows through widening circles)
> that we exist through vibrations
> from one being to another — endlessly.[22]

Guidacci deals with women's sense of displacement in 'Madame X', an ironic hymn to women's search for identity:

> I am not my body.
> It is alien, an enemy to me.
> Worse still is my soul,
> nor in it do I see myself.
> From a distance I watch
> the boorish acrobatics of this couple.[23]

Self-discovery and irony are also at the core of Insana's verse, which, by echoing Woolf, blurs the depiction of the poet's alienated 'I' with a reflection on language and tradition: ' — to know me... tell you what... begin with yourself [...] — you see: they are all women, all with their own room laboriously conquered and sometimes not even that... all women poets and writers'.[24]

The question of the female self is brought to the fore through the exploration of metaliterary motifs. Poets such as Frabotta and Guiducci offer a feminist interpretation of the act of writing: 'I am not a poet the way you are | I am a poetess and whole I do not belong to anyone' (Frabotta);[25] 'at once man's strength and weakness; a lack in nature | relegating me to a note — at the bottom of the page' (Guiducci).[26] Borrowing Cixous's words and imagery, on the threshold between poetry and philosophy, Guiducci's 'Upon Closing the Book' introduces the idea of the female body as writable space:

I will lie down like a book just closed
[...]
And you — having read me in full
will know [...]
You will grasp the whole: what I was
— in one breath.[27]

Other poets move away from these feminist positions to engage with broader philosophical topics: from the existentialist conception of language as the poet's house, a metaphor that echoes Poggioli's postwar slogan (Bettarini's 'The Poet's Home') to the recognition of the reader's authorship (Spaziani's 'To the Readers').

Despite the multiple forms and guises of the lyrical 'I', it is the projection of the female self onto the others that represents the most compelling example of diasporic movement (Pole B). As the case of Guiducci's 'Parto' has already shown, women's search for identity cannot be detached from a meditation on love and motherhood (which explains why the relationship between A and B is biunivocal). From Allen's selection onwards, being a mother was rarely seen as a privilege; more often it was associated with an acute sense of responsibility towards other creatures. In her 'Fragment for the Mother', Bettarini assimilates the challenges of motherhood to those of being naturally a woman: 'In her lap woman gathers all labors [...] My mother gathers them in thought'.[28] Likewise, Lamarque's prayer-like verse relates children's sense of abandonment to the solitude of humans on earth:

Oh child let yourself
[...]
for each of those years be compensated
for when you called us and we weren't there
or were there but were lost to ourselves
or were there but wouldn't see.[29]

In the anthology, a contradictory reflection on love informs the poets' attraction towards a man or another woman. For contemporary female writers, love is a dominant passion as well as an occasion to avenge women's role within society. Some poets demystify the traditional rhetoric of love by playing with conventional metres; I think, for instance, of Daria Menicanti's 'Epigram For a Worm'. Others stress the sensual dimension of love by focusing on desire's destructive forces: 'I am the caressing ruination | quaking furiously at your hands'.[30] Others again exploit the experience of love to deal with women's social marginalisation. Just as men long relegated women to secondary roles, society ostracised them to the point of cultural and political exclusion. This is what Spaziani epitomises in 'Role Reversal', a poem that challenges conventional societal boundaries by pointing out women's nomadic condition:

> The key is always nomadic.
> The lock is still.
> I, yes, a key, furiously a key,
> butterfly in a thousand circles
> around your portal.[31]

The idea of women's submission to society's masculine rules is particularly evident in Sica's poetry as she compares men's attitude to war with women's closeness to nature:

> Women resemble the clouds
> like tidal waters they slowly recede
> and return on the moon's fixed time.
> Men threatening like lightening
> rumble in the world enraged and foolish
> similar to the thundering before war.
> Perhaps now you would like to strike me?[32]

In 'Women's Time' (1978), Kristeva linked female subjectivity to 'cyclical' (repetitive) and 'monumental' (eternal) time by showing that both ways conceptualise time from a female perspective. BLUM AND TRUBOWITZ 2001 pushes Kristeva's model even further when it lets the contrast between time and myth emerge directly from its poets' selection (see points C and D of the diasporic model). In the symbolic order, which can be identified with history, language, and society, there is little, if any, space for women. Ostriker elaborated the concept of 'revisionist mythmaking' to represent American women poetry's subversion of history, literature, and culture. From this viewpoint, mythological revisionism is used 'whenever a poet employs a figure or a story previously accepted and defined by culture' with the purpose of appropriating and transforming it.[33] In an essay published in 1996, Re applied Ostriker's definition to the case of women poets in Italy. In particular, she distinguished between a constructive and a deconstructive approach to describe either the foundation of an alternative mythology or the impossibility of proposing one.[34] Interestingly enough, both Ostriker and Re exploited the figure of Eurydice to exemplify women's attempt to create a new mythological order. Just as Orpheus is thought to be one of the chief (male) poets of all time — able to coax beasts, trees, and rocks by dint of his verse — the silent Eurydice embodies a new, gendered way of thinking literary creation from the standpoint of the voiceless and the excluded.

BLUM AND TRUBOWITZ 2001 made its own use of the concept of mythological revisionism; the anthologised poems are punctuated by mythological and/or legendary figures: not only Eurydice herself, but also Persephone, Diana, Ophelia, Heloise, and one of the Sibyls. Among the poets who appropriated Eurydice's story, Frezza stands out as one of the most original. In 'Places' she used the figure of the nymph to define the relationship between the poet and her urban environment:

Eurydice
watched much too long
my city calls me to feasts of shadows,
and still I won't stop returning.[35]

Milan becomes an image of the Underworld, a place of illusions, columns of smog and stations that impede the poet's flight into the paradise of nature:

Here the green vein of life
does not disappear
in the foams of dawn
[...]
but it is shortened in perspective,
in time.[36]

In another poem, significantly entitled 'Eurydice', Frezza takes the voice of the nymph that reprimands Orpheus' mistake:

If you had fallen from sleep
out there on the grass
in the wake of the snake
you would have seen me Orpheus
you would have crossed without weight
the prohibition of the Places.[37]

Frezza's treatment of myth as a predominantly spatial dimension can be read as a revisionist strategy: as the masculine symbolic order has relegated myth to the sphere of time (namely, the past), her poetry transforms the mythological geography of ancient Greek (the Underworld) into the topography of a modern city (Milan).

The continuous tension between myth and time, oppression and liberation, is also visible in Copioli's interpretation of Eurydice's death. Reproducing a conversation between the two lovers, she stages the conflict between male and female language suggesting the idea that Orpheus fell victim to his own art:

'I will bend a spell-bound music
toward you, the word
that will carry you back
to our house.'
But as the sun struck, she said:
'I am now where you are not looking. And besides,
would you come to me with strings and bundles,
bearing your cage?[38]

Conversely, Valduga plays with Orpheus' thirst for immortality, thus offering an ironic interpretation of the myth; in the vividness of an almost theatrical piece, the poet shows the vanity of Orpheus' ambitions before the reality of death:

But that shmuck, why did he turn back?
Is this what poets do?
Perhaps he wanted to remain in desperation?
to feel even more 'inspiration'? Bah. [Laughing hard] The great
love, mortality...[39]

Other mythological figures serve Blum and Trubowtiz's programme of revisionist mythmaking: from Frabotta's 'lesson of wayfaring Diana' to Merini's identification with Persephone's tragic destiny.[40] By turning myth into a diasporic thread, the editors unearth one of the fundamental ways in which Italian women poets 'are calling into question the ideological underpinnings of a male-centered tradition'.[41] Whereas feminism offered a way of looking at literary tradition from a deconstructed perspective, revisionist mythmaking refounded it within the fluidity of postmodern culture. The anthologists' use of mythological patterns reinforced their diasporic poetics, not only because women's 'subjectivity in progress' is never destined and always in transit, from one wor(l)d to the other, but also because it provides the flexibility for them to escape, migrate, and write.

★ ★ ★ ★ ★

This chapter has elicited a series of theoretical issues and critical dangers. Gradually emerging from the mosaic of the American avant-gardes, Italian women's poetry inhabited the circuits of the transnational and the diasporic. The analysed anthologies gave shape to a new poetic genealogy which interpolates critical conceptions usually kept apart: French and American feminism, deconstructionism, postmodernism, and transnationalism. Although some important names are missing, such as those of Mariangela Gualtieri and Antonella Anedda (the latter appears in comprehensive anthologies of the new millennium), this foreign canon is the point of arrival of a long anthological path that rooted itself in a 'literary archaeology inspired by a recognition of the significance of gender in cultural power dynamics'.[42] In its journey across space and time, women's poetry looked for the mythical, female foundations of contemporary language and culture, thus interweaving a mobile poetics of loss, reinvention, and retrieval. As Marina Zancan observed, 'serve distanza per vedere oltre l'assenza' [distance enables us to see beyond absence]; this is why trans-lated and dis-placed writers have become the privileged metre with which to measure, and contrast, any univocal representations of the self and the world.[43]

Notes to Chapter 11

1. See Bond, 'Towards a Trans-National Turn in Italian Studies?'.
2. Cinzia Sartini Blum, *Rewriting the Journey in Contemporary Italian Literature: Figures of Subjectivity in Progress* (Toronto, Buffalo & London: University of Toronto Press, 2008), p. 5.
3. Ibid., pp. 3–4.
4. Rebecca Walker, 'Becoming the Third Wave', *Ms. Magazine*, 11 (1992), 39–41.
5. See Carol Lazzaro-Weis, *From Margins to Mainstream: Feminism and Fictional Modes in Italian Women's Writing, 1968–1990* (Philadelphia: University of Pennsylvania Press, 1993); and *Feminist Encyclopaedia of Italian Literature*, ed. by Rinaldina Russell (Westport, CT: Greenwood Press, 1997).
6. *L'altro Novecento nella poesia italiana: critica e testi*, ed. by Vittoriano Esposito, 6 vols (Bari: Bastogi, 1995–2001), II (*La poesia femminile in Italia, con rassegna storica dal '200 all'800*).
7. Alberto Asor Rosa, *Un altro Novecento* (Florence: La Nuova Italia, 1999).
8. Cinzia Sartini Blum and Lara Trubowitz, 'Introduction', in BLUM AND TRUBOWITZ 2001, pp. xv–l (p. xxxv).

9. For a full list of poets included in Brock 2012 and Montorfani 2014, see Appendix 2.2.
10. *Femminile plurale: voci della poesia italiana dal 1968 al 2002*, ed. by Maria Pia Quintavalla and Ornella Palumbo (Catanzaro: Abramo, 2002), p. 8.
11. See Oreste Macrì, *La teoria letteraria delle generazioni*, ed. by Anna Dolfi (Florence: F. Cesati, 1995).
12. Blum and Trubowitz, 'Introduction', in Blum and Trubowitz 2001, pp. xxxiii–xxxiv.
13. *Italian Women Poets of the Twentieth Century*, ed. by Catherine O'Brien (Dublin: Irish Academic Press, 1996).
14. Blum and Trubowitz, 'Introduction', in Blum and Trubowitz 2001, p. xvii.
15. Ibid.
16. Blum, *Rewriting the Journey in Contemporary Italian Literature*, p. 5.
17. The essays came out in 1993 and 1996 respectively: Biancamaria Frabotta, 'La viandanza', in *Scrittori, tendenze letterarie e conflitto delle poetiche in Italia*, ed. by Rocco Capozzi and Massimo Ciavolella (Ravenna: Longo, 1993), pp. 87–89; and 'La viandanza femminile e la poesia', *Horizonte*, 1 (1996), 73–79. The poetry collection was published in 1995: Biancamaria Frabotta, *La viandanza, 1982–1992* (Milan: Mondadori, 1995).
18. Blum, *Rewriting the Journey in Contemporary Italian Literature*, p. 105.
19. Ibid., p. 103.
20. Elena Clementelli, from *Etruscan Notebook*, trans. by Cinzia Sartini Blum and Lara Trubowtiz, in Blum and Trubowitz 2001, p. 41.
21. Kristeva, 'Women's Time'.
22. Armanda Guiducci, 'Delivery', trans. by Cinzia Sartini Blum and Lara Trubowtiz, in Blum and Trubowitz 2001, p. 35.
23. Margherita Guidacci, 'Madame X', trans. by Cinzia Sartini Blum and Lara Trubowtiz, in Blum and Trubowitz 2001, p. 35.
24. Jolanda Insana, 'To Know Me?', trans. by Cinzia Sartini Blum and Lara Trubowtiz, in Blum and Trubowitz 2001, pp. 169–73.
25. Biancamaria Frabotta, 'It is True: I am Not a Poet the Way You Are', trans. by Cinzia Sartini Blum and Lara Trubowtiz, in Blum and Trubowitz 2001, p. 215.
26. Armanda Guiducci, 'Readings', trans. by Cinzia Sartini Blum and Lara Trubowtiz, in Blum and Trubowitz 2001, p. 33.
27. Armanda Guiducci, 'Upon Closing the Book', trans. by Cinzia Sartini Blum and Lara Trubowtiz, in Blum and Trubowitz 2001, p. 31.
28. Mariella Bettarini, 'Fragment for the Mother', trans. by Cinzia Sartini Blum and Lara Trubowtiz, in Blum and Trubowitz 2001, p. 31.
29. Vivian Lamarque, 'Prayer of Mothers Who Unintentionally Failed Their Children', trans. by Cinzia Sartini Blum and Lara Trubowtiz, in Blum and Trubowitz 2001, p. 231.
30. Alda Merini, 'Dies Irae', trans. by Cinzia Sartini Blum and Lara Trubowtiz, in Blum and Trubowitz 2001, p. 103.
31. Maria Luisa Spaziani, 'Role Reversal', trans. by Cinzia Sartini Blum and Lara Trubowtiz, in Blum and Trubowitz 2001, p. 55.
32. Gabriella Sica, 'The Lightening', trans. by Cinzia Sartini Blum and Lara Trubowtiz, in Blum and Trubowitz 2001, p. 251.
33. Ostriker, *Stealing the Language*, p. 212.
34. Lucia Re, 'Mythic Revisionism: Women Poets and Philosophers in Italy Today', in *Italian Women Writers from the Renaissance to the Present*, ed. by Marotti, pp. 187–233.
35. Luciana Frezza, 'Places', trans. by Cinzia Sartini Blum and Lara Trubowtiz, in Blum and Trubowitz 2001, p. 63.
36. Ibid., p. 61.
37. Luciana Frezza, 'Eurydice', trans. by Cinzia Sartini Blum and Lara Trubowtiz, in Blum and Trubowitz 2001, p. 67.
38. Rosita Copioli, 'Eurydice', trans. by Cinzia Sartini Blum and Lara Trubowtiz, in Blum and Trubowitz 2001, p. 243.
39. Patrizia Valduga, 'Why Are Those Who Are Loved So Dull and Leaden?', trans. by Cinzia Sartini Blum and Lara Trubowtiz, in Blum and Trubowitz 2001, p. 263.

40. See Biancamaria Frabotta, 'Dianae Sumus in Fide', trans. by Cinzia Sartini Blum and Lara Trubowtiz, in BLUM AND TRUBOWITZ 2001, p. 219; and Alda Merini, 'I Was Born the Twenty-First in Spring', trans. by Cinzia Sartini Blum and Lara Trubowtiz, in BLUM AND TRUBOWITZ 2001, p. 109.
41. Re, 'Mythic Revisionism', p. 228.
42. Allen, 'From One Closet to Another?', p. 31.
43. Marian Zancan, *Il doppio itinerario della scrittura: la donna nella tradizione letteraria italiana* (Turin: Einaudi, 1998), p. 5.

PART IV

Dialects and Diaspora

CHAPTER 12

Dialect Poetry and the Paradoxes of Glocalisation

The nexus between diaspora and dialect literature has been explored by critics and poets alike. Zanzotto pointed out the supranational vocation of dialects (one of his collections of dialect poetry being entitled *In nessuna lingua in nessun luogo* [In Any Language Nowhere]), whereas anthologists Maurizio Cucchi and Stefano Giovanardi set the 'physiological marginality' of dialect poets against the 'centrifugal' vocation of their writing.[1] Similarly, Franco Brevini observed that contemporary dialect poets use a language that is locally inspired, but potentially universal, especially in terms of values and themes: connection with origins, nostalgia for the past, and dialogue with the dead.[2] In contradiction to these views, however, dialect literature has become accessible to fewer and fewer people, a process that began with the standardisation of the Italian language in the 1950s.

Italy has been a dialect-speaking country since the Middle Ages. The passage from Latin to the vernaculars, and to the vernaculars to the Italian language, is at the core of a centuries-long debate over the so-called 'question of language', where dialects represented both a challenge and a driving force towards the making of the Italian literary tradition. Although attempts at a linguistic standardisation date back to the thirteenth century (Dante), Italy remained a multilingual country until the advent of television in the 1950s. Up to the end of the Second World War, dialects used to be the language of communication, whereas Italian was the language of education and bureaucracy. As a result, the majority of Italian critics, from Benedetto Croce to Gianfranco Contini, interpreted the flourishing of dialect literature in linguistic terms, rather than as an anthropological marker.

The US is also a multilingual country. Unlike Italy, however, its linguistic variety sprang from cultural collisions (African-American, Chinese-American, Italian-American etc.), rather than from the historical evolution of a common language such as Latin. Bonaffini, the editor of four of the anthologies analysed hereafter, outlined this difference when stating that the meaning of the term 'dialect' underwent considerable variations in Anglophone areas. Whereas an Italian dialect is a regional language with a Romance derivation, in the US the term dialect 'stands for anormality, departure from a well-defined linguistic standard, so that even a local or regional pronunciation can be regarded as a form of dialect'.[3] Therefore, American 'vernacular style' is a 'special category of "substandard" or "common" usage that serves as an indicator for class, regional, or "age-group" affiliation'; Italian dialects, by contrast, do not represent a simple divergence from the national standard, but a series of 'autonomous linguistic system[s]'.[4] These opposite perspectives resulted in two different ways of understanding dialect poetry: as an engendered, almost elitist language in Italy, and as an instance of ethnic literature in the US.

Among all foreign speaking populations in the US, Italian speakers constitute the earliest immigrant group.[5] Over eighty per cent of the immigrants who settled in America at the beginning of the last century came from the south of Italy and had no Italian. In order to communicate among each other, Italian Americans used a complex combination of idioms composed from their native dialects, Italian, and English. These historical data are particularly relevant for us; not only do they partly explain American editors' interest in dialect poetry from Italy, but they also provide a critical explanation for the differences between this poetry's Italian and American dimensions. Without sounding overdramatic, we may say that dialect poetry from Italy lost its natural audiences, but found a new, diasporic public. Written in disappeared, or disappearing, languages (languages that are preserved within migrant communities), it now engages with a population that is both geographically and culturally displaced.

I choose the term 'glocalisation' as a paradigm to describe the alternation 'from the universal to the particular, from world to home' which is at the core of Italian dialect poetry.[6] This term has the merit of capturing the disjuncture between universalism and particularism that 'has come to constitute something like a global-cultural form, a major axis of the structuration of the world as a whole'.[7] First appearing in a 1980s publication of the *Harvard Business Review*, 'glocalisation' was coined to define a marketing strategy that allows the integration of local markets into world markets.[8] Later applications of this word quickly extended to the cultural and literary domains, an example being Eugene Chen Eoyang's study (2007) on the different meanings of globalisation both in the Asian and Western contexts.[9] The more we are exposed to the effects of globalisation, the more we witness the growing of local literatures in minor languages. By suggesting the idea that the local and the universal are articulated in ways that are best expressed in contemporary diasporic poetics, I define the nature of Italian dialect poetry in the US as 'glocal'.

The coexistence of these opposite poles has historical explanations, which are linked to the history of Italian migration to North America. According to historian Donna Gabbaccia, there is not a single Italian population that dispersed throughout the world, but rather a series of Italian communities that diverge both in terms of language and culture. Since Italians nourished their 'regional, city, and village identities' more than their national sense of belonging, the arrival of Italian migrants on the new continent presented the features not of a single exodus, but of many diasporas. 'It is not an accident,' Gabbaccia observes, that 'the modern Italian word for country is the same as its word for village (paese)'.[10]

The appreciation of dialect poetry as the result of these antipodal forces pushing in and out of Italy's national boundaries is all the more revolutionary if one considers the 'imperialismo centripeto' [centripetal imperialism] of Italian lyric across the centuries.[11] Literary criticism in Italy has been dominated by two main models of interpretations: a Dantean line, privileging expressionistic and multilingual texts, and a Petrarchan line, favouring the monolingualism of the author of the *Rerum vulgarium fragmenta* [Fragments of Vernacular Matters].[12] Although the Dantean model stretches out to include both experimental and dialects poets, it does not do justice to the transnational ramifications of Italian literature as a whole. American editors, instead, emphasised the circulation of Italian texts (a perspective that is essentially anthropological), thus liberating dialect poetry from its hyperliterary dimensions.

These differences notwithstanding, it is possible to illuminate at least two points of contact between the Italian and the American ways of looking at regional literatures. The first similarity concerns the diasporic natures of dialects, which reminds us of the unsolved tension between their centripetal and centrifugal spheres. Dialects can be used as an affirmation of regional identity; yet, at the same time, they are relational and contextual to the global culture to which they refer.[13] The second analogy pertains to the political meaning of marginal, sometimes endangered languages. Both American vernaculars (African American, Italian American, Jewish American etc.) and Italian dialects (Milanese, Genoese, Sicilian etc.) are minor languages in opposition to dominant linguistic model. The translation into English of dialect poetry from Italy problematises these power relationships even further: on the one hand, it adds a third linguistic dimension to a binary structure; and, on the other, it reinforces the idea that migrations from and to Italy trace 'nonlinear paths in the definition of a multicultural Italy whose roots are unmistakably present throughout the centuries', and outside its national borders.[14]

Employed as an instrument of enquiry into the complexities of today's world, the glocal lens, a paradox in itself, makes distortions bigger and contradictions more profound. It enables us to embrace dialect poetry's many paradoxes, from its experimental, Poundian vocation to the rejection of the neo-avant-garde experience; and from its attempt to renew the language of poetry to its sense of nostalgia for the past. Constantly shuttled between the cosmopolitan and the local (from their local villages to New York and San Francisco, and back), Italian dialect poets embody the sense of innovation, contradiction, and loss from which American culture was born.

Notes to Chapter 12

1. *Poeti italiani del secondo Novecento*, ed. by Maurizio Cucchi and Stefano Giovanardi, *1945–1995* (Milan: Mondadori, 1996), p. xliii. See Andrea Zanzotto, *In nessuna lingua in nessun luogo: le poesie in dialetto 1938–2009*, with an introduction by Giorgio Agamben and a preface by Stefano Dal Bianco (Macerata: Quodlibet, 2019).
2. See Franco Brevini, *Le parole perdute: dialetti e poesia nel nostro secolo* (Turin: Einaudi, 1990), p. 76.
3. Luigi Bonaffini, 'Translating Dialect Literature', *World Literature Today*, 7 (1997), 279–88 (p. 282).
4. Ibid., pp. 282–83.
5. Linda Susman Sartarelli, 'Linguistic History of Italian Dialects in the United States', in *The Italian American Experience: An Encyclopaedia*, ed. by Salvatore LaGumina (New York: Garland, 2000), pp. 40–42 (p. 41).

6. Roland Robertson, 'The Universalism-Particularism Issue', in *Literature and Globalization: A Reader*, ed. by Liam Connell and Nicky Marsh (London & New York: Routledge, 2011), pp. 24–26 (p. 24).
7. Ibid.
8. I retrieve this piece of information from Jerry Wind, Stan Sthanunathan, and Rob Malcom, 'Great Advertising is Both Local and Global', *Harvard Business Review*, 29 March 2013 <https://hbr.org/2013/03/great-advertising-is-both-loca> [accessed 20 October 2020].
9. Eugene Chen Eoyang, *Two-way Mirrors: Cross-cultural Studies in Glocalization* (Lanham, MD: Lexington Books, 2007).
10. Donna Gabbaccia, *Italy's Many Diasporas* (London: Routledge, 2000), p. 3.
11. *Poeti italiani del secondo Novecento*, ed. by Cucchi and Giovanardi, p. xliii.
12. The distinction has been famously made by Gianfranco Contini, 'Saggio introduttivo', in Carlo Emilio Gadda, *La cognizione del dolore* (Turin: Einaudi, 1963), pp. 7–28.
13. This argument has been developed by Arjun Appadurai, *Modernity at Large: Cultural Dimensions of Globalization* (Minneapolis: University of Minnesota Press, 1996).
14. Graziella Parati and Anthony Julian Tamburri, 'Thinking Anew: An Introduction', in *The Cultures of Italian Migration*, ed. by Parati and Tamburri, pp. 1–8 (p. 2).

CHAPTER 13

'Future's Profound Night': Dialect Canons 1940s–1960s

This chapter investigates the emergence of dialect poetry in comprehensive anthologies from the 1940s to the 1960s. Moving on from Poggioli's theoretical foundations, it describes the growth of a southern-dialect ramification from the main avant-garde trunk. The quotation in the title, which refers to dialect poetry's double vocation, at once future-oriented and profoundly traditional, is a line taken from a poem by Giacomo Vit entitled 'Dialetto'.[1]

The Origins of Glocalism: Renato Poggioli and the Italian Dialect Tradition

Poggioli, the founder of the Italian diasporic canon in America, was also the first anthologist to foster the inclusion of dialect poetry in this transplanted tradition (see Chapter 3). Although he did not include any dialect poems in his anthologies, dialect literature is at the forefront of his theoretical works. In 1946, concerned with the future of Italian letters, he offered three remedies to the crisis brought about by the end of the Second World War: the engagement with sociopolitical issues; the opening towards foreign traditions; and the recovery of dialect literature:

> Se non avesse avuto tanta superbia, la letteratura italiana si sarebbe accorta di avere a portata di mano un bell'esempio di rettitudine artistica, una via di salvezza. Questo esempio e questa via glieli additava la letteratura dialettale, non sorella minore, ma piuttosto originale rivale della letteratura in lingua: dove la lirica non si dissolve in arcadici o petrarcheggianti platonismi, dove vivono generi popolari come la favola o l'apologo, dove il comico è ancora ricco e sanguigno, dove lo scrittore non sdegna la caricatura sociale e la satira politica, dove non s'è mai del tutto dimenticata la 'gaia scienza' dell'uomo. La letteratura italiana deve imparare questa lezione, e con essa quella che le possono insegnare i grandi maestri nazionali e stranieri.[2]

> [If it had not been so haughty, Italian literature would have realised that it had a fine example of artistic rectitude at hand, a way of salvation. This example and this way came from dialect literature, which is not the younger sister, but rather the original rival of literature in the standard language. Dialect literature does not exhaust itself in the platonic imitation of Petrarch and the Arcadia; it welcomes popular genres such as the fable and the allegory; it uses a rich and visceral comic form; it does not disdain the social caricature or the political

> satire; it has never forgotten the 'joyous science' of man. Italian literature should learn this lesson, together with the lesson taught by the great national and foreign masters.]

As we gather from Poggioli's introductory words to the first issue of *Inventario*, the reappraisal of dialect poetry was neither a matter of nostalgic restoration nor of ethnic survival. Rather, it was part of a broader project of cultural and political reconstruction, a path of liberation that would save the nation from its own idiosyncrasies. Italian letters would have been responsible for their own implosion if they had remained unable to incorporate the unconventional styles and themes that were typical of dialect literature, i.e. the 'gaia scienza' that engages concretely with people's lives. Poggioli understood writings in dialect as a minor, yet complementary branching-out of the mainstream lyric, one able to question those values that were neglected by writers in the standard language.

A few years later, Poggioli reiterated the originality of dialect literature as he mapped the reception of Italian culture in America. In 'The Italian Success Story' (1953), which appeared in both *Inventario* and *The Harvard Wake*, he interlaced his apology for dialect with the notions of fatherland and exile. This is the first time that Italian dialect poetry entered the ambit of the diasporic. 'After the Renaissance,' Poggioli argued, but also 'in more recent times, many writers turned [...] toward the small fatherlands of the peninsula'. Whereas the humanists, preceded by Petrarch, considered themselves cosmopolitan citizens of the Republic of Letters, modern Italians have been 'organically connected' with their local communities. The model for Italians' attachment to their own native place is the poet Dante, who lived and wrote in memory of 'la *gran villa* (the great city) or, endearingly, his "nest"'.[3] By comparing the differing attitudes of Dante and Petrarch towards their home towns, Poggioli traced an anti-Petrarchan lineage beginning with the author of the *Divine Comedy*, passing through nineteenth-century dialect poetry (Giuseppe Gioachino Belli) and reaching contemporary neorealism. In this genealogy, it is no accident that Dante's *Divine Comedy* was written in a vernacular language rather than in Latin, the official language in fourteenth-century Italy.

Poggioli's Dantean model anticipates Gianfranco Contini's (and then Cesare Segre's) 'plurilinguistic line'. As these critics explained in a series of publications that came out between the 1960s and 1980s, two opposing linguistic and stylistic modes have threaded their way through Italian literature from its origins to the present: a high monolinguistic style, starting with Petrarch, on the one hand, and a low plurilinguistic one starting with Dante and culminating with Pascoli, Pasolini, and Carlo Emilio Gadda on the other.[4] However, despite this striking resonance of features and names, Poggioli's genealogy had a cultural, rather than a linguistic, foundation. His exilic perspective reinforced the eccentric roots of Italian literature by pointing out the conflictual relationship between writers, their local identity, and the production of universal meanings. By using the example of fascist dictatorship, Poggioli showed us that the ideal of an Italian fatherland was linked to the migratory experience. This is true not only because the fascist regime tried to destroy regional cultures in the name of a patriotic, 'totemic symbol', but also because it denied any kind of European and cosmopolitan participation, especially through the endorsement of the ideology of *strapaese*.[5] An exile himself, Poggioli referred in this essay to the activity of two fellow antifascist expatriates: Salvemini and Borgese. The former created 'first in the old, and later in the new, continent a "little Italy" of [his] own'; and the latter provided with *Goliath: The March of Fascism* (1937), originally written in English, a 'new synthesis of the two contrasting Italian political myths, the national and the universal one'.[6] As early as 1953, Italian dialect poetry in the US was already an expression of Italy's many homelands and diasporas. Poggioli was a glocal thinker ahead of his time, if not a precursor of Gabbaccia's theories. The creator of the Italian diasporic canon has the merit of revaluating Italy's national works in the light of their glocal forces. At the same time, he crucially associated the representation of Italian poets' exilic experience with literature in dialect.

Poggioli's contribution to the creation of the dialect canon in the US went far beyond his theoretical conceptions. Indirectly, Poggioli was responsible for putting together a canon of southerners and political refugees, which would absorb the dialect tradition in complex ways. This is visible less in his poetry anthologies (where the only poet from southern Italy is the widely-known Quasimodo, who did not write in dialect) than in his prose selections, which largely focused on exilic figures: Vittorini and Ferrero (already anthologised in POGGIOLI 1947A), but also Silone, Lussu, and Borgese. As a result of these poetic choices, Poggioli's legacy translated into the development of two distinctive yet overlapping branches: a southern Italian canon on the one hand, and a dialect canon on the other. These two trajectories are autonomous, but not separate; they crisscrossed and converged in order to reflect the focus on diversity that was to characterise American criticism in the decades to follow.

Lost Words: Southern Canons and Dialect Canons in the 1960s

In this section, I shall analyse two different yet convergent anthological threads: the southern branch, initiated by De Palchi's and Bradshaw's anthologies on the one hand (DE PALCHI 1961, DE PALCHI 1966A, DE PALCHI 1966B, BRADSHAW 1964, BRADSHAW 1971); and the dialect branch, started by Burnshaw and Bergin on the other (BURNSHAW 1960, BERGIN 1964).

At the beginning of the 1960s, these comprehensive anthologies began to allow ample space to poetry from the southern regions, either within an avant-garde (De Palchi) or a broader, pluralistic context (Bradshaw). The distinction between southern and dialect poetry is a functional one, and in no way does it suggest that poetry from a certain geographical area, or written in a particular Italian dialect, should be ghettoised or considered separately from the main poetic trends. Rather, these parallel forces mutually influenced each other, and ultimately converged into the same diasporic rhetoric. Poets from southern Italy have always been marginalised from the mainstream Italian canon, which was made for, and by, northern elites.[7] To compensate for the absence of voices from the Mezzogiorno (the so-called 'midday' regions of southern Italy), thematic anthologies were compiled in Italy, such as Esposito's six-volume anthology *L'altro Novecento* [Another Twentieth Century] (1995–2001) — a volume of which was devoted entirely to poetry from the central, southern, and insular regions — and, more recently, Giorgio Linguaglossa's *Il rumore delle parole: 28 poeti del Sud* [The Noise of Words: 28 Poets from the South] (2014).[8]

Conversely, southern Italian poets gained a place in the American canon at quite an early stage of the history of Italian poetry's anthologisation. The reasons for this early appearance are to be found in the literary climate of the time. First, poetry from southern Italy was one of the threads (avant-garde, female, religious etc.) brought to light by diasporic poetics in North America. Second, the interest in southern poetry coincided with the beginnings of ethnic studies and the revival of American folklore in the 1950s and 1960s.

Among the nine poets anthologised by De Palchi in the tenth issue of the *Chelsea* review (De Palchi 1961), five were from the south: Cattafi, Gatto, Quasimodo, Scotellaro, and Leonardo Sinisgalli. Cattafi also appeared in the special issue of *Chelsea* that the anthologists co-edited in 1966 (De Palchi 1966a); other names came out in the Italian section prepared for the contemporary, multilingual volume of *Modern European Poetry*: Scotellaro, Quasimodo, Sinisgalli, and Piccolo (De Palchi 1966b). It is worth noticing that whereas the number of southern poets diminished between the 1961 and 1966 issues of *Chelsea*, it increased again in this last volume. This discrepancy is probably due to the avant-garde standpoint of this special issue of *Chelsea*, which overtly dealt with 'iconoclastic writers' by devoting an entire issue to visual poetry. The presence of these ignored, southern voices reinforced De Palchi's avant-garde programme underlying his anthologies without suggesting an alternative path of interpretation. For him, there is virtually no difference between southern poetry and the avant-garde, Cattafi being 'one of the many Sicilians who continually vitalize Italian literature'.[9]

De Palchi's contribution is not limited to the southern sphere. His collections also touch directly upon the question of dialect poetry in the section dedicated to Carlo Della Corte, whom he describes as the descendant of a dialect tradition (namely, the Venetian), and, more specifically, as one of Giacomo Noventa's followers. 'Noventa,' De Palchi argued, 'used dialect for themes normally ignored by other dialect poets but dear instead to the usual Italian or simply European poets, Goethe first among them all'.[10] This anthological choice reveals two important, critical trajectories: the anthologists' belief in the continuity between dialect, Italian, and European poetry (a glocal feature already present in Poggioli) on the one hand; and their particular interest in the orbit of Venetian dialect on the other. This last point seems to be at odds with the southern origins of Italian dialect poetry in the US, and yet it is a further confirmation of the diasporic experience that underlay it. A migrant from the Veneto region, De Palchi arrived in New York in 1956 after travelling around France and Spain; this is why he looked back at the poets of his native region.

The themes featuring in De Palchi's southern selection concentrate on the displacement of the lyrical 'I', a sense of estrangement that is expressed in two opposing yet corresponding ways: through the description of a state of inbetweenness (Cattafi), and through the poets' attachment to their homelands and its people (Piccolo, Scotellaro).

In a continuation of De Palchi's collections, anthologist Bradshaw gave shape to a canon with a largely southern look. Calogero, Piccolo, Scotellaro, and Francesco Leonetti featured in her 1964 selection for the *Italian Quarterly* review (four southern poets out of nineteen), whereas her 1971 anthology added Cattafi, Vittorio Fiore, and Marco Pirro, so seven southerners out of thirty-eight; this proportion, although still uneven, nonetheless testifies to a new focus on the Mezzogiorno that will be a typical trait of American editorship. Bradshaw dedicated her volume to Sicilian poet Piccolo, first cousin of Giuseppe Tomasi di Lampedusa, the author of *Il gattopardo* (1958). Piccolo must have had a major influence on the compilation of the anthology given that it is to this poet's 'warm encouragement and intelligent criticism' that Bradshaw owed her work. The anthology opens with the poetry of another southerner, Calogero, the 'last gleam' of the interwar period of hermetism. It is not accidental that Italian poetry's contemporary era starts here with a Sicilian doctor who died just a few years before the anthology's publication.

In BRADSHAW 1971, the dialectics between local and global perspectives is palpable in the 'anguish of the poetic self' who is torn between parochialism and migration, primitive laws and social justice.[11] As Piccolo put it in a letter to fellow poet Sereni, 'the more we penetrate our inmost depths the more we attain a sense of universality'.[12] As discussed previously with reference to women's poetry (see Chapter 9), the emphatic treatment of thoughts and feelings was a sign of confessional poetics in the 1950s. Biography became a poetic model for those who rejected 'modernist difficulty and New Critical complexity in favour of a more [...] personal voice'.[13] Bradshaw's preference for southern poetry was arguably influenced by the confessional style as much as by the growing presence of Italian diasporic communities in America. This double mode, both confessional and diasporic, is at work in a series of poems dealing with memory, landscape, and migration:

Just as my enchanted land,
you are harsh and sweet,
land of South,
scent of brambles and maize.[14]

The migratory theme may be associated with political tones and the longing for social redemption:

Southland today
I liked you better wild
when you wore misery
and were sincere.[15]

Alternatively, it becomes an elegy for the dying motherland, its tradition and people:

Apulia of emigrants and swamps,
there are towns where months drag on and on,
you are sick with the plain.[16]

My village is becoming a ghost town, they embark without songs.[17]

Whereas there exists a consistent number of southern poets anthologised in the 1960s, with Cattafi and Scotellaro being at the forefront of this selection, there does not seem to be a dialect counterpart. Very few dialect poems featured in comprehensive anthologies, which generally excluded texts written in languages other than Italian. From 1945 to 1974, the only dialect poets anthologised in America were Belli, Noventa, and Mario Dell'Arco, all included in two selections edited by the American scholar and translator Bergin: *The Poem Itself*, a collection of modern poetry from Europe supervised by the American poet Burnshaw (Bergin was the editor of the Italian section) (BURNSHAW 1960); and Bergin's own comprehensive anthology, the *Italian Sampler*: *An Anthology of Italian Verse* (BERGIN 1964), which includes three dialect poets out of twenty-seven (Belli, Dell'Arco, and Noventa, as already specified). Despite the fact that the volume was printed in Italy and published in Montreal, I consider this anthology a product of the culture of the United States; an American by birth, Bergin spent most of his life as a Professor of Romance Languages at Yale, proof of his ongoing engagement with the American literary establishment.

Written in Roman dialect, Belli's 'Tre mmaschi e nnove femmine' remained untranslated in BURNSHAW 1960, an anthology which may be read as the travel journal of a British migrant (Burnshaw's parents migrated from England to the US at the turn of the twentieth century). Bergin commented on Belli's sonnet in a way that transcends its literal meaning. After drawing a comparison between Belli, Leo Tolstoy, and Honoré de Balzac — the 'life-breathing and life-scale creators' of European literature — Bergin went on to consider the impact of dialect poetry on American readers. For him 'the effect of spoken Roman on the non-Roman Italian ear is faintly comic and at the same time seductive; perhaps a little like the impression the speech of our deep South makes on the Northern ear'.[18] Bergin conceived of Italian dialects as a sort of American vernacular; by opting for a cultural rather than for a literary translation, he bypassed the obstacle of unfaithful renditions (see Chapter 19).

Known mostly for his translations of Dante, Niccolò Machiavelli, and Giambattista Vico, Bergin might easily be mistaken for a conservative of Italian letters. His 1964 anthology, however, reveals something unexpected. Out of twenty-seven contemporary poets, three wrote in dialect (Belli, Dell'Arco, and Noventa) and seven came from the south (Scotellaro, Quasimodo, Gatto, Sinisgalli, Giuseppe Villaroel, Raffaele Carrieri, and Vittorio Bodini). Opening with 'The Life of Man' (1833), a tragicomic poem by Belli representing the decay of the human body from cradle to grave, the *Italian Sampler* begins in an irreverent way: with an exception to its own criteria (the inclusion of living poets only) and with the affirmation of a series of buried, intercultural influences. 'The spirit of Belli,' Bergin observed, 'ironic, revolutionary, "social-minded", walks abroad again now that hermeticism has become a war casualty'.[19] Belli's surprise presence is placed here at the origins of contemporary Italian poetry, a position occupied by Pascoli and D'Annunzio in domestic anthologies published in Italy. The insurgence of southern and dialect poetry in the 1960s is therefore the fruit of a transnational interpolation mixing the

Italian with the American dimension; introduced as a confessional and/or satirical genre at the beginning, it turned into the expression of America's multiethnic culture at a later stage of its anthological evolution.

Notes to Chapter 13

1. Giacomo Vit, 'Dialetto', cited in Brevini, *Le parole perdute*, p. 49.
2. Poggioli, 'Non programma ma premio', p. 5.
3. Poggioli, 'The Italian Success Story', in *The Spirit of the Letter*, p. 204.
4. In addition to Contini's 'Saggio introduttivo' (previously mentioned), see, by the same author, 'Espressionismo letterario', in *Ultimi esercizî ed elzeviri* (Turin: Einaudi, 1989), pp. 41–105. See also Cesare Segre, 'Polemica linguistica ed espressionismo dialettale nella letteratura italiana', in *Lingua, stile e società* (Milan: Feltrinelli, 1974), pp. 397–426.
5. Poggioli, 'The Italian Success Story', p. 568. *Strapaese*, literally meaning 'super-village', is a literary and cultural movement that started in Italy in the 1920s. Critic Peter Hainsworth defines *strapaese* as 'the vision of peasant wholesomeness and a corresponding earthy pithiness of style which was promoted particularly by Mino Maccari apropos of Tuscany and Tuscan in *Il Selvaggio* in the interwar years. It was polemically opposed to the internationalism of stracittà associated with Bontempelli and the 900 (Novecento) group. Both tendencies claimed to be in tune with the true spirit of Fascism, but strapaese gained the ascendency in the 1930s'. Peter Hainsworth, '*Strapaese*', in *The Oxford Companion to Italian Literature*, ed. by Peter Hainsworth and David Robey (Oxford: Oxford University Press, 2005), p. 154.
6. Poggioli, 'The Italian Success Story', p. 208.
7. The reasons for this marginalisation have been cultural as much as political. Critic Pasquale Verdicchio has compellingly discussed 'the construction of the Italian South and its inhabitants as "racially other"'. To make this claim, Verdicchio draws on Antonio Gramsci's study *La questione meridionale* [The Southern Question], according to which 'the Northern bourgeoisie has subjugated the South of Italy and the Islands, and reduced them to exploitable colonies'. Pasquale Verdicchio, *Bound by Distance: Rethinking Nationalism Through the Italian Diaspora* (Madison, NJ: Farleigh Dickinson University Press, 1997), pp. 12, 14.
8. See *L'altro Novecento nella poesia italiana: critica e testi*, ed. by Esposito; and *Il rumore delle parole: 28 poeti del Sud*, ed. by Giorgio Linguaglossa (Rome: Edilazio, 2014).
9. De Palchi 1966a, p. 74.
10. Ibid., p. 86.
11. Bradshaw 1971, p. 88.
12. Lucio Piccolo, 'From a Letter to Vittorio Sereni', trans. by Vittoria Bradshaw, in Bradshaw 1971, p. 257.
13. Christopher Beach, *The Cambridge Introduction to Twentieth-Century American Poetry* (Cambridge: Cambridge University Press), p. 155.
14. Vittorio Fiore, 'Portrait', trans. by Vittoria Bradshaw, in Bradshaw 1971, p. 87.
15. Marcello Pirro, 'To My Land', trans. by Vittoria Bradshaw, in Bradshaw 1971, p. 571.
16. Vittorio Fiore, 'Fill Me with Words', trans. by Vittoria Bradshaw, in Bradshaw 1971, p. 81.
17. Rocco Scotellaro, 'Psalm to My Home and the Emigrants', trans. by Vittoria Bradshaw, in Bradshaw 1971, p. 103. Note the religious connotation of the title.
18. Burnshaw 1960, pp. 282–83.
19. Bergin 1964, pp. viii–x.

CHAPTER 14

Dialect Poetry in 1970s America

Dialect Poetry, *Spoon River*, and the Beat Generation

From 1971 to 1986, the year that marked the appearance of the first anthology of dialect verse by Haller, dialect poetry from Italy renounced its archaic, satirical vein in order to embrace the forms of the American avant-garde. Feldman and Swann's anthologies showed the first sign of this transformation (SWANN 1972, WEISSBORT, FELDMAN, AND SWANN 1975, and FELDMAN AND SWANN 1979). All anthologies use multiple translators, a sign of experimentation in its own right. SWANN 1972 is a heterogeneous volume mixing fiction, non-fiction and poetry.[1] WEISSBORT, FELDMAN, AND SWANN 1975, which came out in Oxford for *Modern Poetry in Translation*, focuses on poetry only.[2]

An important couple of editor-translators (who, like De Palchi and Raiziss, were also partners in life), Feldman and Swann made a significant contribution to the dissemination of southern/dialect poetry in the US. Except for the publication of three anthologies (the first of which was edited by Swann only, the second in conjunction with Daniel Weissbort), they published a series of monographic collections of poetry by Piccolo (1973), Zanzotto (1976), Cattafi (1981), Scotellaro (1980), and Bodini (1980), all in translation.[3] Among the poets they anthologised, Danilo Dolci is a significant presence as his verse combines a strenuous anti-mafia commitment with a caring attitude towards the people of the south: peasants, fishermen, street urchins, and prostitutes. Almost forgotten in Italy, Dolci became a cultural hero in the Anglophone world, a further example of the unexpected ways in which Italian poets were received abroad.

Two dialect poets appeared in FELDMAN AND SWANN 1979: Pasolini, writing in his mother's Friulan idiom, and Vivaldi, from Genoa; they were thus, respectively, the second and third dialect poets to reach America after Belli. In the introduction to the volume, Cambon argued that Pasolini's best achievement 'must be seen in the Friulano dialect verse which began and concluded his stormy career', rather than in his 'experimental temper'. Pasolini was praised not only for his dialect poetry, but also for 'his ear for the venerable, if sometimes despised, phenomenon of dialect', an interest that led him to publish his own dialect anthology in 1952. Conversely, Vivaldi was appreciated for standing apart from the 'literary squabbles', an attitude that allowed him to 'perfect his unmistakable voice'.[4] This dialect selection concentrates on parental and local themes, with Pasolini and Vivaldi mourning the loss of their ancestral world and its human beings:

> All the world is silver and silk,
> only I am made of though glasses,
> son of a woman of Siest.[5]
>
> I find your face
> in the sea and I know that you are dead.[6]

It is worth noting that, in this experimental anthology, the theme of travel and migration is embodied by female poets (Elizabeth Ferrero and Spaziani) rather than by southern or dialect authors; the latter, however, communicate the sense of nostalgia and uncertainty that is typical of diasporic writing.

American editors treated both female and dialect poetry as an inflection of the avant-garde tradition, even though dialect and women authors fiercely opposed neo-avant-garde trends in Italy. At the same time, Italian anthologists dismissed female poetry as a secondary genre, whereas the same form of exclusion did not apply to the case of dialect poetry. This difference is probably due to the interest of Italian critics in philological and linguistic matters, rather than in questions of gender and ethnic revival.[7] A case in point is Pier Vincenzo Mengaldo's *Poeti italiani del Novecento*, published by Mondadori in 1978. Often conceived as the last anthology proposing a 'universal canon' in Italy, Mengaldo's selection remains an important document for the different treatment reserved for minor poetry in Italy.[8] According to Mengaldo, only Rosselli is worth critical recognition among the rich array of twentieth-century female writers. Conversely, nine dialect poets, some of whom also wrote in Italian, find their place in a selection of fifty-one, all male and northern: Noventa, Pasolini, Zanzotto, Pierro, and Loi, Delio Tessa, Biagio Marin, Tonino Guerra, and Virgilio Giotti. More recently, Segre and Carlo Ossola's *Antologia della poesia italiana* (1999) reiterated Mengaldo's formula counting thirteen dialect poets out of sixty, only two of whom are women: Rosselli and Pozzi.

Seen from an Italian perspective, American editors' presentation of Italian dialect poetry as an avant-garde genre might appear problematic. To be able to understand the ways in which dialect writers from Italy rejected a nostalgic, backward gaze in order to embrace ideas of innovation, it is necessary to look at dialect poetry's literary sources. As Brevini pointed out in *Le parole perdute* (1990), the second half of the twentieth century was characterised by the emergence of a decentralised, experimental literature written in peripheral dialects, i.e. languages spoken outside the main urban areas. Although inspired by the Italian classics, these works reached out centrifugally both to foreign and ancient traditions: Provençal literature on the one hand, usually accessed through Pound (see Chapter 19); and American poetry on the other, namely the poets of the Beat Generation. More specifically, the free verse of Edgar Lee Masters directly informed Italian dialect poets' postwar shift towards experimental forms.

Published in 1943 in Fernanda Pivano's translation, the *Spoon River Anthology* presented these uprooted Italian writers as an interesting mixture of tradition and innovation.[9] Set in the small village of Spoon River (an ideal, yet not idyllic, microcosm), this book covered the totality of human experience seen from the perspective of the dead. The guardians of their dying languages, dialect poets from Italy found in Masters's work a source for glocal, diasporic writing: half-local — if not autochthonous, as in the case of Provençal poetry — and half-American, namely Beat. Charged with a sense of both finitude and ungraspable distance, dialect poetry became a genre at once ancient and modern, self-centred and all-inclusive, one that could bridge the gap between the ethical and the political. As Brevini himself put it:

> Il contatto con i dialetti, uccisi e mai morti, puntiformi ma con agganci ed echi nelle più incredibili lontananze, è capace di inquadrare anche se in termini cifrati la più smagliante apertura su alterità, futuri, attive dissolvenze.
>
> [The contact with killed yet never-dying dialects enables us to identify mysteriously the most dazzling possibilities of alterity, active fading, and the future. Dialects are point-like and yet fixed sources which echo the most incredible distances].[10]

Rebuilding the House of God: Dialect Poetry between Mysticism and the Avant-garde

In this section, I shall focus on the following three anthologies: Tusiani 1974, Marchione 1974, and Lind 1974. Despite being driven by the common aspiration to bring minor poets in the limelight, these three anthologies adopted divergent, if not antipodal, approaches. Tusiani's poetic contribution to the creation of a diasporic Italian culture in the US will be discussed in Chapter 16; instead, what I would like to stress here is his activity as an editor. Presenting itself as a sequel to *Italian Poets of the Renaissance* (1971), Tusiani 1974 is a comprehensive collection of Italian verse from the beginnings of the seventeenth century to the early twentieth century.[11] Tusiani endorsed an antiacademic perspective, insisting on poets (e.g., Vittoria Aganoor), periods (the Italian Risorgimento), and genres (religious poetry) that are generally neglected by literary historians. Simultaneously, he set boundaries for the Italian experimental line, which started with Baroque poetry and stretched until Marinetti's and Domenico Gnoli's futuristic works.

According to Tusiani, in the universe of Italian literature some planets rotate perfectly, 'like satellites, around their centripetal planet'; other planets, by contrast, follow 'a small yet noticeable eccentricity of their own'. Dialect poetry naturally follows the second, centrifugal stream. 'The reader,' Tusiani specified, 'will have to see for himself in which poetic constellation belong the four greatest dialectal stars on the Italian horizon — Belli, Meli, Porta, and Di Giacomo'.[12] This is the first time that a number of dialect poets feature in a comprehensive anthology in English translation. Writing from different centuries (Giovanni Meli was born in 1740) and places (Milan, Rome, Naples, and Sicily), these dialect poets are juxtaposed with the representatives of both Italian romanticism (Ugo Foscolo, Vittorio Alfieri, Giovanni Berchet, and Alessandro Manzoni) and the twentieth-century avant-garde. The satirical vein in which dialect poetry from Italy was introduced to the Americans is recovered here through the examples of Porta and Belli; at the same time, the diasporic theme surfaces in poems such as 'The Lament of Polemuni'

(Meli) and 'Morning at Toledo' (Salvatore di Giacomo) where the poet's sense of wandering is linked to a painful attachment to his native place:

> What's the difference to me
> if the world is wide and great
> when this bleak cliff in the sea
> is my own and only state.[13]

No dialect poets are included in Lind 1974, which opens conventionally with the triad Carducci-Pascoli-D'Annunzio and not with Belli's rebellions, like in Bergin. Yet, Lind's selection presents numerous southern writers, among whom Borgese, Quasimodo, Sinisgalli, Gatto, Scotellaro, and Federico De Maria. Gatto and Sinisgalli stand out for their diasporic writing, Sinisgalli the author of a touching elegy for the poet's memory and his homeland:

> The spirit of silence reigns in the communes
> of my sorrowful province.
> [...]
> I will return alive under your red rains
> [...]
> Shall I hear the she-cats
> wail on the tombs?[14]

Another important characteristic of Lind's selection is its debt to Poggioli's avant-garde line. Of thirty-four poets, seven are shared with Poggioli 1947a, Poggioli 1947b, and Poggioli 1948: Borgese, Campana, Palazzeschi, Ungaretti, Montale, De Libero, and Giglio. Poets such as Montale, Ungaretti, Campana, and Palazzeschi were widely anthologised by this time.[15] De Libero featured less frequently (he is only present in Guenther and Sellin 1959, De Palchi 1961, and Golino 1962), the exile Borgese is considered for his prose, whereas Giglio would not make a third appearance after Poggioli's and Lind's selections.

This avant-garde inheritance influenced Marchione 1974 as well. A member of the Religious Teachers Filippini, as well as Professor of Italian Language and Literature at Farleigh Dickinson University, this editor and nun was the daughter of immigrants from Campania. Her contribution to the shaping of the Italian canon in the US is important on at least two levels: as a diasporic scholar (she is known for her studies on the eighteenth-century Florentine immigrant Philip Mazzei); and as the first editor who considered religion a unifying thread in Italian poetic history. In 1971, Vittoria Bradshaw had already dedicated a section of her anthology to three mystic poets, two of whom were women: Guidacci and Merini (see Chapter 9). Yet, it is the third poet, Father Turoldo, a priest of the Servite order, who provides us with the most compelling case, his poetry being practically ubiquitous in the period 1961–79. During this time, Turoldo appeared in nine anthologies: De Palchi 1961, De Palchi 1962, De Palchi 1966a, Bradshaw 1964, Bradshaw 1971, Miller, O'Neal, and McDonnell 1970, Lind 1974, Marchione 1974, and Feldman and Swann 1979. The success of Italian religious verse, a minor genre both in Italy and the US, is an expression of the American editors' diasporic poetics. Catholicism was a fundamental element of cohesion in Italian American diasporic communities; not only did it inform people's lives, but it also shaped the architecture of the foreign cities they settled in.[16]

These were also the years of Giuseppe Prezzolini's professorship at Columbia University, New York, where he served as head of the university's *Casa Italiana*. An American citizen since 1940, Prezzolini was Marchione's teacher and mentor in the period during which she completed her doctorate at Columbia. Marchione told the story of their friendship in one of the appendices to her anthology, 'Prezzolini Mio Maestro', as well as in a passionate memoir, *The Fighting Nun* (2000).[17] Despite defining himself as a sceptic, Prezzolini published widely on religious matters, from his early essay on communism and Catholicism to *Cristo e/o Machiavelli* [Christ and/or Machiavelli] and *Dio è un rischio* [God is a Risk], which came out in 1969 and 1971 respectively.[18] As Marchione underlines, Prezzolini's output is constellated by his reflections on reason, politics, and faith, and his influence has been fundamental to the development of the Italian literary canon in America.

Far from being narrow in focus, Marchione's selection offers a wide range of poets who overcome the boundaries of religious poetry in the narrow sense. Alongside Turoldo, Clemente Rebora, Cesare Angelini, and Carlo Martini (or even the more exotic Gherardo Del Colle, a Capuchin friar), the anthology includes less obvious voices, such as the socialist activist Dolci and Corrado Alvaro. Out of twenty-three poets, seven came from the south (Alvaro, Dolci, Quasimodo, Giuseppe Centore, Donata Doni, and Giovanni Titta Rosa) and two wrote in dialect (Marin and Trilussa). Marchione's subtle, avant-garde poetics becomes manifest when she explains that 'of the ninety poems presented, there are twenty-two, some of them in their respective authors' handwriting, that appear for the first time'; the anthology is also enriched with images of hand-written letters, evidence of Marchione's enduring friendship with the poets she anthologised.[19]

A longstanding literary acquaintance might well have been the reason for the inclusion of Marin and Trilussa. Both poets, however, will have an important follow-up, recurring in the majority of the dialect anthologies published from the 1980s onwards. Trilussa's case, in particular, is crucial as his first anthological appearance here was preceded by a collection of his poetry in Roman dialect in 1945 (reprinted in 1979); other two collections of his poetry were soon published in 1976 and 1990, edited by Blossom Kirschenbaum and John Du Val respectively.[20]

Whereas dialect poetry's satirical tone emerges in Trilussa's 'After the Deluge', a playful hymn to the cycle of life, Marin's verse insists on the image of the house as both a spiritual and physical dwelling place. Distance and the vertigo of space reflect both the poet's diasporic perspective and the caducity of things:

> At present I have my home
> in the wind's mouth everywhere
> [...]
> But tomorrow. No place
> will be my home.[21]

> On my shores
> a hurt God's
> windowless and shutterless house.[22]

Distance is born,
gateway to the hereafter!'[23]

The Bible is sprinkled with images of tents, houses, and temples as metaphors for the presence of God. The human body, in particular, is presented as the place of God's favourite manifestation: 'Don't you know that you yourselves are God's temple, and that God's Spirit dwells in you?' (1 Corinthians 3:16). Marchione's monothematic section on Marin's poetry can be seen as a tribute to Poggioli's poetics of the 'house of man', this time charged with religious meaning; it outlines her original contribution to the development of the Italian dialect line in the direction of mysticism.

Dialect Poets before Dialect Poetry

Since Poggioli's prophetic words in the 1940s, glocal forces have been at play in the configuration of the Italian dialect canon in ways that are at once logical (the migratory fluxes to the US) and paradoxical (both the drama of and the urge for expatriation). In this scenario, Italian authors from the south served as a springboard for dialect poetry's anthologisation, thus reinforcing the transnational tendencies that nourished American diasporic writing from the start. Among the southern poets anthologised from the 1960s to the 1970s, Cattafi, Scotellaro, and Piccolo are the most popular (although it should be mentioned that Scotellaro's first appearance dates back to Guenther and Sellin 1959).

By way of summary, I present below two charts outlining the emergence and steady anthologisation of dialect poets from Italy in the Anglophone world. Table 14.1 shows the presence of Cattafi, Scotellaro, and Piccolo in anthologies that appeared in the span of years 1959–87. The country of origin for the anthologies published outside the US is recorded between parentheses. These numerous entries suggest that Anglophone editors had a consistent interest in these poets' works, despite their marginalisation from the Italian domestic canon. In the years preceding the publication of the first anthology of dialect poetry in America (Haller 1986), dialect authors made an appearance that is at once in line (because avant-garde) and at odds (because more satirical than migratory) with contemporary poetic movements. A proof of this trend is offered by the fact that the theme of diaspora is a prerogative of southern, rather than of dialect writing, the only exceptions being (as this chapter has shown) Marin and, less obviously, Meli and Di Giacomo.

Table 14.2 registers the names of the first dialect poets who reached the US via one or more American anthologies of Italian poetry in translation. Tusiani 1974 is the volume that gathers the highest number of dialect authors: Belli, Porta, Meli, and Di Giacomo. The American precursor of dialect poetry from Italy, Belli happens to be the only dialect writer who appears in more than one anthology, a presence suggesting dialect poetry's gradual yet continuous movement from marginality to recognised status.

Table 14.1. The presence of Bartolo Cattafi, Rocco Scotellaro and Lucio Piccolo in poetry anthologies 1959–87

Cattafi	Scotellaro	Piccolo
De Palchi 1961	Guenther and Sellin 1959	Weaver and Colquhoun, *Italy 1963*, 1963 (UK)
Kay, *The Penguin Book of Italian Verse*, 1965 (UK)	De Palchi 1961	Bradshaw 1964
De Palchi 1966a	Corman 1963	De Palchi 1966a
Singh, *Contemporary Italian Verse*, 1968 (UK)	Bergin 1964	Cookson, *Double Translation Issue*, 1968
Bradshaw 1971	Bradshaw 1964	Perry, *Poetry Australia 22/23*, 1968 (AU)
Judge and Dragosei 1974	De Palchi 1966a	May, *Modern Italian Poetry*, 1970 (AU)
Weissbort, Feldman, and Swann 1975	Lind 1974	Bradshaw 1971
Feldman and Swann 1979	Corman 1975	Swann 1972
Cherchi 1989	Feldman and Swann 1979	Tomlinson, *Translations*, 1983
Smith 1981	Smith 1981	Smith and Gioia 1985
—	Smith and Gioia 1985	—
—	Gentili and O'Brien, *The Green Flame*, 1987 (IRE)	—

Table 14.2. Emergence of Italian dialect poets in poetry anthologies 1960–79

Belli	Porta	Trilussa	Meli	Di Giacomo
Burnshaw 1960	Tusiani 1974	Marchione 1974	Tusiani 1974	Tusiani 1974
Bergin 1964	—	—	—	—
Tusiani 1974	—	—	—	—

Dell'Arco	Noventa	Marin	Pasolini	Vivaldi
Bergin 1964	Bergin 1964	Marchione 1974	Feldman and Swann 1979	Feldman and Swann 1979
—	—	—	—	—
—	—	—	—	—

Notes to Chapter 14

1. For a list of the poets anthologised and their translators see Healey, *Twentieth-Century Italian Literature in English Translation*, pp. 278–79.
2. Ibid., p. 304.
3. Cf. ibid., pp. 1030, 1040–41.
4. FELDMAN AND SWANN 1979, p. 12.
5. Pier Paolo Pasolini, 'Grass for Rabbits', trans. by Dino Fabris, in FELDMAN AND SWANN 1979, p. 154.
6. Cesare Vivaldi, 'Mother, I Won't Forget', trans. by Lawrence Smith, in FELDMAN AND SWANN 1979, p. 219.
7. See Gigliola Sulis, 'Ridefinire il canone: i dialettali e le antologie poetiche del Novecento', *The Italianist*, 24.1 (2004), 77–106.
8. Cristina Crocco, 'La poesia italiana del Novecento: il canone e le interpretazioni' (2015) <http://www.leparoleelecose.it/?p=18439> [accessed 20 October 2020]
9. Edgar Lee Masters, *Antologia di Spoon River*, trans. by Fernanda Pivano (Turin: Einaudi, 1943).
10. Brevini, *Le parole perdute*, p. 31.
11. *Italian Poets of the Renaissance*, ed. by Joseph Tusiani, trans. into English Verse and with an introduction by Joseph Tusiani (New York: Baroque Press, 1971).
12. TUSIANI 1974, p. xxxi.
13. Giovanni Meli, 'The Lament of Polemuni', trans. by Joseph Tusiani, in TUSIANI 1974, p. 77.
14. Leonardo Sinisgalli, 'Lucania', trans. by Bernard Wall, in LIND 1974, pp. 291–93.
15. For an overview of Italian poets translated into English in the 1970s see Healey, *Twentieth-Century Italian Literature in English Translation*, pp. 255–335.
16. See, for instance, Joseph Sciorra, 'Multivocality and Vernacular Architecture: The Our Lady of Mount Carmel Grotto in Roseband, Staten Island', in *Studies in Italian American Folklore*, ed. by Luisa Del Giudice (Logan: Utah State University Press, 1992), pp. 203–44.
17. Margherita Marchione, 'Prezzolini mio maestro', in MARCHIONE 1974, pp. 294–301; *The Fighting Nun: My Story* (New York: Cornwall Books, 2000).
18. Giuseppe Prezzolini, *Cristo e/o Machiavelli*, ed. by Beppe Benvenuto (Palermo: Sellerio, 2004); *Dio è un rischio*, with a preface by Giulio Andreotti (Florence: Vallecchi, 2004).
19. MARCHIONE 1974, p. 17.
20. Healey, *Twentieth-Century Italian Literature in English Translation*, pp. 49, 317, 467.
21. Biagio Marin, 'At Present I Have My Home', trans. by Margherita Marchione, in MARCHIONE 1974, p. 96.
22. Biagio Marin, 'The Sea Does Not Die', trans. by Margherita Marchione, in MARCHIONE 1974, p. 92.
23. Biagio Marin, 'My God is Poor', trans. by Margherita Marchione, in MARCHIONE 1974, p. 100.

CHAPTER 15

❖

Folk, Forgotten and Displaced: Hermann Haller's 'Hidden' Italies

This chapter offers a diasporic reading of Haller's *The Hidden Italy* (HALLER 1986) by relating it to the contemporaneous debate on ethnicity in America. It investigates the anthology's political agenda, thus problematising its predominantly philological legacy. The irruption of ethnic perspectives in the analysis of the Italian diasporic canon opens our field of investigation to the contiguous yet distinct territory of Italian American studies. Concerned with poetry and prose produced by American writers of Italian descent, this discipline does not specifically look at literature in translation.[1] However, American anthologies of Italian poetry, both in dialect and not, could be considered a subcategory of Italian American culture insofar as they refer to the Italian experience in America. Although my analysis is conducted outside the field of Italian American studies strictly speaking, it nonetheless dialogues and negotiates with it in a way that aspires to be both constructive and fertile.

Ethnicity, Poetry, and Migration in 1980s America: A Sociolinguistic Perspective

By some fortunate coincidence, 1986 saw the publication of the two pioneering anthologies that turned Italian poetry into an object of critical investigation. Published together with the first anthology of female Italian poetry in the English language, ALLEN 1986, HALLER 1986 was released by Wayne State University Press, Detroit. The coincidental timing of these publications is significant as it highlights analogous directions in the process of canon formation in the US, directions that also affected the shaping of other canons in translation (African American, Irish American, etc.). As Guido Guglielmi pointed out, 'I dialetti, fatte le debite differenze, corrispondono alle lingue e culture "minori" rivalutate dai Cultural Studies' [Albeit with some variations, dialects are comparable with the 'minor' languages and cultures that are reappraised by Cultural Studies].[2] Yet, whereas the link between the dissemination of gender studies and feminist anthologies is quite a natural one, the interplay between American ethnic theories and the representation of Italian dialects may be debatable.

In Italy, dialect poetry has rarely been a topic of ethnic enquiry, as Italian critics have analysed it from a mainly linguistic-philological and/or historical perspective.[3]

The transplantation of Italian poets into a different context radically modified the literary agenda within which they had been commonly perceived. Seen through the lens of American critics, Italian dialect poetry stopped being a prerogative of linguists and literary historians to become a truly anthropological and supranational affair.

This change in perspective is epitomised by Haller 1986. Long understood as a philological survey of Italy's dialects, this book combined a linguistic approach with an ethnically diasporic one. An understanding of the correlations among linguistics, ethnicity, and migration as presented by Haller is supported by the work of two American scholars who were active at the time of the anthology's publication: Joshua Fishman's *The Rise and the Fall of the Ethnic Revival: Perspectives on Language and Ethnicity* (1985), and Werner Sollors's *Beyond Ethnicity: Consent and Descent in American Culture* (1986) and *The Invention of Ethnicity* (1988).[4] Relating Haller's anthology to the contemporaneous American debate is helpful on at least two levels: not only does it do justice to the prominence of Haller's work, but it also highlights the anthology's diasporic (both Italian and American) traits.

As leading figures in the field of ethnic studies, these critics add an important dimension to the understanding of the revival of Italian dialects in America. As Fishman observed, 'there is a vast amount of evidence pointing to the conclusion that an "ethnic revival" of sorts occurred in the USA between the mid-sixties and the mid-seventies and that it had significantly declined by the late seventies'.[5] Historically, this 'ethnic fall' coincided with the interruption of the Italian migratory waves to the US, which counted 129,368 people in the 1970s and only 32,900 in the 1980s.[6] Yet, these figures notwithstanding, the 1980s saw the publication of a wide range of anthologies, and related criticism, exploring America's multiethnic identity: *The Columbia Book of Later Chinese Poetry* (1986), *Contemporary Chicana Poetry* (1985), and *American Yiddish Poetry* (1986), to name but a few.[7] Concurrently, the Society for the Study of the Multi-Ethnic Literature of the United States (MELUS) launched its First Annual Conference at the University of California Irvine in 1987.[8] On a similar note, a non-profit international society had been founded in Mineola, New York, at the turn of the previous decade (1979), with the purpose of promoting the language and culture of Sicily: Arba Sicula, or Sicilian Dawn.

Haller's conviction that language and ethnicity are inevitably interwoven, a perspective that is often neglected by contemporary literary historians, found a correspondence in Fishman's theories. As Fishman stated in the preface to his 1985 volume, the study of the relationships between the two is able to illuminate 'the intricate processes of change and continuity' that are inherent to any societal transformation, including migration.[9] While advocating the interrelation between sociology and linguistics, Fishman dispelled some of the misconceptions associated with ethnic studies, such as feelings of nostalgia or nationalism. Fishman's observations prove to be essential to my analysis of Haller's anthology. Not only did Haller refer to Fishman's theories directly (see, for instance, his observations in *Una lingua perduta e ritrovata* [A Lost and Found Language]), but he also contributed to one of Fishman's co-edited volumes with an essay entitled 'Italian in New York' (1997), a sign of the mutual influence between the two.[10]

On the other hand, there is no evidence of collaboration between Haller and Sollors. Yet, the theoretical framework provided by Sollors can be applied to Haller, especially his ideas on migratory multilingualism. A Professor of English and African American Studies at Harvard, as well as Global Professor of Literature at New York University Abu Dhabi, Sollors is a resolute advocate of the American melting pot. Together with Marc Shell, he has been the director of the Longfellow Institute since 1994; placed at the core of Harvard University, this academic organisation fosters 'the study of non-English writings in what is now the United States' in order to 're-examine the English language tradition in the context of American multilingualism'.[11] As part of his research at this institution, Sollors published a revolutionary anthology fostering the passage from an 'English only' to an 'English plus' literary canon.[12]

Sollors's views on language, ethnicity, and migration are particularly relevant here as they provide a valid counterpart to Haller's anthology. First, they support the diasporic roots of ethnic writing, which began with immigrant and migrant letters back in the seventeenth century. Sollors noted that ethnic literature underwent a process of growth, which reproduced the development of literature written in the English language: from non-fictional (letters) to fictional forms; and from popular and folk forms to high culture.[13] He also observed that ethnic authors moved 'from "parochial" marginality to "universal" significance in the literary mainstream', as 'the American mainstream now includes more and more writers with identifiable "ethnic" backgrounds'.[14]

In addition to providing historical foundations to the diasporic nature of ethnic literature, Sollors's work explores the connections between ethnicity and the avant-garde. The critic identified in 'Whitman's panethnic, future-oriented poetic' the formal prototype of ethnic, modernist writing; at the same time, he defined the Beat Generation as the 'trans-ethnic' phenomenon that worked as a model for American literature as a whole.[15] Between these two extremities, he placed the vast array of marginal, less assimilated writers who were 'more in tune with international avant-gardist literary movements than their wholly American or fully Americanized colleagues'.[16]

Somewhat reminiscent of Poggioli's suggestions, Sollors claimed that 'ethnic poets who used languages other than English were [...] more willing to work with the new forms of Whitman and the French symbolists than [...] native American poets who wrote in Whitman's native tongue'.[17] In this sense, ethnic writing can be considered a form of the American avant-garde, rather than a different genre, despite critics tending to separate the two. Ethnic writers' 'double consciousness' (alien to both in-group and out-group audiences) is indeed the expression of a 'persistent conflict between consent and descent in America', margins and mainstream, the ongoing collision from which the totality of American literature, including Italian poetry in translation, originated.[18]

Exposed to the American, ethnic controversy, Haller 1986 reveals its radical aspirations. Largely appreciated for its 'linguistic descriptions' and 'scholarly apparatus', this volume retains ethnic implications that are yet to be assessed.[19] From this perspective, Haller's dialect poets can be considered ethnic from both an

American and Italian angle; using special vernaculars and imaginaries, they stepped aside of these countries' boundaries both politically and linguistically.

As Sollors pointed out, defining ethnicity is both a difficult and misleading task; tentatively described as the act of 'belonging and being perceived by others as belonging to an ethnic group', this term does not even appear in the 1933 edition of the *OED* (making instead its first appearance in the 1972 supplement).[20] At the same time, as Sollors himself reminds us, it is precisely this sense of ineffability that turns ethnicity into a powerful tool for engaging with multiethnic America and its cultures in translation. In the following section, I shall discuss how and why Haller's sociolinguistic approach ignited this connection between ethnicity and diaspora, localism and modernity, folklore and bohemia, at a time when the American ethnic revival was supposedly fading.

The 'Dialect Prism': Refraction and Imitation in Haller's Double Mode

The rich interchange between literary theory and historiography in 1980s America directly contributed to the shaping of the Italian diasporic canon. Largely influenced by contemporary works focusing on race and migration, Haller 1986 is the product of the interaction between poetry and cultural studies as well as the expression of his editor's diasporic profile.

Raised in a multilingual country (Switzerland), Haller is another migrant who left the Old World for the New. His scholarly production is deeply informed by his migratory experience as it displays a consistently diasporic angle. Haller published widely on the different kinds of Italian languages and dialects spoken by Italian American communities in the US, bringing to light the significance of the Italian 'diverse ethnic substratum'.[21] An expert of the so-called 'language contact' phenomenon (Italian and English, Italian and dialects, English and dialects), Haller enriched his rigorous philological practice with a broader sociological input. As he stated at the beginning of his 1997 essay 'Italian in New York', 'the story of the Italian language [and of its dialects] in the United States is intimately tied to the history of Italian migration'.[22] From this perspective, Haller 1986 is part of Haller's sociolinguistic research of the diasporic forces that shaped the recovery and/or loss of certain idioms.

How did Haller fit this theoretical apparatus into his project of anthologisation? Where did he stand vis-à-vis the American and the Italian backgrounds? Dedicated to the 'thousands of Italian Americans who have brought to the New World a diversity of mother tongues', Haller 1986 is a bilingual anthology with a migratory focus.[23] Considering the book's rationale, it is not accidental that Tusiani and Alexey Kondratiev, who served as guest editors, are polyglot and migrants themselves. In particular, at the core of Haller's book lies the idea that Italy's 'cultural diversity' and 'polycentric history' produced an eccentric canon expressing itself in languages other than Italian.[24]

Whereas previous anthologists compared Italian dialect poetry to that of other minor voices, Haller is the first editor who pursued a canonising agenda. Aware of the pioneering value of his enterprise, Haller prepared for the English-speaking audience 'a selection of Italian dialect poetry for the first time', as well as a 'comprehensive text including a broad selection of Italian dialect poetry through several centuries'.[25] He engaged with ethnic discourse on the one hand and competed with Italian models on the other, as he observed that 'Pasolini and Dell'Arco compiled an anthology of twentieth-century dialect poetry some forty years ago, while Tesio and Chiesa recently published a similar work for a predominantly Italian public'.[26] His canonising purposes emerge from his editorial choices: a limited selection (only ten Italian regions and twenty-four poets are represented); the creation of a rich web of inter- and intratextual references among the anthologised poets and their foreign, and national sources; and the presentation of the dialect canon's specificities, from the multiplication of genres to the proximity between realistic and experimental choices.

Due to its strong impact, Haller's programme of anthologisation extended beyond his 1986 seminal work when, thirteen years later, he published a companion volume: *The Other Italy* (Haller 1999). Refining his previous investigations both in length and depth, this book not only discusses dialect literature from seventeen regions and since ancient times (looking back to the origins of Italian dialect poetry in the Renaissance), but it also reinforces the editor's pluralistic perspective. The editor extended his analysis to narrative and the theatre, following the idea, formulated in the 1980s, that 'dialect literature is obviously not an entity' as 'it encompasses all literary genres [and] it is not limited to any specific social class'.[27] The volume has a strong scholarly focus aimed at studying and documenting a significant aspect of [Italy's] linguistic and cultural diversity'.[28] Here the boundaries between the anthological and the critical are blurred purposefully and programmatically, a feature that echoes Pound's idea of *logopoeia*.

To express dialect poetry's 'kaleidoscopic diversity', Haller introduced the newly coined concept of the 'dialect prism'. Used as a metaphor to challenge the reader's imagination, the prismatic geometry represents not only a multifaceted complexity, but also the 'hidden unities' of dialects, that is, their 'universality of genres, themes, forms, and human plights'.[29] Haller's statements recall here the mixture of centrifugal and centripetal forces that inform the very concept of 'glocalism'; in this respect, he is an ambassador of the 'other', hidden canon, as he fostered a new way of interpreting Italian poetry's passage from the avant-garde to its ethnic dimension.

Haller 1986 is situated at an important crossroads in the history of Italian poetry's anthologisation. Imbued with both American and Italian values, it is structured in a way that reflects these countries' critical approaches. On the one hand, the anthology's theoretical matrix resonates with contemporaneous studies on ethnicity and migration in the US (something that returns in the poets' themes); on the other hand, the introductions to each region include a phonetical and morphological presentation of the relevant dialects, which adds a firmly linguistic dimension. Moreover, the introduction to the book provides a definition of what a dialect is alongside an overview of Italy's linguistic situation across different centuries and regions (the so-called 'question of language'). Haller's double mode, both domestic and foreign, is at once philological and ethnic; it is inherently diasporic since it stresses 'not the inheritance of an original culture that is either obliterated or recovered, but the experience of the encounter with America which is common to all ethnic groups'.[30]

As far as the selection is concerned, Haller's choices mirror this binary modality that interpolates both Italian and American archetypes. Haller reproposed, or refracted, some of the poets that had already been transplanted into the American context by the editors of the comprehensive anthologies published in the 1960s and 1970s: Belli, Porta, Trilussa, Meli, Di Giacomo, Dell'Arco, Noventa, and Marin. This fact is significant insofar as it illuminates the ways in which the other 'other' canon (i.e. the Italian dialect canon in English translation) followed a path of independence, regardless of the analogous, marginalising situation in Italy.

Simultaneously, Haller's 'hidden' poets are also an imitation of domestic, dialect collections; nineteen poets out of twenty-four were present either in Pasolini and Dell'Arco's *Poesia dialettale del Novecento* (1952) or in Giovanni Tesio and Mario Chiesa's *Il dialetto da lingua della realtà a lingua della poesia da Porta a Belli a Pasolini* (1978), or in both.[31] The only exceptions are Belli, Porta, Meli, Edoardo Ignazio Calvo, and Domenico Tempio, all active in the nineteenth century and therefore not under consideration for these twentieth-century collections. Haller might have drawn the first three poets (Belli, Porta, and Meli) directly from TUSIANI 1974, considering that Tusiani served as a guest editor for HALLER 1986. Haller's twenty-four poets covered northern (eleven), central (four), and southern regions of Italy (nine), which was an innovative move at that time.

Campania and Sicily are well represented, yet none of the poets comes from Apulia, Tusiani's own region. Haller explained that certain regions, such as Umbria, Calabria, Abruzzi, Sardinia, and Apulia, had been excluded 'simply because those regions lack a continuous production of dialect poetry over many centuries'.[32] It is important to bear in mind that these southern regions, together with Umbria, were Haller's only exclusions, and that he would make up for this omission in HALLER 1999 (the systematic recovery of southern dialect traditions would occur with Bonaffini and collaborators in the 1990s).

Table 15.1 shows the complete canon of HALLER 1986. His debt to Pasolini and Dell'Arco's anthology on the one hand, and Tesio and Chiesa's on the other are marked with the initials PD and TS respectively. The poets' dates of death are also provided; those of the nineteenth century are italicised. Haller provided all translations, with the exception of Tusiani's rendering of Carlo Porta's 'La nomina del cappellan' [The Nomination of the Chaplain].

Nineteen poets of the twenty-four had died by the time of the anthology's publication and all of them were present in the contemporaneous Italian anthologies, apart from those of the nineteenth century. Regarding the American models, we would have expected a stronger influence from the US, especially in the light of Haller's interest in marginal and/or ethnic discourses; yet, Haller's selection is only seemingly conservative. First, we should bear in mind that a certain degree of restriction is justified in an anthology that presents itself as the first example of its kind; this partly explains the omission of some regions, the emphasis on older

Table 15.1. Herman Haller's poetic canon by regions, poets, and anthological models

Haller 1986			
Regions	Poets	Italian Models	American Models
Piedmont	*Calvo* (†1804) Costa (†1945)	PD/TC	
Liguria	Firpo (†1957)	PD/TC	
Lombardy	*Carlo Porta* (†1821) Tessa (†1939) Guicciardi (†1974)	 PD/TC PD	Tusiani 1974
Veneto	Noventa (†1960) Giotti (†1957) Marin (†1985)	PD/TC PD/TC PD/TC	 Marchione 1974
Friuli	Pasolini (†1975)	TC	Feldman and Swann 1979
Emilia Romagna	Guerra (†2012)	PD/TC	
Latium	*Belli* (†1863) Pascarella (†1940) Trilussa (†1950) Dell'Arco (†1996)	 PD/TC PD/TC PD/TC	Tusiani 1974; Bergin 1960; Burnshaw 1960 Bergin 1964
Campania	Di Giacomo (†1934) Russo (†1927) Galdieri (†1923) De Filippo (†1984)	PD/TC PD PD TC	Tusiani 1974
Basilicata	Pierro (†1995)	TC	
Sicily	*Meli* (†1815) *Tempio* (†1820) Vann'Antò (†1960) Buttitta (†1997)	 PD/TC TC	Tusiani 1974

poets, and the unsuccessful attempt to balance entries from northern, central, and southern areas. This imbalance came as a punctuation between the domination by southern poets in the comprehensive anthologies that came before and the emphasis on the Mezzogiorno in the dialect anthologies that came after.

Uprootedness, Realism, and Fragmentation: Haller's Poetics of the Diasporic

Despite, of perhaps thanks to, its limited selection, the originality of Haller 1986 lies in its thematics. Like Nino Pedretti, Haller believed that dialect is 'the land of the tragic' as it performs with 'suffering, pain and anger' what is commonly said in the standard literature.[33] Dialect poetry offers 'realistic portrayals of the lower classes, their suffering from social injustice and poverty, and the simplicity of their approach to life, particularly to earthy, sensual experience'.[34] Haller's emphasis on realistic matters took the shape of a mixed exploration of the fragmented and the exilic, something that both critics and reviewers had so far ignored; his realist agenda is a form of diaspora and political commitment. Topics include the tragedy of love (Meli, Di Giacomo, Pierro), the political meanings of animal fables (Calvo, Meli, Trilussa), the irrationality of war (Calvo, Costa, Trilussa), religious hypocrisy (Porta, Belli, Calvo), the fear of death and the fragility of life (Tessa, Giotti, Guerra), and 'the pain caused by forced emigration to a foreign land and the ensuing alienation (Costa, Noventa, Vann'Antò, Ignazio Buttitta)'.[35]

More specifically, the diasporic theme is embodied here by a series of dialect poets experiencing travel, migration, and exile as different kinds of displacement. Some of the poets fall under more than one category. Noventa, for instance, fits all three, as he travelled widely through Italy, wrote some of his poetry in German, and 'was not allowed to reside in any university city in Italy because of his leftist views and literary activity'.[36] However, this tripartition allows us to bring together under the lens of the diasporic a multitude of motifs, from love to death, and from protest to pessimism.

Even more than Noventa, Emilio Guicciardi is the ultimate poet-traveller. Before travelling throughout Europe, the Far East, and Africa, he practiced law; then he settled in Somalia until the Second World War, directing a large farming enterprise. As Haller pointed out, Guicciardi's case is remarkable as 'it was in Africa that he discovered himself as a Milanese poet';[37] the discovery of one's own roots abroad follows a typically 'glocal' pattern. Guicciardi wrote in Milanese about the Koran and Mohammed, using the irony that is particular to most dialect writers:

> I hold in my hands
> the Koran...
> It's a beautiful and clever book,
> full of nonsense perhaps,
> but poetic.[38]

At the same time, he made use of linguistic contaminations, monologues and radio excerpts, in order to represent the confusion of Babel in the contemporary world:

Trasmettiamo...
Qualche musica brillante...
Ouverture...'
'E mocchéla! In dove sémm?'[39]

By contrast, Piedmontese clerk Nino Costa (generally Haller's poets are not professionals) wrote a letter-epitaph 'To the Piedmontese working abroad', tackling directly the issue of migration. 'Sometimes they return,' Costa says:

but more often a lost harvest
or a fever or a misfortune at work
closes them into a naked grave,
lost in a foreign cemetery.[40]

The nexus between dialect and death reminds us of the influence of Lee Masters in Italy. On a similar note, the Sicilian Vann'Antò desperately mourns the town that he is leaving:

I sing to my town my last
very sad farewell:
I'm going very far away,
I'm leaving like an exiled man.[41]

And Cesare Pascarella depicts man's search for meaning as a tragicomic 'Discovery of America':

And imagine those who were there,
imagine what a lark they were having!
Go on! Keep going! They suffered.
And America? Ha! Go find it![42]

Together with travel and migration, the experience of exile is at the centre of Haller's selection. The connection between antifascism and dialect writing is widely represented (Edoardo Firpo and Guerra); yet, Haller suggests that different exilic experiences are linked by a similar feeling of alienation, told through narrations of illness, protest, and autobiography. Calvo was exiled several times for supporting the ideas of the French Revolution during the Austrian-Russian occupation of Turin. Firpo, a landscape painter, wrote out of his imprisonment as an antifascist in 'Fiori de Zena' [The Flowers of Genoa] (1935). Marin was confined to Davos, Switzerland, not for political reasons, but for a severe lung disease he contracted while fighting in the First World War. Guerra knew the horror of deportation and prison exile, which he recalls, for instance, in *La s-ciuptèda* [The Gunshot] (1950). Finally, the socialist Buttitta, who found his shop bombed in 1943, lived in Milan in exile during and after the Second World War. With Haller's anthology, the bond between realism and dialect, politics and ethnic identity, reached its peak.

The editor hints at his political agenda tacitly but insistently, not only by suggesting that dialect literature developed in moments of crisis (for instance, in a concentration camp), but also by representing such crises through the voices of the poets themselves. For instance, the poetic examples of Buttitta, an acute observer of the 'suffering and struggle for survival of the Sicilian working class',[43] range from the condemnation of mine work to the identification of language with the nation:

Mothers,
who send your sons to the mine,
I'm asking you:
Why do you give
eyes to your sons
if they can't see the daylight?[44]
A nation
turns poor and servile,
when they steal its language
[...]
I notice it now,
as I am turning the guitar of the dialect
which loses a string every day.[45]

Themes of migration and displacement are also at the core of Haller's later publications concerned with the presence, and forms, of the Italian language(s) abroad. In a series of theoretical works published from the 1990s onwards, Haller considered multilingualism as the defining feature of Italian American communities. In the already mentioned 'Italian in New York' (1997), he defined Italian as a language of both migration and culture. He observed that 'Italian was long considered an "ethnic" language, the language of immigrants, and as such not particularly encouraged by school authorities'.[46] At the same time, he discussed the image of Italy as the land of music and high culture, thus demonstrating its schizophrenic reception in the US.

* * * * *

Haller 1986 is a landmark in the history of the Italian diasporic canon, although it concentrated on authors writing in languages other than Italian. There is indeed a sense of continuation between the 1970s avant-garde anthologies that introduced dialect poets to the American audience and Haller's work. These ethnic writers followed the Poundian-Whitmanian thread that shaped the secondary American canon since its beginnings. In particular, Haller's anthology filled the gap between linguistic and cultural studies, something that Allen and her collaborators were also accomplishing with respect to gender. The analysis of the interaction between contemporary ethnic critics (Sollors and Fisherman) and Haller's sources has therefore revealed a new face of Italian dialect poetry in America, i.e. its mainly migratory, ethnic traits. After Haller, dialect became the language of migration, the 'primary marker of ethnic identity', and, as such, a plausible vehicle to quench American audiences' thirst for diversity.[47]

Notes to Chapter 15

1. Italian American studies is a well-established and rapidly expanding field of scholarship. The following titles are offered by way of example: *From the Margin: Writings in Italian Americana*, ed. by Anthony Julian Tamburri, Paolo Giordano, and Fred Gardaphé (West Lafayette, IN: Purdue University Press, 1991); and Martino Marazzi, *Voices of Italian America: A History of Early*

Italian American Literature with a Critical Anthology, trans. by Ann Goldstein (New York: Fordham University Press, 2012).

2. Cited in Sulis, 'Ridefinire il canone', p. 79.
3. See Contini, 'Saggio introduttivo'; and Segre, 'Polemica linguistica ed espressionismo dialettale nella letteratura italiana', in *Lingua, stile e società*.
4. Joshua Fishman, *The Rise and the Fall of the Ethnic Revival: Perspectives on Language and Ethnicity* (Berlin & New York: de Gruyter, 1985); Werner Sollors, *Beyond Ethnicity: Consent and Descent in American Culture* (New York: Oxford University Press, 1986); and *The Invention of Ethnicity* (New York: Oxford University Press, 1988).
5. Cited in Sollors, *Beyond Ethnicity*, p. 489.
6. Hermann Haller, 'Italian in New York', in *The Multilingual Apple: Languages in New York City*, ed. by Joshua Fishman and Ofelia García, 2nd edn (Berlin & New York: de Gruyter, 2002), pp. 119–42 (p. 121).
7. *The Columbia Book of Later Chinese Poetry*, ed. by Jonathan Chaves (New York: Columbia University Press, 1986); *Contemporary Chicana Poetry: A Critical Approach to an Emerging Literature*, ed. by Marta Ester Sànchez (Berkeley: University of California Press, 1985); and *American Yiddish Poetry: A Bilingual Anthology*, ed. by Benjamin Harshav and Barbara Harshav (Berkeley: University of California Press, 1986).
8. See the Society for the Study of the Multi-ethnic Literature of the United States <http://www.melus.org/about/> [accessed 28 September 2018].
9. Fishman, *The Rise and the Fall of the Ethnic Revival*, p. iii.
10. Hermann Haller, *Una lingua perduta e ritrovata: l'italiano degli italo-americani* (Florence: Nuova Italia, 1993); and 'Italian in New York'.
11. See the homepage of the Harvard Longfellow Institute website: <> [accessed 20 October 2020].
12. *Multilingual America: Transnationalism, Ethnicity, and the Languages of American Literature*, ed. by Werner Sollors (New York & London: New York University Press, 1998).
13. Alison Games, *Migration and the Origins of the English Atlantic World* (Cambridge, MA: Harvard University Press, 1999); and *Letters Across Borders: The Epistolary Practices of International Migrants*, ed. by Brice Elliott, David Gerber, and Suzanne Sinke (New York: Palgrave Macmillan, 2006).
14. Sollors, *Beyond Ethnicity*, p. 241.
15. Ibid., pp. 14–16, 240.
16. Ibid., p. 248.
17. Ibid.
18. Ibid., p. 249.
19. See John Welle, 'Hermann Haller, The Hidden Italy' [review], *World Literature Today*, 62 (1998), 112.
20. Sollors, *The Invention of Ethnicity*, p. xiv.
21. Hermann Haller, 'Literature in Dialect and Dialect in Literature: A Sociolinguistic Perspective', in *Italian Dialect and Literature: From the Renaissance to the Present*, ed. by Emmanuela Tandello and Diego Zancani (London: Institute of Romance Studies, 1996), pp. 73–80 (p. 73).
22. Haller, 'Italian in New York', p. 119.
23. HALLER 1986, p. 21.
24. Ibid., pp. 31–48.
25. Ibid., p. 21.
26. Ibid.
27. HALLER 1986, p. 32.
28. Hermann Haller, 'Preface', in HALLER 1999, pp. ix-xi (p. ix).
29. Haller, 'Preface', in HALLER 1999, p. x.
30. Marina Cacioppo, *'If the Sidewalks of These Streets Could Talk': Reinventing Italian-American Ethnicity. The Representation and Construction of Ethnic Identity in Italian-American Literature* (Turin: Otto, 2005), p. 7.
31. *Poesia dialettale del Novecento*, ed. by Pierpaolo Pasolini and Mario Dell'Arco (Parma: Guanda, 1952); *Il dialetto da lingua della realtà a lingua della poesia da Porta a Belli a Pasolini*, ed. by Giovanni Tesio and Mario Chiesa (Turin: Paravia, 1978).

32. HALLER 1986, p. 21.
33. Ibid., p. 44.
34. Ibid.
35. Ibid.
36. Ibid., p. 191.
37. Ibid., p. 181.
38. Emilio Guicciardi, 'The Koran', trans. by Hermann Haller, in HALLER 1986, p. 183.
39. Emilio Guicciardi, 'Summer Fury', trans. by Hermann Haller, in HALLER 1986, p. 184. I have quoted the original here as the multilingual traits are lost in translation.
40. Nino Costa, 'To the Piedmontese Working Abroad', trans. by Hermann Haller, in HALLER 1986, p. 87. Note that this poem is taken from a collection entitled *Rassa Nostran-a* [Our Race].
41. Vann'Antò, 'Farewell to the Town', trans. by Hermann Haller, in HALLER 1986, p. 505.
42. Cesare Pascarella, from *The Discovery of America*, trans. by Hermann Haller, in HALLER 1986, p. 335.
43. HALLER 1986, p. 508.
44. Ignazio Buttitta, 'To the Mothers of the Boys in the Mines', trans. by Hermann Haller, in HALLER 1986, p. 521.
45. Ignazio Buttitta, 'Language and Dialect', trans. by Hermann Haller, in HALLER 1986, p. 533.
46. Haller, 'Italian in New York', p. 136.
47. Ibid., p. 125.

CHAPTER 16

❖

'Mother Gone': Transnationalising Italian Dialect Poetry in America

This chapter examines the third movement in the process of dialect poetry's anthologisation, coinciding with its transnational turn. This phase corresponded to the institutionalisation of global studies as an academic discipline and, more specifically, to its application to the literary field. Bonaffini's anthologies both envisaged and embodied this change, as the Italian language had become, in the words of Italian American poet Felix Stefanile, a replacement of these migrants' disappearing mother:

> Like Dante
> I have pondered and pondered
> the speech I was born to,
> lost now, mother gone
> the whole neighbourhood bull-dozed,
> and no one to say it on the TV,
> that words are dreams.[1]

Luigi Bonaffini's Editorial Journey from South to South

Since their appearance in the late twentieth and early twenty-first century, global theories have investigated the 'diminishment of the sovereignty of the nation-state, the emergence of a homogenizing capitalistic culture and the ascendency of a single version of European and American modernity'.[2] Concurrently, postcolonial criticism 'has attempted to shift the dominant ways in which the relations between western and non-western people and their worlds are viewed' in contemporary society.[3] From this perspective, postcolonialism, like feminism, offered a variety of tools to penetrate the secrecy of those 'hidden' worlds whose inhabitants live in the margins, never qualify as the norm, and are not authorised to speak.[4]

A similar interest in marginality is reflected by the editorial trends of the 1990s and the first decades of the twenty-first century, which endorsed a transnational, postcolonial, and/or multidisciplinary focus. The anthologies of dialect poetry in translation that came out in the last twenty years exemplified the double shift from a mainstream to a sidestream corpus, and from a national to a global perspective. If the dynamics between particularism and universalism was a distinctive feature of dialect writing since its origins ('glocalism'), its transnational potential became more and more preponderant in the last span of years.

This direction is particularly visible in the anthologies coedited by Bonaffini, Achille Serrao, and Justin Vitiello between 1997 and 2001, all published by Legas. The first and third volume concentrate on dialect poetry from southern (1997) and northern and central (2001) Italy respectively; the second collection does not have a geographical focus, but privileges younger writers. All volumes rely on the contribution of multiple translators (see Appendix, Part 3.1). While extending Haller's multilingual project to all the Italian regions and idioms, these anthologies opened a new phase in the American reception of dialect poetry from Italy. First, they put forward the issue of translation by presenting a trilingual version (dialect, Italian, and English) for several hundreds of texts. Second, they fostered a transnational, rather than an ethnic, reading of dialect poetry in the context of the Italian diaspora of the late twentieth and early twenty-first century. This global angle led to the compilation of Bonaffini and Joseph Perricone's diasporic anthology in 2014, significantly entitled *Poets of the Italian Diaspora* and discussed later in this chapter. Unlike Haller 1986, Bonaffini's volumes offer a selection of young poets that continues the avant-garde tradition begun with De Palchi and Raiziss. They also grant a certain preponderance to southern poetry, as reflected in *Dialect Poetry from Southern Italy*, the first publication of the series (Bonaffini 1997). As Bonaffini pointed out in the editor's note, 'the focus on southern dialect poetry aims first of all to compensate in part for the scarce attention traditionally — and unfairly — paid to the south by national dialect anthologies, but it also acknowledges the fact that the great Italian diaspora in the United States has a predominantly southern origin, and that most of the dialects spoken by Italian-Americans in this country are from the south'.[5] This declaration summarises my argument sustained throughout, i.e. the fact that southern dialect poetry from Italy and Italian American poetry in the US share the same, diasporic root.

Bonaffini's biography and editorship strengthen this viewpoint. Professor of Italian at Brooklyn College, CUNY, he was born in Isernia, in the Italian region of Molise. The second smallest region after the Aosta Valley, Molise is also the youngest, becoming independent from Abruzzo in 1963. Like the rest of Mezzogiorno, and even more so, Molise suffered from the north-south economic divide in Italy, which resulted in an ongoing process of emigration, especially to the New World. A migrant himself, Bonaffini sistematised the process of anthologisation of Italian dialect poetry in the US and anchored it to the poetics of the diasporic. His contribution to the dissemination of Italian regional literatures is tremendous. In addition to the three volumes analysed here, he edited or coedited two further trilingual anthologies of Italian dialect poetry.[6] Together with Mia Comte, he also published a bilingual anthology of migrant writers in Italy, a proof of the multiple forms that the Italian diaspora has acquired.[7]

In addition to his anthological works, Bonaffini translated both from Italian and various dialects, translating forty-three poets across seven anthologies (see

Appendix 3.3). Amongst the poets he translated are Campana, Luzi, Sereni, Pasolini, Rimanelli, Pierro, Giuseppe Jovine, and Franco Scataglini. Bonaffini published widely both on theoretical matters and single authors, Italian as well as American, his essays on dialect poetry and translation being particularly noteworthy. Being the editor of the *Journal of Italian Translation*, he contributed to the inverse process too, that is, to the dissemination of American poetry (mainly written by Italian Americans) in Italy.

Starting from his Molisan homeland, Bonaffini's editorial journey circularly took him back to the south. And yet, by performing a typical diasporic trajectory, it is less concerned with its origins than with its destinations.[8] In this process of cultural transformations, from the south of Italy to America, and back, Bonaffini was supported by a series of collaborators and two important publishing houses: Legas, based in Ottawa, Ontario, and Fordham University Press, which released the 2014 anthology as part of the Critical Studies in Italian America series. Both companies specialise in multilingual publishing and works by minor authors; Legas however, is located in Canada, and therefore in a nation other than the US. Despite breaking one of this study's criteria, I felt authorised to incorporate Legas anthologies here as they were edited by critics operating in the US. In addition, these volumes were all included in the Italian Poetry in Translation series, whose editor is Gaetano Cipolla. The representative for Legas Publishing in New York as well as president of Arba Sicula, Cipolla significantly contributed to the circulation of southern Italian culture across the Atlantic. Although I shall concentrate on Bonaffini as a linking figure among different publications and initiatives, it is important to bear in mind that his activity can be truly appraised only if considered within the network of people and institutions that constituted the Italian American diasporic community. No anthological enterprise happens, so to speak, in a vacuum.

Mourning the Past, Envisaging the Future: Three Anthologies of Contemporary Dialect Poetry

This section provides a comparative reading of the three dialect anthologies coedited by Bonaffini. Despite dealing with different geographical areas, these volumes are interdependent. Bonaffini 1997 and Bonaffini 2001 are conceived as companion publications, whereas Bonaffini 1999 is the first anthology of contemporary or neo-dialect poetry offering a selection from almost all regions. Only the Aosta Valley and Trentino are missing, but all southern regions are represented. The three anthologies were issued by the same publisher, Legas, with the exception of Bonaffini 1999, first published in Italian by Campanotto, a militant publishing house based in Udine. The editor of the Italian original is Serrao, meaning that Bonaffini and Vitiello mainly worked as translators for the realisation of the English version.

Even though Bonaffini 1999 has a different genetic history, the three anthologies are part of the same programme of cultural transplantation. Bonaffini's mediation in the field of dialect literature spanned more than twenty years, starting with a trilingual volume, *Poesia dialettale del Molise* [Dialect Poetry from Molise] (1993). It is interesting to notice that the peak of the neo-dialect season occurred at different times in the US and Italy, where it was a 1980s phenomenon. Bonaffini 2001 is also the fruit of the cooperation between Bonaffini and Serrao, a further sign of the linkage among the three works.

To put into practice his ambitious project, Bonaffini surrounded himself with a large team of contributors, poets, and translators. Each volume numbers on average nine translators and twelve contributors, most of whom are poets in their own right: see Vivaldi, Dante Maffia, Alberto Bertoni, and Gian Mario Villalta. These anthologies present one or more introductory essays by an Italian critic, whereas the introductions to the various regions are written by a specialist of the area. Thus, Bonaffini 1997 opens with the essays by Giacinto Spagnoletti and Luigi Reina, whereas the northern region of Trentino is introduced by Elio Fox in the companion volume. There are no contributors in bonaffini 1999, where the editors themselves provide all the commentaries.

As far as the selection is concerned, the three anthologies concentrate on young poets, and especially on their unpublished works. In Bonaffini 1999, the poets are all born after 1930 and, therefore, almost all of them were alive at the time of the anthology's publication. Women's presence became more consistent after 1999, whereas it was still hidden in the anthology of southern poetry. There is also a high percentage of experimental writers, including poets who are either bilingual or multilingual. Bonaffini's anthologies display the features of dialect poetry all at once (marginality, novelty, and experimentation), working as an efficient canonising instrument.

The tables below show the canon of dialect poetry as presented by this series of publications. Table 16.1 compares the 1997 selection with the southern regions of Bonaffini 1999. Table 16.2 follows the same principle by juxtaposing Bonaffini 1999 (northern and central regions) with the anthology of northern and central poetry. Female poets are identified with an asterisk; recurrent authors are marked in bold.

Table 16.1. A comparative analysis of Bonaffini 1997 and Bonaffini 1999 by regions and poets

	Bonaffini 1997	Bonaffini 1999
Abruzzo	Clemente Dommarco Giannangeli **Rosato** Savastano	**Rosato** Civitareale Marciani Moretti
Latium	Pascarella Zanazzo Trilussa Dell'Arco **Marè**	**Marè**
Molise	Altobello Trofa Cirese **Jovine** **Rimanelli**	**Jovine** **Rimanelli**
Apulia	Gatti Borazio De Donno Tusiani **Angiuli** **Granatiero**	**Angiuli** **Granatiero**
Campania	Di Giacomo Russo Viviani **Serrao** **Sovente** Pignatelli	**Serrao** **Sovente** Di Natale
Basilicata	Pierro **Riviello** Romeo Lotierzo Brindisi	**Riviello** Nigro
Calabria	Pane Creazzo Giunta Butera Curcio **Maffia**	Marino **Maffia**
Sicily	Di Giovanni Vann'Antò Buttitta Calì Messina Cremona	Di Marco De Vita
Sardinia	Sari Lobina Pinna Mastino	Collu Sole

Table 16.2. A comparative analysis of Bonaffini 1999 and Bonaffini 2001 by regions and poets

	Bonaffini 1999	Bonaffini 2001
Italian Switzerland	—	Bianconi Canonica Orelli Scamara Grignola Quadri
Aosta Valley	—	Cerlogne Martinet* Gal
Piedmont	**Dorato*** **Bertolino**	Costa Pacòt Olivero Bodrìe **Dorato*** **Bertolino**
Lombardy	**Loi** **Grisoni*** Quadri	Tessa **Loi** Marelli Consonni
Liguria	**Bertolani** **Giannoni**	Firpo Panero Vivaldi Cassinelli **Bertolani** **Giannoni**
Veneto	**Bressan** **Cecchinel**	Calzavara Zanotto **Bressan** Caniato **Cecchinel** Villalta Zanzotto Ruffato
Friuli-Venezia Giulia	Zanier Doplicher **Grisancich** **Giacomini** Valleruga* Vit Villalta	Giotti Marin Cergoly **Grisancich** Pasolini Bartolini Naldini **Giacomini** Di Monte*
Trentino	—	Felini Pola Borgogno Francescotti Slomp* Varner

Emilia Romagna	Spadoni **Nadiani**	Stuffler Pezzani Zavattini Guerra Baldassari Baldini Rentocchini **Nadiani**
The Marches	—	Giansanti Grimaldi **Scataglini** **Mancino** Ghiandoni
Umbria	**Ponti**	Fratoni Ronchi Francardi* **Ponti** Zuccherini Ramadori Prugnola

A comparative reading of these charts allows space for some considerations. First, Bonaffini 1999 presents a limited selection of authors; it offers an overview of neo-dialect poetry throughout Italy rather than a selection from a specific geographical area. In addition, this anthology includes a larger number of young and experimental writers, as opposed to Bonaffini 1997, which is closer to Haller's design. In Bonaffini 1997, Bonaffini contributed to the canonisation of dialect poetry from the Mezzogiorno by anthologising a restricted pool of authors (five per region). As a consequence, the poets that are shared with Haller 1986 prove to be canonical within this tradition: Pascarella, Trilussa, and Dell'Arco for Latium; Vann'Antò and Buttitta for Sicily; and Pierro for Basilicata. It is worth noticing that, despite being a seminal figure in southern poetry, Pierro does not appear in Bonaffini 1999 for generational reasons (he was born in 1916).

Bonaffini 2001 strikes a balance between canonical and younger writers. A region like Veneto, for instance, includes samples from Zanzotto (a major poet) and Luciano Caniato (a lesser-known poet); similarly, Pasolini is juxtaposed with Nico Naldini among the poets from Friuli. The dialect-mystical poet Marin resurfaces in the English context after almost thirty years of silence (see Marchione 1974). Another important feature of Bonaffini 2001 is the introduction of women writers. The male presence is still incontestable, with six women out of sixty-nine poets, yet a new sensitivity towards gender issues emerged. In his introduction to Trentino, Fox praised ten contemporary poets, four women and six men, who 'made significant contributions to all the local contemporary poetic culture'.[9] Women are presented as a constituent part of the process of dialect poetry's canonisation in border-line regions such as Trentino and Friuli. All the female poets included in Bonaffini and Serrao's selection — representing Umbria, Trentino, Friuli, Piedmont, Lombardy, and the Aosta Valley — already appeared in Bonaffini 1999 two years before, with the exception of Franca Ronchi Francardi (Umbria) and Ida

Vallerugo (Friuli), replaced by Nelvia Di Monte in BONAFFINI 2001. This emphasis on border regions is crucial. By addressing the question of cultural diversity since its start, the volume opens with a selection of dialects from the Italian Swiss area, a proof of the transnational vibe of this collection.

From a thematic viewpoint, the three anthologies present tropes of diasporic writing on the one hand (autobiography, migration, memory, landscape, mysticism, melancholia), and introduce new themes on the other (ecocriticism and the posthuman), a way of addressing the challenges imposed to human life after the scientific and technological advances of our time. A continuous reflection on language crisscrosses the anthologies, concretising in both metaliterary and experimental practices. There has been a tendency to distinguish between a northern and a southern line; southern poets 'focus on themes of social injustice or emigration', whereas 'linguistic experimentation is more widespread in northern regions'.[10] This paradigm, however, is applicable to Bonaffini's anthologies only partially. The experience of migration is common to the populations of Trentino and Friuli (Irredentism) as much as to southern peasants; at the same time, dialect poets from the north look upon dialect poetry from the south for its freshness and innovation.

The theme of diaspora is inflected in multiple manners. Special attention is paid to Italian American migrants and poets, but their case will be discussed in the next section. Diaspora here encompasses the reality of migration, often to the US (Rimanelli, Michele Pane, Ugo Canonica); the struggles of the exiled self (Luciano Cecchinel, Bianca Dorato, Pasolini); the archetypal image of the mother (Remigio Bartolino, Luigi Antonio Trofa, Vivaldi), and sometimes of the father (Serrao); the liminal geographies of certain Italian regions and cities (Vittorio Felini, Giotti, Marin); and the alternation between local and global perspectives. This last feature emerges from most of the poems; yet, it is also a matter of theoretical discussion in the introductions to individual regions. See, for example, Bertoni and Vincenzo Bagnoli's introduction to Emilia-Romagna, input by a famous quotation by Édouard Glissant, a French writer and critic from Martinique: 'We have reached a moment in history when we realize that man's imagination needs all the languages of the world'.[11]

The following examples illustrate the predominance of a diasporic semantics. In his collection *Latitudine Nord* [North Latitude] (1980), Carlo Cergoly's poems are entitled after the names of deported Jews, a clear instance of the diasporic: 'Aronne Pakitz | [...] of the Krakov ghetto, | [...] who died in Warsaw. | His son Simon | [...] died in Gorizia. | Paola his daughter [...] dead in Mathausen'.[12] Similarly, Renzo Francescotti depicts the harshness of both collective migration ('But who are these poor people | coming down the path [...] | women men and children covering | with their hands cans and jars? | Birds wet with rime | who go far | from Trento') and personal isolation ('From the sea | of my wandering | I arrived | one night of broken street lights | at my old house').[13]

Other poets resort to the symbol of the train to link the necessity of migration to the changes of contemporary life; see, for instance, Buttitta's collection of popular songs, *Lu trenu di lu suli* [The Train of the Sun] (1963), and one of Pasolini's most famous poems, 'La Meglio Gioventù' [The Best of Youth]: 'Come on, trains, take them so far away | roaming the earth to see what they have lost | here. | Trains everywhere scatter these once happy | men, | They will not laugh when leaving home | forever'.[14] A further, important feature of the diasporic is the emphasis on the figure of the outcast, who can be either a prisoner (Guerra, Buttitta) or a woman (Dorato, Franca Grisoni, Lilia Slomp). Valleruga's verse poignantly captures the poet's condition at the fringes of society: 'The last place in the world, the world | a station if it has a station, | however small, the name vanished'.[15]

Directly dependent on dialect poets' unconventional status is their interest in experimentation. The link between dialect poetry and the avant-garde was first underlined by Spagnoletti, as reflected in his introductory essay to Bonaffini 1997:

> What we are speaking of primarily is an avant-garde dialect poetry that was inconceivable before. [...] The experimental tendency has definitely won, and not only in northern Italy, but surprisingly in the south as well, where you no longer find a yearning for the days of old as in the distant past (of Basile and Cortese), but a decided drive towards experimentation. [...] this clash with the new gives rise to a mode of expression which is no longer strictly semantic, but something explosive.[16]

The emancipation of dialect poetry from tradition and the past is crucial on a number of levels: it fosters a new reading of the relationship between dialect poetry and the neo-avant-garde; it connects the most peculiar of the Italian poetic experiences to the American dimension; and it suggests new thematic developments in dialect writing. Some writers contributed to the renewal of dialect poetry through their participation in avant-garde movements, such as the *Gruppo Beta* and the *Alessio Di Giovanni Group*, both based in Sicily. Founded in 1965 by Lucio Zinna, the contributor to Bonaffini 1997's Sicilian section, *Gruppo Beta* was inspired by the contemporaneous *Gruppo 63*, whereas the *Alessio Di Giovanni Group* sought the 'development and adoption of a Sicilian *koine*; syntactic and metric freedom in favour of expressive power; unity of thought, language and reality, in a Sicilian perspective of life and art'.[17] Paolo Messina's poem 'A Flower's Breath' reproduces this search for an expressionistic language: 'Calyx | white | silence — | where you grow | pinch by pinch | I feel the dew | that bathed your finger tips | drying...'.[18] On a similar note, Vann'Antò's verse echoes his youthful Futurist experience: 'Enough! We're all a herd of stupid sheep, | who go about with heads low to the ground, | forced to behave like wolves'.[19]

Tessa (Lombardy), Mauro Marè (Latium), Marco Pola (Trentino), and Ernesto Calzavara (Veneto) are recurring presences in the avant-garde dialect trunk described here, but new buds sprang also from the Umbria and the Molise regions. The more marginal an environment, the more it seems to lean towards experimental solutions. Trofa, for instance, experimented with the dialect of Ferrazzano, Campobasso, and metrics (free verse), appropriating a prerogative of futurist poetry (Bonaffini 1997). Likewise, Gaio Fratini, from Umbria, pursued effects of 'violent expressionism', by combining it with a 'phonosymbolic' use of language: 'In Perugia, Perugians are real men | [...] Hack-lawyers, godfathers, hogs and pigs, | premature corpses, resuscitated | as paunchy nitwits all primped and tasty'.[20] In Piedmont, Tòni Bodriè moved across different registers and tones, thus reproducing his existence 'on the fringe between the Provençal and Piedmontese worlds, [...] country and city, tradition and modernity'.[21] His poems revive the spell of Ariosto's magic: 'Castel resplendent with stars | (they called it Castille | because it castigated | the good and the bad), | lovely, young and old — so much beauty astride the hill'.[22] Furthermore, the anthologies abound in figures of poet-painters and art critics, among whom Pascarella, Sandro Zanotto, Cosimo Savastano, Michele Sovente, Vito Riviello, Santo Calì, and Ferruccio Ramadori, the marriage between writing and the figurative arts being a constant in avant-garde writing.

At the interface between the avant-garde and the diasporic experiences, with all the facets they entail, lies the theme of metaliterature. Parts I to III discussed the relevance of metaliterary practices both in experimental and female anthologies; yet, dialect poetry in self-reflective processes take centre stage. Across Bonaffini's volumes, it is possible to distinguish three possible inflections of the metaliterary element: plurilingualism (which is a form of experimentalism in itself); language as alterity; and language as mourning. The employment of multiple languages, or their superimposition in newly coined words, is a central trait of Bonaffini and Perricone's anthology on the *Poets of the Italian Diaspora* (see the next section). The first signs of this tradition are already visible in the 1990s and, especially, in the words of southern authors. In 'My Husband Wrote to Me', for instance, Trofa intermingles his dialect from Molise with the English language (see 'yes' and 'mèn', with an accent) as well as neologisms deriving from the contact between Italian, dialect, and American: 'ggiòbba' for 'job'; 'nò stèn' for 'I can't understand'; 'uomméne' for 'women'.[23]

Similarly, the poet's sense of alterity is expressed through the attachment to those idioms that make him or her an alien to the society s/he lives in. This is evident from south to north, in Buttitta's poetic manifesto: 'I'm not a poet [...] give me hooked blades | glinting in whites of eyes | of oxen on the block';[24] in Savastano's imploration before his grandmother's grave: 'But tell me, grandma, does the earth speak? | or do they share an ancient tongue, | like you and I, breath and stone?';[25] and in Francescotti's ethical approach to the gift of language: 'I love words that have | a forgotten music | [...] invented by another breed. | A dialect | that trips | the bitter talk | of these wretched times'.[26] The Babel of languages silenced the poets' words, while pollution damaged them to the point of death: 'We have sold our factories | we have polluted the water, the air | and our dialect. With the money | we have changed our thoughts, our way of life | the way we look into each other's eyes. | We are no longer us'.[27] Dialect poets present themselves as the guardians of untold, primitive stories that nobody knowns or recognises: 'I have a story to tell you | about butterflies | [...] Every day we notice | the immortality of nature, | where merit has no place'.[28]

The same concern towards the future of languages and society is at the core of the third, and most important, inflection of the metaliterary motif, i.e. dialect as grief. Within this category, dialect writing may refer to different forms of distance (both temporal and spatial) and/or death, thus expressing feelings of mourning as well as an act of resistance towards the transience of life. Poet Roberto Giannoni remarked that dialect is 'the language of the dead and of the old. | The language itself is old and even now when I love it, | and it will be deader than dead before too long'.[29] Franca Ronchi Francardi expressed a similar idea in a more lyric way when she wrote that 'the tongue breaking from the log | has a short life: | [...] it flees, strays | till it dies lightly | in silence'.[30]

Maffia's poems, which close the Calabria section in BONAFFINI 1997, are entirely devoted to the connections between metaliterature, dialect, and melancholia: 'Can you bring back to life | who had been paper once? Can Lucia walk, can Nausicaa? | A fright after that, the pages | rustled | like human flesh'; 'I lose a page, an insert of the clamor, | who knows | if I'll find a living word'; and 'When was it that we were alive? | When did we die?'.[31] Other poets went even further as they envisaged dialects' afterlives, their verse becoming an elegy for languages' finitude in this world: 'Caught in these drapes | of fog, a cuckoo alone prays, prays | for this language | on the wane, dragging toward its death...';[32] 'Abide don't die | don't die in my hands | abide abide words'.[33]

America and Beyond: *Poets of the Italian Diaspora*

'There's no way out, | I'm a chain of insidious origins' (De Palchi); 'Today's false exile | is a cohort of dreams within and without our world' (Fontanella); 'And so the emigrant leaves, | and in his journey dreams (Nino Provenzano); 'I decided to enter | no-man's-land, | the faraway frontier' (Orazio Tanelli); 'The lie of always | leaving from somewhere else' (Piero Salabè); 'I only wished [...] that all of you | suddenly became emigrants' (Saro Marretta); 'We are a seed dispersed | the fragments of a far-flung diaspora | [...] A bastard race, | we are always fleeing' (Vittorio Fioravanti); 'While traveling everything is disrupted and dispersed | desire is dyed white | [...] the calm terror of discovering that perhaps life is | nothing but this' (Fontanella).[34]

These lines by different authors are taken from *Poets of the Italian Diaspora*, the bilingual anthology of Italian diasporic poetry compiled by Bonaffini and Perricone (BONAFFINI AND PERRICONE 2014). In its 1,532 pages, the editors brought together seventy-nine Italian poets dispersed throughout the world, from Argentina to Croatia, and from Australia to Belgium, thus transcending the Italian and American dimensions. In particular, the Italian American section, edited by Peter Carravetta, numbers twenty poets based in the United States, including three women (Irene Marchegiani, Annalisa Saccà, and Victoria Surliuga, all professors at American universities).

The reason for choosing this anthology as a way of concluding our journey in the land of transplanted dialect poetry is twofold: first, it makes an important selection of dialect writers, mostly, but not solely, from the US; and second, it embodies the passage from the local to the global in its very structure and themes.

As Sante Matteo suggested in his introductory essay to the volume, Italian poetry has gone global; although 'links between particular branches of the Italian diaspora — American, Australian, Venezuelan, Argentinean, and so on — and their Italian roots have already been addressed', this anthology nevertheless 'provides a view of all the branches simultaneously, indeed of the whole global forest where Italian roots have spread and flourished, giving us the poetic voices of the Italian diaspora from around the planet'.[35]

The diasporic canon reaches here both its point of departure and completion. All the thematic threads analysed so far reemerge (migration, experimentation, metaliterature, melancholia, mysticism); other semantic possibilities are either invented or excavated from the past (see, for instance, the philosophical verse by Paolo Valesio and Carravetta himself, reminiscent of Ballerini's ontological theories). The dialect poets anthologised here offer a compelling example of the ways in which this variety of tones, styles, and motifs intermingle. Writers employ their native dialects to connect with their distant homelands, landscape, and people, often insisting on the sense of decay threatening both their languages and lives. For instance, Loredana Bugliun, from Pola, Croatia, makes a metaphysical use of the Istrian language in order to resist the deterioration of the world of Dignano, her birthplace:

> When the house collapses day by day
> I know that the whole of Dignano is crying.
> Today I look at its ruins
> and know it will never return as before.[36]

The image of the damaged house, a topos in diasporic writing since Poggioli, resurfaces in another poem by Bugliun, emblematically entitled 'The Mountain House': 'Empty this house on the mountain, | it slowly crumbles'.[37]

A similar sense of resignation is palpable in the dialect poems that deal with nostalgia for the homeland. This group is by far the most conspicuous, its manifestations including a sample of oral dialect poems from some Aeolian communities in Sydney. At the same time, professionals in disciplines other than poetry wrote diasporic verse from across the Atlantic. A business man who worked in Iran, Libya, and Brazil, Ermanno Minuto was born in Savona, Liguria, whence his dialect poems constantly return:

> When life has hunted me far,
> so far from Savona and my little nest
> [...]
> I carried with me the smell of the earth
> soaked in a sudden downpour.[38]

> Now that I'm living almost at the end of the world
> I can relive a whole bunch of Christmases.[39]

In other cases, melancholia is tied up with the reality of death, experienced through the loss of parental figures, both physical and metaphorical (when the mother is the land itself):

I ask you Slavic mother
who pushes up milky smiles,
which is my original look
heaved from my chest with my first breath?
[...]
But if I try to tear myself from this earth
strips of flesh and bitter blood remain.[40]

Dialect poetry from the US displays a peculiar nostalgic vein that is distinguishable from that of any other country. Italian American poets, such as De Palchi, Tusiani, Rimanelli, Fontanella, and Livorni, are not only viscerally attached to their countries, but also fully immersed into the cultural streams of their new world. They use different languages (up to four, in the case of Tusiani and Rimanelli) and styles as a way of, in the words of Bhabha, facing the 'instability of cultural signification', the 'limits of the nations', and 'the foreignness of languages'; Bhabha also pointed out that, in such conditions, culture is both transnational and translational, becoming a true 'strategy of survival'.[41] Its force lies precisely in the sense of displacement and fragmentation from which dialect poetry originates.

In order 'to sketch a map of the problematic territories inhabited by the Italophone poets of the United States', Carravetta proposed a 'semiotic parallelogram' that provides a 'general interpretation of the situation of writing in a language when actually living in a country where that language is not dominant'.[42] The four apexes of the parallelogram are marked by their own specific tensions, which also contrast with their respective opposites: Apex A (origins/immortality) versus Apex B (home/mortality); and Apex C (poetry/language) versus Apex D (reality/*langue*). As Carravetta observed, 'the tension is owned to the displacement created by having home away from the origin', and poetry away from the usual codes of communication.[43]

Even within this particular hermeneutic context, dialect poetry offers a case in point. An eminent Italian cultural figure in the US, as well as the editor of an anthology of experimental poetry in the 1970s, Tusiani has become the symbol of the 'transformed' writer suspended between the here and the beyond:

There is a song that surges deep inside
and it's an ocean heaving to extend
[...]
This song's the dialect spoken on the side
of that blessed Mountain.[44]

In a similar manner, Tusiani's unsent letter to his native Gargano represents 'the psychic split that emigration brings at all levels':

So, my Gargano, my beautiful Gargano,
I'm writing you this letter so you'll know
that, after forty years of this America,
one thing alone is definite: It seems
almost as I had never made that trip.[45]

Another nomadic figure of Italian literature, who has also been called a 'fleeting writer', Rimanelli embodies 'the subversive and dispersive, eclectic and multiform connotations of the variegated Italian intellectual diaspora of the 1950s'.[46] Forced to migrate to the US following the publication of a wry pamphlet, *Il mestiere del furbo* [The Craft of Being Smart] (1959), Rimanelli's works oscillate among languages, cultures, and genres: from prose to poetry, and from epic to the avant-garde. His dialect poems reproduce the rhythm of oral Italian ballads, finding a correspondent in the American narrative forms:

Italy is a long country
A very very long stretch of land
like a heartsickness
[...]
America is made up of water.[47]

Soft is the voice when she tells me
That love is only what remains.[48]

Further examples of Rimanelli's narrative style occur in 'A Vije du Molise' [The Path to Molise] and in the 'Ballata di Joe Selimo' [The Ballad of Joe Selimo], where the poet compares the consequences of living in a globalised society with the solitude of the lacerated self:

I was born inside a room
that is small as the world.
I went far and I went wide
to find myself another world.[49]

These lines resonate with Tusiani's most famous verse, written in English and included in his 1978 collection, *Gente mia and Other Poems* [My People and Other Poems]: 'Two languages, two lands, perhaps two souls... | Am I a man or two strange halves of one?'.[50]

As Francesco Durante says, Rimanelli's and Tusiani's poetics reflect the 'suspended reality that is at once no longer Italian and not yet — at least not fully — something else', and by extension, whatever these diasporic writers produce is simultaneously 'peripheral and eccentric to Italian literary spheres, as well as to the literary spheres of [their] host country'.[51] As Durante also pointed out, 'one might liken the precariousness of this literary space to a response to Nietzsche's invitation, in *The Gay Science*, to build a house at the foot of a volcano'. Within this space, he continued, 'creativity and expression [...] often become an integral and irrevocable part of that most crucial moment for members of a diaspora: the final dream they dreamed before liquefying themselves into a new identity'.[52] Seen through this lens, Bonaffini and Perricone 2014 prophetically registered the incipient moment in which the 'liquidity' (Bauman) of contemporary identity and culture formed.

* * * * *

To sum up, we may say that Italian dialect poetry was introduced to an American readership via the mediation of ethnic theories and the consequent dissemination of global perspectives in the US. Originally associated with the avant-garde Poundian tradition, it developed as an extension of the Italian plurilingual branch that had begun with Dante in the thirteenth century and ended with neorealism in the

1950s. This multilingual, off-centre body of work was given special attention in the US, where the interest in ethnic writing, prompted by the presence of Italian American communities, became a pretext for investigating the fluidity of American society at large. Concurrently, the diasporic reading of the Italian dialect tradition illuminated new ways of understanding domestic canons, both locally (as a form of conservation) and transnationally (in the spirit of glocalisation).

In the land of poetry, drawing conclusions might be hazardous. Yet, at the end of this journey, it is possible to indicate a handful of names that became canonical in the English-speaking world: Belli, Porta, Trilussa, Meli, Di Giacomo, Dell'Arco, Pasolini, Noventa, Marin, Tessa, Tusiani, and Rimanelli, but also Baldini and Loi, who made their first appearance in Brock 2012. As Brock himself pointed out, contemporary dialect poets 'gain access to fresh storehouses of language, untroubled by the eloquence problem, under-spoiled by eight centuries of tradition'; in other words, they can be considered the heralds of a new transnational avant-garde.[53]

I would like to end this chapter by recalling Acetoso's image of Poggioli as a new Ulysses, the castaway who enjoys his limbic, transatlantic condition, suspended between two different languages, continents, and ages.[54] As Matteo observes, 'reading is a form of migration'. As we move from poem to poem, and from one language to the other, 'we too are "translated" [...] out of our home turf, out of ourselves: like Ulysses, whose travels [...] afflicted him with great nostalgia but also gained him the ability' to see the world with the 'migrant's second eye'.[55] At times Ulysses and Aeneas, Poggioli is both an outcast and an originator who provided new ways of interpreting Italian poetry in a world that had lost its traditional boundaries, points of references, and manners of communication. It is exactly this sense of displacement, perfectly embodied by dialect poetry, that offers the contemporary global reader (Italian, American, both, or other) a deeper understanding of his/her world, as well as that of someone else.

Notes to Chapter 16

1. Felix Stefanile, 'The Americanization of the Immigrant', in *The Country of Absence: Poems and Essays* (West Lafayette, IN: Bordighera, 2000), p. 59.
2. Liam Connell and Nicky Marsh, 'Theorizing Globalization', in *Literature and Globalization: A Reader*, ed. by Liam Connell and Nicky Marsh (London & New York: Routledge, 2011), pp. 1–4 (p. 2).
3. Robert J. C. Young, *Postcolonialism: A Very Short Introduction* (Oxford: Oxford University Press, 2003), p. 1.
4. Ibid.
5. Bonaffini 1997, p. 12.
6. *Poesia dialettale del Molise: testi e critica. A Trilingual Anthology*, ed. by Luigi Bonaffini, Giambattista Faralli, and Sebastiano Martelli (Isernia: Marinelli, 1993); *The Bread and the Rose: A Trilingual Anthology of Neapolitan Poetry from the 16th Century to the Present*, ed. by Luigi Bonaffini, and Achille Serrao (Ottawa: Legas, 2005).
7. *A New Map: The Poetry of Migrant Writers in Italy*, ed. by Luigi Bonaffini and Mia Comte (Ottawa: Legas, 2011).
8. Francesco Durante, 'Seven Points on Poetry of the Italian Diaspora', in Bonaffini and Perricone 2014, pp. xix–xxi (p. xix).
9. Bonaffini 2001, p. 458.

10. Haller, 'Literature in Dialect and Dialect in Literature', p. 77.
11. Bonaffini 2001, p. 513.
12. Carlo Cergoly, 'Aaron Pakitz', trans. by Rina Ferrarelli, in Bonaffini 2001, p. 387.
13. Renzo Francescotti, 'But Who Are These Poor People?' and 'Bed', trans. by Rina Ferrarelli, in Bonaffini 2001, pp. 487–88, 491.
14. Pier Paolo Pasolini, 'The Best of Youth', trans. by Adeodato Piazza Nicolai, in Bonaffini 2001, p. 413.
15. Ida Vallerugo, 'Last Place', trans. by Dino Fabris, in Bonaffini 1999, p. 113.
16. Giacinto Spagnoletti, 'Italian Language and Southern Dialects', in Bonaffini 1997, pp. 13–14 (p. 14).
17. Bonaffini 1997, p. 437.
18. Paolo Messina, 'A Flower's Breath', trans. by Justin Vitiello, in Bonaffini 1997, p. 440.
19. Vann'Antò, 'The Last War', trans. by Gaetano Cipolla, in Bonaffini 1997, p. 410.
20. Gaio Fratini, 'Hymn to Perugia', trans. by Justin Vitiello, in Bonaffini 2001, p. 628.
21. Bonaffini 2001, p. 155.
22. Tòni Bodriè, 'Castle Resplendent with Stars', trans. by Justin Vitiello, in Bonaffini 2001, p. 157.
23. Luigi Trofa, 'My Husband Wrote to Me', trans. by Luigi Fontanella, in Bonaffini 1997, p. 143.
24. Ignazio Buttitta, 'I'm Not a Poet', trans. by Justin Vitiello, in Bonaffini 1997, p. 420.
25. Cosimo Savastano's, 'Breath and Stone', trans. by Anthony Molino, in Bonaffini 1997, p. 63.
26. Renzo Francescotti, 'Words Like a Shout', trans. by Rina Ferrarelli, in Bonaffini 2001, pp. 493–94.
27. Fernando Grignola, 'And So We're Here!', trans. by Gaetano Cipolla, in Bonaffini 2001, p. 63.
28. Marco Gal, 'Butterflies', trans. by John Shepley, in Bonaffini 2001, p. 108.
29. Roberto Giannoni, 'Time and Again I've Tried to Talk About Things', trans. by Michael Palma, in Bonaffini 2001, p. 281.
30. Franca Ronchi Francardi, 'Tongue of Fire', trans. by Justin Vitiello, in Bonaffini 2001, p. 634.
31. Dante Maffia, 'The Protagonists', 'A Stroll in the City', and 'Going by Your House', trans. by Luigi Bonaffini, in Bonaffini 1997, pp. 374–77.
32. Cosimo Savastano, 'Would that My Song Could Find Her', trans. by Anthony Molino, in Bonaffini 1997, p. 66.
33. Ernesto Calzavara, 'Mad Words', trans. by Dino Fabris, in Bonaffini 2001, p. 297.
34. Alfredo De Palchi, 'Who Me, Ashamed? Of This Three-dimensional', trans. by Sonia Raiziss, in Bonaffini and Perricone 2014, p. 1149; Luigi Fontanella, 'The Celestial City', trans. by Carol Lettieri and Irene Marchegiani, in Bonaffini and Perricone 2014, p. 1277; Nino Provenzano, 'There Will Always Be Emigrants', trans. by Nino Provenzano with Peter Carravetta, in Bonaffini and Perricone 2014, p. 1253; Orazio Tanelli, 'No-Man's-Land', trans. by Luigi Bonaffini and Peter Carravetta, in Bonaffini and Perricone 2014, p. 1165; Piero Salabè, 'Waking Brings No Response', trans. by Michael Palma, in Bonaffini and Perricone 2014, p. 955; Saro Marretta, 'Begging Tigers', trans. Adeodato Piazza Nicolai, in Bonaffini and Perricone 2014, p. 1029; Vittorio Fioravanti, 'Mediterannean Race', trans. by Elizabeth Pallitto, in Bonaffini and Perricone 2014, p. 1485; and Luigi Fontanella, 'Traveling', trans. by Carol Lettieri and Irene Marchegiani, in Bonaffini and Perricone 2014, p. 1267.
35. Sante Matteo, 'Italian Roots in Global Soil', in Bonaffini and Perricone 2014, pp. xi–xviii (pp. xii–xiii).
36. Loredana Bugliun, 'My Father the Madonna', trans. by Adeodato Piazza Nicolai, in Bonaffini and Perricone 2014, p. 687.
37. Ibid., p. 689.
38. Ermanno Minuto, 'Christmas 1960-Christmas 1987', trans. by Adria Bernardi, in Bonaffini and Perricone 2014, p. 339.
39. Ermanno Minuto, 'Nostalgia. Yes. Up to a Point', trans. by Adria Bernardi, in Bonaffini and Perricone 2014, p. 337.
40. Laura Marchig, 'Slavic Mother', trans. by Gil Fagiani, in Bonaffini and Perricone 2014, p. 707.
41. Bhabha, *The Location of Culture*, p. 247.

42. See Peter Carravetta's introductory essay to the US section of Bonaffini and Perricone 2014, pp. 1061–71 (p. 1066).
43. Peter Carravetta, 'The United States', in Bonaffini and Perricone 2014, pp. 1061–71 (p. 1066). Carravetta's opposition between 'language' and *langue* reflects the standard linguistic dichotomy between *langue* (abstract rules of a signifying system) and *parole* (speech, concrete use of language).
44. Joseph Tusiani, 'There is a Song', trans. by Luigi Bonaffini, in Bonaffini and Perricone 2014, p. 1091.
45. Joseph Tusiani, 'The Letter Never Sent', trans. by Luigi Bonaffini, in Bonaffini and Perricone 2014, p. 1085. For Carravetta's use of the expression 'psychic split', see p. 1074.
46. Fontanella, *Migrating Words*, p. 95.
47. Giose Rimanelli, 'Italy is a Long Country', trans. by Peter Carravetta, in Bonaffini and Perricone 2014, p. 1117–19.
48. Giose Rimanelli, 'Soft is Her Voice', trans. by Peter Carravetta, in Bonaffini and Perricone 2014, p. 1121.
49. Giose Rimanelli, 'Ballad of Joe Selimo', trans. by Peter Carravetta, in Bonaffini and Perricone 2014, p. 1125.
50. Joseph Tusiani, 'Song of the Bicentennial', in *Gente mia and Other Poems* (Stone Park, IL: Italian Cultural Center, 1978), p. 7.
51. Durante, 'Seven Points on Poetry of the Italian Diaspora', p. xx.
52. Ibid., p. xxi.
53. Brock 2012, p. xxxix.
54. Acetoso, 'Renato Poggioli's Intellectual Project and the Psychology of Exile', p. 143.
55. Matteo, 'Italian Roots in Global Soil', p. xvii.

PART V

❖

Diasporic Translation

CHAPTER 17

Translation as Migration: The Unfolding of a Metaphor

The link between translation and migration has become a commonplace in contemporary criticism. A discursive understanding of migration, in terms of 'mobility of texts, international transfer of knowledge, and transformation in the field of cultural literacy', is fundamental in order to appreciate this enigmatic yet intimate connection.[1] Inspired by recent studies in the field, this chapter will show that the translation-migration nexus is, by definition, metaphorical; it will also demonstrate that this nexus provides the diasporic editor, poet, and translator with a set of rhetorical tools, including translating strategies, that have hitherto remained uncharted.[2]

Translation and migration are related very closely, even more so than the pairings previously analysed (diaspora and the avant-garde, diaspora and the feminine, and diaspora and dialects); in fact, their agendas are so similar that they ultimately coincide. In order to illuminate this link, and despite different contexts and approaches, critics have insisted on a similar range of rhetorical (metaphor) and ideological tropes, including marginality, both societal and poetic, politics, and the ethics of translation. The most compelling study on the metaphorical aspects of translation is Reynolds's *The Poetry of Translation* (2011). Reynolds does not discuss diasporic metaphors directly; yet, he provides us with evidence of the impossibility of divorcing the process of translation from its creative energy. According to Reynolds, stylistic, thematic, and rhetorical aspects of source-texts can affect the ways in which they are themselves translated. 'All poem-translations,' he claims, 'take shape according to some distinguishable metaphor or metaphors, whether knowingly or not, [...] of which "translation as carrying across" — translation rigidly conceived — is only one'.[3] This means, for instance, that erotic texts may elicit erotic translations, just as diasporic texts may activate displacing, translatorly tools.

Time, as well as style, plays a role in translators' engagement with particular practices. There are historical reasons why some metaphors flourish more at some times than others and, therefore, it is not surprising that a global age such as ours has produced diasporic texts. In order to appraise the metaphorical correspondences that link the original to its translation, Reynolds introduces the concept of 'double of translation', which is his definition of the original vis-à-vis the foreign version.[4] When the 'creative interaction' between the source-texts and the way they are translated occurs, translation itself proves to be a kind of poetry: the 'poetics of translation', as Pound called it, or 'the poetry of translation', in Reynolds's words.

Reynolds also explored the link between translation and marginality. By quoting Sherry Simon's major work on *Gender in Translation* (1996), he pointed out that translation can be used as a metaphor to express 'the difficulty of access to language, of a sense of exclusion from the codes of the powerful'.[5] Thus, 'migrants strive to "translate" their past into the present', and women to '"translate themselves" into the language of patriarchy'.[6] Chapter 19 will elucidate this point by providing examples from relevant poetry anthologies.

Whereas Reynolds's study helps us to identify the presence of uprooting metaphors in the translation of migratory texts, Bhabha's *Location of Culture* allows us to consider the effects of the 'poetics of exile' on the split, diasporic subject, and on his/her community. A wellspring of inspiration for cultural historians and poets alike, this work is concerned with the 'emergence of the interstices — the overlap and displacement of domains of difference — [where] the intersubjective and collective experiences of *nationness*, community interest, or cultural value are negotiated'.[7] Exile and the nation, two concepts that equally concern the private and the public sphere, use the 'language of metaphor' in order to 'fill the void left in the uprooting of communities'. Bhabha goes on to say that 'metaphor, as the etymology of the word suggests, transfers the meaning of home and belonging, across the "middle passage", [...] across those distances, and cultural differences, that span the imagined community of the nation-people'.[8] Metaphor is a form of translation as well as of diaspora; the three terms transmute the sense of an original experience, be it the individual's home-country and/or the home-text.

Bhabha's idea of a 'third place', that is the transnational and translational hybrid where culture is both located and produced, has been crucial in dealing with each of the diasporic groups considered so far: avant-garde, female, and dialect poets. Bhabha's exilic thinking, however, is even more pertinent when applied directly to the analysis of poems in translation. In being both subject-centred and deterritorialised, Italian translated poets have become an ideal subject for the investigation of the diasporic postures of modern poets and translators. Strategies of mistranslation and eccentricity, as displayed by the translated poems examined in Chapter 19, epitomise the 'splitting of the national subject', or 'split in storytelling utterance', that lies at the core of Bhabha's reasoning.[9] If the subject is 'graspable only in the passage between telling/told, between "here" and "somewhere else"', then the nation (Italy, the US) 'speaks its disjunctive narrative', one of uncertainty, delay, and cultural difference.[10] The subject-nation, diasporically conceived, is 'dialogical or transferential'; it is created:

> Through the locus of the Other which suggests both that the object of identification is ambivalent, and, more significantly, that the agency of identification is never pure or holistic but always constituted in a process of substitution, displacement or projection.[11]

Bhabha's concept of 'cultural difference' is an elaboration of Walter Benjamin's idea of the 'foreignness of languages'. In 'The Task of the Translator' (1923), Benjamin defended translation's alienating force, thus initiating a literal, unidiomatic practice. In turning to the principle of 'literalness with freedom' (his proposed criterion for any translation exercise), Benjamin saw in the interlinear version of the Bible a 'prototype or ideal' of translation altogether.[12] As they urge us to question critics' dominant line of interpretation, most of the poem-translations analysed in Chapter 19 privilege the literal as opposed to the idiomatic, thus fostering the idea that diasporic texts call for deviant, unnatural solutions. This is possible because, in the act of translation, content and language diverge (scatter), so that all 'cultural languages' become 'foreign, [diasporic images of] themselves'.[13] From this stylistic perspective, the foreignness of languages can be defined as the 'nucleus of the untranslatable', that is the linguistic, metaphorical, and translatorly counterpart to the poetry of diaspora.[14]

Notes to Chapter 17

1. Ewa Kołodziejczyk, 'Editor's Foreword', in *Open Cultural Studies: Migration and Translation*, ed. by Ewa Kołodziejczyk (2017) <https://www.degruyter.com/dg/page/migration-translation/open-cultural-studies-migration-and-translation> [accessed 20 October 2020].
2. See: Loredana Polezzi, 'Translation and Migration', *Translation Studies*, 3 (2013), 345–68; and Moira Inghillieri, *Translation and Migration* (London: Routledge, 2016).
3. Reynolds, *The Poetry of Translation: From Chaucer & Petrarch to Homer & Logue* (Oxford: Oxford University Press, 2011), pp. 6–7.
4. Ibid., p. 7.
5. Reynolds, *The Poetry of Translation*, pp. 8–9. Sherry Simon, *Gender in Translation: Cultural Identity and the Politics of Transmission* (London: Routledge, 1996).
6. Reynolds, *The Poetry of Translation*, pp. 8–9.
7. Bhabha, *The Location of Culture*, p. 2.
8. Ibid., p. 200.
9. Ibid., pp. 211, 231.
10. Ibid., pp. 231–32.
11. Ibid., p. 233.
12. Walter Benjamin, 'The Task of the Translator', in *Illuminations*, ed. and with an introduction by Hannah Arendt (New York: Harcourt, Brace & World, 1968), pp. 69–82 (p. 82). This essay was written in 1921 and first published as an introduction to Harry Zohn's translation of Baudelaire's *Tableaux parisiens* in 1923.
13. Bhabha, *The Location of Culture*, pp. 234–35.
14. Ibid., p. 234.

CHAPTER 18

❖

The Translator's Visibility: Loci of Difference

'In the Margins of Anglophone Poetries': After Venuti

Benjamin's notion of the foreignness of languages is also key to Venuti's history and theory of translation. In his seminal work, *The Translator's Invisibility* (1995), Venuti argued that the history of literary translation in the English language has been one of fluency. Translators renounced their authority (invisibility), effaced their 'manipulation of the translating language' (transparency), and adopted a plain, standard idiom (domestication). A fluent translation is therefore 'written in English that is current ("modern") instead of archaic, [...] widely used instead of specialized ("jargonisation"), [...] standard instead of colloquial ("slangly")', and so on and so forth. Conversely, when 'foreign words or English words and phrases imprinted by a foreign language ("pidgin")' are not avoided but embraced, we practice a form of translation that Venuti has defined as 'foreignization'.[1]

As confirmed by the marginal poets analysed here, 'foreignizing translation in English can be a form of resistance against ethnocentrism and racism, cultural narcissism and imperialism'.[2] According to Venuti, although domestication and foreignisation 'do not establish a neat binary opposition that can simply be superimposed on "fluent" and "resistant" discursive strategies', the two terms 'indicate fundamentally *ethical* attitudes towards a foreign text and culture'. He specifies that these dissident attitudes vary with 'cultural situations and historical moments', as what is foreignising in one translation project may not be so in another one.[3] As a result, foreignising translation suggests a feeling of 'underlying sympathy' between the author and the translator — a form of diasporic identification, a sharing of experiences and values — that allows the latter to 'become [...] an immigrant [...] in relation to [his/her] own language'.[4]

Thanks to its diasporic resonances, foreignisation can be used to justify the poetics of marginality that has inspired the translation of Italian poetry in the US. My idea of an Italian, foreignised canon seems in contradiction with Venuti's argument, according to which the canon of translated literature into English is a domesticated one. Venuti maintained that the figure of an 'English-ed' Montale has hitherto dominated the Anglophone scene, whereas experimental poets from Italy remained 'remarkably underrepresented'. For him, 'Montale's canonical status [...]

rests on his translators' assimilation of his poetry to [the postromantic], mainstream poetics', one that has proclaimed the poet's authoritative, unified, and hence neither split nor marginal subjectivity.[5]

My argument builds upon, and nuances, Venuti's view rather than opposing it. Venuti is right in asserting that Italian texts were 'rewritten to conform to styles and themes that *currently* prevail[ed] in domestic literature' (here 'domestic' refers to American culture), revealing in this way 'exclusions and admissions, centres and peripheries that deviate from those current in the foreign language'.[6] At the same time, however, it is important to note that these themes (religious, confessional, migratory tropes) and styles (e.g., avant-garde poetry) were equally perceived as marginal in America, a fact that problematises any clear-cut distinction between domesticating and foreignising perspectives. Moreover, if it is true that translations of Italian poetry into English 'have reasserted the importance of the authenticity of the lyrical voice (even when arguing in favour of maintaining the experimental potential to it)', they have also brought to the fore 'the complex and often paradoxical ways in which personality, identity and nation are ideologically interconnected'.[7] This is particularly evident in the case of the diasporic, translated subject, who epitomises not only the condition of the translated self, but also that of the national writer in the age of globalisation, a compelling example of this being offered by transnational dialect poetry (see Chapter 16). On the basis of these considerations, I argue that the Italian diasporic canon is a doubly foreignised entity: because it deviates from the dominant, aesthetic values of its target culture; and because it expresses these values in a non-standard language.

The ways in which the Italian canon was shaped and translated in the US are therefore concordant. To a dissident, diasporic canon there corresponds a dissident, diasporic language and imagery. Venuti himself observed that 'a translator can signal the foreignness of the foreign text, not only by using a discursive strategy that deviates from prevailing discourses [...], but also by choosing to translate a text that challenges the contemporary canon'.[8] This horizontal reading of literary canons, which Poggioli called 'active tradition', has been defined as 'symptomatic' by Venuti and 'performative' by Bhabha, further evidence of the correspondences between translation and canonicity on the one hand, and among different conceptions of diaspora on the other.[9]

Such an idea of translation as anthologisation, and vice versa, was already key to the modernist poetics, which motivated 'appropriations of various archaic and foreign poetries to serve modernist cultural agendas in English'.[10] Whereas modernist writing was made canonical, modernist translation has remained marginal, so much so that today's practice 'bears little sign of these developments'.[11] Through the recovery of Pound's poetics of translation, and in line with this study's critical angle, the next section will argue, instead, that the principles of modernist translation (creativity, literality, heterogeneity, and experimentalism) lie in fact at the core of the rewriting of Italian lyric in America.

The Locus of Difference: Poundian Translation and the Diasporic Paradigm

Diasporic translation, just like the canon to which it gave shape, found its roots in the figure of Pound whose understanding of translation as original poetry has mainly been discussed as an exercise in domestication.[12] However, if translation is conceived in terms of semantic equipollence, i.e. as a transfer of the original's content, then the authori(ali)ty of translation is put to the test, and so is the foreign aura that it entails. Recent criticism has tackled this issue by placing an ever-increasing emphasis on the role played by questions of difference, marginality, and alterity in Poundian translation. Two important cases in point are Daniel Katz's *American Modernism's Expatriate Scene* (2007) and Claro's doctoral thesis 'Ezra Pound's Poetics of Translation'.[13] According to these critics, Pound regarded the task of the translation in a Benjaminian way:

> Not solely or primarily as a transmission of information, [...] (it is only the 'bad' translation of philologists which does so, systematically negating the relation with the foreign under its disguise of 'exactness'), but as a transfer of procedures of signification, of the poetic ways of charging language, which is what assures the irruption of a strong difference.[14]

Pound put to use this residue of foreignness by exploring two seemingly antipodal techniques of translation: literalness (see his Cavalcanti versions) and transcreation, or creative translation, as in his famous *Homage to Sextus Propertius.*[15] Both literalness and transcreation produce an alienating effect on the reader, who does not expect to read a text that is unidiomatic and/or unfaithful. Moreover, these practices both result in forms of deviation from the norm, be it the standard English language or the original.

These two Poundian translating modes have been constantly and variously active in the English renditions of Italian lyric produced in the US in the past seventy years. By virtue of their Poundian inheritance and foreignising effects, I call these Italian-into-English translations diasporic (for a presentation of diasporic translation's subcategories see Chapter 19). Far from being mere reflections of the canon they embody, translations shape this canon in a decisive way. They are, in a sense, this canon's *raison d'être* rather than its linguistic surface. The centrality of translation within the rhetoric of the diasporic is justified by the fact that avant-garde, female, and dialect poets from Italy were 'carried across' according to similar translating patterns. Reaching beyond their undeniable specificities, they operated as a single diasporic unit.

Pound honoured the visibility of translation. If we agree with him that translation is an act of criticism, then the criteria for translation deserve at least as much attention as those relating to selection. This task is made ever more difficult by the fact that various, often contradictory, translatorly forces are at play not only in each anthology, but also within the same poem. When looking at our anthological corpus, we are confronted with a spectrum of possibilities that is potentially infinite: from Burnshaw's degree zero prose renditions in BURNSHAW 1960 to Lowell's and Vitiello's transcreations.[16] Although foreignisation is an overarching technique in diasporic anthologies, domestication often worked as a counterweight, especially in

Poggioli's early collections. In translating Ungaretti's 'I Have Lost All' (POGGIOLI 1947A), John Conley attenuated some of the original's lexical poignancy while also levelling out its syntactical twists (domestication , examples of which are marked in bold): 'non potrò mai più | **smemorarmi** in un grido' / 'and never may I more | **lose myself** in tears'.[17] See also:

la vita non mi è più,
arrestata in fondo alla gola,
che una roccia di gridi.

life to me is
no more now
than a rock of cries
massed at
the pit of the throat.[18]

At the same time, Conley foreignised the poem, both by charging it emotionally ('gridi' becomes 'tears') and by creating new semantic associations based on his own metaphorical reading. For instance, 'arrestata' becomes 'massed', justified by the image of the rock. A similar translation procedure, whereby the translator used synecdoche or metonymy, is visible in the poem's final lines: 'ed eccomi perduto | **in infinito delle notti'** translated as 'and behold me lost | **in the infinite nights**'.[19]

Just to add to the complexity of the situation, editors may or may not specify their adopted translation criteria. If they do so, they discuss them in the anthology's introduction, or in an appropriate editor's and/or translator's note. Discussions of the translation process are rare; Poggioli, who dedicated one of his most famous essays to the advantages of creative translation, edited three anthologies without directly dealing with the topic. Similarly, Bonaffini, a key figure in dialect poetry's anthologisation, examines translation possibilities in his essays rather than in his collections. The only meaningful exception to this trend is a sentence placed at the end of the editor's note in BONAFFINI 1997. 'The anthology,' Bonaffini wrote, 'strives to present dialect poetry in translations that are of the same quality as those that accompany poetry in standard Italian, as a further reaffirmation of the fundamental concept that good poetry can be written in any language'.[20]

Whether they were incorporated in the anthologies' paratextual apparatus or published elsewhere, the editors' ideas on the issue of translation gravitated around the two, Poundian poles mentioned before: creative translation and foreignisation. In 'The Added Artificer', Poggioli assumed that 'translation is an interpretative art' that 'endeavours to give the verbal composition a strange clothing, a changed body, and a novel spirit (exoticism)'.[21] In their note 'On Translation', placed after the introduction to BLUM AND TRUBOWITZ 2001, Blum and Trubowitz admitted that, in order to:

> Remain in contact with each poem, [they] had to draw away from it, focusing not on the ways in which individual words transferred from Italian into English, but on how images, cultural allusions, meter, and rhyme moved, or, as was often the case, failed to move from one language to another.[22]

A further expression of their foreignising practice is given by instances of literalness, mistranslation, and contact between the languages, whereby they allowed 'Italian syntax to seep into the English sentence structure'.[23] This approach to translation is clearly diasporic as it celebrates the mobility of both texts and people. The translator-editors are respectively a native speaker of Italian and of English; they conceived their project half-way between Italy and the US, both literally and metaphorically, as if it sprang from the moving waters of the Atlantic Ocean: 'we began this project hoping to make our leaps without getting too wet', but 'it was often in the moments of tripping, of getting our feet wet, that the pleasure of translation arose'.[24] In BRADSHAW 1971, another woman, the editor-translator herself, staged the foreignness of the translated texts from the 'use of "difficult", esoteric terms or neologisms' to 'dislocated' syntax.[25]

Bonaffini's and Brock's reflections are slightly more elaborated, but still comparable to these statements. First of all, when turning to dialect poetry, Bonaffini advocates the necessity of trilingual translation, which is used as an intensifier for the foreignness of languages. Unlike Miller Williams, who noted that every dialect 'is merely the natural way of speaking for people who speak dialect', Bonaffini defends dialects' subversive force.[26] 'Dialect,' he claims:

> Is by nature a distinct and marginal language with respect to a standard language, and all speakers of dialect consider it such, that is, they are conscious of speaking a language which in some way is in opposition to another.[27]

In a sort of sympathetic transmigration, the speakers' awareness becomes that of the translator. This explains why, in Bonaffini's anthologies, dialect poetry not only manifests its diversity in the presence of both the standard and the target language, but also very rarely lends itself to slang, vernacular, or ethnographic translations.

BROCK 2012 is inspired by the principle of creative translation. 'Two Tunnels', Brock's essay on translation which follows the anthology's introduction, makes two important points in this respect. Firstly, translation is 'not a simple transposition, but a re-creation' insofar as the act of translation is 'an instance of metaphor-making' (Reynolds).[28] Brock conceives of poetry translation as a kind of reincarnation, which is a clear elaboration of Benjamin's pioneering essay and mystical views. The second point made by Brock in this essay is one of estrangement. The original and its translation will never coincide, but two poems (or tunnels, if we borrow Attipate Ramanujan's image used by Brock) are better than one; in Brock's own words, they are in fact 'the best we can hope for'.[29] Following up on his argument, he claimed that 'any notion of fidelity must therefore include an understanding of the kinds of liberties necessary to find poetry in the translation'. 'Translators,' he continues, 'must always be listening *as poets* to their own translations, even while listening *as translators* to the original'.[30] This idea encouraged Brock to include, among his translators, many English-speaking poets, such as Pound, Samuel Beckett, Robert Fitzgerald, Allen Ginsberg, Seamus Heaney, Ted Hughes, and Geoffrey Hill. Their presence may be seen 'as a partial survey of the engagement of Anglophone poets with their twentieth-century Italian counterparts' and, therefore, as a further proof of Italian poetry's diasporic dimension.[31]

In negotiating Italian 'tone, mood, imagery, story, logic [and even] motion', American editors invalidated Venuti's concerns over the translator's invisibility by providing us with a canon that challenges the idea of a fluent, domesticated regime.[32] Through, and beyond, its editors' declarations, the translated Italian canon speaks for itself. Its language is an echo of Pound's theory of translation, whose diasporic implications it exacerbates. Sound over meaning, ultra-close versions, formal freedom, deletion, exaggeration, distortion, topical allusions, homophones, all Pound's techniques are at work in this diasporic output.[33]

Notes to Chapter 18

1. Venuti, *The Translator's Invisibility*, p. 4.
2. Ibid., p. 16.
3. Ibid., p. 20.
4. Ibid., p. 237.
5. Ibid., pp. 240, 242.
6. Ibid., p. 67.
7. Caselli, 'Value and Authority in Anthologies of Italian Poetry in English (1956–1992)', p. 67.
8. Venuti, *The Translator's Invisibility*, p. 125.
9. Ibid., p. 21; Bhabha, *The Location of Culture*, p. 208.
10. Venuti, *The Translator's Invisibility*, p. 164.
11. Ibid.
12. Steven Yao, *Translation and the Languages of Modernism: Gender, Politics, Language* (New York: Palgrave Macmillan, 2002).
13. Daniel Katz, *American Modernism's Expatriate Scene: The Labour of Translation* (Edinburgh: Edinburgh University Press); and Claro, 'Ezra Pound's Poetics of Translation'.
14. Claro, 'Ezra Pound's Poetics of Translation', p. 231.
15. See John Sullivan, *Ezra Pound and Sextus Propertius: A Study in Creative Translation* (London: Faber & Faber, 1965); and *Creative Constraints*, ed. by Wilson and Gerber.
16. See Robert Lowell, *Imitations, 1917–1977* (London: Faber & Faber, 1961).
17. Giuseppe Ungaretti, 'I Have Lost All', trans. by John Conley, in Poggioli 1947a, p. 13 (the use of bold here is mine).
18. Ibid.
19. Ibid.
20. Luigi Bonaffini, 'Editor's Note', in Bonaffini 1997, p. 12.
21. Poggioli, 'The Added Artificer', p. 355.
22. Cinzia Sartini Blum and Lara Trubowitz, 'On Translation', in Blum and Trubowitz 2001, pp. li–liv (p. li).
23. Ibid., p. lii.
24. Ibid., p. liii.
25. Bradshaw 1971, p. vii.
26. Cited in Bonaffini, 'Translating Dialect Literature', p. 283.
27. Ibid., p. 283.
28. Geoffrey Brock, 'Two Tunnels: A Note on Translation', in Brock 2012, pp. xli–iii (p. xlii).
29. Ibid., p. xliii.
30. Ibid., p. xlii.
31. Ibid., p. xliii.
32. Ibid., p. xlii.
33. For an analysis of Pound's translatorly techniques see Ronnie Apter, *Digging for the Treasure: Translation after Pound* (New York: Peter Lang, 1984).

CHAPTER 19

❖

Forms of Diasporic Translation: Transliterality, Erraticness, and Multilingualism

This chapter provides examples of diasporic translation. Given the number of anthologies examined in this book (including the extremely high number of translators involved), a detailed scrutiny of the translation criteria of each individual anthology would be unrealistic. BROCK 2012, for instance, features seventy-three poets and one hundred and forty-seven translators, as one poet is translated by more than one translator. Instead of offering an exhaustive review of the situation, my analysis aims to discuss the most typical techniques of translation through the consideration of target samples. In the book so far, I have explored the contexts of publication and the role of individuals; now I want to illustrate trends in translation strategies in this corpus of diasporic Italian poetry anthologies. Considered as a whole, these anthologies are hospitable to certain methods, whoever is doing the translating; as a result, the anthologies offer their readers not only instances of poetry, but also instances of modes of translation. By bundling them all together, I am wary of the risk of downplaying the agency and circumstances of individual translators as well as of different editorial, historical, and cultural contexts. Yet, I believe that the focus on fragments (syntagms, lines, and sections), rather than on full poems, reflects the poems' essentially dislocated nature, thus mapping this changing landscape of poetry in transition in a reliable way. It also conforms to the principle of kaleidoscopic reading adopted throughout the book.

The corpus of American anthologies selected for study in this chapter, eighteen titles in total, merges two anthological groups: some of the key collections that shaped the reception of Italian lyric and that have been analysed in this volume; and a number of anthologies which, without featuring prominently here, confirm and reinforce the diasporic paradigm. Table 19.1 illustrates our primary materials (left-hand column). The right-hand column records the presence of multiple (M) or single (S) translators. In the case of multiple translators, the number is given between parentheses; in the case of single translators, often the editor/s themselves, I give the name. For a full list of the translators, accompanied by the poets they translated, see the Appendix 3.1.

Table 19.1. List of examined anthologies with an indication of single or multiple translators

Anthology	Translator(s)
Poggioli 1947a	M (4)
Poggioli 1948	M (2)
Caetani 1950	S (William Weaver)
De Palchi 1961	M (8)
De Palchi 1966a	M (22)
De Palchi 1966b	M (19)
Bradshaw 1971	S (Vittoria Bradshaw)
Feldman and Swann 1979	M (30)
Smith 1981	S (Lawrence Smith)
Allen 1986	S (Muriel Kittel)
Bonaffini 1997	M (11)
Bonaffini 1999	M (7)
Bonaffini 2001	M (8)
Blum and Trubowitz 2001	M (2)
Condini 2009	S (Ned Condini)
Brock 2012	M (147)
Bonaffini and Perricone 2014	M (40)
Montorfani 2014	M (29)

As far as the translators' profiles are concerned, I would like to highlight a recurring phenomenon, that is the conflation of different professional figures into one, the poet, the editor, and the translator often being the same person. As a result, many of the anthologists analysed feature as translators in the work of other editors (Bonaffini himself, for example, translates Campana and Sereni in Brock 2012); similarly, American poets have either edited (Ned Condini, Guenther, Corman, Burnshaw, Brock) or translated (Pound, Moore, Stefanile, Vitiello) for an anthology of Italian lyric. It is important to stress that Weaver, Bergin, Bonaffini, Feldman, Guenther, Raiziss, and Vangelisti, who are amongst the most frequent translators in the corpus, are anthologists themselves (see Appendix 3.3).

I have identified three categories, or types, of diasporic translation: (i) transliteral, i.e. a form of literal translation conceived and practiced in a transnational context; (ii) erratic, a development of the Poundian concept of transcreation; and (iii) multilingual. Each type may present subcategories therein; so, erratic translation can assume an intensified, metaphorical, or properly erroneous form, just as the multilingual type contemplates the use of neologisms, or the insertion of a third (or fourth, fifth...) language. Some of the types may work in synergy; for instance, transvisuality, the translation technique used for avant-garde visual texts, is a combination of transliterality and multilingualism (see Chapter 20). Similarly, transliterality can contemplate forms of error. And yet, despite this vast array of solutions, the three main practices share common motivations and results, as they underline the foreignness of the original in a complementary fashion.

Transliterality

This section deals with the first kind of diasporic translation, that is transliterality. This practice consists in a faithful reproduction of the source text with foreignising effects on the English-speaking reader. Strict adherence to the original can be pursued structurally, phonetically, morphologically (through the insertion of neologisms and/or foreign words), and, more often, syntactically; yet, the result is never a static reproduction. The language of the poem-translation happens to be a fictional hybrid; although it uses English words, it sounds unnatural to the native reader, thus performing its displacing function. This composite language, half-English and half-Italian, is a vivid expression of Bhabha's idea of the third place, as well as a powerful metaphor for diasporic poetics *tout court*. The prefix 'trans-', with which I characterise this particular mode of literal-diasporic translation, highlights therefore both its transnational origins and responses.

Weaver, by far the most popular translator of contemporary Italian literature into English (see Appendix 3.3), is an heir of Pound's diasporic, literary renditions (especially from the Provençal and of Cavalcanti), which are a model for this approach. The editor of several anthologies, both in prose and poetry (the latter published in the UK), Weaver translated major Italian novelists (Italo Calvino, Umberto Eco, Luigi Pirandello, Gadda, and Svevo), poets (Montale, Quasimodo, Ungaretti) and librettos (Giacomo Puccini, Giuseppe Verdi) throughout his fifty-year-long career. He was also an anthologist of literature in translation. Together with Archibald Colquhoun, he edited the 1963 poetry issue of *The London Magazine, Italy 1963*; in addition, he was the editor of a prose anthology entitled *Open City: Seven Writers in Postwar Rome* (1999).[1] His translations feature in Poggioli's anthologies, and CAETANI 1950 used Weaver as the sole translator. Weaver's transliteral translations often renounce rhyme schemes in favour of more faithful lexical choices. At the same time, the loss of rhyming couplets is counteracted by the stressing of alliterating phonemes in the English translation: 'Dunque toccami il cuore; gli occhi no, non la mente | non la lingua insolente, la bocca ove m'ascondo'/ 'Touch my heart then, not the eyes, the mind, | the insolent tongue, the mouth wherein I hide'.[2] Occasionally, Weaver modifies the punctuation or the semantics of certain words, a trait that problematises his poetics of literalness; see, for instance, the different ways in which he translates the key, invariable word *funicolare* in Caproni's homonymous poem ('fluent cable', 'muted harp', 'ark', 'boat').[3] After Weaver, this complex, often contradictory, understanding of literalness, whereby the original is not simply reproduced but also altered, became a crucial aspect in the translation of Italian poetry into English.

If it is true that examples of transliterality traverse the entire anthological corpus considered here, they are particularly striking in translations of women's and avant-garde poems. Whereas in the first case literality conveys female writers' sense of 'permanent strangeness', in the second case the same strategy, often combined with multilingualism, is employed in order to enhance the avant-garde's metaliterary dimensions.[4] The privilege of looking at poetry, and language, in the very process of its creation is a constituent feature of the diasporic canon. Just as the experience of migration shaped the anthologies' selections, translation reveals to us the inner mechanisms of exilic language. With this in mind, the following samples will concentrate on poetry written and/or translated by women, and on the combination of literal and multilingual approaches in the translation of avant-garde texts.

Despite Weaver's seminal role as a diasporic-literal translator, it is only with Allen 1986 that transliterality became a systematic trait in the translation of modern Italian poetry. As José Santaemilia reminds us, 'translation is an archetypically "feminine" activity'; it is therefore not accidental that 'the intersection between translation (which is contradictory and multiple per se — subservient and subversive at the same time) and gender/sex' makes possible phenomena such as the reconceptualisation of original and copy, fidelity and betrayal.[5] In the passage from one language to the other, transliterality aims to preserve women poets' original voice as well as the sense of alienation associated with it.

Whereas transliterality is mainly a matter of syntax, forms of erroneous translation are most often linked to the lexis. This is the case not only in Allen's anthology, but in diasporic anthologies in general. Yet, the distinction between literal solutions and semantic divergences (which can also be seen as forms of unidiomatic expressions or errors) is not clear-cut, especially since certain terms, such as *patria* or *madrelingua*, can be translated both in literal and deviant, or even defiant, ways. Similarly, the syntactical calque of the originals may result in forms of semantic ambiguity, with the logical subject placed ungrammatically after the object: 'Quel gran problema scioglierà la morte'/ 'That great problem death will solve'.[6] Kittel, a co-editor of Allen 1986 and the translator of most of its poems, made use of transliterality through the adoption of a twisting English syntax. This allowed her to imitate the movements of the Italian sentences on the one hand, and to navigate women's sense of estrangement on the other. In these poem-translations, both punctuation and the enjambments are faithfully reproduced:

> Molte volte novembre è ritornato
> Nella mia vita, e questo che oggi ha inizio
> Non è il peggiore: quieto.
>
> Many times November has come back
> Into my life, and the one starting today
> Is not the worst: peaceful.[7]

Occasionally, Kittel's English renditions resort to forms of hypercorrection deriving from the over-application of the principle of literalness (the use of bold hereafter is mine): 'Ma poi lo so già tornerà a spendere il sole | sui **petti rossi dei pettirossi**' ['But then I know the sun will come back to shine again | on the **red breasts of the robin-redbreasts**'.[8]

Transliteral practices continued in and dominated Bradshaw 1971. In the introduction to this almost eight-hundred-page anthology, the female editor-translator explains that the difficult Italian style is preserved at the expense of an artificial 'uniform simplicity'.[9] This sense of heterogeneity is visible, again, in the use of syntactical fragmentation, reached both through subordination and inversions, a style that turned the language of Italian lyric into a foreignising code, as here:

e forse il letto
e la morte meditate
piangendo.

and maybe the bed
and death meditated
by weeping.[10]

Further examples include: 'e lui, già cittadino, non lo vogliono'/ 'and him, already a citizen, they don't want';[11] 'il tocco di solitudine | che ogni cosa in sé custodiva ed a noi rendeva, liberando'/ 'the touch of solitude | Each thing in itself kept and to us rendered, freeing'.[12]

Blum and Trubowitz 2001, which also features women poets, editors, and translators, presents similar translating patterns seeking 'an intimate but not mimetic' relationship with the originals.[13] The editors' translations play around with the position of adjectives, prepositions, and verbs, thus challenging grammatical hierarchies. The reader's patriarchal and/or literary expectations are unsettled, as shown by the following series of inversions: 'Ancora peggio è l'anima'/ 'Worse still is my soul';[14] 'Buio miele che odori'/ 'Dark honey fragrant';[15] 'Lunga è stata la frangia di quel tempo | e fitti i nodi che non so sbrogliare'/ 'Long has been the fringe of that time | and thick the knots I can't untangle';[16] 'Allegri e mesti erano i ricordi'/ 'Happy and mournful were the memories';[17] 'parli di | di soluzioni radicali'/ 'you speak of | of radical solutions'.[18]

Together with multilingualism, explored later in this chapter, transliterality is also a key practice in the translation of avant-garde verse. This is true both for comprehensive and thematic anthologies, which share the challenge of translating the neo-avant-garde's idiosyncratic language. In Bradshaw 1971, Sanguineti's words are meticulously transposed from the Italian to the English, as if played on a well-tuned keyboard:

Ellie tenue corpo di peccaminose escrescenze
che possiamo roteare
e rivolgere e odorare e adorare nel tempo
desiderantur (essi).

Ellie tenuous body of sinful excrescences
which we can rotate
and revolve and savor and adore in time
desiderantur (they).[19]

The Latin passive indicative, 'desiderantur' [they are desired], by remaining unchanged, adds a further linguistic layer to the poem-melody. The sense of a perfect correspondence, however, is only apparent, as the phonic and semantic transplantation has an alienating effect to both the Italian and the American ear. Very much in the style of the Italian neo-avant-garde, this poem is in fact a strident meditation on the philosophy of language and the possibilities of desire, conducted through similarly convoluted images.

Future anthologies of the Italian avant-garde, both comprehensive and thematic, explored the potential of literal translation further. FELDMAN AND SWANN 1979 opens with Balestrini's 'The Instinct of Preservation', an avant-garde hymn to the fragility, rather than the magnificence, of species. Preservation appears to offer a double-edged language, able to describe both life and death conditions on earth; it is a way of demystifying our own idiosyncrasies by acknowledging them verbally. In this scenario, literalness is a form of conservation just like instinct is:

> Qui conta come (può un pesce vivere
> a lungo sulla sabbia secca? Dormire
> senza cuscino?) la vita dell'uomo è
> tutta un tentativo (non ne ho la minima
> idea, non sono mai stato così triste).
>
> The story's about (can a fish live
> long on dry sand? sleep without
> a pillow?) man's life is all
> an attempt (I don't have the slightest
> idea, I've never felt sadder).[20]

It is interesting to notice how the practice of transliterality is taken to its extremes in Smith's almost contemporaneous translation. Nonetheless, here a major lexical change occurs, as the adjective *triste*, translated as 'depressed', assumes a medical connotation:

> What matters here is (can a fish live
> for long on dry sand? Sleep
> without a pillow?) man's life is
> just an attempt (I don't have the least idea
> about it, I've never been so depressed).[21]

BALLERINI 1978, SMITH 1981, and SPATOLA AND VANGELISTI 1982 all present a vast selection of avant-garde poems translated literally. The multilingual halo of the original is kept, with the non-Italian and non-English insertions remaining unchanged, as poems take the form of a vertiginous tower of Babel:

> è soltanto essere (sein) ma essere
> [...]
> être à l'égard d'être
> être c'est montrer
> être impassible pour connaître l'être tel qu'il est
> [...]
> ÊTRES AUTRES.
>
> it is only being (sein) but to be
> [...]
> être à l'égard d'être
> être c'est montrer

> être impassible pour connaître l'être tel qu'il est
> [...]
> ÊTRES AUTRES.[22]

Similarly, '(e allora, | anche, *onze, rue Payenne*)'/ '(and then, | as well, *onze, rue Payenne*)',[23] and:

> les lèvres
> aveugles
> devenues.[24]

In these instances of translingual fidelity, where different languages are layered, it is interesting to observe how poets and translators highlighted the presence of foreign verse and/or words; they did so either by avoiding their translation (see the last, French example) or by keeping, and/or resorting to, the use of italics. Sometimes, foreign expressions are normalised, as happens in the following poem by Rosselli:

> passato il tempo in cui nello *slip*
> ti guardavi contenta, accontentata
> d'un umore qualsiasi
> *follie-bergères* dietro ogni
> mobile, spostabile definitivamente
> ogni mattina.
>
> time past when you looked at yourself
> happily in the slip, satisfied
> by just any old whim
> *folies-bergères* behind every
> piece of furniture, definitively moveable
> every morning.[25]

Female, multilingual poets, such as Rosselli and Niccolai, were privileged not only for embodying the poetics of the diasporic, but also for their original contribution to the avant-garde. Dedicated to her friend and colleague Villa, Niccolai's 'E.V. Ballad' performs a composite, experimental language mixing Italian, English, French, German, and neologisms of various sorts; the resultant compound reveals the magmatic and disconcerting nature of exilic verse:

> *Ev*ening and the *Everest*
> ist vers la poetry learning er
> [...]
> Ça au national park
> But all america la calzi
> come un guanto zeus rabelais.[26]

Alongside multilingualism, the use of neologisms plays a crucial role in the English renderings of Italian avant-garde poems. This type of literal translation, springing from the coinage of foreignising words in the two languages, results in the annihilation of their distance. This is visible not only in the thematic anthologies of the 1970s and 1980s, but also in most recent collections; see, for example, Fontanella's creative grammar as presented by MONTORFANI 2014: 'fa che questo momento | si faccia **tuttotempo**'/ 'let this moment | become **alltime**'.[27] As Pound himself conceived it, literal translation is therefore the opposite of mundane and/or pedantic imitation. As these examples have shown, it is in fact a springboard for the transformation of the original, first transposed and then reshaped in the suspended territory of the diasporic.

Erraticness

The words 'erratic' and 'error' have the same etymological root. The Latin verb *errāre*, from which they both derive, means 'to wander' in its literal form and 'to be mistaken', or to err, in its metaphorical one; therefore, they both express a sense of deviation from the norm, be it a 'conduct, habit, or opinion' (*OED*). On the basis of their etymological quintessence, I have called the second kind of diasporic translation 'erratic' because it retains this double dimension, diasporic and irregular at once.

The history of literary translation is one of mistakes, more or less deliberate. Yet, as Reynolds observes, 'translation errors, or mere differences, do not matter much in themselves. Their effects depend on their interpretation and use'.[28] Reynolds's view is corroborated by Pym's distinction between 'error' and 'mistake' whereby, in any translated text, 'mistake only becomes error when the difference between equivalence and mistranslation assumes a non-trivial meaning on its own'. Pym warns us that 'criticism has to be very careful when invoking apparently immutable rules' since 'there are many ways of translating, many things that can be said through translation, and bad explicit theorization is apt to do more harm than is mere poverty on the level of practice'.[29] From this perspective, there is no such a thing as a right, or wrong, poem-translation; mistranslations of the source text can be in fact foreignising renditions taking on board the original's eccentric potential.

This critical angle, based on the study of the interaction between these two different yet complementary spheres, the erroneous and the erratic, is new to the field of translation studies. So far, error theory has concentrated on moral philosophers, such as David Hume, Bertrand Russell, and Ludwig Wittgenstein, and specific authors, such as James Joyce, but there does not seem to be an analysis of the role of mistakes in translated literature.[30] This absence is particularly surprising if one considers that translation has long been defined as the art of failure and loss, i.e. the perfect counterpart to a theory of mistakes. By looking at the functions of translation-errors, broadly conceived, this section aims to be a pragmatic exploration of the potential of error theory when applied to the study of diasporic translation.

An evolution of Pound's principle of creative translation, erraticness is an extremely varied subcategory, the site where the metaphoric potential of both diaspora and translation comes to the fore. By exploiting the original's supply of eccentric images, it encompasses all forms of infidelity, distortion, and exaggeration inherent in it. Among the roles that it enacts, erraticness works as an intensifier of certain impressions and ideas, but it also takes the form of a rhetorical reconfiguration, a semantic transformation, a betrayal of the punctuation, a lacuna, a temporal and/or spatial shift, or an actual mistake. This range of possibilities is justified by the fact that translators of different approaches and generations variously contributed to the transplantation of Italian lyric into the American domain; what strikes one most, however, is the ultimate consistency of their choices. Whereas transliterality was a common translatorly strategy in avant-garde and female poetry, erraticness is present across all anthological genres. It is particularly interesting to notice how errors, broadly defined, have been methodologically employed by translators of dialect poetry as a way of responding to the difficulty of transposing it into English.

Erraticness insists on the themes that are proper to diasporic poetry (religion, metaliterature, politics, mourning, and the body) by using them as a platform for metaphoric transpositions. Thus, different semantic clusters may be enhanced in accordance with the source poem's peculiar texture. The American translated canon of Italian lyric is therefore an extreme, deeper, and sometimes darker version of its domestic counterpart, one that has sharpened the original's language and imaginary. From this viewpoint, erraticness is an extension of Reynolds's theory on the poetry of translation, based on the poems' inherent, and latent, metaphoricity.

In the segment of BRADSHAW 1971 dedicated to the poetry of the Resistance, Bradshaw opted for a politicising translation underlying the poets' sense of protest. Her version of Morandini's 'The Executed', by playing with the ambiguity of certain words, intensifies the experience first of seclusion, 'piccole **case** | di sasso'/ 'small stone | **huts**', then of destruction, '**colsero** le stele'/ 'they **pierced** the stars', and finally of death undergone by the partisans, 'i campi senza **germoglio**'/ 'fields with no **shoots**'.[31] Elsewhere, in translating Turoldo's 'poetry of protest through prayer' (her definition), Bradshaw eroticises the original so much so that sex becomes a metaphor for the encounter with the divine: 'Tu celato in ogni desiderio, | o Infinito, che pesavi negli **abbracci**'/ 'You concealed in each longing, | oh Endless, you weighing in **love making**'.[32] Bradshaw seems to develop here De Palchi's translatorly mode, which, just like his own poetry and anthological selection, is rooted in the language of anatomy and desire:

Nulla è più misterioso
e adorabile e **proprio**
della tua carne spogliata.

Nothing is more mysterious
and adorable and **becoming**
than your naked flesh.[33]

This corporeal, translatorly approach is adopted up to and including Bonaffini's versions, where dialect is depicted as the language not only of memory and affection, but also of passion and longing: 'dialèto, la lingua de l'**afèto**'/ 'dialect, **love**'s tongue'.[34] Yet, in the passage from Italian to English, the language of the original is not always made sensual. Bradshaw herself promoted forms of spiritualisation, especially, but not exclusively, in the translation of women's verse. Some of her renditions highlight the translator's journey from reason to faith, 'Guarda l'acqua **inesplicabile**'/ 'Behold the **unfathomable** water',[35] and from the natural to the metaphysical, 'raggio | che s'acqueta d'un **cielo** ove cadere'/ 'ray | allayed with **heavens** where to fall'.[36] Other verbal choices underline Bradshaw's preference for devotional terms, variously linked to religious rituals, worship, doctrine, or liturgy: 'La sera umana che lenta **sconfina** | nella notte?'/ 'The human eve as it **transcends** slowly | into night?';[37] and:

> Quando sarò bassorilievo al tempo
> della Tua eternità, non avrò fronti
> contro cui **capovolgere** la faccia.
>
> When I shall be bas-relief by the time
> of Your eternity, I will not have brows
> whereupon to **prostrate** my face.[38]

Poet Adeodato Piazza Nicolai, who translated Marin's poetry in Bonaffini 2001, took this tendency further, as he manipulated the original with the insertion of Christian formulas, 'che dentro l'ore | ogni to passo xe lisier'/ 'and **may your steps travel light** | at each turn of the hour', and biblical echoes, 'Godi nel pensier'/ '**Rejoyce and be glad**'.[39] On a similar note, Condini 2009 and Montorfani 2014 intensified the religious dimension either by personifying the divine or deifying the human: 'il viaggio è un **altro**'/ 'the journey is **Other**';[40] 'O medio Oriente disteso dalla **sua** voce'/ 'O middle East created by **His** voice'.[41]

Other forms of semantic intensification pursued through translation revolve around the representation of solitude and melancholia, death and grief. Carried from one language to the other, including disappearing dialects, experiences of distance, anguish, and loss acquire a more sombre, pessimistic tone, especially when linked to the experience of migration. The most compelling example, almost a paradigm, is offered by the translation of *moltitudine* as diaspora: 'sperdü **badalüff**'/ 'who knows where in the **diaspora**'.[42] In a similarly erratic way, *gridare* and *chiamare* are translated as 'to wail', rather than as 'to shout' and 'to call' respectively: '**grido** all'ara | del tuo amore perfetto'/ '**I wail** | to the altar of your perfect love';[43] and 'e chela voce chiama, **chiame**'/ 'as a voice calls out, and **wails**'.[44] Likewise, *nero, triste,* and *pianto* become 'bleak', 'gloom', and 'grief': 'Viene il giorno dei **neri** pensieri'/ 'Come the day of the **bleak** thoughts';[45] 'né sai decidere quale sia **la più triste**'/ 'nor can you decide which one is **the gloomiest**';[46] 'le cose son ebbre di **pianto**!'/ 'The world is drunk with **grief**'.[47] The temporal concept of *durata* is seen as a form of spatial flatness inspiring feelings of disorientation and sorrow: ''l è altro che **durare**'/ 'nothing else but **flat time**'.[48]

On a similar note, the verb *abbandonare* sharpens its spatial connotation as it incorporates the impression of a desert's empty distance: 'La speranza di pure rivederti | **m'abbandonava**'/ 'The hope of even seeing you again | was **deserting me**'.[49] Sometimes, translators added adverbs and/or adjectives in order to intensify negative feelings, a procedure that is particularly visible in dialect poems dealing with the experience of migration. In Nicolai's version of 'The Best of Youth', a Friulian poem by Pasolini, the translator transferred the young people's departure into a suspended, infinite dimension (see the insertion of the adverb 'forever', which does not appear in the original): 'Puartàit, trenos, pal mond a no ridi mai pì | chisciu legris fantàs paràs via del paìs' / 'Trains everywhere scatter these once happy men, | they will not laugh when leaving home **forever**'.[50] Yet, at the same time,

Nicolai gave these migrants responsibility for their own leaving, since the phrasal verb 'paràs via', i.e. 'rejected', is charged with an active meaning, 'leave forever'. Similarly, translator Adria Bernardi added the adverb 'still' to the ending of Tomino Baldassari's poem 'The Keys of the Air', thus increasing the sense of dismay in the original:

e nun a 'taren d'astê al mateni biânchi
quânt us svegia la chêrna
par dis ch'a sen a e' mònd.

and we will wait for white mornings
when the flesh wakes up
to tell us we're **still** in the world.[51]

The introduction of the adjective 'new' has a comparable effect of actualisation in Brock's translation of 'A Memory' by Saba: 'E domani non venne. Fu **un dolore**'/ 'Tomorrow he did not come: a **new pain**'.[52]

Erraticness also contemplates cases of semantic reconfiguration, where the original syntagms are purposely mistranslated, and therefore foreignised, so as to stress their sense of melancholic isolation. A compelling example is offered by Vitiello's translation of 'Who Is It?' by Grisoni, where solitude is made absolute by the use of the indefinite pronoun 'no one' instead of the personal pronoun *lui*. The sense of detachment and confinement is further underlined by the introduction of the enjambment in the translation: 'e se ghe fős **gna lü**?'/ 'what if there's | **no one else**?'.[53] Again, this erratic-erroneous practice, based on the betrayal of the original, is very popular in dialect poetry's translations. The following examples show further instances of this mode across Bonaffini's anthologies; notice that 'to remain' is translated as 'to tear', 'to be born' as 'to ripen', and 'dreaming' as 'failing': 'Eccu cce mme **rrumane**'/ 'from me this can't **be torn**!';[54] 'fine **me buta** la parola inchièta'/ 'the subtle disquieting word **ripens** within me';[55] 'Addia addia | core de ru mia **core addupeiate**'/ 'Goodbye, | heart of my **failing heart**'.[56]

Alternatively, it is the phonic resemblance with the original that triggers translation mistakes. Obviously, 'dissetarsi' [to quench one's thirst] and 'dissect', which share the same beginning in *disse-*, are not synonyms; yet, they are used as such in Smith's translation of Erba's poem 'Tabula Rasa?': 'in corsa a **dissetarsi** di vento'/ 'moving **to be dissected** by wind'.[57] A similar procedure, based on translatorly false friends, occurs in Vitiello's translation of the title of a poem by Riviello, '**L'aria** della luna', which becomes 'Moon **Aura**'.[58] On a similar note, Bonaffini systematically translates dialect poetry by following phonetically rhyming patterns, whereby the original is semantically modified (e.g., 'fiscanne' [whistle] becomes 'roar') but phonetically reassembled:

Hann' 'a I'èsse cchiù di mill'anne
ca ie mi sente accussì:
come nd'u terramote di nu trene
ca nun arrìvete mèie
ma ca nnatèrne pàssete fiscanne
dasupr'a mmi.

It must be a thousand years
I've felt this way:
in the earthquake of a train
that never nears
but eternally hurtles over me
with its roar.[59]

In addition to metaphorical intensification and phonetic affinity, other two sub-categories of erratic translation are personification and synecdoche/metonymy. Just like the first type, these two clusters share a certain degree of freedom from the original, also achieved by means of metaphorical developments. Personification, in particular, often works as a concretising tool in the translation of poems that present an anatomical and/or material focus. Abstract nouns are replaced by concrete nouns, whereas indefinite articles and pronouns become personal: 'Parlo coi **lutti**'/ 'I talk to the **departed**';[60] '**Chiunque** vorrebbe i tuoi occhi per guardarsi'/ '**We** would all like your eyes to look at ourselves';[61] 'Avaste cu tte rusce **na** palore'/ 'Just by whispering **your** word'.[62] Similarly, the agent of passive actions is generally suggested or introduced: '**Si ripiegano** i bianchi abiti estivi'/ 'the white summer clothes **are folded** away';[63] 'Mare c ò **zbandonà**'/ 'Mother **I've left**'.[64] Another distinguishable use of personification is noticeable in the attribution of anatomical terminology to architecture, the landscape, silence, and even spatial distance: 'campanili **diroccati**'/ '**maimed** steeples';[65] 'colonne **mozze**'/ '**maimed** columns';[66] '**rami** gonfi'/ 'swollen **limbs**';[67] 'in ste silèinsi **pótt**'/ 'in this | **naked** silence';[68] '**deserta** misura'/ '**forsaken** measure'.[69] The English, foreignising effect reaches its peak when the adverb *lontano*, after a double process of materialisation and archaisation, disintegrates in this memorable incipit: 'Moriremo **lontani**'/ 'We will die **asunder**'.[70]

Synecdoche and metonymy complement each other as forms of diasporic translation, the former by offering a quantitative, less abstract reading of the source text and the latter by modifying the associations between names and qualifiers in the original. Examples of synecdochic translation, where the whole stands for the part or vice versa, are mainly drawn from the imagery of nature and the body, and are fairly consistent throughout the anthologies: "nzi lo **mare**'/ 'towards the **shore**';[71] 'tante nta mille **vucche**'/ 'so many on a thousand **lips**';[72] 'quel suo baciarmi la **spalla**'/ 'she kisses my **back**';[73] 'questa è la direzione dello **sguardo**'/ 'this is the direction of the **eye**'.[74] Concurrently, the rhetorical centre of some of the poems is moved around the different elements of the sentence — from the noun to the adjective, from the adjective to the adverb, from the verb to the subject and so on — as the poems' overarching metaphors swirl around an ever-changing metonymic prism: 'Folta la nuvola bianca delle falene **impazzite** | Turbine'/ 'The dense white cloud of the mayflies **crazily** | Whirls';[75] 'Nel becco | il **rosso tragico senza grido**'/ 'its beak open **not to cry** | **a sorrow of red**';[76] 'e i cucù, | chi **ne gomìsse** dae costèle'/ 'and **melancholy** calls | of cuckoos from the little hills';[77] 'l'**angustia** delle biografie'/ 'the **cramped** biographies';[78] 'gli ubriachi **del nulla**'/ '**worthless** drunks'.[79]

As shown by the examples above, these linguistic wanderings can be a precious source for the study of translated literature and critical translation. By pursuing different forms of intensification, erraticness reinforces the metaphor of migration experienced by the editor, the poet, and the translator alike in definite, almost absolute terms. The poem-translations deriving from this practice, variously diverging from the original, testify to the different roles played by 'mistakes' in translation. From this viewpoint, diasporic errors and erroneous paths appear to be an authentic guise for the translator, the way by which s/he reveals his/her own presence; their deforming, misleading effect is the result of his/her nomadic sensitivity.

Multilingualism

In the section of this chapter entitled 'Transliterality', I analysed the function of multilingual insertions in transliterary practices. Multilingualism, however, is a type of diasporic translation in its own right and, among the three modes considered here, is the one that is most obviously associated with the language of migration. A hallmark of Pound's *Cantos*, multilingualism defies both the idea of national literature and the concept of translation as simple transfer of meaning. Often confronted with multilingual texts, which had become popular in contemporary Italian poetry, English translators had to deal with the challenge of using more than one target language. As a result, their poem-translations went against the so-called 'nondifficult English prose', thus offering a compellingly foreignising case.[80]

Italy has a long tradition of multilingual authors, from Dante to Ruzante, and from Alfieri to the poets of the neo-avant-garde. As well as Latin, French, and their native dialects, contemporary poets are adopting new languages (English, German, Spanish, Romanian, Croat, Arabic), a distinct expression of their migration experience. BONAFFINI AND PERRICONE 2014 includes some of the youngest and/or most recent multilingual voices, such as Vera Lúcia de Oliveira and Bogliun. This anthology is indeed the point of arrival for a decade of effort to shape a multilingual Italian canon, one which could not have been conceived without the intermedium of translation. Multilingual translations were already present at the time of BRADSHAW 1971 for poems by Sereni, Guidacci, and Giovanni Raboni, and increased considerably in the anthologies of the 1980s and 1990s. Whereas at the beginning the multilingual poets anthologised in the US were mostly avant-garde representatives (Sanguineti, Oberto) and women (Rosselli, Niccolai), nowadays they are generally dialect writers and/or migrants. What does not change from one generation to the next is the poets' concern with metaliterary topics, which are explored from both a semantic and semiotic perspective. In this context, diaspora is, at once, the form and the content of representation.

Instances of metaliterary texts translated multilingually are numerous due to the anthologies' selections, which focused on multilingual and/or multicultural authors rather than on traditional, monolingual ones. The translators may keep the original's plurilingual texture, or deliberately introduce words from languages other than Italian and English — often misspelt French words commonly used in English — in order to challenge the reader's expectations. The intrusive French words, which can be playful (*voilà*), historical (*flambeaux*) [torchlight], or technical (*réveille*) [reveille, the military morning bugle call] enrich the poem-translations with a further foreignising dimension: '**ecco**, scopro l'America'/ '**voilà**, I discover America';[81] 'i barbagli delle mie **faci**'/ 'the dazzle of my **flambeaus**'.[82] In a similar way, by translating the title of Levi's poem 'Alzarsi' [Awakening] with the word 'Reveille', Feldman and Swann play with the double sense of this term, which, whereas it has a military connotation in English (the poem evokes life in Auschwitz), it refers to the act of getting up and/or rising in French (*réveille, se réveiller*).[83] In these poems, metaliterature is a disguised motif more than a central theme. Things, however, are profoundly different when it comes to the poets of the neo-avant-garde, for whom the reflection on language is an unavoidable trope.

In Chapters 10 and 11, I touched upon the multilingual nature of Niccolai's poetry. Her 'Hetty's Bar Ballad' is a typical multilingual poem, dedicated to Marcello Angioni, a Sardinian polyglot married to a Swedish woman, as well as a contributor to the avant-garde review *Analfabetica*. This text is built upon four languages (Italian, German, French, and English), the last somehow disappearing in the translation, which used it as the main language of communication:

Des dry martini! Neuf!
[...]
Anche un Americano che chiede
nine dry martini
corre il rischio di non riceverne neanche uno.
Des dry martini! Neuf!
[...]

Des dry martini! Neuf!
[...]
An American who orders
nine dry martini
also runs the risk of not getting even one.
Des dry martini! Neuf!
[...][84]

Niccolai's metaliterary imagination goes even further in 'The Geographical History', a poem dedicated to another contemporary of hers, the feminist publisher Laura Lepetit. When interlaced with the theme of diaspora, metaliterature becomes a form of meta-translation justified by the poet's own reflection on the translatorly act. This is one of the most compelling testimonies of the poet-translator's experience of travelling as writing as being:

Questa poesia la sto cominciando a Brescia. (Continua)
Me voiçi a Paris.
[...]
È viaggiare che porta a fare giochi di parole.

I am beginning this poem in Brescia. (*To be continued*)
Me voiçi a Paris.
[...]
It is travel that leads to creating word games.[85]

Also, in the same poem:

> Si vede si vede eccome si vede
> che sto traducendo Gertude Stein.
> Ma se sono portata a fare giochi di parole in proprio
> [...]
> come si farà a vedere finita la mia traduzione di
> *The Geographical History of America.*
> Beh l'inizio c'è già nel titolo e io sono a buon punto.
>
> It's obvious it's obvious it's certainly obvious
> that I am translating Gertrude Stein.
> But if I'm driven to create my own word games
> [...]
> how we will get to see the completion of my translation of
> *The Geographical History of America.*
> Well the beginning is already there in the title and I'm at a good point.[86]

Similarly, the poetry of Niccolai, Giuliani, and Sanguineti is also constitutionally multilingual, as reflected in the translations of their major works from the 1960s until now. De Palchi 1966a includes a handful of avant-garde, multilingual poets, both established (Sanguineti) and unknown, such as Acutis. Bradshaw 1971 recasts the Babelic confusion of languages, with 'Poem 23', from Sanguineti's *Laborintus*, layering (unaccented) ancient and modern languages, abbreviations, and dates; the Italian idiom, and its English translation, echo in the distance: 's.d. ma 1951 (unruhig) και κρινουσιν e socchiudo gli occhi'/ 's.d. but 1951 (unruhig) και κρινουσιν and I squint my eyes'.[87] Bradshaw's translations play with multilingualism in all its forms, including mathematics and music. In this poem by Orelli, 'Spring at Nocca', words flow (or roam) like notes on a score:

> *Au bois il y a un oiseau* — torna l'andante
> affettuoso — *son chant vous arrête*
> *et vous fait rougir.*
>
> *Au bois il y a un oiseau* — the *andante*
> *affettuoso rom* — *son chant vous arrête*
> *et vous fait rougir.*[88]

In the first decades of the twenty-first century, translators have highlighted the metaliterary, translingual traits of the Italian neo-avant-garde even more, as revealed in these lines, again by Sanguineti:

> La lingua è già, da sola, un'ansiogena anfibologia: sessualmente
> sensata, per l'appunto)
> [...]
> come da programma, intiera, un sexy-booze and — schmooze:
> (gaio usque ad mortem).
>
> The tongue already, in itself, is an anxiolytic amphibology: sexually
> sensate, which is the whole point)
> [...]
> as planned, a complete sexy-booze and — schmooze:
> (cheerful usque ad mortem).[89]

It is worth noticing the sexually philosophical representation of language, which also works as a foreignising strategy; and the 'erroneous', indeed semantically reversed, translation of the adjective 'ansiogena' [anxiogenic], here offered in its opposite meaning, 'anxiolytic'.

As well as women and avant-garde poets, dialect authors also were translated multilingually. Sometimes, dialect is paired with Latin insertions, which are an ironic and/or cultural reference to the language of philosophy, and the Church:

Füma or vapor, ma-güüt,
ma-güüt! Mater mea, oi che dolor!
Smoke the vapor
Ma-güüt, ma-güüt! Mater mea,
oh what a pain![90]

'*Sunt animae rerum*'
[...]
Sunt linguae rerum
sighi pianti tremiti
[...]
pensièri *rerum*
sunt sunt.

'*Sunt animae rerum*'
[...]
Sunt linguae rerum
shouts cries tremblings
[...]
thoughts *rerum*
sunt sunt.[91]

Most often a residue of the original dialect remains, especially in refrains, dialogues, and definitions that spring to the mind of the diasporic poet:

So' uomméne le fémmene,
ri màschere so' men,
e yes, a Bruccheli,
signìfeca: pe'scì

'Uommene' here are women,
and the males are 'men,'
and 'yes' in 'Bruccheli'
stands for our 'scì'.[92]

In the migrants' language, 'Bruccheli' is a corruption of 'Brooklyn'. The habit of creating and using an invented language, generally a combination of the poet's native dialect, Italian, and English, has become more and more popular in transnational writers of the twenty-first century. Bonaffini and Perricone 2014 abounds in examples of this kind, as shown by Totaro's invented verb *forgettare*, a provokingly diasporic compound: 'Oh forgetta | forgetta le parole'/ 'Oh, forgetta | forgetta the words'.[93]

In its evolution from female and avant-garde poetry through dialect verse up to the present inhabited by transnational writers, the practice of multilingualism is therefore an identifying symbol of eccentric translations, and of diasporicity.

Notes to Chapter 19

1. *Italy 1963*, ed. by Weaver and Colquhoun; and *Open City: Seven Writers in Postwar Rome*, ed. by William Weaver (South Royalton, VT: Steerforth Press, 1999).
2. Giorgio Bassani, 'Poems', trans. by William Weaver, in Caetani 1950, p. 92.
3. Giorgio Caproni, 'The Funicular', trans. by Williams Weaver, in Caetani 1950, p. 181.
4. Lucia Aiello, Jou Charnley, and Mariangela Palladino, 'Foreword', in *Displaced Women: Multilingual Narratives of Migration in Europe*, ed. by Lucia Aiello, Jou Charnley, and Mariangela Palladino (Newcastle upon Tyne: Cambridge Scholars, 2014), pp. ix–x.
5. José Santaemilia, *Gender, Sex and Translation: The Manipulation of Identities* (Abingdon & New York: Routledge, 2014), p. 6.
6. Annie Vivanti, 'Ego', trans. by Muriel Kittle, in Allen 1986, pp. 40–41.
7. Margherita Guidacci, 'Many Times November Has Come Back', trans. by Muriel Kittle, in Allen 1986, pp. 60–61.
8. Vivian Lamarque, 'Weather Forecast', trans. by Muriel Kittle, in Allen 1986, pp. 116–17.
9. Bradshaw 1971, p. vii.
10. Lorenzo Calogero, 'CLX', trans. by Vittoria Bradshaw, in Bradshaw 1971, pp. 10–11.
11. Rocco Scotellaro, 'America', trans. by Vittoria Bradshaw, in Bradshaw 1971, pp. 102–03.
12. Margherita Guidacci, 'VI', trans. by Vittoria Bradshaw, in Bradshaw 1971, pp. 208–09.
13. Blum and Trubowitz 2001, p. lii.
14. Margherita Guidacci, 'Madame X', trans. by Cinzia Sartini Blum and Lara Trubowitz, in Blum and Trubowitz 2001, pp. 12–13.
15. Cristina Campo, 'Love, Today My Lip', trans. by Cinzia Sartini Blum and Lara Trubowitz, in Blum and Trubowitz 2001, pp. 24–25.
16. Elena Clementelli, 'Moviola', trans. by Cinzia Sartini Blum and Lara Trubowitz, in Blum and Trubowitz 2001, pp. 44–45.
17. Maria Luisa Spazini, 'The Present', trans. by Cinzia Sartini Blum and Lara Trubowitz, in Blum and Trubowitz 2001, pp. 46–47.
18. Vera Gherarducci, 'October 27th', trans. by Cinzia Sartini Blum and Lara Trubowitz, in Blum and Trubowitz 2001, pp. 74–75.
19. Edoardo Sanguineti, 'Laborintus 1', trans. by Vittoria Bradshaw, in Bradshaw 1971, pp. 730–31.
20. Nanni Balestrini, 'The Instinct for Preservation', trans. by 'C. F.', in Feldman and Swann 1979, p. 17. I am unable to identify the translator.
21. Nanni Balestrini, 'The Instinct of Self-preservation', trans. by Lawrence Smith, in Feldman and Swann 1979, pp. 396–97.
22. Martino Oberto, 'Ana of Esserialism', trans. by Rosa Maria Salamone, in Ballerini 1978, pp. 90–91.
23. Edoardo Sanguineti, from *Purgatory of Hell*, trans. by Lawrence Smith, in Smith 1981, pp. 382–83.
24. Emilio Villa, '1 Soirée', in Spatola and Vangelisti 1982, p. 116. The poem is not translated.
25. Amelia Rosselli, 'No One', trans. by Lawrence Smith, in Smith 1981, pp. 362–63.
26. Giulia Niccolai, 'E.V. Ballad', in Spatola and Vangelisti 1982, p. 74. A translation is not provided.
27. Luigi Fontanella, 'When the Evenings', trans. by Luigi Bonaffini, in Montorfani 2014, pp. 80–81.
28. Matthew Reynolds, *Translation: A Very Short Introduction* (Oxford: Oxford University Press, 2016), p. 64.
29. Pym, *Translation and Text Transfer*, pp. 187, 186.
30. See Jonas Olson, *Moral Error Theory: History, Critique, Defence* (Oxford: Oxford University Press, 2014); and Tim Conley, *Joyce's Mistakes: Problems of Intention, Irony, and Interpretation* (Toronto: University of Toronto Press, 2003).
31. Luigi Morandini, 'The Executed', trans. by Vittoria Bradshaw, in Bradshaw 1971, pp. 66–67.
32. David Maria Turoldo, 'Love and Death', trans. by Vittoria Bradshaw, in Bradshaw 1971, pp. 196–97.

33. Vincenzo Cardarelli, 'Adolescent', trans. by Sonia Raiziss and Alfredo De Palchi, in De Palchi 1966b, pp. 280–81.
34. Luciano Caniato, 'Valedictions, II', trans. by Dino Fabris, in Bonaffini 2001, p. 323.
35. Lucio Piccolo, 'The Sundial', trans. by Vittoria Bradshaw, in Bradshaw 1971, pp. 266–67.
36. Andrea Zanzotto, 'III Eclogue: The Vintage', trans. by Vittoria Bradshaw, in Bradshaw 1971, pp. 322–23.
37. Margherita Guidacci, 'All Saints Day: VII', trans. by Vittoria Bradshaw, in Bradshaw 1971, pp. 218–19.
38. Alda Merini, 'The Flight', trans. by Vittoria Bradshaw, in Bradshaw 1971, pp 233–34.
39. Biagio Marin, 'The River's Water', trans. by Adeodato Piazza Nicolai, in Bonaffini 2001, pp. 381–82.
40. Ermanno Krumm, 'Of Course There Might Have Been', trans. by Simon Carnell and Erica Segre, in Mortorfani 2014, pp. 66–67.
41. Cristina Campo, 'Now I Want All My Letters Back, ...', trans. by Ned Condini, in Condini 2009, pp. 270–71.
42. Piero Marelli, 'And When My Pages No Longer', trans. by Justin Vitiello, in Bonaffini 2001, p. 225.
43. Alda Merini, 'I Have Renewed for You', trans. by Vittoria Bradshaw, in Bradshaw 1971, pp. 234–35.
44. Giuseppe Rosato, 'To Hear, Again, Years Later, a Voice', trans. by Anthony Molino, in Bonaffini 1997, p. 56.
45. Roberto Roversi, 'Red Black', trans. by Vittoria Bradshaw, in Bradshaw 1971, pp. 426–27.
46. Margherita Guidacci, 'Might Awakening', trans. by Vittoria Bradshaw, in Bradshaw 1971, pp. 212–13.
47. Giovanni Pascoli, 'Mist', trans. by E. J. Scovell, in Brock 2012, pp. 10–11.
48. Luigi Bressan, 'Look, The Air's Turning Bad', trans. by Dino Fabris, in Bonaffini 2001, p. 316.
49. Eugenio Montale, from *Motets*, 6, trans. by George Kay, in Brock 2012, pp. 188–89.
50. Pier Paolo Pasolini, 'The Best of Youth', trans. by Adeodato Piazza Nicolai, in Bonaffini 2001, pp. 412–13.
51. Tolmino Baldassari, 'The Keys to the Air', trans. by Adria Bernardi, in Bonaffini 2001, pp. 550–21.
52. Umberto Saba, 'A Memory', trans. by Geoffrey Brock, in Brock 2012, pp. 96–97.
53. Franca Grisoni, 'Who Is it?', trans. by Justin Vitiello, in Bonaffini 2001, p. 242.
54. Nicola Giuseppe De Donno, 'Horn of Plenty', trans. by Justin Vitiello, in Bonaffini 1997, p. 202.
55. Luciano Caniato, 'Little Incipient Poem', trans. by Dino Fabris, in Bonaffini 2001, p. 321.
56. Cosimo Savastano, 'Hailstorm', trans. by Anthony Molino, in Bonaffini 1997, p. 70.
57. Luciano Erba, 'Tabula Rasa?', trans. by Lawrence Smith, in Smith 1981, pp. 230–31.
58. Vito Riviello, 'Moon Aura', trans. by Justin Vitiello, in Bonaffini 1999, p. 244.
59. Albino Pierro, 'Among People Laughing', trans. by Luigi Bonaffini, in Bonaffini 1997, p. 297.
60. Lorenzo Calogero, 'LXXXVII', trans. by Vittoria Bradshaw, in Bradshaw 1971, pp. 8–9.
61. Biancamaria Frabotta, 'Myopia', trans. by Cinzia Sartini Blum and Lara Trubowitz, in Blum and Trubowitz 2001, pp. 220–21.
62. Pietro Gatti, 'You're Reading a Romance of Merlin', trans. by Justin Vitiello, in Bonaffini 1997, p. 189.
63. Cristina Campo, 'The White Summer Clothes Are Folded Away', trans. by Cinzia Sartini Blum and Lara Trubowitz, in Blum and Trubowitz 2001, pp. 22–23.
64. Luciano Caniato, 'Finished Poem', trans. by Dino Fabris, in Bonaffini 2001, p. 322.
65. Luciano Luisi, 'A Tale', trans. by Vittoria Bradshaw, in Bradshaw 1971, pp. 54–55.
66. Margherita Guidacci, 'The Sand and the Angel', trans. by Vittoria Bradshaw, in Bradshaw 1971, pp. 206–07.
67. Nelo Risi, 'Apple Trees Apple Trees Apple Trees', trans. by Lawrence Smith, in Smith 1981, pp. 236–37.
68. Emilio Rentocchini, 'You Remain, in Order to Lose Track of Time', trans. by Adria Bernardi, in Bonaffini 2001, p. 569.

69. Cristina Campo, 'At Time I Say: Let's Try to Be Joyful', trans. by Vittoria Bradshaw, in Bradshaw 1971, pp. 246–47.
70. Cristina Campo, 'We Will Die Asunder', trans. by Vittoria Bradshaw, in Bradshaw 1971, pp. 246–47.
71. Tommaso Pignatelli, 'Death', trans. by Luigi Bonaffini, in Bonaffini 1997, p. 279.
72. Dante Maffia, 'Other Names', trans. by Luigi Bonaffini, in Bonaffini 1999, p. 259.
73. Antonella Anedda, 'For My Daughter', trans. by Sarah Arvio, in Brock 2012, pp. 576–77.
74. Roberto Mussapi, 'The Poet's Gaze', trans. by Patrizia Villani, in Montorfani 2014, pp. 256–57.
75. Eugenio Montale, 'The Hitler Spring', trans. by Maurice English, in Poggioli 1948, p. 317.
76. Alfredo De Palchi, 'Black Glasses', trans. by Sonia Raiziss, in De Palchi 1961, pp. 22–23.
77. Paolo Bertolani, 'On Summer', trans. by Michael Palma, in Bonaffini 2001, p. 275.
78. Antonella Anedda, 'To Unearth the Reason for a Verb', trans. by Jaime McKendrick, in Brock 2012, pp. 574–75.
79. Vera Lúcia de Oliveira, 'Third Universe of the Sky', trans. by Adria Bernardi, in Bonaffini and Perricone 2014, pp. 346–47.
80. Brian Lennon, *In Babel's Shadow: Multilingual Literatures, Monolingual States* (Minneapolis: University of Minnesota Press, 2010), p. 4.
81. Mariella Bettarini, 'Biography', trans. by Cinzia Sartini Blum and Lara Trubowitz, in Blum and Trubowitz 2001, pp. 198–99.
82. Margherita Guidacci, 'Epulon', trans. by Vittoria Bradshaw, in Bradshaw 1971, pp. 212–13.
83. Primo Levi, 'Reveille', trans. by Ruth Feldman and Brian Swann, in Brock 2012, pp. 346–47.
84. Giulia Niccolai, 'Harry's Bar Ballad', trans. by Cinzia Sartini Blum and Lara Trubowitz, in Blum and Trubowitz 2001, pp. 138–39.
85. Giulia Niccolai, 'The Geographical History', trans. by Cinzia Sartini Blum and Lara Trubowitz, in Blum and Trubowitz 2001, pp. 140–41.
86. Ibid., pp. 142–43.
87. Edoardo Sanguineti, from *Laborintus*, 23, trans. by Vittoria Bradshaw, in Bradshaw 1971, pp. 738–39.
88. Giorgio Orelli, 'Spring at Nocca', trans. by Vittoria Bradshaw, in Bradshaw 1971, pp. 284–85.
89. Edoardo Sanguineti, from *Libretto*, XV, trans. by Pádraig J. Daly, in Brock 2012, pp. 480–83.
90. Gabriele Alberto Quadri, 'A Vision', trans. by Gaetano Cipolla, in Bonaffini 2001, p. 72.
91. Ernesto Calzavara, 'Throw Yourself In', trans. by Dino Fabris, in Bonaffini 2001, p. 301.
92. Luigi Antonio Trofa, 'My Husband Wrote to Me', trans. by Luigi Fontanella, in Bonaffini 1997, p. 143.
93. Paolo Totaro, 'First Ballad Cavalcanti: Words', trans. by Gaetano Cipolla, in Bonaffini And Perricone 2014, pp. 190–91.

CHAPTER 20

Translating Degree Zero: The Case of Visual Poetry

In *Writing Degree Zero* (1953), Roland Barthes reflected on the nature and history of writing; by exploring the relationship between the author and society, he claimed that contemporary writers' oral style, which can be seen as an absence of style itself, constitutes the 'degree zero' of literary creation.[1] After almost seventy years, and applied to the contemporary global context, I borrow Barthes's fortunate definition for looking at the process of transplantation of Italian visual poetry into the American system as an exemplary case of diasporic translation. Text-images of this kind were translated in a hyperliteral way, to the point where, very often, transvisuality (which I define as a particular kind of transliterality) resulted in forms of non-translation. Multilingual insertions, invented alphabets, and/or nonsense sentences transmigrated with little, if any, adaptation. This combination of diasporic modes (transliterality and multilingualism), or the absence thereof, gave shape to the most exilic of poem-translations, where the crossing of languages intersects with the crossing of media.[2]

Yet, the degree zero of translation, or non-translation, does not define the horizon of untranslatability; rather, it is the ultimate, most dramatic representation of the 'foreignness of languages' as described in Chapter 18. Presented with a non-translated visual poem, the English-speaking reader is offered a manifestation of the irreconcilability of poetry and translation on the one hand, and of the 'interpermeability between word and image' on the other.[3] The boundaries between the verbal and the visual, the intelligible and the unintelligible, blur, thus revealing the paradoxical complexities of literary writing.

Surprisingly, little analysis of the relationship between visual poetry and translation has been undertaken thus far. For the purposes of this book, I present seven examples of Italian concrete and/or abstract poems from American anthologies examined in this study: Pignotti, 'La Dolce Avanguardia' (De Palchi 1966a, p.184); Maurizio Nannucci, 'Chromatic Poem/Red' (Ballerini 1973, p. 62); Sandri, 'AA Galaxy OP 238.738' (Ballerini 1973, p. 40); Sarenco, 'Omaggio alla poesia' (Spatola and Vangelisti 1982, p. 102); Sandri, 'From: Uomo/ o il Tempo' (Spatola and Vangelisti 1982, p. 97); Claudio Parmiggiani, 'Found Poem' (Spatola and Vangelisti 1982, p. 83); and Pino Masnata, 'Ambition' (Brock 2012, p. 221). The poems are illustrated below (Figures 20.1–7).[4]

Fig. 20.1. 'La Dolce Avanguardia' (1966) by Lamberto Pignotti[5]

NANNUCCI, Maurizio, "Chromatic poem/red," 1972

FIG. 20.2. 'Chromatic Poem/Red' (1973) by Maurizio Nannucci

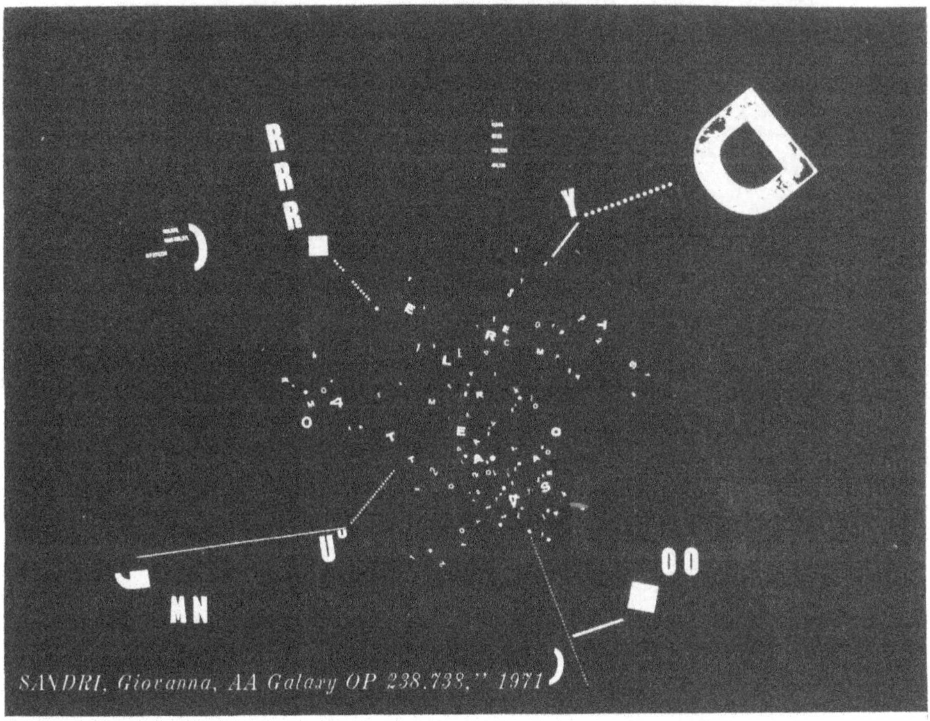

FIG. 20.3. 'AA Galaxy OP 238.738' (1973) by Giovanna Sandri

Sarenco

[*Omaggio alla poesia*]

Fig. 20.4. 'Omaggio alla poesia' (1982) by Sarenco

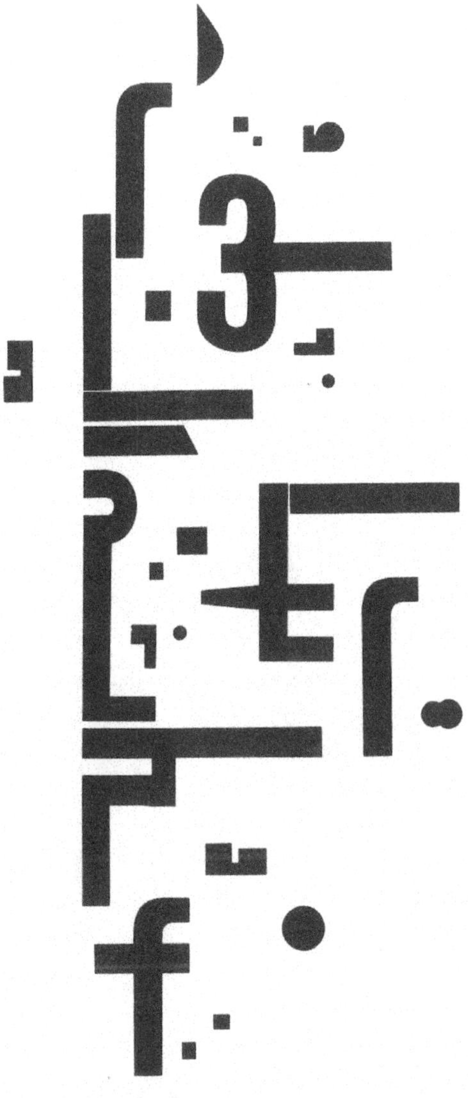

[FROM: *Uomo / o il Tempo*]

Fig. 20.5. 'From: Uomo/o il Tempo' (1982) by Giovanna Sandri

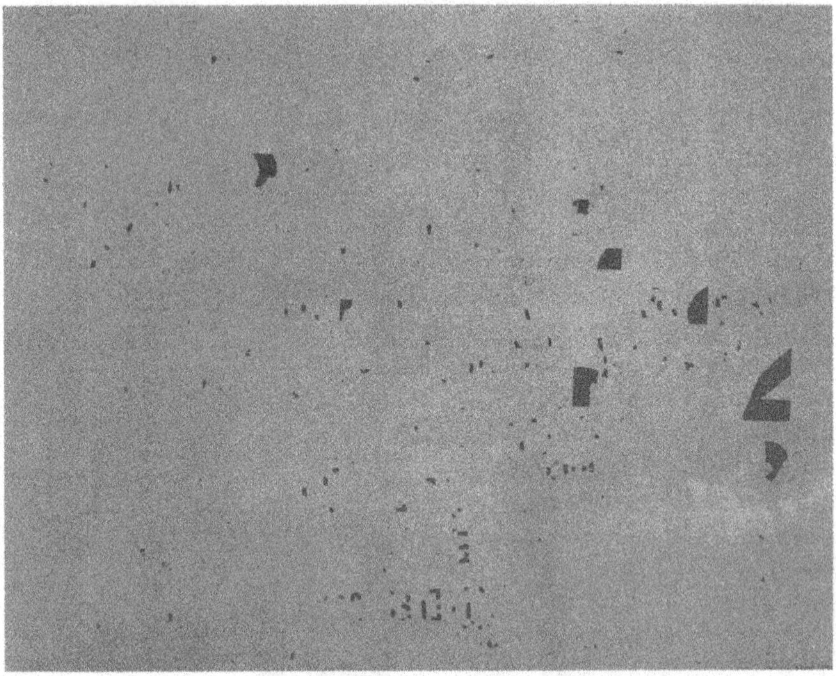

FIG. 20.6. 'Found Poem' (1982) by Claudio Parmiggiani

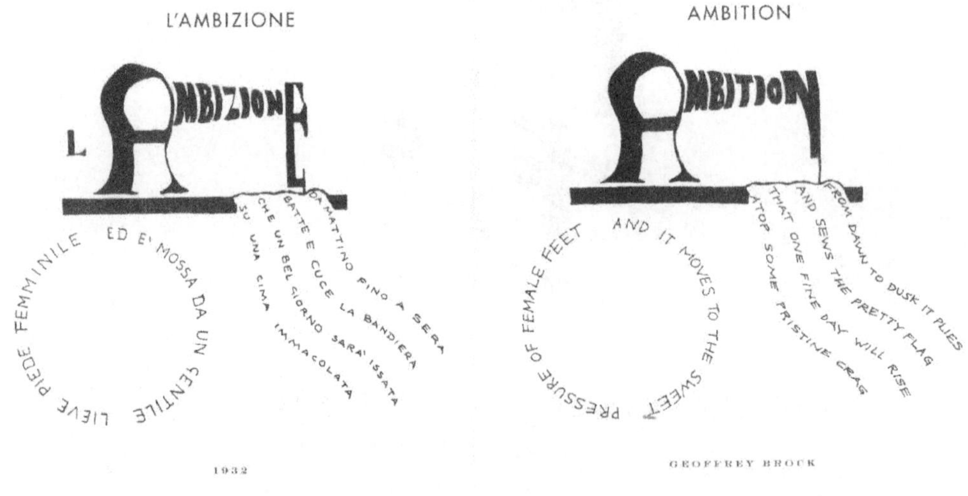

FIG. 20.7. 'Ambition' (2012) by Pino Masnata

These poems, published from the 1960s to the 1980s, make very limited (if any) use of words; the languages they foreground suggest hieroglyphics (Sandri), red brush strokes (Nannucci), cosmic alphabets (Sandri), and exploded letters (Parmiggiani). They elicit the most challenging translation conundrums — how to translate an image, an abstraction, or even a colour? Can the (visual) arts still speak a national language? — whilst often remaining untranslated. Only their titles, placed at the bottom of the page, are sometimes given in English. Masnata's poem originally of 1932, however, is an exception to this trend. Edited and translated by the poet-anthologist Brock, it is offered both in its original and in its visually, almost unsettlingly, faithful rendition, an operation that both enhances and maximises the responsibilities of the diasporic translator.

This pictorial ending testifies to the ultraverbal nature of the diasporic canon; it is an ideal point of departure for future, interdisciplinary investigations, which, I hope, will be carried on beyond the domain of this study.

I have argued that forms of diasporic translation — transliterality (including transvisuality), erraticness, and multilingualism — have characterised the transmission of Italian poetry in the US. Despite these forms seeming to be in contradiction with one another, they are in fact complementary and concurrent, insofar as they foreground the idea that 'traduire apparaît comme une mauvaise transmission du sens [...], tantôt trop libre, tantôt trop servile' [translation appears to be a bad transmission of meaning [...], sometimes too free, sometimes too servile].[6] What made this paradox possible is the same metaphor of diaspora, which encompasses both the faithful and the unfaithful, the close and the distant. Diasporic translation, which refers to a series of foreignising practices, proves to be the natural counterpart to the poetry of displacement. By using unidiomatic language, it turns its diasporic themes (melancholia, metaliterature, religion etc.) into words at the margin.

This emphasis on the borderline and the other does not come without important consequences. First, it fosters 'a new conception of originality [...], one which would also imply new conceptions of literary tradition, linguistic appurtenance, and symbolic debt on the level of both culture and the subject'.[7] The most evident product of this reversed perspective is the figure of the translator as author. Second, it reinforces the idea that translation is at origin an ethical act, consisting in 'reconnaître et [...] recevoir l'Autre en tant qu'Autre' [acknowledging and receiving the Other as an Other].[8] As Venuti pointed out, 'a translation ethics [...] can't be restricted to a notion of fidelity'; instead, it stages 'an opening, a dialogue, a cross-breeding, a decentring' of languages and views.[9] Therefore, the ethicisation of the translation process, which Venuti called the 'ethics of difference', went hand in hand with the anthologies' selections; their diasporically ethical design developed from Poggioli's imperative 'to rebuild the house of man' to be further explored in contemporary attempts to incorporate the cry of the migrant in the age of globalisation. Finally, as a corollary, this ethically-oriented translating practice suggests that, if diasporic poems allow the transnational subject to grieve (see Ramazani's 'poetry of mourning'), diasporic translations provide the space for his/her reconnection with life, or resurrection.[10] This mystical understanding of translation, already present in Poggioli's *Inventario* project and brought to completion by Brock 2012, was prefigured by Benjamin in his 1923 essay, crucial to all future foreignising theories (Venuti, Antoine Berman, Paul De Man etc.).

At the end of this anthological journey, distance is not just a coordinate, but a poetics and a stylistics. This vision of the Italian poetic canon in English translation certainly owes much to Moretti's notion of distant reading as a way of transcending the philological confines of literary texts, be they canonical or marginal.[11] Yet, it also moves away from Moretti's work as it engages with the texts' spiritual (mystical, metaphysical) as well as material (sociological, economical) tenets. As mediators of opposites, American translators of Italian poetry bridged the gap between the national and the supranational, the self and the other, the dead and the alive, thus removing the veil of their alleged anonymity. In this manner, the *auberge* (or the canon) of the present, with its levels of idiomaticness and uncontrollable idiosyncrasies, has creatively become the *auberge* of the absent and the distant.

Notes to Chapter 20

1. Roland Barthes, *Le degré zéro de l'écriture* (Paris: Seuil, 1953); *Writing Degree Zero*, trans. by Annette Lavers (New York: Farrar Straus & Giroux, 1968).
2. Matthew Reynolds, *Likenesses: Translation, Illustration, Interpretation* (Oxford: Legenda, 2013), p. 16.
3. Ibid., p. 51.
4. I thank the poets, translators, editors, and publishers of these works for generously granting me permission to reproduce them.
5. Dates of publication in the American anthologies are reported here. These dates do not refer to the years in which the works were created and/or first published.
6. Antoine Berman, *La Traduction et la lettre, ou l'auberge du lointain* (Paris: Seuil, 1991), p. 45.
7. Katz, *American Modernism's Expatriate Scene*, p. 72.
8. Berman, *La Traduction et la lettre*, p. 74.
9. Lawrence Venuti, *The Scandals of Translation: Towards an Ethics of Difference* (London: Routledge, 1998), pp. 81–82.
10. Jahan Ramazani, *Poetry of Mourning: The Modern Elegy from Hardy to Heaney* (Chicago & London: University of Chicago Press, 1994).
11. Moretti, *Distant Reading*.

CONCLUSIONS

❖

'Today is Profound'

The translated canon of Italian lyric in the US — a poetic internation, or 'interzone', that I define as diasporic — has presented ethical, performative, and historical features. Initiated by a political émigré in the aftermath of the Second World War, and imbued with Pound's translational poetics, it immediately embraced an ethical cause, not only by foregrounding poetry's civic mission, but also by turning towards the margins of the literary establishment. By following intersecting, non-linear trajectories, it gradually accommodated the poetry of the avant-garde, of women, and of dialect writers, thereby eliciting the metamorphosis of the diasporic editor into a diasporic author. The formation of a 'second [poetic] tradition', one that is marginal, eccentric, and displaced, did not develop in the denial of the canon's Italian roots, but rather blended them with the multilayered soil of America.[1] This newly forged canon, therefore, gravitated around two centres rather than one; its two spaces interfered with one another to the point that, to use the image of a famous Polish-American poet and exile, they ultimately 'coalesce[d]' (Czesław Miłosz).[2]

Because of, and thanks to, its ethical implications, the Italian diasporic canon has been concerned with its present more than with its past, an attitude that I have explained in the light of three distinctive yet comparable concepts: Poggioli's idea of 'active tradition' (1948), Bhabha's theory of performativity (1994), and Venuti's notion of 'symptomatic reading' (1995). This idiosyncratic gaze, both nostalgic and outward-looking, justifies this canon's potential for transformation, its sense of instability, as well as its tendency to repositioning, a posture that has been most visible in its metaliterary inflections. By reflecting on and challenging its own languages and meanings, the diasporic canon has presented itself as a work in progress; suspended in a horizontal, almost 'sidereal' space, to use Jean Baudrillard's term, it still fights 'la distance fébrile du regard culturel' [the febrile distance of the cultural gaze], of its prejudices, and categories.[3]

Thirdly, the diasporic canon has proved to be a paradoxical combination of personal and societal forces. Lyrical and cultural at once, it has brought together poetry and (literary) history in a compelling fashion. This dual perspective has been elicited by the anthological genre insofar as any macroscopic investigation of the canon at large, including of its theoretical frameworks (see Pound's concept of *logopoeia*), cannot overlook its authors' microscopic, or intimate, dimensions.

By exploring Italian poetry's potential for mobility and transformation, this study puts forward a refreshed image of literature in translation and of its significance. Neither Italian nor American, Italian translated poetry is no less important than any other aspect of its domestic and receiving cultures. A unique compound, it also distinguishes itself from the vast corpus of Italian American writing, thus occupying an exclusive place in contemporary literary history. While literature in translation has often been 'regarded as [an] exotic or multicultural [sideshow] to literary histories of formal advancement or the growth of discrete national poetries', this study shows us that its 'cross-cultural dynamics are among the engines of modern and contemporary poetic development and innovation'.[4] Translation as presented here is a form of canonicity whereby nations and their literatures 'no longer signify a definite event but carry the ambiguity of comparison within them'.[5]

Yet, as Bhabha says, the products of translation 'cannot forever sustain [their] position in the academy as the adversarial cutting-edge of Western idealism', and as he has pointed out, translational thinking should stop being a counterdiscourse so that it could become a norm: 'what is required is to demonstrate another territory of translation, another testimony of analytical argument, a different engagement in the politics of and around cultural domination'.[6] The diasporic canon has suggested a way of making this change. Its emphasis on the trans-N/L-ational, which coincides with Bhabha's third place and Apter's translation zone, 'demands that we rethink our perspective on the identity of culture', which is never unitary nor 'simply dualistic in the relation of Self to Other'.[7] In Bhabha's words, 'the meanings and symbols of culture have no primordial unity or fixity' as 'even the same signs can be appropriated, translated, rehistoricized and read anew', as through the facets of a prism (Reynolds).[8]

This canon's state of in-betweenness has important effects on the reader. On the one hand, it invites us to revisit the hendiadys literature-nation, thus reversing 'il senso da attribuire alla stessa attività storiografica' [the meaning we should attribute to historiography itself] both within and outside its national borders.[9] On the other hand, it offers us a new image of the author (be s/he the poet and/or the translator) and of the reader him/herself, one that is nomadic (see Deleuze and Guattari's 1982 study), 'schizomorphic', and dispersed (BALLERINI 2017).[10] At the same time, it has also 'protected' the Italian translated canon from any risk of cultural appropriation, if we accept that migration can be an act of 'civilization', 'ethical responsibility', and 'political dissent'.[11] From this perspective, it would make no sense to express an aesthetic judgment on the value of the diasporic canon vis-à-vis its domestic counterpart. Even though, as Asor Rosa put it, 'non sempre ciò che sta ai confini rappresenta lo "spirito dei tempi" meglio di quanto non faccia ciò che eventualmente intende collocarsi al "centro"' [not always what stands at the margins represents the 'spirit of times' better than what potentially aims to occupy the centre], it is precisely where 'la ricerca letteraria si sfrangia, si decompone, entra in contatto con altri universi linguistici e comunicativi' [literary criticism unravels, breaks up, and comes into contact with other linguistic and communicational worlds] that we are most able to appreciate its artistic value.[12]

Translated canons are not dependent on domestic tradition(alism)s and/or dominant languages; they are literary objects in their own right and, as such, actively contribute to the 'literary polysystem' (Even-Zohar). Undoubtedly, there exist 'concrete differences in power between languages and literatures', English being the 'hypercentral' language and Italian being one of the five 'semicentral' languages.[13] Nonetheless, distinctions based on power and/or cultural dominancy should not prevent us from practicing a fairer criticism. At this time 'when the global hegemony of English invites a cultural narcissism and complacency on the part of British and American readers, translation can illuminate the heterogeneity that characterises any culture'.[14] It is only when:

> We understand that all cultural statements and systems are constructed in [a translational] space of enunciation, that we begin to understand why hierarchical claims to the inherent originality or 'purity' of cultures are untenable, even before we resort to empirical historical instances that demonstrate their hybridity'.[15]

Translation's transformative energy has turned the history of modern Italian poetry in the US into a new history of modern Italian poetry *tout court*. It has enlarged, rather than erased, its boundaries. It has enlightened the ways in which, in countries other than Italy, (1) the most prominent feature of twentieth-century Italian lyric is not hermeticism, but the avant-garde; (2) feminism, religious poetry, and dialect verse are transnationally interlinked; and (3) a truly comparative analysis of Italian and American poetry cannot overlook the role played by French poets and critics. By the same token, we have learnt that the birth of America's most influential and experimental publishing house, New Directions, took place in Italy, a fact that reinforces American multiculturalism on the one hand, and problematises its already complex literary foundations on the other.

Given the diasporic canon's metamorphic nature, the attempt to draw any conclusive remarks may appear too limiting an operation; it is nonetheless possible to identify a number of poets, translators, and editorial trends that contributed to its evolution in a significant way. For American anthologists, the roots of modern Italian lyric are to be found in authors such as Belli, Campana, and Ungaretti, a dialect, mystical, and cosmopolitan trio that challenges the domestic Pascoli-D'Annunzio model. The editors' diasporic sensitivity gave shape to hybrid forms of anthologisation which sponsored not just poets who had reached canonical status in Italy (such as Nobel Prize recipients Montale and Quasimodo), but also highly controversial and/or subaltern figures. Amongst the latter, Pasolini, the most anthologised poet overall (see Appendix 2.3), strikingly incarnates the anthologists' diasporic stance. The other and the self, the political and the spiritual, the pictorial and the cinematic, the 'glocal' and the epic, these are just some of the many aspects that make Pasolini a diasporic poet by definition.[16] By a twist of fate, Pasolini met Ezra Pound in 1960s Venice, where they discussed the directions of the Italian *Neoavanguardia*. Now that we can 'watch' this encounter from a distance, it is not surprising that the two ends of the diasporic thread converged in the most literary and intercontinental of Italian cities. As such, Venice is to be added to the map of diasporic landmarks (Tokyo, Paris, New York, but also Rapallo, Trieste, Croatia, Gargano, and Ninfa) which have been revealed by this study to form this canon's underpinning geography.

Poets such as Pasolini, Giuliani, Niccolai, Risi, Rosselli, Scotellaro, Turoldo, and Zanzotto, to name but a few, triggered some of the main diasporic clusters (dialect and avant-garde poetry) and themes (religion, politics, and exile) which are still at the core of the Italian translated canon today. And yet, this poetic constellation would not have existed without the mediation of the canon's translators. Weaver, already well-known as a translator of prose and opera libretti, was also, as this study has shown, an established poetry translator. As the data in Appendix 3.3 shows, he is, by far, the most prolific translator across the corpus, his translations appearing in almost a quarter of the featured anthologies, all the way from POGGIOLI 1947A to BROCK 2012, even though the number of poets he translated (nineteen) is relatively low compared to other popular translators such as Bonaffini (forty-three) and Feldman (thirty-six). Weaver specialised in poets such as Campana, Montale, Ungaretti, and Pasolini, a further sign of his impact on the formation of this diasporic tradition.

As far as anthological trends are concerned, early collections tended to be published in monolingual journals (English only), whereas the most recent publications are bilingual, trilingual, or multilingual volumes. Simultaneously, there has been an increase in thematic, poetry-only anthologies, even though comprehensive volumes still appear (see Appendix 2.1). As I summarise these data by way of conclusion, I appreciate that observations of this kind may appear simplistic; in the very way in which they suggest alternative anthological histories and perspectival modes, they open up, rather than put an end to, diasporic discourse. In this search for a coherent narrative, I have now reached the point where I realise that I could have written a very different book had I focused on poets and/or translators rather than on editors. Yet, this is a compromise and a limitation that I have been willing to accept from the very start, in the hope that readers will nuance, enrich, and challenge the story that I chose to recount, now that the story contained in these pages becomes, as it should, no longer mine, but yours.

The diasporic canon has also shown a certain degree of adaptability, if not universality. Despite being rooted in a specific historical period and cultural context, it speaks of the transnational nexus between poetry and globalisation at a time when it is impossible to keep nations (and literatures) apart. In this 'liquid' (Bauman) scenario, the US and Italy have functioned as systems, the former by embodying 'modernity' whilst the latter has been of necessity a 'perennially hyphenated cross-space', suspended between centre and periphery, literariness and diglossia.[17] More specifically, the Italian nation, 'with its peculiar process of formation, the continuous tensions between its own northern and southern regions, and its history of emigration, provides an important case for complicating and [comparatively] reassessing' the divide between East and West, North and South, as well as for questioning 'concepts of national, racial, economic, and cultural dominance'.[18] By putting forward an 'eccentric' image of Italy, this study has demonstrated that critical bigotry and literary misconceptions — from the abberancy of a white male literary canon to the absurdity of showing national, racial and/or ethnic passports in the 'world republic of letters' (Pascale Casanova) — can be overcome by means of poetry and its translations, i.e. through the same media that are generally considered the least impactful and transformative of all.[19]

The exemplary role played by these two countries may now allow us to apply the diasporic paradigm elsewhere, for instance: (i) to English-language anthologies of contemporary Italian poetry published in countries other than the US; (ii) to translated anthologies of contemporary Italian poetry published in languages other than English (French, Spanish, German etc.); (iii) to anthologies of literature in self-translation (postcolonial, italophone, francophone etc.); (iv) to translated anthologies of other historical periods (the Middle Ages, the Renaissance etc.); or (v) to other forms and media of anthologisation (online anthologies, visual, oral, and textile exhibitions, and so on and so forth). There is also a need for quantitative approaches which, in line with emerging research in the field of the sociology of poetry translation, could outline different translation histories by using and expanding the preliminary data collected in the Appendix.

It goes without saying that not all canons are diasporic; however, we can agree on the fact that all canons include in themselves the seed of their own metamorphoses. For this reason, I used diaspora not as a synonym for migrant, minor, or translated literature, but as a particular way (ethical, performative, and historical at once) of looking at, and speaking of, all of the above. As a result, diaspora has presented us with a new poetics, a new stylistics, and a new idea of translation-based canonicity, one that moves along its spatial coordinates as much as along its temporal dimension. To paraphrase Rushdie, we have all emigrated from the country of our past, even more so when we (have been asked to) abandon and/or transform our languages and countries.[20]

And yet, even though the diasporic canon has proved to be an inverted, almost mystifying entity, built upon distortions and even errors, it is neither an anti-canon nor a countercanon. It does not want to compete with, or oppose, its Italian equivalent; rather, it complements and illuminates it by giving it 'new eyes, new thought, new distance'.[21] This transformational awareness comes from the migrant's peculiar 'way of seeing', to use Berger's expression, one that is blurred and fragmentary as much as it is sharp, just like the image reflected by a 'broken mirror', or the vision of a reversed tower of Babel (see Diana Al-Hadid's sculpture at the end of this chapter).[22] Very importantly, this broken glass, and/or reversed world, is not merely a 'mirror of nostalgia'; it is in fact 'a useful tool with which to work in the present', rebuild it, and see it anew.[23] This privileged vision explains why the Italian diasporic canon included 'nation-crossing figurations of death and mourning' while also promoting their transcultural sublimation into the language and forms of translation.[24] Migrants see, and help us see, through the fog-light of another alphabet.

Finally, as a corollary, the diasporic lens has freed us from the idea that all tradition is relegated to the past or, in other words, is conservative.[25] At times, as in the case of Italian poetry's transpositions into the English language, tradition can be a daring leap towards the future. As Perloff reminded us with the words of Cendrars, 'today is profound'.[26] In this horizontal and eccentric journey out of Italy's national, linguistic, and aesthetic borders, we had the opportunity to 'toccare con mano quel macigno inamovibile, e spesso insondabile, che è l'altro, il diverso' [feel tangibly that immovable, and often unfathomable, boulder that is the other, the diverse], exactly as if we were feeling ourselves.[27] As the current migration crisis imposes on us a new awareness of the transcultural dimensions of literature, the diasporic canon has given us a chance — as Italians, as Americans, or as neither of the above — to be 'contemporanei e non antenati di noi stessi' [contemporaries to and not ancestors of ourselves].[28]

FIG. C.1. 'Self-melt' (2008) by Diana Al-Hadid.[29]

Notes to the Conclusion

1. Salman Rushdie, *Imaginary Homelands: Essays and Criticism 1981–1991* (London: Granta Books/ Penguin, 1991), p. 20.
2. Czesław Miłosz, 'Notes on Exile', *Books Abroad*, 50 (1976), 281–84 (p. 283).
3. Jean Baudrillard, *Amérique* (Paris: Grasset, 1986), p. 55.
4. Ramazani, *A Transnational Poetics*, p. 1.
5. Apter, *The Translation Zone*, p. 248.
6. Bhabha, *The Location of Culture*, p. 47.
7. Ibid., p. 52.
8. Ibid., p. 55.
9. Martino Marazzi, *A occhi aperti: letteratura dell'emigrazione e mito americano* (Milan: Franco Angeli, 2011), p. 12.
10. Gilles Deleuze and Félix Guattari, 'What is a Minor Literature?', trans. by Robert Brinkley, *Mississippi Review*, 11 (1982), 13–33.
11. Claro, 'Ezra Pound's Poetics of Translation', p. 230.
12. Asor Rosa, *Un altro Novecento*, p. ix.
13. Blakesley, 'Introduction', in *Sociologies of Poetry Translation*, p. 10. The categorisation of languages as either hyper-central, central, semi-central, or peripheral, ranging from the most hegemonic to the least hegemonic, is to be attributed to Johan Heilbron, 'Le Système mondial des traductions', in *Les Contradictions de la globalisation éditoriale*, ed. by Gisèle Saphiro (Paris: Nouveau Monde, 2009), pp. 253–74.
14. Venuti, *The Scandals of Translation*, p. 104.
15. Bhabha, *The Location of Culture*, pp. 54–55.
16. The relation between Pasolini and the American avant-gardes, especially the Beat Generation, has been the object of an essay by Ara H. Merjian, '"Howls from the Left": Pier Paolo Pasolini, Allen Ginsberg, and the Legacies of Beat America', in *Pier Paolo Pasolini, Framed and Unframed: A Thinker for the Twenty-first Century*, ed. by Luca Peretti and Karen T. Raizen (London: Bloomsbury Academic, 2018), pp. 37–62.
17. Bond, 'Towards a Trans-national Turn in Italian Studies?', p. 421. For a perceptive study of 'America's role as a model of modernity in contemporary European history', see David Ellwood, *The Shock of America: Europe and the Challenge of the Century* (Oxford: Oxford University Press, 2012), p. 1.
18. Verdicchio, *Bound by Distance*, p. 11.
19. See Pascale Casanova, *The World Republic of Letters*, trans. by M. B. Debevoise (Cambridge, MA: Harvard University Press, 2004).
20. Rushdie, *Imaginary Homelands*, p. 12.
21. Miłosz, 'Notes on Exile', p. 281.
22. Rushdie, *Imaginary Homelands*, p. 12.
23. Ibid.
24. Ramazani, *A Transnational Poetics*, p. 71.
25. Marazzi, *A occhi aperti*, p. 19.
26. The expression is the title of one of Blaise Cendrars' proses (1917). Perloff adopts it to name the first chapter of *The Futurist Moment*, p. 2.
27. Asor Rosa, *Un altro Novecento*, p. 118.
28. Ibid., p. 122.
29. I am deeply grateful to Syrian-American artist Diana Al-Hadid for granting me permission to reproduce 'Self-melt', and to photographer Thomas Powel who captured it. There could not be a more sensitive, striking, and relevant way to close: the image of the diasporic canon's reversed Tower of Babel.

APPENDIX

❖

Contents

Part 1
North American Anthologies of Modern and Contemporary Italian Poetry: Chronological Order (1940–2018)

N.B. Not all the anthologies listed in Part 1 are analysed in this book (see Part 2 for those that are).

1940–49

MANN 1943: *Heart of Europe: An Anthology of Creative Writing in Europe 1920–1940*, ed. by Klaus Mann (New York: Fisher, 1943).
POGGIOLI 1947A: 'Contemporary Italian Literature', ed. by Renato Poggioli, *Briarcliff Quarterly*, 3.12 (1947), 225–75.
POGGIOLI 1947B: *Italian-French Issue*, ed. by Renato Poggioli and Henri Peyre, special issue of *Voices: A Quarterly of Poetry*, 128 (1947) [Italian section edited by Renato Poggioli, pp. 3–22].
POGGIOLI 1948: 'A Little Anthology of Italian Poetry', ed. by Renato Poggioli, *New Directions in Prose and Poetry*, 10 (1948), 309–29.

1950–59

CAETANI 1950: *An Anthology of New Italian Writers, Selected from the Pages of the Review 'Botteghe Oscure'*, ed. by Marguerite Caetani (New York: New Directions, 1950).
WILLIAMSON 1951/1952: 'Contemporary Italian Poetry', ed. by Edward Williamson, *Poetry*, 79.3 (1951), 159–81, and 79.4 (1952), 233–44.
PUCELLI 1955: *Anthology of Italian and Italian-American Poetry*, ed. by Rodolfo Pucelli (Boston, MA: Bruce Humphries, 1955).
PACIFICI 1957: *The Promised Land and Other Poems: An Anthology of Four Contemporary Italian Poets. Umberto Saba, Giuseppe Ungaretti, Eugenio Montale, Salvatore Quasimodo*, ed. by Sergio Pacifici with a preface by Henri Peyre (New York: S. F. Vanni, 1957).
MILLER 1958: 'Italian Poetry of the *Novecento*', ed. by Peter Miller, *Folio*, 23.3 (1958), 11–34.
SELLIN 1959: 'Contemporary Italian Poems', ed. by Eric Sellin, *The Literary Review*, 2.3 (1959), 376–82.
GUENTHER AND SELLIN 1959: 'Contemporary Italian Poets', ed. by Charles Guenther and Eric Sellin, *The Literary Review. Italian Number*, 3.1 (1959), 101–62.
GUENTHER 1959: 'Contemporary Italian Poets', ed. by Charles Guenther, *The Literary Review*, 3.2 (1959), 249–59.

1960–69

BURNSHAW 1960: *The Poem Itself*, ed. by Stanley Burnshaw (Cleveland, OH: World Publishing Company, 1960) [Italian section edited by Thomas Bergin, pp. 269–327].
DE GAETANO 1961: 'Some New Trends in Italian Poetry of our Times', ed. by Armand De Gaetano, *Italica*, 38.2 (1961), 116–29.
DE PALCHI 1961: 'Poems', ed. by Alfredo De Palchi and others, *Chelsea*, 10 (1961), 7–25.
DE PALCHI 1962: 'Poems', ed. by Alfredo De Palchi and others, *Chelsea* 11 (1962), 82–93.
GUENTHER 1961: *Modern Italian Poets*, ed. by Charles Guenther (San Francisco: Inferno Press, 1961).

GOLINO 1962: *Contemporary Italian Poetry: An Anthology*, ed. by Carlo Luigi Golino (Berkeley: University of California Press, 1962).

CORMAN 1963: 'Post-war Italian Poetry', ed. and trans. by Cid Corman, *Origin: Second Series. Response*, 9 (1963), 9–62.

BERGIN 1964: *Italian Sampler: An Anthology of Italian Verse*, ed. by Thomas Bergin (Montreal: Mario Casalini, 1964).

BRADSHAW 1964: 'An Anthology of Post-war Italian Poets', ed. by Vittoria Bradshaw, *Italian Quarterly*, 31.8 (1964), 14–64.

DE PALCHI 1966A: *New Italian Writing*, ed. by Alfredo De Palchi and Sonia Raiziss, special issue of *Chelsea*, 18/19 (1966).

DE PALCHI 1966B: *Modern European Poetry: French, German, Greek, Italian, Russian, Spanish*, ed. by Willis Barnstone (New York: Bantam Books, 1966), 269–370. [Italian editors Alfredo De Palchi and Sonia Raiziss]

DE LUCA AND GIULIANO 1966: *Selections from Italian Poetry: A Bilingual Selection*, ed. by Michael De Luca and William Giuliano, foreword by Thomas G. Bergin, illus. by Ann Grifalconi (Irvington-on-Hudson, NY: Harvey House, 1966).

DE' LUCCHI 1967: *An Anthology of Italian Poems, 13th-19th Century*, ed. by Lorna De' Lucchi. With a Preface by Cesare Foligno (New York: Biblio and Tannen, 1967).

CARY 1969: *Three Modern Italian Poets: Saba, Ungaretti, Montale*, ed. by Joseph Cary (Chicago, IL, & London: University of Chicago Press, 1969; repr. 1993).

REBAY 1969: *Italian Poetry: A Selection from St. Francis to Salvatore Quasimodo*, ed. by Luciano Rebay (New York: Dover, 1969).

1970–79

GARRIGUE 1970: *Translations by American Poets*, ed. by Jean Garrigue (Athens: Ohio University Press, 1970).

MILLER, O'NEAL, AND MCDONNELL 1970: *Italian Literature in Translation*, ed. by James Miller Jr., Robert O'Neal, and Helen McDonnell (Glenview, IL: Scott, Foresman, 1970).

BRADSHAW 1971: *From Pure Silence to Impure Dialogue: A Survey of Post-war Italian Poetry, 1945–1965*, ed. by Vittoria Bradshaw (New York: Las Américas, 1971).

KIRBY 1971: *Futurist Performance*, ed. by Michael Kirby and Victoria Nes Kirby (New York: Dutton, 1971).

NIMS 1971: *Sappho to Valéry: Poems in Translation*, ed. by John Frederick Nims (New York: Rutgers University Press, 1971).

SMITH 1972: *Poems from Italy*, ed. by William Jay Smith, illus. by Elaine Raphael, calligraphy by Don Bolognese (New York: Crowell, 1972).

SWANN 1972: *Contemporary Italian Writing in English Translation*, ed. by Brian Swann, special issue of *Mediterranean Review*, 11 (1972).

APOLLONIO 1973: *Futurist Manifestos*, ed. by Umbro Apollonio (New York: Viking Press, 1973).

BALLERINI 1973: *Italian Visual Poetry, 1912–1972*, ed. by Luigi Ballerini (New York: Finch College Museum, Istituto Italiano di Cultura, 1973).

JUDGE AND DRAGOSEI 1974: *Special Italian Issue*, ed. by Franck Judge and Francesco Dragosei, special issue of *Vanderbilt Poetry Review*, 1 (1974).

LIND 1974: *Twentieth-Century Italian Poetry: A Bilingual Anthology*, ed. by Levi Robert Lind, intro. and biographical notes by Edward Williamson (Indianapolis, IN: Bobbs-Merrill, 1974).

MARCHIONE 1974: *Twentieth-Century Italian Poetry: A Bilingual Anthology*, ed. by Margherita Marchione, sketches by Filomena Puglisi (Rutherford, NJ: Fairleigh Dickinson University Press, 1974).

TUSIANI 1974: *From Marino to Marinetti: An Anthology of Forty Italian Poets*, ed. and tr. by Joseph Tusiani (New York: Baroque Press, 1974).
CORMAN 1975: *The Gist of Origin, 1951–1971: An Anthology*, ed. by Cid Corman (New York: Grossman, 1975).
WEISSBORT, FELDMAN, AND SWANN 1975: 'Contemporary Italian Poetry', ed. by Daniel Weissbort, Ruth Feldman and Brian Swann, *Modern Poetry in Translation*, 26 (1975), 1–25.
BALLERINI 1978: *The Waters of Casablanca: Analogic and Ablative Poiesis Towards Ontological Writing in Italy*, ed. by Luigi Ballerini, special issue of *Chelsea*, 37 (1978).
FELDMAN AND SWANN 1979: *Italian Poetry Today: Currents and Trends*, ed. by Ruth Feldman and Brian Swann (St. Paul, MN: New Rivers Press, 1979).

1980–89

STEFANILE 1980: *The Blue Moustache: Some Futurist Poets*, tr. by Felix Stefanile (New Rochelle, NY: Elizabeth Press, 1980).
SMITH 1981: *The New Italian Poetry, 1945 to Present: A Bilingual Anthology*, ed. by Lawrence Smith (Berkeley: University of California Press, 1981).
SPATOLA AND VANGELISTI 1982: *Italian Poetry: 1960–1980. From Neo to Post-avanguardia*, ed. by Adriano Spatola and Paul Vangelisti (San Francisco & Los Angeles: Invisible City/Red Hill Press, 1982).
HARRISON 1983: *The Favorite Malice: Ontology and Reference in Contemporary Italian Poetry*, ed. by Thomas Harrison (New York: Out of London Press, 1983).
PAOLINI 1985A: *Italian Writing Today*, ed. by Pier Francesco Paolini, special issue of *The Literary Review*, 28.2 (1985).
PAOLINI 1985B: 'A Meaningful Handful: Sixteen Contemporary Italian Poets', edited by Pier Francesco Paolini, *The Literary Review*, 29.1 (1985), 87–122.
SMITH AND GIOIA 1985: *Poems from Italy*, ed. by William Smith and Dana Gioia (St Paul, MN: New Rivers Press, 1985).
ALLEN 1986: *The Defiant Muse: Italian Feminist Poems from the Middle Ages to the Present. A Bilingual Anthology*, ed. by Beverly Allen, Muriel Kittel, and Keala Jane Jewell, introduction by Beverly Allen (New York: Feminist Press, 1986).
HALLER 1986: *The Hidden Italy: A Bilingual Edition of Italian Dialect Poetry*, ed. by Hermann Haller (Detroit: Wayne State University Press, 1986).
CHERCHI 1989: *Italian Poetry Since World War II. A Special Issue*, ed. by Paolo Cherchi, special issue of *Poetry*, 155 (1989).
VANGELISTI 1989: Emilio Villa, Giulia Niccolai, and Luciano Caruso, *Foresta ultra naturam*, ed. by Paul Vangelisti, tr. by Ippolita Rostagno, Pasquale Verdicchio, and Paul Vangelisti (Los Angeles: Red Hill Press, 1989).

1990–99

GIOIA AND PALMA 1991: *New Italian Poets*, ed. by Dana Gioia and Michael Palma (Brownsville, OR: Story Line Press, 1991).
REBAY 1991: *Introduction to Italian Poetry: A Dual-language Book*, ed. by Luciano Rebay (New York: Dover Publications, 1991).
BALLERINI 1992: *Shearsmen of Sorts: Italian Poetry, 1975–1993*, ed. by Luigi Ballerini, special issue of *Forum Italicum* (1992).
DE STASIO, CAMBON, AND ILLIANO 1992: *Twentieth-Century Italian Poets*, ed. by Giovanna Wedel de Stasio, Glauco Cambon and Antonio Illiano, first series (Detroit: Gale Research, 1992).

Vitiello 1992: *Italy's Ultramodern, Experimental Lyrics: Corpo 10,* ed. by Justin Vitiello (New York & London: Peter Lang, 1992).
Bohn 1993: *The Dada Market: An Anthology of Poetry*, ed. by Willard Bohn (Carbondale: Southern Illinois University Press, 1993).
De Stasio, Cambon, and Illiano 1993: *Twentieth-Century Italian Poets*, ed. by Giovanna Wedel de Stasio, Glauco Cambon and Antonio Illiano, second series (Detroit: Gale Research, 1993).
Smith and Picchione 1993: *Twentieth-Century Italian Poetry: An Anthology*, ed. by Lawerence Smith and John Picchione (Toronto, Buffalo & London: University of Toronto Press, 1993).
Giuliani 1995: *I Novissimi: Poetry for the Sixties*, ed. by Alfredo Giuliani (Los Angeles: Sun & Moon Press, 1995).
Ridinger and Renello 1996: *Italian Poetry, 1950–1990*, ed. by Gayle Ridinger and Gian Paolo Renello (Boston, MA: Dante University of America Press, 1996).
Vivante 1996: *Italian Poetry: An Anthology from the Beginning to the Present*, ed. by Arturo Vivante (Wellfleet, MA: Delphinium Press, 1996).
Bonaffini 1997: *Dialect Poetry of Southern Italy: Texts and Criticism. A Trilingual Anthology*, ed. by Luigi Bonaffini (Brooklyn, Ottawa & Toronto: Legas, 1997).
Claypole 1997: *Sicilian Erotica: A Bilingual Anthology of Erotic Poems by Giovanni Meli, Domenico Tempio and Giuseppe Marco Calvino*, ed. by Onat Claypole, intro. by Justin Vitiello (Brooklyn, NY: Legas, 1997).
Rothenberg and Joris 1998: *Poems for the Millennium: The University of California Book of Modern & Postmodern Poetry. Volume 2: From Postwar to Millenium*, ed. by Jerome Rothenberg and Pierre Joris (Berkeley, Los Angeles & London: University of California Press, 1998).
Haller 1998: *The Other Italy: The Literary Canon in Dialect* (Toronto & Buffalo: University of Toronto Press, 1999).
Ballerini 1999: *The Promised Land: Italian Poetry after 1975. A Bilingual Edition*, ed. by Luigi Ballerini and others (Los Angeles: Sun & Moon Press, 1999).
Bonaffini 1999: *Via Terra: An Anthology of Contemporary Italian Dialect Poetry*, ed. by Achille Serrao, Luigi Bonaffini and Justin Vitiello (Brooklyn, Ottawa & London: Legas, 1999).

2000–18

Blum and Trubowitz 2001: *Contemporary Italian Women Poets: A Bilingual Anthology*, ed. by Cinzia Sartini Blum and Lara Trubowitz (New York: Italica Press, 2001).
Bonaffini 2001: *Dialect Poetry of Northern & Central Italy: Texts and Criticism. A Trilingual Anthology*, ed. by Luigi Bonaffini and Achille Serrao (Brooklyn, Ottawa & Toronto: Legas, 2001).
Frabotta 2002: *Italian Women Poets*, ed. by Biancamaria Frabotta, tr. by Corrado Federici (Toronto, Buffalo & Lancaster: Guernica, 2002).
Malinconico 2003: *Look, Stranger: A Bilingual Anthology of Italian Poets*, ed. by Alfonso Malinconico (Stony Brook, New York: Gradiva, 2003).
Payne 2004: *A Selection of Modern Italian Poetry in Translation*, ed. by Roberta Payne (Montreal & London: McGill-Queen's University Press, 2004).
Harrison and Stewart 2007: *Contemporary Italian Poetry*, ed. by Robert Harrison and Susan Stewart, special issue of *TriQuarterly*, 127 (2007).
Brock 2007: '*Poetry*'s Italian Portfolio', ed. by Gianluigi Simonetti and Geoffrey Brock, *Poetry*, 191 (2007), 209–42.
Miller and Prufer 2008: *New European Poets*, ed. by Wayne Miller and Kevin Prufer (St Paul, MN: Graywolf Press, 2008).

MOSCÈ 2008: *New Italian Poetry*, ed. by Alessandro Moscè (Stony Brook, NY: Gradiva, 2008).
CONDINI 2009: *An Anthology of Modern Italian Poetry in English Translation with Italian Text*, ed. by Ned Condini (New York: Modern Language Association of America, 2009).
BROCK 2012: *The FSG Book of Twentieth-Century Italian Poetry*, ed. by Geoffrey Brock (New York: Farrar, Straus & Giroux, 2012).
BONAFFINI AND PERRICONE 2014: *Poets of the Italian Diaspora: A Bilingual Anthology*, ed. by Luigi Bonaffini and Joseph Perricone (New York: Fordham University Press, 2014).
MONTORFANI 2014: *Canone Inverso: Anthology of Contemporary Italian Poetry*, ed. by Pietro Montorfani (New York: Gradiva, 2014).
BALLERINI 2017: *Those Who from Afar Look Like Flies: An Anthology of Italian Poetry from Pasolini to the Present*, ed. by Luigi Ballerini, Beppe Cavatorta, and Marjorie Perloff (Toronto & London: University of Toronto Press, 2017).

Part 2
North American Anthologies of Modern and Contemporary Italian Poetry: Structural Features and Lists of Poets

2.1 *Main Features*

The American anthologies listed here are the ones that have been analysed in this book. Their main features are marked as follows: [J] = journal publication, [V] = volume publication or [C] = exhibition catalogue; [M] = monolingual, [B] = bilingual or [T] = trilingual anthology; [P] = poetry only, [Pr] = poetry and prose collection and/or [PE] = poetry and essays collection; [CO] = comprehensive (without a specific focus on poetic genres, authors and/ or themes), [T] = thematic (single-sex, selected authors and/or specific genre), [H] = historical (with modern and/or contemporary section) or [PL] = anthology of European literature, or in which Italian features among other languages.

1945–79

Anthology	[J]/[V]/[C]	[M]/[B]/[T]	[P]/[Pr]/[PE]	[CO]/[T]/[H]/[PL]
Poggioli 1947a	[J]	[M]	[Pr, PE]	[CO]
Poggioli 1947b	[J]	[M]	[Pr, PE]	[CO], [PL]
Poggioli 1948	[J]	[M]	[P]	[CO]
Caetani 1950	[V]	[M]	[Pr]	[CO]
Pacifici 1957	[V]	[B]	[P]	[T]
Sellin 1959	[J]	[M]	[P]	[CO]
Guenther and Sellin 1959	[J]	[M]	[Pr]	[CO]
Guenther 1959	[J]	[M]	[P]	[CO]
Burnshaw 1960	[V]	[M- Italian only]	[P]	[PL]
De Palchi 1961	[J]	[M]	[Pr, PE]	[CO], [PL]
Guenther 1961	[V]	[M]	[P]	[CO]
De Palchi 1962	[J]	[M]	[Pr]	[CO], [PL]
Golino 1962	[V]	[B]	[P]	[CO]
Corman 1963	[J]	[M]	[P]	[CO]
Bergin 1964	[V]	[B]	[P]	[H]
Bradshaw 1964	[J]	[B]	[P]	[CO]
De Luca and Giuliano 1966	[V]	[B]	[P]	[H]
De Palchi 1966a	[J]	[M]	[Pr, PE]	[CO]

De Palchi 1966b	[V]	[M]	[P]	[PL]
Bradshaw 1971	[V]	[B]	[PE]	[CO]
Smith 1972	[V]	[B]	[P]	[H]
Swann 1972	[J]	[M]	[Pr, PE]	[CO]
Ballerini 1973	[C]	[M]	[Pr, PE]	[T]
Lind 1974	[V]	[B]	[P]	[CO]
Marchione 1974	[V]	[B]	[P]	[CO]
Tusiani 1974	[V]	[M]	[P] /[Pr]	[H]
Ballerini 1978	[J]	[B]	[P]	[T]
Feldman and Swann 1979	[V]	[M]	[P]	[CO]

1980–2018

Anthology	[J]/[V]	[M]/[B]/[T]	[P]/[Pr]/[PE]	[CO]/[T]/[H]/[PL]
Stefanile 1980	[V]	[M]	[P]	[T]
Smith 1981	[V]	[B]	[P]	[CO]
Spatola and Vangelisti 1982	[V]	[M]	[P]	[T]
Harrison 1983	[V]	[B]	[PE]	[T]
Smith and Gioia 1985	[V]	[B]	[P]	[H]
Allen 1986	[V]	[B]	[P]	[T], [H]
Haller 1986	[V]	[B]	[P]	[T]
Gioia and Palma 1991	[V]	[B]	[P]	[CO]
Ballerini 1992	[J]	[B]	[P]	[CO]
Vitiello 1992	[V]	[B]	[P]	[T]
Smith and Picchione 1993	[V]	[M]	[P]	[CO]
Bonaffini 1997	[V]	[T]	[P]	[T]
Ballerini 1999	[V]	[B]	[P]	[CO]
Bonaffini 1999	[V]	[T]	[P]	[T]
Blum and Trubowitz 2001	[V]	[B]	[P]	[T]
Bonaffini 2001	[V]	[T]	[P]	[T]
Moscè 2008	[V]	[B]	[P]	[CO]
Condini 2009	[V]	[B]	[P]	[CO]
Brock 2012	[V]	[B]	[P]	[CO]

Bonaffini and Perricone 2014	[V]	[B]	[P]	[CO]
Montorfani 2014	[V]	[B]	[P]	[CO]
Ballerini 2017	[V]	[B]	[PE]	[CO]

2.2. List of Poets

The American anthologies considered here are the ones that have been analysed in the book. In the case of historical and/or multilingual anthologies, only the modern and/or Italian selections are given. Poets are listed in alphabetical order. The number of poems per poet is given in brackets. A number marked with an asterisk signals the presence of excerpts from one or more poetry collection(s), rather than a selection of single poems.

Poggioli 1947a: Dino Campana (1*); Libero De Libero (2); Eugenio Montale (2); Aldo Palazzeschi (2); Salvatore Quasimodo (2); Umberto Saba (1); Giuseppe Ungaretti (1).

Poggioli 1947b: Libero De Libero (2); Francesco De Pisis (1); Mario Luzi (3); Eugenio Montale (4); Francesco Monterosso (1); Aldo Palazzeschi (2); Umberto Saba (5); Giuseppe Ungaretti (4).

Poggioli 1948: Tommaso Giglio (1*); Mario Luzi (1*); Eugenio Montale (1*); Giuseppe Ungaretti (1*).

Caetani 1950: Giorgio Bassani (7); Attilio Bertolucci (1*); Giorgio Caproni (1); Franco Fortini (3); Alfonso Gatto (1*); Antonio Rinaldi (2); Roberto Roversi (3).

Pacifici 1957: Eugenio Montale (16*); Salvatore Quasimodo (10); Umberto Saba (9); Giuseppe Ungaretti (10).

Sellin 1959: Enrico Fracassi (1); Alfonso Gatto (1); Eugenio Montale (1); Sandro Penna (1); Salvatore Quasimodo (1); Vittorio Sereni (2); Leonardo Sinisgalli (1); Giuseppe Ungaretti (1).

Guenther and Sellin 1959:[1] Attilio Bertolucci; Giorgio Caproni; Libero De Libero; Alfonso Gatto; Mario Luzi; Pier Paolo Pasolini; Sandro Penna; Rocco Scotellaro; Vittorio Sereni; Leonardo Sinisgalli; Maria Luisa Spaziani.

Guenther 1959: Carlo Betocchi (2); Raffaele Carrieri (3); Libero De Libero (1); Ugo Fasolo (1); Luigi Fiorentino (1); Alessandro Parronchi (1); Salvatore Quasimodo (4); Nelo Risi (1); Sergio Solmi (1); Camillo Sbarbaro (1); Diego Valeri (1).

Burnshaw 1960: Dino Campana (2); Giosuè Carducci (1); Gabriele D'Annunzio (1); Guido Gozzano (1); Eugenio Montale (4); Giovanni Pascoli; Salvatore Quasimodo (1); Umberto Saba (3); Giuseppe Ungaretti (5). It also includes poems by the nineteenth-century poets Giacomo Leopardi and Giuseppe Gioachino Belli.

De Palchi 1961: Bartolo Cattafi (2); Alfredo De Palchi (2); Alfonso Gatto (2); Salvatore Quasimodo (2); Nelo Risi (2); Rocco Scotellaro (2); Vittorio Sereni (2); Leonardo Sinisgalli (2); David Maria Turoldo (1).

De Palchi 1962: Pietro Cimatti (1); Luciano Erba (2); Mario Luzi (1); Giorgio Orelli (1); Pier Paolo Pasolini (1); David Maria Turoldo (2).

Guenther 1961: Carlo Betocchi (3); Raffaele Carrieri (2); Libero De Libero (1); Ugo Fasolo (2); Luigi Fiorentino (2); Alessandro Parronchi (4); Salvatore Quasimodo (7); Nelo Risi (8); Camillo Sbarbaro (1); Sergio Solmi (3); Diego Valeri (2).

Golino 1962: Luigi Bartolini (2); Carlo Betocchi (2); Dino Campana (6); Vincenzo Cardarelli (5); Sergio Corazzini (2); Libero De Libero (1); Alfonso Gatto (3); Corrado Govoni (3); Guido Gozzano (3); Margherita Guidacci (1); Piero Jahier (1); Mario Luzi (3); Eugenio Montale (9); Aldo Palazzeschi (5); Giovanni Papini (1); Pier Paolo Pasolini

(1); Cesare Pavese (2); Sandro Penna (5); Salvatore Quasimodo (12); Clemente Rebora (2); Umberto Saba (8); Camillo Sbarbaro (1); Vittorio Sereni (3); Giuseppe Ungaretti (8).

CORMAN 1963: Luciano Erba (9); Enzo Fabiani (1*); Giuliano Gramigna (4); Margherita Guidacci (1*); Eugenio Montale (7); Pier Paolo Pasolini (1*); Cesare Pavese (1*); Nelo Risi (8); Alberico Sala (11); Emilio Tadini (1*); Paolo Volponi (1*).

BERGIN 1964: Vittorio Bodini (1); Vincenzo Cardarelli (2); Raffaele Carrieri (3); Mario Dell'Arco (7); Luciano Erba (1); Alfonso Gatto (2); Corrado Govoni (2); Carlo Michelstaedter (1); Eugenio Montale (2); Giacomo Noventa (2); Aldo Palazzeschi (5); Pier Paolo Pasolini; Cesare Pavese (2); Salvatore Quasimodo (2); Nelo Risi (2); Umberto Saba (9); Alberico Sala (1); Roberto Sanesi (1); Camillo Sbarbaro (1); Rocco Scotellaro (3); Vittorio Sereni (2); Leonardo Sinisgalli (3); Giorgio Soavi (2); Sergio Solmi (2); Giuseppe Ungaretti (7); Giuseppe Villaroel (10). It includes a poem by Giuseppe Giochino Belli.

BRADSHAW 1964: Giovanni Arpino (1); Nanni Balestrini (1*); Giorgio Bassani (1); Lorenzo Calogero (2); Luciano Erba (2); Franco Fortini (1); Alfredo Giuliani (1); Francesco Leonetti (1); Elio Pagliarani (1); Pier Paolo Pasolini (1); Lucio Piccolo (1); Marco Pirro (1); Antonio Porta (1); Nelo Risi (1); Roberto Roversi (1); Rocco Scotellaro (1); David Maria Turoldo (1); Paolo Volponi (1*); Andrea Zanzotto (1).

DE LUCA AND GIULIANO 1966: Vincenzo Cardarelli (1); Giosuè Carducci (5); Gabriele D'Annunzio (2); Guido Gozzano (1); Eugenio Montale (1); Aldo Palazzeschi (1); Giovanni Pascoli (1); Salvatore Quasimodo (5); Umberto Saba (2); Giuseppe Ungaretti (3).

DE PALCHI 1966A: Sergio Acutis (1); Nanni Balestrini (1*); Bartolo Cattafi (6); Giorgio Cesarano (1); Carlo Della Corte (4); Franco Fortini (4); Elio Pagliarani (1*); Pier Paolo Pasolini (1*); Lamberto Pignotti (1); Nelo Risi (8); Edoardo Sanguineti ()1; Vittorio Sereni (2); Andrea Zanzotto (3). It also includes a collection of facsimiles of visual poetry from *Il Dissenso* (1965): Danilo Giorgi (1); Alfredo Giuliani e Toti Scialoja (1); Emilio Isgrò (1); Lucia Marcucci (1); Steliomaria Martini (2); Eugenio Miccini (1); Luciano Ori (1); Lamberto Pignotti (1); Antonio Porta e Romano Ragazzi (2); Adriano Spatola e Giuseppe Landini (1); Arrigo Lora Totino (1).

DE PALCHI 1966B: Dino Campana (4); Vincenzo Cardarelli (3); Bartolo Cattafi (6); Luciano Erba (4); Mario Luzi (4); Eugenio Montale (10); Giorgio Orelli (5); Pier Paolo Pasolini (2*); Cesare Pavese (5); Lucio Piccolo (4*); Salvatore Quasimodo (7); Umberto Saba (4); Rocco Scotellaro (7); Vittorio Sereni (8); Leonardo Sinisgalli (5); David Maria Turoldo (3); Giuseppe Ungaretti (7*).

BRADSHAW 1971: Elio Filippo Accrocca (6); Giovanni Arpino (6); Nanni Balestrini (6); Lorenzo Calogero (6); Cristina Campo (4); Bartolo Cattafi (7); Giorgio Cesarano (6); Corrado Costa (5); Luciano Erba (9); Vittorio Fiore (4); Franco Fortini (19); Giovanni Giudici (10); Alfredo Giuliani (9); Margherita Guidacci (11); Francesco Leonetti (4); Luciano Luisi (5); Biagia Marniti (4); Alda Merini (6); Luciano Morandini (6); Giorgio Orelli (6); Elio Pagliarani (5); Pier Paolo Pasolini (10); Cesare Pavese (4); Lucio Piccolo (6); Lamberto Pignotti (6); Marcello Pirro (6); Antonio Porta (4); Giovanni Raboni (10); Nelo Risi (9); Angelo Romano (2); Roberto Roversi (7); Edoardo Sanguineti (10); Rocco Scotellaro (10); Vittorio Sereni (6); David Maria Turoldo (5); Cesare Vivaldi (1); Paolo Volponi (4); Andrea Zanzotto (12).

SMITH 1972: Carlo Betocchi (1); Gabriele D'Annunzio (1); Corrado Govoni (1); Guido Gozzano (1); Mario Luzi (1); Eugenio Montale (4); Aldo Palazzeschi (1); Giovanni Pascoli (1); Sandro Penna (1); Salvatore Quasimodo (2); Umberto Saba (2); Vittorio Sereni (1); Giuseppe Ungaretti (3); Diego Valeri (1).

SWANN 1972: Guido Ballo (3*); Alfredo De Palchi (9*); Alberto Lattuada (1*); Mario Luzi (2*); Alberto Mario Mariconi (2*); Eugenio Montale (5); Nelo Risi (1*); Umberto Saba (1*); Roberto Sanesi (4*); Vittorio Sereni (1); Andrea Zanzotto (3*).

BALLERINI 1973[2]: Vincenzo Accame; Giacomo Balla; Marco Balzarro; Gianfranco Baruchello; Carlo Belloli; Benedetto Fra Le Donne; Mirella Bentivoglio; Mario Betuda; Umberto Boccioni; Sylvano Bussotti; Paolo Buzzi; Francesco Cangiullo; Giorgio Carmelich; Carlo Carrà; Ugo Carrera; Luciano Caruso; Paolo Castaldi; Giorgio Cegna; Giuseppe Chiari; Tullio D'Albissola; Gianni De Bernardi; Fortunato Depero; Mario Diacono; Julius Evola; Luisa Gardini; Corrado Govoni; Emilio Isgrò; Guglielmo Jannelli; Arrigo Lora-Totino; Filippo Tommaso Marinetti; Stelio Maria Martini; Pino Masnata; Armando Mazza; Eugenio Miccini; Rolando Mignani; Magdalo Mussio; Maurizio Nannucci; Giulia Niccolai; Gastone Novelli; Anna Oberto; Martino Oberto; Anna Parapatti; Claudio Parmiggiani; Lamberto Pignotti; Luigi Russolo; Giovanna Sandri; Sarenco; Gino Severini; Gianni Emilio Simonetti; Ardengo Soffici; Adriano Spatola; Gabriele Stocchi; Emilio Villa; Volt.

LIND 1974: Angelo Barile (2); Attilio Bertolucci (4); Carlo Betocchi (2); Giuseppe Antonio Borgese (5); Paolo Buzzi (2); Dino Campana (4); Giorgio Caproni (1); Vincenzo Cardarelli (4); Giosuè Carducci (2); Gabriele D'Annunzio (5); Libero De Libero (6) Federico De Maria (1); Alfonso Gatto (3); Tommaso Giglio (1); Corrado Govoni (3); Guido Gozzano (4); Piero Jahier (1); Mario Luzi (2); Eugenio Montale (26); Saturno Montanari (5); Aldo Palazzeschi (5); Giovanni Pascoli (1); Pier Paolo Pasolini (1); Sandro Penna; Salvatore Quasimodo (17); Roberto Roversi (1); Umberto Saba (8); Rocco Scotellaro (4); Vittorio Sereni (2); Leonardo Sinisgalli (6); David Maria Turoldo (4); Giuseppe Ungaretti (14); Diego Valeri (3); Giorgio Vigolo (9).

MARCHIONE 1974: Corrado Alvaro (1); Cesare Angelini (2); Carlo Betocchi (3); Marcello Camilucci (1); Giuseppe Centore (4); Gherardo Del Colle (3); Danilo Dolci (1); Donata Doni (4); Domenico Giuliotti (1); Corrado Govoni (1); Adriano Grande (1); Giuseppe Longo (1); Biagio Marin (3); Carlo Martini (6); Arturo Onofri (1); Giovanni Papini (2); Salvatore Quasimodo (6); Clemente Rebora (23); Giovanni Titta Rosa (4); Trilussa (1); David Maria Turoldo (9); Giuseppe Ungaretti (11).

TUSIANI 1974: Vittoria Aganoor Pompili (3); Giosuè Carducci (11); Gabriele D'Annunzio (12); Salvatore Di Giacomo (4); Antonio Fogazzaro (3); Domenico Gnoli (2); Guido Gozzano (3); Arturo Graf (6); Filippo Tommaso Marinetti (2); Ada Negri (3); Giovanni Pascoli (11).

BALLERINI 1978: Nanni Cagnone (2*); Alfredo Di Legge (1*); Mario Diacono (2*); Rubina Giorgi (1*); Martino Oberto (1*); Raffaele Perrotta (2*); Emilio Villa (4*).

FELDMAN AND SWANN 1979: Nanni Balestrini (3); Luigi Ballerini (5); Dario Bellezza (3); Piero Bigongiari (2); Alfredo Bonazzi (4); Edith Bruck (2); Ferdinando Camon (2); Giorgio Caproni (1); Giovanni Cecchetti (3); Guido Ceronetti (1); Giorgio Chiesura (3); Pietro Cimatti (3); Elena Clementelli (4); Roberto Coppini (6); Raffaele Crovi (3); Maurizio Cucchi (2); Brandolino Brandolini d'Adda (2); Milo De Angelis (3); Alfredo De Palchi (4); Arnaldo Di Benedetto (1); Luciano Erba (3); Elizabeth Ferrero (3); Gilberto Finzi (1); Andrea Genovese (2); Amedeo Giacomini (3); Alfredo Giuliani (3); Renato Gorgoni (2); Margherita Guidacci (1*); Armanda Guiducci (4); Federico Hindermann (2); Gina Labriola (2); Mario Lunetta (1); Giorgio Luzzi (1); Giancarlo Majorini (2); Giorgio Manacorda (3); Giorgio Mannacio (3); Dacia Maraini (3); Elsa Morante (2); Alberto Mario Moriconi (2); Giampiero Neri (2); Giulia Niccolai (3); Stanislao Nievo (3); Rossana Ombres (1); Giorgio Orelli (4); Elio Pagliarani (3); Pier Paolo Pasolini (3); Camillo Pennati (3); Alessandro Peregalli (2); Danilo Plateo (1); Antonio Porta (2); Vasco Pratolini (1*); Giovanni Raboni (2); Silvio Ramat (3); Franco Rella (1); Nelo Risi (2); Roberto Roversi (1*); Sergio Salvi (2); Giovanna Sandri (3); Roberto Sanesi (4); Edoardo Sanguineti (2*); Francesco Smeraldi (1); Adriano Spatola (3*); Maria Luisa Spaziani (2); David Maria Turoldo (4); Carlo Villa (2); Cesare Vivaldi (2); Paolo Volponi (1).

STEFANILE 1980: Libero Altomare (1); Paolo Buzzi (4); Enrico Cavacchioli (1); Auro D'Alba (2); Luciano Folgore (2); Corrado Govoni (6); Gian Pietro Lucini (1); Gesualdo Manzella-Frontini (1); Filippo Tommaso Marinetti (1); Aldo Palazzeschi (3); Ardengo Soffici (2).

SMITH 1981: Nanni Balestrini (7); Bartolo Cattafi (8); Luciano Erba (6); Franco Fortini (9); Giovanni Giudici (3); Alfredo Giuliani (8); Giancarlo Majorino (5); Giancarlo Marmori (4); Elio Pagliarani (5); Pier Paolo Pasolini (7); Lamberto Pignotti (3); Antonio Porta (8); Nelo Risi (7); Amelia Rosselli (5); Roberto Roversi (4); Edoardo Sanguineti (3); Rocco Scotellaro (6); Adriano Spatola (2); Cesare Vivaldi (5); Paolo Volponi (6); Andrea Zanzotto (7).

SPATOLA AND VANGELISTI 1982: Vincenzo Accame (1); Marcello Angioni (1); Nanni Balestrini (1); Luig Ballerini (1); Dino Bedino (1); Gianfranco Baruchello (1); Franco Beltrametti (1); Mirella Bentivoglio (1); Gianni Bertini (1); Irma Blank (1); Tomaso Binga (1); Edoardo Cacciatore (3); Nanni Cagnone (1*); Luciano Caruso (1); Giorgio Celli (1*); Agostino Contò (1*); Corrado Costa (5); Maurizio Cucchi (1); Michelangelo Coviello (1); Betty Danon (1); Milo De Angelis (1); Enzo Di Mauro (2); Giuliano Della Casa (1); Fabio Doplicher (1); Flavio Ermini (1); Gilberto Finzi (1); Giovanni Fontana (1); Luigi Fontanella (1); Biancamaria Frabotta (1); Alfredo Giuliani (2); Milli Graffi (1); Giuliano Gramigna (1); Massimo Gualteri (1); Giuseppe Guglielmi (1); Tomaso Kemeny (1); Giulio Leoni (1); Arrigo Lora-Totino (2); Nino Majellaro (1); Lucia Marcucci (1); Angelo Maugeri (1*); Stelio Martini (1); Eugenio Miccini (1); Giuseppe Morrocchi (1); Maurizio Nannucci (1); Giulia Niccolai (4); Martino Oberto (1); Piera Oppezzo (2); Luciano Ori (1); Elio Pagliarani (1); Anna Oberto (1); Renzo Paris (2); Claudio Parmiggiani (1); Lamberto Pignotti (2); Raffaele Perrotta (2); Giancarlo Pontiggia (1); Antonio Porta (2); Mario Ramous (1); Vittorio Reta (1); Franco Rella (1); Giovanni Sandri (3); Amelia Rosselli (1*); Edoardo Sanguineti (1*); Aldo Selleri; Sarenco (1); Gregorio Scalise (1*); Carlo Sitta (1); Adriano Spatola (5); Paolo Valesio (1); Franco Verdi (1); Sebastiano Vassalli (2); Patrizia Vicinelli (1); Carlo Villa (2); Emilio Villa (4); Luigi Viola (1); Cesare Vivaldi (1); Cesare Viviani (1); William Xerra (1).

HARRISON 1983[3]: Luigi Ballerini (10); Nanni Cagnone (1*); Jacques Garelli (1*); Alfredo Giuliani (11); Angelo Lumelli (4); Raffaele Perrotta (3*); Antonio Porta (8); Andrea Zanzotto (6).

SMITH AND GIOIA 1985: Carlo Betocchi (2); Dino Campana (5); Giosuè Carducci (2); Gabriele D'Annunzio (2); Corrado Govoni (1); Guido Gozzano (4); Mario Luzi (3); Filippo Tommaso Marinetti (1); Eugenio Montale (14); Aldo Palazzeschi (2); Giovanni Pascoli (3); Pier Paolo Pasolini (2); Cesare Pavese (2); Sandro Penna (3); Lucio Piccolo (2); Salvatore Quasimodo (8); Nelo Risi (3); Umberto Saba (7); Rocco Scotellaro (3); Vittorio Sereni (2); Giuseppe Ungaretti (9); Diego Valeri (2).

ALLEN 1986: Vittoria Aganoor Pompili (1); Sibilla Aleramo (3); Anonymous Popular Songs (5); Silvia Batisti (1); Mariella Bettarini (2); Livia Candiani (1); Franca Maria Catri (1); Liana Catri (1); Patrizia Cavalli (2); Marta Fabiani (1); Marianna Fiore (1); Biancamaria Frabotta (2); Luciana Frezza (1); Rosanna Guerrini (1); Margherita Guidacci (1); Armanda Guiducci (3); Amalia Guglielminetti (2); Jolanda Insana (1); Vivian Lamarque (1); Anna Malfaiera (1); Sandra Mangini (1); Dacia Maraini (2); Daria Menicanti (1); Loretta Merenda (1); Ada Negri (1); Giulia Niccolai (2); Rossana Ombres (1); Piera Oppezzo (1); Antonia Pozzi (2); Amelia Rosselli (2); Gabriella Sica (1); Maria Luisa Spaziani (2); Ida Vallerugo (1); Annie Vivanti (1).

HALLER 1986: Ignazio Buttitta (13); Nino Costa (12); Eduardo De Filippo (6); Mario Dell'Arco (9); Salvatore Di Giacomo (20); Edoardo Firpo (13); Rocco Galdieri (5); Virgilio Giotti (15); Tonino Guerra (14); Emilio Guicciardi (3); Biagio Marin (25); Giacomo Noventa (11); Cesare Pascarella (10); Pier Paolo Pasolini (11); Albino Pierro (14); Ferdinando Russo (3); Delio Tessa (7); Trilussa (10); Vann'Antò (5).

Gioia and Palma 1991: Patrizia Cavalli (19); Milo De Angelis (15); Rodolfo Di Biasio (4); Fabio Doplicher (7); Luigi Fontanella (12); Valerio Magrelli (19); Rossana Ombres (9); Umberto Piersanti (3); Paolo Ruffilli (2); Maria Luisa Spaziani (18).

Ballerini 1992: Luigi Ballerini (9); Edoardo Cacciatore (9); Nanni Cagnone (2); Biagio Cepollaro (3); Sebastiana Comand (5); Alfredo Giuliani (9); 'Gruppo '93 e dintorni' (Mario Baino [1*], Lorenzo Durante [6], Gabriele Frasca [1], Marcello Frixione [3], Vittorio Liberti [4], Tommaso Ottonieri [6], Lello Voce [1*]); Angelo Lumelli (2); Mario Luzi (2); Antonio Porta (2); Amelia Rosselli (4*); Adriano Spatola (5); Emilio Villa (3*); Cesare Viviani; Paolo Volponi (1); Andrea Zanzotto (5).

Vitiello 1992: Cristina Annino (1*); Massimo Bettini (1*); Vincenzo Bonazza (1*); Giusi Busceti (1*); Giovanna Carnazza (1*); Giuliano Corti (1*); Michelangelo Coviello (1*); Ivano Fermini (1*); Gabriele Frasca (1*); Silvio Giussani (1*); Alberto Mari (1*); Tommaso Ottonieri (1*); Mario Parrinello (1*); Gennaro Pessini (1*); Carmelo Pistillo (1*); Justin Vitiello (1*).

Smith and Picchione 1993: Vincenzo Accame (1); Nanni Balestrini (7); Edoardo Cacciatore (5); Dino Campana (8); Livia Candiani (1); Ugo Carrega (1); Biagio Cepollaro (1); Giuseppe Conte (3); Sergio Corazzini (7); Maurizio Cucchi (1); Gabriele D'Annunzio (10); Corrado Govoni (8); Luciano Erba (8); Marta Fabiani (1); Franco Fortini (8); Gabriele Frasca (3); Giovanni Giudici (9); Alfredo Giuliani (6); Guido Gozzano (6); Emilio Isgrò (1); Mario Luzi (8); Valerio Magrelli (3); Lucia Marcucci (1); Filippo Tommaso Marinetti (3); Stelio Maria Martini (1); Eugenio Miccini (1); Eugenio Montale (19); Giulia Niccolai (11); Luciano Ori (1); Tommaso Ottonieri (3); Elio Pagliarani (3); Aldo Palazzeschi (8); Giovanni Pascoli (11); Pier Paolo Pasolini (4); Cesare Pavese (6); Lamberto Pignotti (1); Antonio Porta (12); Salvatore Quasimodo (12); Nelo Risi (10); Amelia Rosselli (6); Umberto Saba (12); Edoardo Sanguineti (7); Sarenco (1); Camillo Sbarbaro (8); Vittorio Sereni (9); Ardengo Soffici (5); Adriano Spatola (1); Giuseppe Ungaretti (17); Cesare Viviani (1); Andrea Zanzotto (9).

Bonaffini 1997: Giuseppe Altobello (6); Lino Angiuli (5); Francesco Paolo Borazio (1); Rocco Brindisi (5); Vittorio Butera (2); Ignazio Buttitta (4); Santo Calì (3); Eugenio Cirese (6); Vittorio Clemente (6); Pasquale Creazzo (3); Antonio Cremona (4); Achille Curcio (2); Nicola Giuseppe De Donno (5); Mario Dell'Arco (8); Salvatore Di Giacomo (5); Alessio Di Giovanni (1); Alessandro Dommarco (4); Pietro Gatti (7); Ottaviano Giannangeli (4); Nicola Giunta (2); Francesco Granatiero (5); Giuseppe Jovine (5); Benvenuto Lobina (4); Antonio Lotierzo (4); Dante Maffia (5); Mauro Marè (6); Cesarino Matino, known as Ziu Gesaru (4); Paolo Messina (5); Michele Pan (3); Cesare Pascarella (6); Albino Pierro (6); Tommaso Pignatelli (6); Mario Pinna (5); Giose Rimanelli (5); Vito Riviello (5); Mario Romeo (3); Giuseppe Rosato (4); Ferdinando Russo (3); Rafael Sari (5); Cosimo Savastano (5); Achille Serrao (5); Michele Sovente (3); Trilussa (5); Luigi Antonio Trofa (5); Joseph Tusiani (6); Vann'Antò (4); Raffaele Viviani (3); Gigi Zanazzo (4).

Ballerini 1999: Raffaello Baldini (4); Nanni Balestrini (4); Luigi Ballerini (1); Edoardo Cacciatore (9); Nanni Cagnone (2*); Biagio Cepollaro (3); Sebastiana Comand (5); Corrado Costa (9); Maurizio Cucchi (9*); Milo De Angelis (7); Biancamaria Frabotta (2); Alfredo Giuliani (9); Milli Graffi (3); Franco Loi (6*); Angelo Lumelli (2); Mario Luzi (4*); Giancarlo Majorino (4*); Mauro Marè (15); Giulia Niccolai (2*); Rossana Ombres (1); Elio Pagliarani (9*); Antonio Porta (3); Amelia Rosselli (17); Giovanna Sandri (11); Edoardo Sanguineti (2*); Adriano Spatola (5); Emilio Villa (3*); Cesare Viviani (2*); Paolo Volponi (1); Andrea Zanzotto (7).

Bonaffini 1999: Lino Angiuli (3); Remigio Bartolino (4); Paolo Bertolani (4); Luigi Bressan (9); Pietro Civitareale (4); Luciano Cecchinel (4); Efisio Collu (4); Nino De Vita

(1); Salvatore Di Marco (6); Salvatore Di Natale (6); Fabio Doplicher (4); Bianca Dorato (4); Amedeo Giacomini (8); Roberto Giannoni (1); Francesco Granatiero (4); Claudio Grisancich (5); Franca Grisoni (9); Giuseppe Jovine (5); Franco Loi (8); Dante Maffia (6); Leonardo Mancino (4); Marcello Marciani (5); Mauro Marè (4); Stefano Marino (4); Vito Moretti (3); Giovanni Nadiani (3); Raffaelle Nigro (3); Antonio Carlo Ponti (4); Gabriele Alberto Quadri (6); Giose Rimanelli (4); Vito Riviello (3); Giuseppe Rosato (5); Franco Scataglini (9); Achille Serrao (3); Leonardo Sole (2); Michele Sovente (4); Nevio Spadoni (5); Ida Vallerugo (3); Gian Maria Villalta (6); Giacomo Vit (4); Leonardo Zanier (3).

BLUM AND TRUBOWITZ 2001: Mariella Bettarini (12*); Cristina Campo (8); Anna Cascella (6); Patrizia Cavalli (10); Elena Clementelli (6*); Rosita Copioli (4); Biancamaria Frabotta (8); Luciana Frezza (8); Vera Gherarducci (5); Margherita Guidacci (9*); Armanda Guiducci (8); Jolanda Insana (6*); Vivian Lamarque (12); Gabriella Leto (10); Dacia Maraini (9); Daria Menicanti (10); Alda Merini (10); Giulia Niccolai (7); Luciana Notari (6); Rossana Ombres (6); Piera Oppezzo (5*); Amelia Rosselli (10); Gabriella Sica (6*); Maria Luisa Spaziani (10); Patrizia Valduga (5).

BONAFFINI 2001: Tomino Baldassari (6); Raffaello Baldini (3); Elio Bertolini (7); Paolo Bertolani (5); Remigio Bertolino (8); Giovanni Bianconi (5); Tòni Bodrìe (4); Arcadio Borgogno (5); Luigi Bressan (5); Ernesto Calzavara (5); Luciano Caniato (5); Ugo Canonica (5); Giuseppe Cassinelli (5); Luciano Cecchinel (5); Jean-Baptiste Cerlogne (2); Giancarlo Consonni (6); Nino Costa (4); Nelvia Di Monte (4); Bianca Dorato (5); Vittorio Felini (4); Edoardo Firpo (5); Franca Ronchi Francardi (4); Renzo Francescotti (5); Gaio Fratini (3); Marco Gal (8); Carlo Gergoly (5); Gabriele Ghiandoni (7); Amedeo Giacomini (7); Roberto Giannoni (5); Odoardo Giansanti, known as Pasqualon (1); Virgilio Giotti (5); Fernando Grignola (5); Giulio Grimaldi (5); Claudio Grisancich (5); Franca Grisoni (8); Tonino Guerra (4); Franco Loi (10); Leonardo Mancino (3); Piero Marelli (4); Biagio Marin (5); Eugenia Martinet (7); Giovanni Nadiani (3); Nico Naldini (8); Luigi Olivero (3); Giovanni Orelli (5); Pinin Pacòt (5); Luigi Panero (5); Pier Paolo Pasolini (8); Renso Pezzani (1); Marco Pola (5); Antonio Carlo Ponti (6); Alessandro Prugnola (2); Gabriele Alberto Quadri (5); Ferruccio Ramadori (2); Emilio Rentocchini (5); Cesare Ruffato (5); Elio Scamara (5); Franco Scataglini (9); Lilia Slomp (5); Enrico Stuffler, known as Fulminànt (3); Delio Tessa (6); Italo Varner (5); Gian Mario Villalta (5); Cesare Vivaldi (5); Andrea Zanzotto (8); Sandro Zanzotto (5); Cesare Zavattini (4); Renzo Zuccherini (4).

MOSCÈ 2008: Antonella Anedda (2); Dario Bellezza (5); Mariella Bettarini (2); Franco Buffoni (4); Patrizia Cavalli (2); Giuseppe Conte (4); Claudio Damiani (3); Milo De Angelis (5); Eugenio De Signoribus (2); Fabio Doplicher (4); Umberto Fiori (2); Luigi Fontanella (4); Valerio Magrelli (5); Roberto Mussapi (2); Remo Pagnanelli (4); Feliciano Paoli (3); Plinio Perilli (2); Umberto Piersanti (4); Giancarlo Pontiggia (2); Paolo Ruffilli (2); Giovanna Sicari (3); Michele Sovente (2); Adriano Spatola (2); Patrizia Valduga (3); Cesare Viviani (2); Valentino Zeichen (4).

CONDINI 2009: Sibilla Aleramo (1); Carlo Betocchi (3); Dino Campana (2); Cristina Campo (2); Giorgio Caproni (3); Vincenzo Cardarelli (2); Sergio Corazzini (1); Gabriele D'Annunzio (2); Milo De Angelis (3); Alfredo De Palchi (3); Luigi Fontanella (3); Franco Fortini (3); Alfredo Giuliani (3); Corrado Govoni (3); Guido Gozzano (2); Amalia Guglielminetti (1); Giorgio Guglielmino (3); Gian Pietro Lucini (2); Mario Luzi (5); Valerio Magrelli (4); Anna Malfaiera (2); Fausto Maria Martini (1); Eugenio Montale (7); Arturo Onofri (1); Aldo Palazzeschi (3); Giovanni Pascoli (3); Pier Paolo Pasolini (2); Sandro Penna (3); Antonia Pozzi (2); Salvatore Quasimodo (2); Amelia Rosselli (2); Umberto Saba (2); Roberto Sanesi (2); Edoardo Sanguineti (2); Camillo Sbarbaro (3); Maria Luisa Spaziani (2); Giuseppe Ungaretti (6); Andrea Zanzotto (3).

BROCK 2012: Antonella Anedda (4); Raffaello Baldini (5); Giacomo Balla (1); Giorgio Bassani (3); Attilio Bertolucci (6); Carlo Betocchi (3); Franco Buffoni (4); Dino Campana (6*); Giorgio Caproni (5); Vincenzo Cardarelli (2); Bartolo Cattafi (4); Patrizia Cavalli (8); Annalisa Cima (3); Sergio Corazzini (1*); Gabriele D'Annunzio (3); Gianni D'Elia (3); Milo De Angelis (6); Alfredo De Palchi (2); Eugenio De Signoribus (3); Salvatore Di Giacomo (2); Luciano Erba (7); Farfa (4); Fillia (2); Umberto Fiori (3); Franco Fortini (8); Gabriele Frasca (1); Alfonso Gatto (4); Giovanni Giudici (3); Alfredo Giuliani (2); Corrado Govoni (3); Guido Gozzano (4); Margherita Guidacci (3*); Vivian Lamarque (3); Primo Levi (2); Franco Loi (3); Mario Luzi (7); Valerio Magrelli (8); Dacia Maraini (2); Lucio Mariani (2); Filippo Tommaso Marinetti (3*); Pino Masnata (2); Alda Merini (7); Eugenio Montale (16); Saturno Montanari (2); Giorgio Orelli (3); Aldo Palazzeschi (4); Giovanni Pascoli (9); Pier Paolo Pasolini (5); Cesare Pavese (6); Sandro Penna (18); Camillo Pennati (1); Antonio Porta (4*); Antonia Pozzi (2); Fabio Pusterla (4); Salvatore Quasimodo (11); Giovanni Raboni (5); Clemente Rebora (1); Nelo Risi (5); Amelia Rosselli (6); Umberto Saba (13*); Edoardo Sanguineti (4*); Camillo Sbarbaro (3); Leonardo Sciascia (2); Rocco Scotellaro (4); Vittorio Sereni (7); Leonardo Sinisgalli (6); Ardengo Soffici (3); Maria Luisa Spaziani (5); Trilussa (4); Giuseppe Ungaretti (14); Patrizia Valduga (5*); Diego Valeri (2); Andrea Zanzotto (8).

BONAFFINI AND PERRICONE 2014: Vlada Acquavita (5); Alida Airaghi (5); Antonio Aliberti (2); Cristina Alziati (5); Giovanni Andreoni (3); Maria J. Ardizzi (1*); Alberto Avolio (4); Luigi Ballerini (4); Ester Sardoz Barlessi (6); Adelia Biasol (6); Franco Biondi (6); Pino Bosi (6); Alfredo Bufano (2); Loredana Bogliun (6); Dino Campana (4); Franco Caporossi (5); Lisa Carducci (3); Peter Carravetta (8); Alessandro Carrera (6);Gino Chiellino (10); Lino Concas (6); Ned Condini (7); Marcella Continanza (1); Mariano Coreno (8); Giovanni Costa (5); Alessandro Damiani (6); Vera Lúcia de Oliveira (11); Nino Del Duca (4); Alfredo De Palchi (7); Severino Di Giovanni (2); Enoe Di Stefano (7); Roberto Dobran (6); Vittorio Fioravanti (5); Luigi Fontanella (7); Valeriano Garbin (3); Andrea Genovese (7); Giuseppe Giambusso (8); Gianni Grohovaz (4); Anna Maria Guidi (5); Bruno Gulli (2); Marianna Jelicich (5); Silvana Lattmann (10); Ernesto Livorni (5); Marco Lucchesi (6); Irene Marchegiani (3); Laura Marchig (6); Saro Marretta, known as Saraccio (6); Lucifero Martini (6); Corrado Mastropasqua (5); Ermanno Minuto (7); Giorgio Mobili (3); Giovanni Montagna (3); Mario Moroni (4); Romano Perticarini (5); Adeodato Piazza Nicolai (6); Oral Dialect Poets (3); Fruttuoso Piccolo, known as Mao (3); Giancarlo Pizzi (5); Nino Provenzano (5); Osvaldo Ramous (6); Giose Rimanelli (6); Annalisa Saccà (1*); Piero Salabè (5); Filippo Salvatore (5); Salvatore A. Sanna (6); Franco Sepe (6); Mario Schiavato (6); Giacomo Scotti (5); Luigi Strano (8); Victoria Surliuga (2*); Orazio Tanelli (4); Pietro Tedeschi (6); Paolo Totaro (3); Maurizio Tremul (5); Joseph Tusiani (6); Paolo Valesio (10); J. Rodolfo Wilcock (6); Silvano Zamaro (6); Leonardo Zanier (6); Eligio Zanini (6).

MONTORFANI 2014: Antonella Anedda (5); Dario Bellezza (5); Danilo Bramati (5); Franco Buffoni (5); Aurelio Buletti (5); Patrizia Cavalli (5); Giuseppe Conte (5); Rosita Copioli (5); Maurizio Cucchi (5); Gianni D'Elia (5); Milo De Angelis (5); Eugenio De Signoribus (5); Umberto Fiori (5); Luigi Fontanella (5); Ermanno Krumm (5); Valerio Magrelli (5); Roberto Mussapi (5); Alberto Nessi (5); Umberto Piersanti (5); Giancarlo Pontiggia (5); Fabio Pusterla (5); Roberto Rossi Precerutti (5); Giovanna Sicari (5); Patrizia Valduga (5); Cesare Viviani (5).

BALLERINI 2017: Nanni Balestrini (4); Fernando Bandini (7); Edoardo Cacciatore (9); Lorenzo Calogero (1*); Giorgio Caproni (4); Bartolo Cattafi (18); Giorgio Celli (1); Giorgio Cesarano (2*); Corrado Costa (11); Raffele Crovi (1); Antonio Delfini (11); Mario Diacono (6); Luciano Erba (12); Massimo Ferretti (3); Franco Fortini (10);

Giovanni Giudici (2); Alfredo Giuliani (19); Giuseppe Guglielmi (4); Emilio Isgrò (7); Francesco Leonetti (11); Giancarlo Majorino (1*); Giulia Niccolai (19); Rossana Ombres (1); Elio Pagliarani (11); Pier Paolo Pasolini (4); Alessandro Peregalli (3); Lamberto Pignotti (1); Antonio Porta (5); Giovanni Raboni (9); Vittorio Reta (11); Nelo Risi (6); Amelia Rosselli (29); Tiziano Rossi (15); Roberto Roversi (8); Edoardo Sanguineti (3*); Leonardo Sinisgalli (3); Adriano Spatola (9); Emilio Villa (18); Cesare Vivaldi (10); Andrea Zanzotto (14).

2.3 Most Frequently Anthologised Poets

The poets recorded in the table below (first column) appear more than six times across the fifty anthologies examined (second column). The occurrence of each poet across the fifty anthologies is also expressed as a percentage (third column). The number six has been taken as an arbitrary threshold value beyond which I have considered a poet to be frequently represented.

Poet	Occurrences [>6/50]	Percentage
Pier Paolo Pasolini	19	38%
Eugenio Montale	18	36%
Salvatore Quasimodo	18	36%
Giuseppe Ungaretti	17	34%
Nelo Risi	15	30 %
Mario Luzi	15	30%
Umberto Saba	15	30%
Vittorio Sereni	14	28%
Alfredo Giuliani	13	26%
Andrea Zanzotto	13	26%
Aldo Palazzeschi	12	24%
Antonio Porta	12	24%
Corrado Govoni	11	22%
Dino Campana	10	20%
Luciano Erba	10	20%
Amelia Rosselli	10	20%
Edoardo Sanguineti	10	20%
Rocco Scotellaro	10	20%
Adriano Spatola	10	20%
Nanni Balestrini	9	18%
Carlo Betocchi	9	18%
Franco Fortini	9	18%
Elio Pagliarani	9	18%
Milo De Angelis	8	16%
Giulia Niccolai	8	16%

Leonardo Sinisgalli	8	16%
David Maria Turoldo	8	16%
Giorgio Caproni	7	14%
Vincenzo Cardarelli	7	14%
Bartolo Cattafi	7	14%
Libero De Libero	7	14%
Margherita Guidacci	7	14%
Lamberto Pignotti	7	14%
Roberto Roversi	7	14%
Maria Luisa Spaziani	7	14%
Luigi Fontanella	6	12%
Filippo Tommaso Marinetti	6	12%
Emilio Villa	6	12%

Part 3
North American Anthologies of Modern and Contemporary Italian Poetry: Lists of Translators

3.1 List of Translators

The American anthologies considered here are the ones that have been referred to and/or analysed in the volume with respect to translation issues. In the case of historical and/or European anthologies, only the translators for the modern and/or Italian sections are given. The surnames of the poets translated by each translator are given in brackets.

Poggioli 1947a: Maurice English (Montale); Frederick Mortimer Clapp (Palazzeschi, Saba); Warren Ramsey (Campana); William Weaver (Quasimodo, Ungaretti).

Poggioli 1947b: John Glynn Conley (Ungaretti); Maurice English (Montale); Frederick Mortimer Clapp (De Libero, De Pisis, Palazzeschi, Saba); William Weaver (Montale).

Poggioli 1948: Maurice English (Montale); William Weaver (Giglio, Luzi, Ungaretti).

Caetani 1950: William Weaver (Bassani, Bertolucci, Caproni, Fortini, Gatto, Rinaldi, Roversi).

Pacifici 1957: Thomas Bergin (Saba); Irma Brandeis (Montale); John Glynn Conley (Ungaretti); Maurice English (Montale, Ungaretti); Creighton Gilbert (Quasimodo, Ungaretti); Ben Johnson and James Mirrill (Montale); Frederick Mortimer Clapp (Saba); Sergio Pacifici (Quasimodo); Bernard Wall (Quasimodo); William Weaver (Montale, Quasimodo, Ungaretti).

Sellin 1959: Eric Sellin (Fracassi, Gatto, Montale, Penna, Quasimodo, Sereni, Sinisgalli, Ungaretti).

Guenther and Sellin 1959: Eric Sellin and Charles Guenther (Bertolucci, Caproni, De Libero, Gatto, Luzi, Pasolini, Penna, Scotellaro, Sereni, Sinisgalli, Spaziani).

Guenther 1959: Charles Guenther (Betocchi, Carrieri, De Libero, Fasolo, Fiorentino, Parronchi, Quasimodo, Risi, Sbarbaro, Solmi, Valeri).

Burnshaw 1960: John Frederick Nims (Campana, Gozzano, Montale, Saba, Ungaretti); Glauco Cambon (Carducci, D'Annunzio, Montale, Pascoli, Ungaretti); Mario Praz

(Montale); Wallace Fowlie (Quasimodo); Jonathan Levy (Saba); Thomas Bergin (Belli, Saba).

De Palchi 1961: Thomas Bergin (Scotellaro); Glauco Cambon (Cattafi, Gatto); Ursule Molinaro (Quasimodo, Sereni); Sonia Raiziss (De Palchi); Margo Viscusi and Anthony Viscusi (Quasimodo, Risi, Sinisgalli, Turoldo).

Guenther 1961: Charles Guenther (Betocchi, De Libero, Fasolo, Fiorentino, Parronchi, Quasimodo, Risi, Sbarbaro, Solmi, Valeri).

De Palchi 1962: Charles Guenther (Luzi); Lynee Lawner (Erba, Orelli, Pasolini); Margo Viscusi and Anthony Viscusi (Turoldo); William Weaver (Cimatti).

Golino 1962: Thomas Bergin (Saba); Cosimo Corsano (Cardarelli); Norman Thomas Di Giovanni (Pavese); Ronald Ferrar (Corazzini); Carlo Golino (Bartolini, Betocchi, Bertolucci, Campana, De Libero, Govoni, Gozzano, Guidacci, Jahier, Luzi, Montale, Papini, Palazzeschi, Penna, Rebora, Sbarbaro, Sereni); Allen Mandelbaum (Quasimodo); Lowry Nelson (Ungaretti); William Weaver (Pasolini).

Corman 1963: Cid Corman (Erba, Fabiani, Gramigna, Guidacci, Montale, Pasolini, Pavese, Risi, Sala, Tadini, Volponi).

Bradshaw 1964: Vittoria Bradshaw (Arpino, Balestrini, Bassani, Calogero, Erba, Fortini, Giuliani, Leonetti, Pagliarani, Pasolini, Piccolo, Pirro, Porta, Risi, Roversi, Scotellaro, Turoldo, Volponi, Zanzotto).

Bergin 1964: Thomas Bergin (Bodini, Cardarelli, Carrieri, Dell'Arco, Erba, Gatto, Govoni, Michelstaedter, Montale, Noventa, Palazzeschi, Pasolini, Pavese, Quasimodo, Risi, Saba, Sala, Sanesi, Sbarbaro, Scotellaro, Sereni, Sinisgalli, Soavi, Solmi, Ungaretti, Villaroel).

De Palchi 1966a: Cid Corman (Risi); Donald Gardner (Pasolini); Charles Guenther (Fortini); Barbara Guest and Nicola La Bianca (Pignotti); Baxter Hathaway (Acutis, Sanguineti); Venable Herndon (Risi); Oswald LeWinter (Zanzotto); Sonia Raiziss (Della Corte, Sereni); I. L. Salomon (Balestrini); Felix Stefanile (Ceserano); Robert White (Cattafi); Charles Wright (Pagliarani).

De Palchi 1966b: Thomas Bergin (Scotellaro); Irma Brandeis (Montale); Glauco.

Cambon (Cattafi); Norman Thomas Di Giovanni (Pavese); Robert Fitzgerald (Erba); George Garrett (Quasimodo); Charles Guenther (Luzi, Quasimodo, Scotellaro); Lynee Lawner (Erba, Orelli, Saba); Robert Lowell (Montale); Allen Mandelbaum (Quasimodo, Ungaretti); John Frederick Nims (Campana, Montale, Saba, Ungaretti); Sonia Raisizz (Cattafi, Sereni); Sonia Raiziss and Alfredo De Palchi (Campana, Cardarelli, Montale, Piccolo, Sinisgalli, Ungaretti); Sonia Raiziss and Glauco Cambon (Sereni); Eric Sellin (Luzi, Sereni); Felix Stefanile (Saba); Margo Viscusi and Anthony Viscusi (Turoldo); William Weaver (Scotellaro, Sinisgalli, Ungaretti); Charles Wright (Pasolini).

De Luca and Giuliano 1966: Arletta Abbott (Pascoli); Thomas Bergin (Saba); G. L. Bickersteth (Carducci); Michael De Luca (Carducci, Quasimodo, Saba); William Giuliano (Cardarelli, D'Annunzio, Ungaretti); Carlo Golino (Palazzeschi); Allen Mandelbaum (Quasimodo); Lowry Nelson Jr. (Ungaretti); Frank Sewall (Carducci); Ruth Shepard Phelps (Gozzano); William Weaver (Montale).

Bradshaw 1971: Vittoria Bradshaw (Accrocca, Arpino, Balestrini, Calogero, Campo, Cattafi, Cesarano, Costa, Erba, Fiore, Fortini, Giudici, Giuliani, Guidacci, Leonetti, Luisi, Marniti, Merini, Morandini, Orelli, Pagliarani, Pasolini, Pavese, Piccolo, Pignotti, Pirro, Porta, Raboni, Risi, Romano, Roversi, Sanguineti, Scotellaro, Sereni, Turoldo, Vivaldi, Volponi, Zanzotto).

Swann 1972: William Alexander (Sanesi); Richard Burns (Ballo); Patrick Creagh (Zanzotto); Ruth Feldman and Brian Swann (Lattuada, Saba, Sereni); Anne Griguoli (Moriconi); Dora Pettinella (Sereni); Sonia Raiziss (De Palchi, Luzi, Sereni); I. L. Salomon (De Palchi, Luzi); Ghan Singh (Montale).

Ballerini 1973: 'The texts (if any) of the works are frequently glossed in English. Also included are essays by F. T. Marinetti (translated by R. W. Flint and A. Coppotelli), Anna and Martino Oberto, Ugo Carrera (translated by Julia Cullinan), Mario Diacono, Daniela Palazzoli, Eugenio Miccini and M. Perfetti (translated by Rowena Fajardo), and Arrigo Lora-Totino'.[4].

Lind 1974: C. M. Bowra (Quasimodo); Arthur Boyars (De Libero); Irma Brandeis (Montale); D. S. Carne-Ross (Luzi); Cecil Clifford Palmer (Valeri); Margaret Crosland (Quasimodo); Maurice English (Montale); G. S. Fraser (D'Annunzio); Creighton Gilbert (Sinisgalli, Turoldo, Ungaretti); Francis Henchy (Penna, Ungaretti, Vigolo); Hamish Henderson (Gatto, Govoni); Levi Robert Lind (Barile, Betocchi, Bertolucci, Borgese, Campana, Carducci, D'Annunzio, De Maria, Gatto, Govoni, Luzi, Pascoli, Quasimodo, Saba, Sereni, Sinisgalli, Vigolo); Frederick Mortimer Clapp (De Libero, Palazzeschi, Quasimodo, Saba); Elizabeth Paragallo (Gozzano, Montale); Ezra Pound (Montanari); Samuel Putnam (Buzzi, Cardarelli, Jahier, Montale, Valeri); Olga Ragusa (Carducci, D'Annunzio, Montale, Ungaretti); Bernard Wall (Campana, Montale, Quasimodo, Sinisgalli, Ungaretti); William Weaver (Bertolucci, Campana, Caproni, Cardarelli, Giglio, Montale, Pasolini, Penna); Richard Wilbur (Quasimodo).

Marchione 1974: Margherita Marchione (Alvaro, Angelini, Betocchi, Camilucci, Centore, Del Colle, Dolci, Doni, Giuliotti, Govoni, Grande, Longo, Marin, Martini, Onofri, Papini, Quasimodo, Rebora, Titta Rosa, Trilussa, Turoldo, Ungaretti).

Tusiani 1974: Joseph Tusiani (Pompili, Carducci, D'Annunzio, Di Giacomo, Fogazzaro, Gnoli, Gozzano, Graf, Marinetti, Negri, Pascoli).

Weissbort, Feldman, and Swann 1975: Luigi Ballerini and Brian Swann (Finzi); Patrick Creagh (Giudici, Luzi, Pasolini, Risi, Zanzotto); W. S. Di Piero (Penna, Sanguineti); Ruth Feldman and Brian Swann (Bodini, Cattafi, Erba, Giudici, Giuliani, Morante, Pasolini, Porta, Raboni, Risi, Sereni); Allen Mandelbaum (Giudici); Edgar Pauk (Labriola, Maraini, Ombres).

Ballerini 1978: Julia C. Ballerini (Villa, Di Legge); Luigi Ballerini (Diacono); Richard Milazzo (Cagnone, Di Legge, Diacono, Villa); Faust Pauluzzi (Giorgi, Villa); Rosa Maria Salamone (Oberto); Daniel Scanlon (Perrotta); David Verzoni (Cagnone).

Feldman and Swann 1979: William Alexander (Sanesi); John Ashbery and Ruth Feldman (Ferrero); Anita Barrows (Ramat); Peter Burian (Mannaccio); Giovanni Cecchetti and Karen Antonelli (Pratolini); Mary Jane Ciccarello (Gorgoni); Ann Deagon (Hindermann); W. S. Di Piero (Finzi, Manacorda, Pennati, Sanguineti); D. J. Dutschke (Cecchetti); Dino Fabris (Pasolini); Ruth Feldman (Bellezza, Caproni, Cimatti, Crovi, Cucchi, Erba, Genovese, Lunetta, Neri, Raboni, Spaziani); Ruth Feldman and Brian Swann (Ballerini, Bellezza, Bruck, Clementelli, Erba, Ferrero, Giuliani, Guidacci, Guiducci, Morante, Moriconi, Neri, Niccolai, Porta, Raboni, Risi, Sandri); Rina Ferrarelli (Balestrini, Chiesura, Giuliani, Guiducci, Turoldo); Jonathan Galassi (Salvi); Katherine Jason (Villa); Frank Judge (Bonazzi, Cimatti); Richard Lansing (Bigongiari, Ceronetti); Donald Louire (Peregalli); Charles Matz (Brandolini D'Adda); Richard Milazzo (Ballerini); Rose Anna Mueller (Plateo, Rella); Ida Nolemi (Nievo); Jan Pallister (Giacomini); Edgar Pauk (Labriola, Maraini, Ombres); John Pellerzi and Art Neisberg (Coppini, Luzzi, Pagliarani); John Pellerzi and Marisa Gatti-Taylor (Smeraldi); Sonia Raiziss (De Palchi, Di Benedetto); Martin Robbins (Camon); Lawrence Smith (Majorino, Roversi, Sanguineti, Vivaldi, Volponi); Lawrence Venuti (De Angelis, Orelli, Spatola); John Yau and Ruth Feldman (Ferrero).

Stefanile 1980: Felix Stefanile (Altomare, Buzzi, Cavacchioli, D'Alba, Folgore, Govoni, Lucini, Manzella-Frontini, Marinetti, Palazzeschi, Soffici)..

Smith 1981: Lawrence Smith (Balestrini, Cattafi, Erba, Fortini, Giudici, Giuliani, Majorino, Marmori, Pagliarani, Pasolini, Pignotti, Porta, Risi, Rosselli, Roversi, Sanguineti, Scotellaro, Spatola, Vivaldi, Volponi, Zanzotto).

SPATOLA AND VANGELISTI 1982: Evelyn Bradshaw (Majellaro); John Cairncross (Cacciatore); Peter Carravetta (Ermini, Perrotta); A. Chili (Rella); Silvana Colonna (Cucchi); Luigi Fontanella (Fontanella); Luigi Fontanella and Judith Davies (Doplicher); Clive Foster (Balestrini); Giulia Niccolai (Sanguineti, Sitta); Thomas Harrison (Ballerini); David Holzapfel (Giuliani); Keala Jewell (Frabotta); Tomaso Kemeny (Kemeny); Angela Locatelli and Carla Locatelli (Maugeri); Luciano Martinengo (Oppezzo); Robert Miller (Viviani); Antonio Mungai (De Angelis); Giulia Niccolai and Paul Vangelisti (Niccolai); Faust Paulussi (Sandri); Alfredo Rizzardi (Ramous); Margaret Straus (Carlo Villa); Catherine Suppan (Pignotti); Paolo Valesio (Valesio); Paul Vangelisti (Baruchello, Beltrametti, Celli, Costa, Coviello, Di Mauro, Graffi, Gramigna, Gualtieri, Guglielmi, Pagliarani, Paris, Pontiggia, Porta, Rosselli, Spatola, Vassalli, Vivaldi); David Verzoni (Cagnone); Edgar Vincenzi (Leoni); Loraine Willis (Porta).

HARRISON 1983: Thomas Harrison (Ballerini, Cagnone, Garelli, Giuliani, Lumelli, Perrotta, Porta, Zanzotto).

SMITH AND GIOIA 1985: William Arrowsmith (Pavese); Thomas Bergin (Saba); Jack Bevan (Quasimodo); G. L. Bickersteth (Carducci); George Campster (D'Annunzio); Alfred Corn (Montale); Patrick Creagh (Ungaretti); Norman Thomas Di Giovanni (Pavese); W. S. Di Piero (Penna); Maurice English (Montale); Gavin Ewart (Risi); Jonathen Galassi (Montale); Isabella Gardner (Ungaretti); Dana Gioia (Luzi, Montale); William Giuliano (D'Annunzio); Carlo Golino (Govoni, Gozzano); Levi Robert Lind (Campana);Robert Lowell (Montale); Norman MacAfee (Pasolini); Allen Mandelbaum (Quasimodo); Luciano Martinengo (Pasolini); James Merrill (Montale); J. G. Nichols (Gozzano); Michael Palma (Gozzano, Valeri); I. L. Salomon (Betocchi, Luzi, Valeri); E. J. Scovell (Pascoli); Ghan Singh (Montale); William Jay Smith (Carducci, Montale, Pascoli, Quasimodo, Risi, Saba, Ungaretti); Felix Stefanile (Govoni, Marinetti, Palazzeschi, Saba); Henry Taylor (Penna, Saba, Sereni); Charles Tomlinson (Gozzano, Piccolo, Ungaretti); Paul Vangelisti (Scotellaro, Sereni); William Weaver (Campana, Quasimodo); Richard Wilbur (Quasimodo, Ungaretti); Charles Wright (Campana).

ALLEN 1986: Beverly Allen (Niccolai); Keala Jane Jewell (Frabotta, Insana); Muriel Kittel (Aganoor Pompili, Aleramo, Anonymous Popular Songs, Batisti, Bettarini, Candiani, Franca Maria Catri, Liana Catri, Cavalli, Fabiani, Fiore, Frezza, Guerrini, Guidacci, Guiducci, Guglielminetti, Lamarque, Malfaiera, Mangini, Maraini, Menicanti, Merenda, Negri, Ombres, Oppezzo, Pozzi, Rosselli, Sica, Spaziani, Vallerugo, Vivanti).

HALLER 1986: Hermann Haller (Buttitta, Costa, De Filippo, Dell'Arco, Di Giacomo, Firpo, Galdieri, Giotti, Guerra, Guicciardi, Marin, Noventa, Pascarella, Pasolini, Pierro, Russo, Tessa, Trilussa, Vann'Antò).

GIOIA AND PALMA 1991: Beverly Allen (Spaziani); Judith Baumel (Cavalli); W. S. Di Piero (Fontanella); Ruth Feldman (Ombres); Jonathan Galassi (Magrelli); Dana Gioia (Doplicher, Magrelli); Kenneth Koch (Cavalli); Roberto McCracken (Cavalli); Roberto McCracken and Patrizia Cavalli (Cavalli); Roberto McCracken and Pietro Pedace (Ombres); Michael Palma (Fontanella); Stephen Sartarelli (Di Biasio, Doplicher, Piersanti); Felix Stefanile (Ruffilli); Lawrence Venuti (De Angelis).

BALLERINI 1992: Richard Collins (Lumelli); Bradley Dick (Volponi); David Jacobson (Cacciatore); Michael Moore (Cepollaro, Giuliani); Lucia Re and Paul Vangelisti (Rosselli); Stephen Sartarelli (Ballerini, Cagnone, Luzi); Paul Vangelisti (Comand, Baino, Durante, Frasca, Frixione, Liberti, Ottonieri, Spatola, Viviani, Voce); Pasquale Verdicchio (Porta); Pascale Verdicchio and Chris Luzwiak (Villa); Elizabeth Wilkins (Zanzotto).

VITIELLO 1992: Justin Vitiello (Annino, Bettini, Bonazza, Busceti, Carnazza, Corti, Coviello, Fermini, Frasca, Giussani, Mari, Ottonieri, Parrinello, Pessini, Pistillo, Vitiello).

Smith and Picchione 1993: Italian texts only, English notes at the end of each chapter (Accame, Balestrini, Cacciatore, Campana, Candiani, Carrega, Cepollaro, Conte, Corazzini, Cucchi, D'Annunzio, Govon, Erb, Fabiani, Fortini, Frasca, Giudici, Giuliani, Gozzano, Isgrò, Luzi, Magrelli, Marcucci, Marinetti, Martini, Miccini, Montale, Niccola, Ori, Ottonieri, Pagliarani, Palazzeschi, Pascoli, Pasolini, Pavese, Pignott, Porta, Quasimodo, Risi, Rosselli, Saba, Sanguineti, Sarenco, Sbarbaro, Sereni, Soffici, Spatola, Ungaretti, Viviani, Zanzotto).

Bonaffini 1997: Luigi Bonaffini (Altobello, Calì, Cirese, Creazzo, Curcio, Dommarco, Dell'Arco, Giunta, Granatiero, Jovine, Maffia, Mastino, Pane, Pierro, Pignatelli, Rimanelli, Russo, Trofa, Tusiani, Sari, Serrao, Sovente); Novella Bonaffini (Angiuli, Dommarco, Zanazzo); Gaetano Cipolla (Calì, Cremona, Di Giovanni, Vann'Antò); John Du Val (Pascarella, Trilussa); Luigi Fontanella (Trofa); Ruth Feldman (Pinna); Anthony Molino (Clemente, Giannangeli, Rosato, Savastano); Michael Palma (Brindisi, Di Giacomo, Lotierzo, Riviello, Romeo, Viviani); Joseph Perricone (Borazio, Granatiero); John Shepley (Lobina); Justin Vitiello (Buttitta, De Donno, Gatti, Maré, Messina).

Ballerini 1999: Luigi Ballerini and Paul Vangelisti (Cucchi, Pagliarani); Jill Bennett (Balestrini); Richard Collins (Lumelli, Majorino, Sanguineti); Carmen Di Cinque (Ombres); Bradley Dick (Volponi); Hermann Haller (Baldini, Loi, Maré); David Jacobson (Cacciatore); Keala Jewell and Paul Vangelisti (Frabotta); Michael Moore (Cepollaro, Giuliani); Jeremy Parzen (Ballerini, Graffi, Sandri); Lucia Re and Paul Vangelisti (Rosselli); Stephen Sartarelli (Cagnone, Luzi); Paul Vangelisti (Comand, Costa, Niccolai, Spatola, Viviani); Lawrence Venuti (De Angelis); Pasquale Verdicchio (Porta); Pasquale Verdicchio and Chris Juzwiak (Villa); Elizabeth Wilkins (Zanzotto).

Bonaffini 1999: Luigi Bonaffini (Angiuli, Bertolani, Bertolini, Di Natale, Dorato, Granatiero, Jovine, Maffia, Mancino, Marino, Rimanelli, Scataglini, Serrao, Sovente); Gaetano Cipolla (De Vita, Di Marco); Dino Fabris (Bressan, Doplicher, Giacomini, Grisancich, Vallerugo, Villalta); Michael Palma (Civitareale, Giannoni, Marciani, Moretti, Ponti, Rosato, Vit, Zanier); Adeodato Piazza Nicolai (Nicolai); Joseph Perricone (Angiuli, Granatiero); Justin Vitiello (Collu, Grisoni, Loi, Marè, Nadiani, Nigro, Quadri, Riviello, Sole, Spadoni).

Blum and Trubowtiz 2001: Cinzia Sartini Blum and Laura Trubowitz (Bettarini, Campo, Cascella, Cavalli, Clementelli, Copioli, Frabotta, Frezza, Gherarducci, Guidacci, Guiducci, Insana, Lamarque, Leto, Maraini, Menicanti, Merini, Niccolai, Notari, Ombres, Oppezzo, Rosselli, Sica, Spaziani, Valduga).

Bonaffini 2001: Adria Bernardi (Baldassari, Baldini, Guerra, Nadiani, Pezzani, Rentocchini, Stuffler, Zavattini); Gaetano Cipolla (Bianconi, Canonica, Grignola, Orelli, Quadri, Scamara); Luigi Bonaffini (Giansanti, Ghiandoni, Grimaldi, Mancino, Scataglini); Dino Fabris (Bressan, Calzavara, Caniato, Cecchinel, Ruffato, Villalta, Zanotto, Zanzotto); Rina Ferrarelli (Borgogno, Felini, Francescotti, Pola, Slomp, Varner); Adeodato Piazza Nicolai (Bartolini, Cergoly, Di Monte, Giacomini, Giotti, Grisancich, Marin, Naldini, Pasolini); Michael Palma (Bertolani, Cassinelli, Firpo, Giannoni, Panero, Vivaldi); John Shepley (Cerlogne, Gal, Martinet); Justin Vitiello (Bertolani, Bodrie, Consonni, Costa, Dorato, Francardi, Fratini, Grisoni, Loi, Marelli, Olivero, Pacot, Ponti, Prugnola, Ramadori, Tessa, Zuccherini).

Moscè 2008: Emanuel Di Pasquale (Anedda, Bellezza, Bettarini, Buffoni, Cavalli, Conte, Damiani, De Angelis, De Signoribus, Doplicher, Fiori, Fontanella, Magrelli, Mussapi, Pagnanelli, Paoli, Perilli, Piersanti, Pontiggia, Ruffilli, Sicari, Sovente, Spatola, Valduga, Viviani, Zeichen).

Condini 2009: Ned Condini (Aleramo, Betocchi, Campana, Campo, Caproni, Cardarelli, Corazzini, D'Annunzio, De Angelis, De Palchi, Fontanella, Giuliani, Govoni, Gozzano,

Guglielminetti, Guglielmino, Lucini, Luzi, Magrelli, Malfaiera, Martini, Montale, Onofri, Palazzeschi, Pascoli, Pasolini, Penna, Pozzi, Quasimodo, Rosselli, Saba, Sanesi, Sanguineti, Sbarbaro, Spaziani, Ungaretti, Zanzotto).

Brock 2012: V. Joshua Adams (De Signoribus); Beverly Allen (Spaziani); Al Alvarez (Levi); William Arrowsmith (Montale, Pavese); Sarah Arvio (Anedda, Ungaretti); Patrick Barron (Zanzotto); Douglas Basford (Merini); Judith Baumel (Cavalli); Samuel Beckett (Montale); Nicholas Benson (Bertolucci); Adria Bernardi (Baldini); Carla Billitteri (D'Elia, Merini); Willard Bohn (Fillia); Luigi Bonaffini (Campana, Sereni); Vittoria Bradshaw (Risi); Geoffrey Brock (Balla, Bertolucci, Betocchi, Buffoni, Cattafi, Cavalli, D'Annunzio, Fiori, Fortini, Frasca, Govoni, Gozzano, Lamarque, Luzi, Masnata, Montale, Pascoli, Pavese, Penna, Pusterla, Raboni, Rebora, Saba, Sbarbaro, Sciascia, Sinisgalli, Soffici, Spaziani, Valduga, Valeri); Van K. Brock (Fortini, Risi); Barry Callaghan and Francesca Valente (Cavalli); Emanuel Carnevali (Di Giacomo, Palazzeschi); Cyrus Cassells (Bertolucci); Wayne Chambliss (Zanzotto); Fred Chappell (Farfa); Frederick Mortimer Clapp (Palazzeschi); Martha Collins (Maraini); Ned Condini (Caproni); Cid Corman (Guidacci, Scotellaro, Ungaretti); Peter Corvino (Lamarque); Patrick Creagh (Ungaretti); Padraig J. Daly. (Sanguineti); Donald Davie (Bassani); Peter Davinson (Trilussa); Chad Davidson and Marella Feltrin-Morris (Pusterla); Mary Di Michele (Pasolini); W. S. Di Piero (Erba, Fortini, Penna, Sereni, Sinisgalli); Laurie Duggan (Soffici); Riccardo Duranti and Anamaria Crowe Serrano (Magrelli); John DuVal (Trilussa); Michael Egan (Quasimodo); Moira Egan and Damiano Abeni (Buffoni, Cavalli, Lamarque, Penna); Alistair Elliot (D'Annunzio, Fiori, Pascoli); Ruth Feldman (Guidacci); Ruth Feldman and Brian Swann (Cattafi, Levi, Scotellaro, Zanzotto); Lawrence Ferlinghetti and Francesca Valente (Pasolini); Rina Ferrarelli (Cattafi, Sinisgalli); Robert Fitzgerald (Erba); R. W. Flint (Marinetti); Andrew Frisardi (Loi, Ungaretti); Jonathan Galassi (Cima, D'Annunzio, Magrelli, Montale); Adam Giannelli (Penna, Quasimodo); Estelle Gilson (Saba); Allen Ginsberg (Ungaretti); Dana Gioia (Cattafi, Luzi, Magrelli, Montale); David Goldstein (Caproni); Eamon Grennan (Montale); Charles Guenther (Quasimodo); Robert Hahn and Michela Martini (Sanguineti); Peter Hainsworth (Zanzotto); Michael Hamburger (Fortini); Kevin Hart (Ungaretti); Seamus Heaney (Pascoli); Anthony Hecht (Ungaretti); Geoffrey Hill (Montale); Ted Hughes (Pennati); Peter Jay (Ungaretti); Stephanie Jed and Pasquale Verdicchio (Merini); George Kay (Montale); Kenneth Koch (Cavalli); Stanley Kunitz (Ungaretti); Lynne Lawner (Erba, Orelli, Pozzi); Paul Lawton (Fortini); Robert Lowell (Montale); Thomas Lux (Campana); Rob MacKenzie (Quasimodo); Allen Mandelbaum (Cardarelli, Quasimodo, Ungaretti); J. D. McClatchy (Montale); Jaime McKendrick (Anedda, Bassani, Magrelli, Montale); James Merrill (Montale); Anthony Molino (Magrelli, Mariani, Porta); Marianne Moore (Cima); Michael Moore (Giuliani); Paul Muldoon (Montale); Elizabeth Napier and Barbara Studholme (Marinetti); John Frederick Nims (Campana); Catherine O'Brien (Guidacci); Desmond O'Grady (Pozzi, Spaziani); Jacqueline Osherow (Saba); Michael Palma (Buffoni, Corazzini, Di Giacomo, Gozzano, Palazzeschi, Raboni, Risi, Valeri); Don Peterson (Quasimodo); Roberta Payne (Gatto); Marcus Perryman (Saba); Giovanni Pontiero (Gatto); Ezra Pound (Montanari); Sonia Raiziss and Alfredo De Palchi (Sinisgalli); Lucia Re and Paul Vangelisti (Rosselli); Gayle Ridinger (Sbarbaro); Blake Robinson (Penna); Peter Robinson (Bassani, Caproni, Spaziani); Peter Robinson and Marcus Perryman (Erba, Sereni); Peter Russell (Quasimodo); J. L. Salomon (De Palchi, Luzi); Stephen Sartarelli (Luzi, Pasolini, Saba); Cinzia Sartini Blum and Lara Trubowitz (Merini); Jennifer Scappettone (Rosselli); E. J. Scovell (Pascoli); George Scrivani (Penna); Olivia Sears (Soffici); Gail Segal (De Palchi); Hal Steven Shows (Gatto); Ghan Singh and Gabrielle Barfoot (Luzi); Lawrence Smith (Fortini, Rosselli); William Jay Smith (Giudici, Penna, Risi, Sereni); Kendrick

Smithyman (Gatto); W. D. Snodgrass (Govoni); A. E. Stallings (Pascoli); Felix Stefanile (Govoni, Palazzeschi); Susan Stewart (Merini); Susan Stewart and Gian Maria Annovi (Anedda); Susan Stewart and Brunella Antomarini (Cavalli); Susan Stewart and Patrizio Ceccagnoli (De Angelis); David Stivender and J. D. McClatchy (Raboni); Laura Stortoni (Spaziani); Henry Taylor (Penna); Harry Thomas (Montale); Diana Thaw (Rosselli); Charles Tomlinson (Bertolucci, Sanguineti, Ungaretti); Paul Vangelisti (Porta); Lawrence Venuti (De Angelis, Orelli); Pasquale Verdicchio (Caproni); Rosanna Warren (Mariani); William Weaver (Cardarelli, Penna, Scotellaro, Sinisgalli); Christopher Whyte (De Signoribus); Christopher Whyte and Marco Fazzini (D'Elia, Valduga); Richard Wilbur (Quasimodo, Ungaretti); Miller Williams (Porta); Alan Williamson (Pavese, Risi); Charles Wright (Campana, Erba, Giudici, Pavese); Andrew Wylie (Ungaretti); David Young (Montale).

Bonaffini and Perricone 2014: Adria Bernardi (Minuto, De Oliveira); Luigi Bonaffini (Carducci Lisa, Piccolo, Sanna, Salvatore, Tanelli); Novella Bonaffini (Alziati, Biondi, Chiellino, Continanza); Barbara Carle (Caporossi, Lucchesi); Peter Carravetta (Carravetta, Rimanelli); Alessandro Carrera and D. F. Brown (Carrera, Surliuga); Gaetano Cipolla (Bosi, Genovese, Saccà, Strano, Totaro); Ned Condini (Condini); Paul D'Agostino (Alberti, Di Giovanni, Wilcock); Celestino De Iuliis (Ardizzi); Emanuel Di Pasquale (Moroni); John DuVal (Andreoni, Coreno, Garbin, Tedeschi); Gil Fagiani (Acquavita, Avolio, Biasol, Concas, Dobran, Marchig); Rodger Friedman (Del Duca); Bruni Grulli and Rosemary Manno (Gulli); Thomas Harrison (Ballerini); Jason Laine (Livorni); Irene Marchegiani (Di Stefano, Guidi, Marchegiani); Giorgio Mobili and Peter Carravetta (Mobili); Elizabeth Pallitto (Fioravanti); Michael Palma (Costa, Fontanella, Giambusso, Mastropasqua, Salabè, Sepe, Zamaro); Adeodato Piazza Nicolai (Airaghi, Bogliun, Grovohaz, Lottman, Marretta, Martini, Piazza Nicolai, Ramous, Schiavato, Scotti, Zanier, Zanini); Nino Provenzano and Peter Carravetta (Provenzano); Sonia Raiziss (De Palchi); Graziella Sidoli (Valesio); Robert Test Redy (Perticarini); Thomas Van Order (Tusiani); Justin Vitiello (Burlessi, Damiani, Jelicich, Montagna, Pizzi, Tremul).

Montorfani 2014: Damiano Abeni and Moira Egan (Bramati, De Signoribus, Pusterla, Sicari); Sarah Arvio (Anedda); Judith Baumel (Cavalli); Johanna Bishop (Cavalli, De Signoribus, Valduga, Viviani); Luigi Bonaffini (Fontanella, Pontiggia); Geoffrey Brock (Fiori, Valduga); Simon Carnell and Erica Segre (Bellezza, Krumm); Emanuele Di Pasquale (De Angelis, Sicari); Richard Dixon (Buffoni); Alistair Elliot (Fiori); Simon Knight (Pusterla); David Lummus, Susan Stewart, and Robert Harrison (Valduga); Enrica Martinengo (Rossi Precerutti); Jaime McKendrick (Anedda, Magrelli); Catherine O'Brien (Valduga); Michael Palma (Fontanella); Douglas Reid Skinner and Marco Fazzini (D'Elia); Gayle Ridinger (De Angelis); Matthew Rusnack (Piersanti); Marco Sonzogni (Buletti, Cucchi, Fiori, Nessi); Susan Stewart and Patrizio Ceccagnoli (De Angelis); Laura Anna Stortoni (Conte); Renata Treitel (Copioli); Pasquale Verdicchio (Conte); Patrizia Villani (Mussapi).

Ballerini 2017: Luigi Ballerini (Giuliani, Niccolai); Philip Balma (Bandini, Ceserano, Crovi, Peregalli); Adriana Baranello (Isgrò); Jacob Blakesley (Rosselli, Zanzotto); Luigi Bonaffini (Celli, Reta, Roversi); Bradley Dick (Sanguineti); Adam Bregman (Giuliani); Barbara Carle (Caproni, Giudici); Beppe Cavatorta (Delfini, Niccolai); Gianpiero Doebler (Pignotti, Raboni); Lyn Embree (Roversi); Ruth Feldman (Zanzotto); Rina Ferrarelli (Fortini); Surian Figueroa (Majorino); Polly Geller (Pasolini); Brendan Hennesse (Erba, Sinisgalli); David Jacobson (Cacciatore); Claire Lavagnino, Patrick Rumble, and Erica Westhoff (Arbasino, Diacono, Ferretti, Pagliarani, Rondi, Sanguineti, Straniero); Evgenia Matt (Cattafi, Leonetti, Ombres, Vivaldi); Gianluca Rizzo (Villa); Peter Robinson (Erba); Patrick Rumble (Pagliarani); Federica Santini (Giuliani); Anna Santos

(Guglielmi); Stephen Sartarelli (Balestrini, Pasolini); Dominic Siracusa (Delfini, Villa); Brian Swann (Zanzotto); Emma Van Ness (Calogero, Risi); Paul Vangelisti (Costa, Giuliani, Pasolini, Porta, Rossi, Spatola); Erica Westhoff (Ferretti, Sanguineti, Pasolini); Elizabeth Wilkins (Zanzotto).

3.2 Most Anthologised Poets and Their Translators

The four tables below list the translators of the most anthologised poets: Pasolini, Montale, Quasimodo, and Ungaretti. The anthologies in which these translations appear are given in the column 'Anthologies'.

Pasolini

Translators	Anthologies
Bergin, Thomas	BERGIN 1964
Bradshaw, Vittoria	BRADSHAW 1964 BRADSHAW 1971
Condini, Ned	CONDINI 2009
Corman, Cid	CORMAN 1963
Creagh, Patrick	WEISSBORT, FELDMAN, AND SWANN 1975
Di Michele, Mary	BROCK 2012
Fabris, Dino	FELDMAN AND SWANN 1979
Ferlighetti, Lawrence and Francesca Valente	BROCK 2012
Gardner, Donald	DE PALCHI 1966A
Geller, Polly	BALLERINI 2017
Haller, Hermann	HALLER 1986
Lawner, Lynne	DE PALCHI 1962
MacAfee, Norman	SMITH AND GIOIA 1985
Martinengo, Luciano	SMITH AND GIOIA 1985
Piazza Nicolai, Adeodato	BONAFFINI 2001
Sartarelli, Stephen	BROCK 2012 BALLERINI 2017
Sellin, Eric and Charles Guenther	GUENTHER AND SELLIN 1959
Smith, Lawrence	SMITH 1981
Vangelisti, Paul	BALLERINI 2017
Weaver, William	GOLINO 1962 LIND 1974
Westhoff, Erica	BALLERINI 2017
Wright, Charles	DE PALCHI 1966B

Montale

Translators	Anthologies
Arrowsmith, William	Brock 2012
Beckett, Samuel	Brock 2012
Bergin, Thomas	Bergin 1964
Brandeis, Irma	Pacifici 1957 De Palchi 1966b Lind 1974
Brock, Geoffrey	Brock 2012
Condini, Ned	Smith and Gioia 1985
Corman, Cid	Corman 1963
Corn, Alfred	Smith and Gioia 1985
English, Maurice	Poggioli 1947a Poggioli 1947b Poggioli 1948 Pacifici 1957 Lind 1974 Smith and Gioia 1985
Galassi, Jonathan	Smith and Gioia 1985 Brock 2012
Gioia, Dana	Smith and Gioia 1985 Brock 2012
Golino, Carlo	Golino 1962
Grennan, Eamon	Brock 2012
Hill, Geoffrey	Brock 2012
Johnson, Ben and James Mirrill	Pacifici 1957
Kay, George	Brock 2012
Lowell, Robert	De Palchi 1966b Smith and Gioia 1985 Brock 2012
McClatchy, J.D.	Brock 2012
Merrill, James	Smith and Gioia 1985 Brock 2012
Muldoon, Paul	Brock 2012
Nims, John Frederick	Burnshaw 1960 De Palchi 1966b
Paragallo, Elizabeth	Lind 1974
Praz, Mario	Burnshaw 1960
Putnam, Samuel	Lind 1974
Ragusa, Olga	Lind 1974
Sellin, Eric	Sellin 1959
Singh, Ghan	Swann 1972 Smith and Gioia 1985

Smith, William Jay	SMITH AND GIOIA 1985
Thomas, Harry	BROCK 2012
Wall, Bernard	LIND 1974
Weaver, William	POGGIOLI 1947B PACIFICI 1957 DE LUCA AND GIULIANO 1966 LIND 1974
Young, David	BROCK 2012

Quasimodo

Translators	Anthologies
Bergin, Thomas	BERGIN 1964
Bevan, Jack	SMITH AND GIOIA 1985
Bowra, C.M.	LIND 1974
Boyars, Arthur	LIND 1974
Condini, Ned	CONDINI 2009
Gilbert, Creighton	PACIFICI 1957
Crosland, Margaret	LIND 1974
De Luca, Michael	DE LUCA AND GIULIANO 1966
Egan, Michael	BROCK 2012
Fowlie, Wallace	BURNSHAW 1960
Garret, George	DE PALCHI 1966B
Giannelli, Adam	BROCK 2012
Guenther, Charles	GUENTHER 1959 GUENTHER 1961 DE PALCHI 1966B BROCK 2012
Lind, Levi Robert	LIND 1974
MacKenzie, Rob	BROCK 2012
Mandelbaum, Allen	GOLINO 1962 DE PALCHI 1966B DE LUCA AND GIULIANO 1966 SMITH AND GIOIA 1985 BROCK 2012
Marchione, Margherita	MARCHIONE 1974
Molinaro, Ursule	DE PALCHI 1961
Pacifici, Sergio	PACIFICI 1957
Peterson, Don	BROCK 2012
Putnam, Samuel	LIND 1974
Russell, Peter	BROCK 2012
Sellin, Eric	SELLIN 1959

Viscusi, Margo and Anthony Viscusi	DE PALCHI 1961
Wall, Bernard	PACIFICI 1957
Wall, Bernard	LIND 1974
Weaver, William	POGGIOLI 1947A PACIFICI 1957 SMITH AND GIOIA 1985
Wilbur, Richard	LIND 1974 SMITH AND GIOIA 1985 BROCK 2012

Ungaretti

Translators	Anthologies
Arvio, Sarah	BROCK 2012
Bergin, Thomas	BERGIN 1964
Cambon, Glauco	BURNSHAW 1960
Condini, Ned	CONDINI 2009
Conley, John Glynn	POGGIOLI 1947B PACIFICI 1957
Corman, Cid	BROCK 2012
Creagh, Patrick	SMITH AND GIOIA 1985 BROCK 2012
De Luca, Michael	DE LUCA AND GIULIANO 1966
English, Maurice	PACIFICI 1957
Frisardi, Andrew	BROCK 2012
Gardner, Isabella	SMITH AND GIOIA 1985
Gilbert, Creighton	PACIFICI 1957 LIND 1974
Ginsberg, Allen	BROCK 2012
Hart, Kevin	BROCK 2012
Hill, Geoffrey	BROCK 2012
Jay, Peter	BROCK 2012
Kunitz, Stanley	BROCK 2012
Mandelbaum, Allen	DE PALCHI 1966B BROCK 2012
Marchione, Margherita	MARCHIONE 1974
Nelson, Lowry	GOLINO 1962 DE LUCA AND GIULIANO 1966
Nims, John Frederick	BURNSHAW 1960
Putnam, Samuel	LIND 1974
Ragusa, Olga	LIND 1974
Raiziss, Soni and Alfredo De Palchi	DE PALCHI 1966B

Sellin, Eric	SELLIN 1959
Smith, William Jay	SMITH AND GIOIA 1985
Tomlinson, Charles	SMITH AND GOIA 1985 BROCK 2012
Wall, Bernard	LIND 1974
Weaver, William	POGGIOLI 1947A POGGIOLI 1948 PACIFICI 1957 DE PALCHI 1966B
Wilbur, Richard	SMITH AND GIOIA 1985 BROCK 2012
Wylie, Andrew	BROCK 2012

3.3 Most Frequent Translators and Poets Translated

The seven tables below display a list of the most popular translators featuring in the analysed anthologies: William Weaver (the most popular translator featuring in 12 anthologies out of 50), Thomas Bergin, Luigi Bonaffini, Ruth Feldman, Charles Guenther, Sonia Raiziss, and Paul Vangelisti. The tables register the names of the anthologies featuring each translator as well as the names of the poets translated.

Translator	Occurrences	Poets Translated
Weaver, William	POGGIOLI 1947A POGGIOLI 1947B POGGIOLI 1948 CAETANI 1950 PACIFICI 1957 DE PALCHI 1962 GOLINO 1962 DE PALCHI 1966B DE LUCA AND GIULIANO 1966 LIND 1974 SMITH AND GIOIA 1985 BROCK 2012	Bassani Bertolucci Campana Caproni Cardarelli Cimatti Fortini Gatto Giglio Luzi Montale Pasolini Penna Quasimodo Rinaldi Roversi Scotellaro Sinisgalli Ungaretti
Bergin, Thomas	PACIFICI 1957 BURNSHAW 1960 DE PALCHI 1961 GOLINO 1962 DE PALCHI 1966B DE LUCA AND GIULIANO 1966 SMITH AND GIOIA 1985	Belli Bodini Cardarelli Carrieri Dell'Arco Erba Gatto Govoni Michelstaedter Montale Noventa Palazzeschi Pasolini Pavese Quasimodo Risi Saba Sala Sanesi Sbarbaro Scotellaro Sereni Sinisgalli Soavi Solmi Ungaretti Villaroel

Bonaffini, Luigi	BONAFFINI 1997 BONAFFINI 1999 BONAFFINI 2001 BROCK 2012 BONAFFINI AND PERRICONE 2014 MONTORFANI 2014 BALLERINI 2017	Altobello Angiuli Bertolani Bertolini Calì Campana Carducci (Lisa) Celli Cirese Creazzo Curcio Dell'Arco Di Natale Dommarco Dorato Ghiandoni Giansanti Giunta Granatiero Grimaldi Jovine Maffia Mancino Marino Mastino Pane Piccolo Pierro Pignatelli Reta Rimanelli Roversi Russo Salvatore Sanna Sari Scataglini Sereni Serrao Sovente Tanelli Trofa Tusiani

Feldman, Ruth	Swann 1972 Weissbort, Feldman, and Swann 1975 Feldman and Swann 1979 Gioia and Palma 1991 Bonaffini 1997 Brock 2012 Ballerini 2017	Ballerini (with Brian Swann) Bellezza Bellezza (with Brian Swann) Bodini (with Brian Swann) Bruck (with Brian Swann) Caproni Cattafi (with Brian Swann) Cimatti Clementelli (with Brian Swann) Crovi Cucchi Erba Erba (with Brian Swann) Ferrero (with John Ashbery) Ferrero (with Brian Swann) Ferrero (with John Yau) Genovese Giudici (with Brian Swann) Giuliani (with Brian Swann) Guidacci Guidacci (with Brian Swann) Guiducci (with Brian Swann) Lattuada (with Brian Swann) Levi (with Brian Swann) Lunetta Morante (with Brian Swann) Moriconi (with Brian Swann) Neri Neri (with Brian Swann) Niccolai (with Brian Swann) Ombres Pasolini (with Brian Swann) Pinna Porta (with Brian Swann) Raboni Raboni (with Brian Swann) Risi (with Brian Swann) Saba (with Brian Swann) Sandri (with Brian Swann) Scotellaro (with Brian Swann) Sereni (with Brian Swann) Spaziani Zanzotto Zanzotto (with Brian Swann)

Guenther, Charles	Guenther and Sellin 1959 Guenther 1959 Guenther 1961 De Palchi 1962 De Palchi 1966a De Palchi 1966b Brock 2012	Bertolucci (with Eric Sellin) Betocchi Caproni (with Eric Sellin) Carrieri De Libero De Libero (with Eric Sellin) Fasolo Fiorentino Fortini Gatto (with Eric Sellin) Luzi Luzi (with Eric Sellin) Montale Parronchi Pasolini (with Eric Sellin) Penna (with Eric Sellin) Quasimodo Risi Scotellaro Scotellaro (with Eric Sellin) Sereni (with Eric Sellin) Sinisgalli (with Eric Sellin) Sbarbaro Spaziani (with Eric Sellin) Valeri
Raiziss, Sonia	De Palchi 1961 De Palchi 1966a De Palchi 1966b Swann 1972 Feldman and Swann 1979 Brock 2012 Bonaffini and Perricone 2014	Campana (with Alfredo De Palchi) Cardarelli (with Alfredo De Palchi) De Palchi Della Corte Di Benedetto Luzi Montale (with Alfredo De Palchi) Piccolo (with Alfredo De Palchi) Sereni Sereni (with Glauco Cambon) Sinisgalli (with Alfredo De Palchi) Ungaretti (with Alfredo De Palchi)

Vangelisti, Paul	Spatola and Vangelisti 1982 Smith and Gioia 1985 Ballerini 1992	Baino Baruchello Beltrametti Celli Comand Costa Coviello Di Mauro Durante Frasca Frixione Graffi Gramigna Gualtieri Guglielmi Liberti Niccolai (with Giulia Niccolai) Ottonieri Pagliarani Paris Pontiggia Porta Rosselli Rosselli (with Lucia Re) Scotellaro Sereni Spatola Vassalli Viviani Vivaldi Voce

Part 4
Transcription and Translation of Ennio Contini's Letter to Ezra Pound

A letter written by Ennio Contini to Ezra Pound on Christmas Day 1958 is conserved at the Beinecke Rare Books and Manuscript Library, Yale University, a precious piece of evidence of the importance of Pound to Italian outsiders.[5]

Natale 1958

Il tuo grande ammiratore e compagno delle primissime ore buie (quando, ad amor del vero, in Italia nessuno voleva ricordarsi di Lei, neppure gli amici), quello che con Lei e per Sua bontà fece squillare L'Alleluja, Le invia il "Pax et bonum" di Un tale.

Ennio Contini
Prà Sottano-Ferrania
(Savona)

[Christmas 1958

Your great admirer and companion during the very first dark hours (when, to tell the truth, in Italy nobody wanted to remember You, not even friends), the companion who with You and out of Your goodwill made the Alleluja ring, sends to You the "Pax et bonum" of A certain unknown person.

Ennio Contini
Prà Sottano-Ferrania
(Savona)]

Notes to the Appendix

1. This anthology presents excerpts of poems by the anthologised authors. The excerpts are accompanied by the editors' commentary.
2. Please note that not all of the poets have works illustrated in this exhibition catalogue. Due to the nature and structure of this anthology, I have decided not to include numbers.
3. The anthology includes critical texts by Stefano Agosti, Fredi Chiappelli, and Gianni Vattimo, the boundaries between poetry and hermeneutics being purposefully blurred.
4. I gather these pieces of information from Healey, *Twentieth-Century Italian Literature in English Translation*, p. 285.
5. For an image of this letter, see <https://brbl-zoom.library.yale.edu/viewer/11890285> [accessed 8 June 2021].

BIBLIOGRAPHY

❖

Primary Literature

Allen, Beverly, Muriel Kittel, and Keala Jane Jewell, eds, *The Defiant Muse: Italian Feminist Poems from the Middle Ages to the Present. A Bilingual Anthology*, introduction by Beverly Allen (New York: Feminist Press, 1986) [Allen 1986]

Allen, Donald, *The New American Poetry, 1945–1960* (New York: Grove Press, 1960)

Alvarez, Alfred., ed., *The Faber Book of Modern European Poetry* (London: Faber & Faber, 1992)

Anceschi, Luciano, ed., *Lirici nuovi* (Milan: Mursia, 1964)

Antomarini, Brunella, Berenice Cocciolillo, and Rosa Filardi, eds, *Italian Poets in Translation* (Rome: John Cabot University Press, 2008)

Apollonio, Umbro, ed., *Futurist Manifestos* (New York: Viking Press, 1973) [Apollonio 1973]

Ballerini, Luigi, ed., *Italian Visual Poetry, 1912–1972* (New York: Finch College Museum, Istituto Italiano di Cultura, 1973) [Ballerini 1973]

—— *The Waters of Casablanca: Analogic and Ablative Poiesis Towards Ontological Writing in Italy*, special issue of *Chelsea*, 37 (1978) [Ballerini 1978]

—— *Che figurato muore*, trans. into English by Thomas Harrington (Milan: All'Insegna del Pesce D'Oro, 1988)

—— *Shearmen of Sorts: Italian Poetry, 1975–1993*, special issue of *Forum Italicum* (1992) [Ballerini 1992]

Ballerini, Luigi, and Richard Milazzo, eds, *La rosa disabitata: poesia trascendentale americana, 1960–1980* (Milan: Feltrinelli, 1981)

Ballerini, Luigi, and others, eds, *The Promised Land: Italian Poetry after 1975. A Bilingual Edition* (Los Angeles: Sun & Moon Press, 1999) [Ballerini 1999]

Ballerini, Luigi, and Paul Vangelisti, eds, *Nuova poesia americana: Los Angeles* (Milan: Mondadori, 2005)

Ballerini, Luigi, and Paul Vangelisti, eds, *Nuova poesia americana: San Francisco* (Milan: Mondadori, 2006)

Ballerini, Luigi, and Federica Santini, eds, *Perché New York?* (Piacenza: Scritture, 2007)

Ballerini, Luigi, Beppe Cavatorta, and Marjorie Perloff, eds, *Those Who from Afar Look Like Flies: An Anthology of Italian Poetry from Pasolini to the Present* (Toronto & London: University of Toronto Press, 2017) [Ballerini 2017]

Barnstone, Willis, ed., *Modern European Poetry: French, German, Greek, Italian, Russian, Spanish* (New York: Bantam Books, 1966) [Italian section ed. by Alfredo De Palchi and Sonia Raiziss, pp. 269–370] [De Palchi 1966b]

Bergin, Thomas, ed., *Italian Sampler: An Anthology of Italian Verse* (Montreal: Mario Casalini, 1964) [Bergin 1964]

Blum, Cinzia Sartini, and Lara Trubowitz, eds, *Contemporary Italian Women Poets: A Bilingual Anthology* (New York: Italica Press, 2001) [Blum and Trubowitz 2001]

Bodini, Vittorio. *The Hands of the South*, trans. by Ruth Feldman and Brian Swann (Washington: Charioteer Press, 1980)

BOHN, WILLARD, ed., *The Dada Market: An Anthology of Poetry* (Carbondale: Southern Illinois University Press, 1993) [BOHN 1993]

BONAFFINI, LUIGI, ed., *Dialect Poetry of Southern Italy: Texts and Criticism. A Trilingual Anthology* (Brooklyn, Ottawa & Toronto: Legas, 1997) [BONAFFINI 1997]

BONAFFINI, LUIGI, GIAMBATTISTA FARALLI, and SEBASTIANO MARTELLI, eds, *Poesia dialettale del Molise: testi e critica. A Trilingual Anthology* (Isernia: Marinelli, 1993)

BONAFFINI, LUIGI, and ACHIELLE SERRAO, eds, *Dialect Poetry of Northern & Central Italy: Texts and Criticism. A Trilingual Anthology* (Brooklyin, Ottawa & Toronto: Legas, 2001) [BONAFFINI 2001]

BONAFFINI, LUIGI, and ACHILLE SERRAO, eds, *The Bread and the Rose: A Trilingual Anthology of Neapolitan Poetry from the 16th Century to the Present* (Ottawa: Legas, 2005)

BONAFFINI, LUIGI, and MIA COMTE, eds, *A New Map: The Poetry of Migrant Writers in Italy* (Ottawa: Legas, 2011)

BONAFFINI, LUIGI, and JOSEPH PERRICONE, eds, *Poets of the Italian Diaspora: A Bilingual Anthology* (New York: Fordham University Press, 2014) [BONAFFINI AND PERRICONE 2014]

BRADSHAW, VITTORIA, ed., 'An Anthology of Post-war Italian Poets', *Italian Quarterly*, 31.8 (1964), 14–64 [BRADSHAW 1964]

——*From Pure Silence to Impure Dialogue: A Survey of Post-war Italian Poetry, 1945–1965* (New York: Las Américas, 1971) [BRADSHAW 1971]

BROCK, GEOFFREY, ed., '*Poetry*'s Italian Portfolio', *Poetry*, 191 (2007), 209–42 [BROCK 2007]

BROCK, GEOFFREY, ed., *The FSG Book of Twentieth-Century Italian Poetry* (New York: Farrar, Straus & Giroux, 2012) [BROCK 2012]

BUFFONI, FRANCO, ed., *Italian Contemporary Poets: An Anthology* (Rome: FUIS, 2016)

BURNSHAW, STANLEY, ed., *The Poem Itself* (Cleveland, OH: World Publishing Company, 1960) [BURNSHAW 1960]

BUTTITTA, IGNAZIO, *Lu trenu di lu suli, Il treno del sole: storie, canti di protesta, canzoni in dialetto siciliano con traduzioni a fronte. La vera storia di Salvatore Giuliano, introduzione polemica di Leonardo Sciascia* (Rome: Nuova Editrice Avanti!, 1963)

CAETANI, MARGUERITE, ed., *An Anthology of New Italian Writers, Selected from the Pages of the Review 'Botteghe Oscure'* (New York: New Directions, 1950) [CAETANI 1950]

CARNEVALE, GIORGIO, and STEFANIA PASTORE, 'Omaggio a John Tedeschi', in *Intellettuali in esilio: dall'Inquisizione romana al fascismo*, ed. by John Tedeschi, Giorgio Caravale, and Stefania Pastore (Rome: Storia e Letteratura, 2012), pp. vii–xiv

CARUSO, LUCIANO, ed., *Poesia visiva in Italia, 1962–1974* (Catanzaro: Studio d'Arte il Meridione, 1974)

CARY, JOSEPH, ed., *Three Modern Italian Poets: Saba, Ungaretti, Montale* (Chicago, IL, & London: University of Chicago Press, 1969; repr. 1993) [CARY 1969]

CATTAFI, BARTOLO, *The Dry Air of the Fire: Selected Poems*, tr. by Ruth Feldman (Edinburgh: Rowan Tree Press, 1981)

CENDRARS, BLAISE, *Profond aujourd'hui* (Paris: A la Belle Edition, 1917)

CERGOLY, CAROLUS L., *Latitudine Nord* (Milan: Mondadori, 1980)

CHAVES, JONATHAN, ed., *The Columbia Book of Later Chinese Poetry* (New York: Columbia University Press, 1986)

CHERCHI, PAOLO, ed., *Italian Poetry Since World War II: A Special Issue*, special issue of *Poetry*, 155 (1989) [CHERCHI 1989]

CLAYPOLE, ONAT, ed., *Sicilian Erotica: A Bilingual Anthology of Erotic Poems by Giovanni Meli, Domenico Tempio and Giuseppe Marco Calvino*, introduction by Justin Vitiello (Brooklyn, NY: Legas, 1997) [CLAYPOLE 1997]

CONDINI, NED., ed., *An Anthology of Modern Italian Poetry in English Translation with Italian Text* (New York: Modern Language Association of America, 2009)

Contini, Ennio, *L'alleluja: poesie di Ennio Contini e la prima decade dei 'Cantos' di Ezra Pound tradotti da Mary de Rachewiltz* (Rome: Siciliana, 1952)

Cookson, William, ed., *Double Translation Issue*, special issue of *Agenda*, 6 (1968)

Corman, Cid, ed., 'Post-war Italian Poetry', *Origin: Second Series. Response*, 9 (1963), 9–62 [Corman 1963]

—— *The Gist of Origin, 1951–1971: An Anthology* (New York: Grossman, 1965) [Corman 1975]

Cox, Virginia, ed., *Lyric Poetry by Women of the Italian Renaissance* (Baltimore, MD: John Hopkins University Press, 2009)

Croce, Elena, ed., *Poeti del Novecento italiani e stranieri* (Turin: Einaudi, 1960)

Cucchi, Maurizio, and Stefano Giovanardi, eds, *Poeti italiani del secondo Novecento, 1945–1995* (Milan: Mondadori, 1996)

De Gaetano, Armand, ed., 'Some New Trends in Italian Poetry of our Times', *Italica*, 38.2 (1961), 116–29 [De Gaetano 1961]

De Libero, Libero, *Il libro del forestiero* (Milan: Mondadori, 1945)

De Luca, Michael, and William Giuliano, eds, *Selections from Italian Poetry: A Bilingual Selection*, foreword by Thomas G. Bergin, illus. by Ann Grifalconi (Irvington-on-Hudson, NY: Harvey House, 1966) [De Luca and Giuliano 1966]

De' Lucchi, Lorna, ed., *An Anthology of Italian Poems, 13th-19th Century* (New York: Biblio and Tannen, 1967) [De' Lucchi 1967]

De Palchi, Alfredo, *Sessions with My Analyst: Poems* (Stonington, CT: October House, 1970)

——, *Paradigma: Tutte le poesie, 1947–2005* (Milan: Mimesis/Hebenon, 2006)

De Palchi, Alfredo, and others, eds, 'Poems', *Chelsea*, 10 (1961), 7–25 [De Palchi 1961]

—— 'Poems', *Chelsea*, 11 (1962), 82–93 [De Palchi 1962]

De Palchi, Alfredo, and Sonia Raiziss, eds, *New Italian Writing*, special issue of *Chelsea*, 18/19 (1966) [De Palchi 1966a]

De Stasio, Giovanna Wedel, Glauco Cambon, and Antonio Illiano, eds, *Twentieth-Century Italian Poets*, first series (Detroit: Gale Research, 1992) [De Stasio, Cambon, and Illiano 1992]

—— *Twentieth-Century Italian Poets*, second series (Detroit: Gale Research, 1993) [De Stasio, Cambon, and Illiano 1993]

Devlin, Denis, ed., *Translations into English from French, German and Italian Poetry* (Dublin: Dedalus, 1992)

Di Nola, Laura, ed., *Poesia femminista italiana* (Rome: Savelli, 1978)

Dionisotti, Carlo, ed., *The Oxford Book of Italian Verse: XIIIth Century-XIXth Century. Chosen by St. John Lucas. Second Edition Revised with XXth Century Supplement* (Oxford: Clarendon Press, 1952)

Edmonds, Ursula, ed., *Lyrical Poems Including Some Original Lyrics and Some Translations from Italian Verse* (Taunton: Goodman, 1962)

Edwards, Michael, Diego Giuliano, and Margaret Straus, eds, *Directions in Italian Poetry: Prospice 6* (Aquila: The Phaeton Press, 1976)

Elliot, Alistair, ed., *Italian Landscape Poems* (Newcastle upon Tyne: Bloodaxe Books, 1993)

Esposito, Vittoriano, ed., *L'altro Novecento nella poesia italiana: critica e testi*, 6 vols (Bari: Bastogi Editrice, 1995–2001)

Feldman, Ruth, and Brian Swann, eds, *Italian Poetry Today: Currents and Trends* (St. Paul, MN: New Rivers Press, 1979) [Feldman and Swann 1979]

Frabotta, Biancamaria, ed., *Donne in poesia: antologia della poesia femminile in Italia dal dopoguerra a oggi* (Rome: Savelli, 1976)

——*Italian Women Poets*, trans. by Corrado Federici (Toronto, Buffalo & Lancaster: Guernica, 2002) [FRABOTTA 2002]
FULTON, ROBIN, ed., *An Italian Quartet: Saba, Ungaretti, Montale, Quasimodo* (London: London Magazine Edition, 1966)
GARRIGUE, JEAN, ed., *Translations by American Poets* (Athens: Ohio University Press, 1970) [GARRIGUE 1970]
GELLI, PIERO, and GINA LAGORIO, eds, *Poesia italiana: il Novecento* (Milan: Garzanti, 1980)
GENTILI, ALESSANDRO, and CATHERINE O'BRIEN, eds, *The Green Flame: Contemporary Italian Poetry with English Translations* (Dublin: Irish Academy, 1987)
GIOIA, DANA, and MICHAEL PALMA, eds, *New Italian Poets* (Brownsville, OR: Story Line Press, 1991) [GOIA AND PALMA 1991]
GIULIANI, ALFREDO, ed., *I Novissimi: poesie per gli anni '60* (Milan: Rusconi e Paolazzi, 1961)
——*I Novissimi: Poetry for the Sixties* (Los Angeles: Sun & Moon Press, 1995) [GIULIANI 1995]
GOLINO, CARLO LUIGI, ed., *Contemporary Italian Poetry: An Anthology* (Berkeley: University of California Press, 1962) [GOLINO 1962]
GUENTHER, CHARLES, ed., 'Contemporary Italian Poets', *The Literary Review*, 3.2 (1959), 249–59 [GUENTHER 1959]
——, ed., *Modern Italian Poets* (San Francisco: Inferno Press, 1961) [GUENTHER 1961]
GUENTHER, CHARLES, and ERIC SELLIN, eds, 'Contemporary Italian Poets', *The Literary Review*, 3.1 (1959), 101–62 [GUENTHER AND SELLIN 1959]
GUERNERI, LUCA, ed., *Contemporary Italian Poets*, special issue of *Modern Poetry in Translation*, 15 (1999)
GUERRA, TONINO, *La s-ciuptèda* (Faenza: Lega, 1950)
GUIDACCI, MARGHERITA, *La sabbia e l'angelo* (Florence: Vallecchi, 1946)
HAINSWORTH, PETER, and EMMANUELA TANDELLO, eds, 'Italian Poetry since 1956', *The Italianist: Supplement 1*, 15 (1995), 1–199
HAJDARI, GËZIM, *Stigmata*, trans. by Cristina Viti (Bristol: Shearsman Books, 2016)
HALL, DONALD, and ROBERT PACK, eds, *New Poets of England and America* (Cleveland: Meridian Books, 1962)
HALLER, HERMANN, ed., *The Hidden Italy: A Bilingual Edition of Italian Dialect Poetry* (Detroit: Wayne State University Press, 1986) [HALLER 1986]
HALPERN, DANIEL, ed., *The Antaeus Anthology* (New York: Bantam Dell, 1986)
HARRISON, THOMAS, ed., *The Favorite Malice: Ontology and Reference in Contemporary Italian Poetry* (New York: Out of London Press, 1983) [HARRISON 1983]
HARRISON, ROBERT, and SUSAN STEWART, eds, *Contemporary Italian Poetry*, special issue of *TriQuarterly*, 127 (2007) [HARRISON AND STEWART 2007]
HARSHAV, BENJAMIN, and BARBARA HARSHAV, eds, *American Yiddish Poetry: A Bilingual Anthology* (Berkeley: University of California Press, 1986)
HOWE, FLORENCE, and ELLEN BASS, eds, *No More Masks! An Anthology of Poems by Women* (Garden City, NY: Anchor Press, 1973)
JACOBBI, RUGGERO, ed., *Poesia futurista italiana* (Parma: Guanda, 1968)
JONES, FREDERIC, ed., *The Modern Italian Lyric* (Cardiff: University of Wales Press, 1986)
JUDGE, FRANCK, and FRANCESCO DRAGOSEI, eds, *Special Italian Issue*, special issue of *Vanderbilt Poetry Review*, 1 (1974) [JUDGE AND DRAGOSEI 1974]
KAY, GEORGE, ed., *The Penguin Book of Italian Verse: With Plain Prose Translations of Each Poem* (Harmondsworth: Penguin, 1958) [repr. 1965]
KIRBY, MICHAEL, and VICTORIA NES KIRBY, eds, *Futurist Performance* (New York: Dutton, 1971) [KIRBY 1971]
KONEK, CAROL, and DOROTHY WALTERS, eds, *I Hear My Sisters Saying: Poems by Twentieth-Century Women* (New York: Crowell, 1976)

LIND, LEVI ROBERT, ed., *Twentieth-Century Italian Poetry: A Bilingual Anthology*, (Indianapolis, IN: Bobbs-Merrill, 1974) [LIND 1974]

LINGUAGLOSSA, GIORGIO, ed., *Il rumore delle parole: 28 poeti del Sud* (Rome: Edilazio, 2014)

LOWELL, ROBERT, *Imitations, 1917–1977* (London: Faber & Faber, 1961)

LUZI, MARIO, *Quaderno gotico* (Florence: Vallecchi, 1947)

MALINCONICO, ALFONSO, ed., *Look, Stranger: A Bilingual Anthology of Italian Poets* (Stony Brook, NY: Gradiva, 2003) [MALINCONICO 2003]

MANN, KLAUS, ed., *Heart of Europe: An Anthology of Creative Writing in Europe 1920–1940* (New York: Fisher, 1943) [MANN 1943]

MARCHIONE, MARGHERITA, ed., *Twentieth-Century Italian Poetry: A Bilingual Anthology*, sketches by Filomena Puglisi (Rutherford, NJ: Fairleigh Dickinson University Press, 1974) [MARCHIONE 1974]

MARINETTI, FILIPPO TOMMASO, *Marinetti: Selected Writing*, ed. by R. W Flint (New York: Ferra, Straus Giroux, 1972)

—— *Stung by Salt and Water: Creative Texts of the Italian Avant-gardist F. T. Marinetti*, ed. and trans. by Richard J. Pioli (New York: Peter Lang, 1987)

—— *The Futurist Cookbook*, ed. by Leslie Chamberlain (Bedford, MA: Bedford Arts, 1989)

MASTERS, EDGAR LEE, *Antologia di Spoon River*, trans. by Fernanda Pivano (Turin: Einaudi, 1943)

MAY, FREDERICK, ed., *Modern Italian Poetry: Selections with English Parallel*, compiled by Vanni Scheiwiller (Sidney: South Head Press, 1970)

MCGUINNESS, PATRICK, *L'età della sedia vuota*, ed. and trans. by Giorgia Sensi (Rovigo: Il Ponte del Sale, 2011)

MCKENDRICK, JAMIE, ed., *The Faber Book of 20th-century Italian Poems* (London: Faber & Faber, 2004)

MENGALDO, PIER VINCENZO, ed., *Poeti italiani del Novecento* (Milan: Mondadori, 1978)

MILLER, PETER, ed., 'Italian Poetry of the *Novecento*', *Folio*, 23.3 (1958), 11–34 [MILLER 1958]

MILLER, JAMES JR., ROBERT O'NEAL, and HELEN MCDONNELL, eds, *Italian Literature in Translation* (Glenview, IL: Scott, Foresman, 1970) [MILLER, O'NEAL, AND MCDONNELL 1970]

MILLER, WAYNE, and KEVIN PRUFER, eds, *New European Poets* (St Paul, MN: Graywolf Press, 2008) [MILLER AND PRUFER 2008]

MONTALE, EUGENIO, *La bufera e altro* (Venice: Neri Pozza Editore, 1956)

MONTORFANI, PIETRO, ed., *Canone inverso: Anthology of Contemporary Italian Poetry* (New York: Gradiva, 2014) [MONTORFANI 2014]

MORGAN, EDWARD, *Rites of Passage: Selected Translations* (Manchester: Carcanet, 1976)

MORRISON, ROBERT, ed., *Australia's Italian Poets* (Adelaide: Andor Publishers, 1976)

MOSCÈ, ALESSANDRO, ed., *New Italian Poetry* (Stony Brook, NY: Gradiva, 2008) [MOSCÈ 2008]

NICCOLAI, GIULIA, *Harry's Bar e altre poesie, 1969–80* (Milan: Feltrinelli, 1981)

NIMS, JOHN FREDERICK, ed., *Sappho to Valéry: Poems in Translation* (New York: Rutgers University Press, 1971) [NIMS 1971]

Ó CEALLACHÁIN, ÉANNA, ed., *Twentieth-Century Italian Poetry: A Critical Anthology. 1900 to the Neo-avant-garde* (Leicester: Troubador, 2007)

O'BRIEN, CATHERINE, ed., *Italian Women Poets of the Twentieth Century* (Dublin: Irish Academic Press, 1996)

O'GRADY, DESMOND, *Trawling Translation: Translations 1954–1994* (Salzburg: University of Salzburg, 1994)

PACIFICI, SERGIO, ed., *The Promised Land and Other Poems: An Anthology of Four Contemporary Italian Poets. Umberto Saba, Giuseppe Ungaretti, Eugenio Montale, Salvatore Quasimodo* (New York: S. F. Vanni, 1955) [PACIFICI 1999]

PAOLINI, PIER FRANCESCO, ed., *Italian Writing Today*, intro. by Alfredo Giuliani, special issue of *The Literary Review*, 28 (1985) [PAOLINI 1985A]

——, ed., 'A Meaningful Handful: Sixteen Contemporary Italian Poets', *The Literary Review*, 29 (1985), 87–122 [PAOLINI 1985B]

PASOLINI, PIERPAOLO, and MARIO DELL'ARCO, eds, *Poesia dialettale del Novecento* (Parma: Guanda, 1952)

PAYNE, ROBERTA, ed., *A Selection of Modern Italian Poetry in Translation* (Montreal & London: McGill-Queen's University Press, 2004) [PAYNE 2004]

PERROTTA, RAFFAELE, ed., *Italian Poetry Today: A Critical Anthology* (Sydney: Frederick May Foundation for Italian Studies, University of Sydney, 1980)

PERRY, GRACE, ed., *Poetry Australia 22/23* (Sydney: South Head Press, 1968)

PICCOLO, LUCIO, *The Collected Poems of Lucio Piccolo*, ed. by Brian Swann and tr. by Ruth Feldman (Princeton, NJ: Princeton Legacy Library, 1972)

POGGIOLI, RENATO, ed., 'Contemporary Italian Literature', *Briarcliff Quarterly*, 3.12 (1947), 225–75 [POGGIOLI 1947A]

——, ed., 'A Little Anthology of Italian Poetry', *New Directions in Prose and Poetry*, 10 (1948), 309–29 [POGGIOLI 1948]

POGGIOLI, RENATO, and HENRY PAYRE, eds, *Italian-French Issue*, special issue of *Voices: A Quarterly of Poetry*, 128 (1947) [POGGIOLI 1947B]

PORTA, ANTONIO, *As If It Were a Rhythm*, trans. by Paul Vangelisti (San Francisco: Red Hill Press, 1978)

——*Passenger: Selected Poems, 1958–79*, trans. by Pasquale Verdicchio (Toronto: Guernica, 1986)

——*Kisses from Another Dream*, trans. by Antony Molino (Los Angeles: City Lights Publisher, 1987)

POUND, EZRA, ed., *Des imagistes: An Anthology* (New York: Charles and Albert Boni, 1914)

——*Confucius to Cummings: An Anthology of Poetry* (New York: New Directions, 1964)

PUCELLI, RODOLFO, ed., *Anthology of Italian and Italian-American Poetry* (Boston: Bruce Humphries, 1955) [PUCELLI 1955]

QUASIMODO, SALVATORE, *Poesie e discorsi sulla poesia*, ed. by Gilberto Finzi (Milan: Mondadori, 1966)

QUINTAVALLA, MARIA PIA, and ORNELLA PALUMBO, eds, *Femminile plurale: voci della poesia italiana dal 1968 al 2002* (Catanzaro: Abramo, 2002)

RANSFORD, TESSA, ed., 'Fourteen Italian Poets for the Twenty-first Century', trans. by Marco Fazzini and Christopher Whyte, *Lines Review*, 130 (1994), 1–64

REBAY, LUCIANO, ed., *Italian Poetry: A Selection from St. Francis to Salvatore Quasimodo* (New York: Dover, 1969) [REBAY 1969]

——*Introduction to Italian Poetry: A Dual-language Book* (New York: Dover Publications, 1991) [REBAY 1991]

RIDINGER, GAYLE, and GIAN PAOLO RENELLO, eds, *Italian Poetry, 1950–1990* (Boston, MA: Dante University of America Press, 1996) [RIDINGER AND RENELLO 1996]

RIMANELLI, JOSE, *Il mestiere del furbo: panorama della narrativa italiana contemporanea* (New York: Bordighera Press, 1959)

ROSSELLI, AMELIA, *War Variations*, trans. by Lucia Re and Paul Vangelisti (Los Angeles: Otis Books, 2016)

ROTHENBERG, JEROME, and PIERRE JORIS, eds, *Poems for the Millennium: The University of California Book of Modern and Postmodern Poetry. Volume 2: From Postwar to Millenium* (Berkeley: University of California Press, 1998) [ROTHENBERG AND JORIS 1998]

SÀNCHEZ, MARTA ESTER, ed., *Contemporary Chicana Poetry: A Critical Approach to an Emerging Literature* (Berkeley: University of California Press, 1985)

SANDRI, GIOVANNA, *From K to S: Ark of the Asymmetric* (New York: Out of London Press, 1976)
SANGUINETI, EDOARDO, ed., *Poesia del Novecento* (Turin: Einaudi, 1969)
SEGRE, CESARE, and CARLO OSSOLA, eds, *Antologia della poesia italiana* (Turin: Einaudi, 1999)
SELLIN, ERIC, ed., 'Contemporary Italian Poems', *The Literary Review*, 2.3 (1959), 376–82 [SELLIN 1959]
SCAMMACCA, NAT, *Bye Bye America: ricordi di un wop* (Palermo: Libri siciliani, 1972)
——*Analisi antigruppo* (Trapani: Antigrouppo, 1973)
SCOTELLARO, ROCCO, *The Dawn is Always New: Selected Poems of Rocco Scotellaro*, trans. by Ruth Feldman and Brian Swann (Princeton, NJ: Princeton Legacy Library, 1980)
SERRAO, ACHILLE, LUIGI BONAFFINI, and JUSTIN VITIELLO, eds, *Via Terra: An Anthology of Contemporary Italian Dialect Poetry* (Brooklyn, Ottawa & London: Legas, 1999) [BONAFFINI 1999]
SINGH, GHAN, ed., *Contemporary Italian Verse* (London: London Magazine Editions, 1968)
SKLAR, MORTY, and DARRELL GRAY, eds, *The Actualist Anthology* (Iowa City, IA: The Spirit that Moves Us Press, 1977)
SMITH, WILLIAM JAY, ed., *Poems from Italy* (New York: Crowell, 1972) [SMITH 1972]
SMITH, LAWRENCE, ed., *The New Italian Poetry, 1945 to Present: A Bilingual Anthology* (Berkeley: University of California Press, 1981) [SMITH 1981]
SMITH, WILLIAM, and DANA GIOIA, eds, *Poems from Italy* (St Paul, MN: New Rivers Press, 1985) [SMITH AND GIOIA 1985]
SMITH, LAWRENCE, and JOHN PICCHIONE, eds, *Twentieth-Century Italian Poetry: An Anthology* (Toronto, Buffalo & London: University of Toronto Press, 1993) [SMITH AND PICCHIONE 1993]
SOUTHERLAND, GRAY, ed., *Splinters of Light: Antonella Anedda, Milo De Angelis and Fabio Pusterla* (Ferrara: Kolibris, 2013)
SPATOLA, ADRIANO, *Majakovskiiiiiiij* (Turin: Geiger, 1971)
—— *Various Devices*, ed. and trans. by Paul Vangelisti (Los Angeles: Red Hill Press, 1978)
SPATOLA, ADRIANO, and PAUL VANGELISTI, eds, *Italian Poetry: 1960–1980. From Neo to Post–avanguardia* (San Francisco & Los Angeles: Invisible City/ Red Hill Press, 1982) [SPATOLA AND VANGELISTI 1982]
SPAZIANI, MARIA LUISA, *Il gong* (Milan: Mondadori, 1962)
STEFANILE, FELIX, ed., *The Blue Moustache: Some Futurist Poets* (New Rochelle, NY: Elizabeth Press, 1980) [STEFANILE 1980]
—— *The Country of Absence: Poems and Essays* (West Lafayette, IN: Bordighera, 2000)
STORTONI, LAURA ANNA, and MARY PRENTICE LILIE, eds, *Women Poets of the Italian Renaissance: Courtly Ladies and Courtesans* (New York: Italica Press, 1997)
SWANN, BRIAN, ed., *Contemporary Italian Writing in English Translation*, special issue of *Mediterranean Review*, 11 (1972) [SWANN 1972]
TANDELLO, EMMANUELA, and DIEGO ZANCANI, eds, *Italian Dialect and Literature: From the Renaissance to the Present* (London: Institute of Romance Studies, 1996)
TESIO, GIOVANNI, and MARIO CHIESA, eds, *Il dialetto da lingua della realtà a lingua della poesia da Porta a Belli a Pasolini* (Turin: Paravia, 1978)
TOMASI DI LAMPEDUSA, GIUSEPPE, *Il gattopardo*, ed. and with a preface by Giorgio Bassani (Milan: Feltrinelli, 1958)
TOMLINSON, CHARLES, ed., *The Oxford Book of Verse in English Translation* (Oxford: Oxford University Press, 1980)
—— *Translations* (Oxford & New York: Oxford University Press, 1983)
TREVELYAN, RALEIGH, ed., *Italian Writing Today* (Harmondsworth: Penguin, 1967)
TUSIANI, JOSEPH, *Gente mia and Other Poems* (Stone Park, IL: Italian Cultural Center, 1978)

TUSIANI, JOSEPH, ed., *Italian Poets of the Renaissance*, trans. into English Verse and with an introduction by Joseph Tusiani (New York: Baroque Press, 1971)

TUSIANI, JOSEPH, ed., *From Marino to Marinetti: An Anthology of Forty Italian Poets*, trans. by Joseph Tusiani (New York: Baroque Press, 1974) [TUSIANI 1974]

UNGARETTI, GIUSEPPE, *Allegria di naufragi* (Florence: Vallecchi, 1919)

——*Il porto sepolto: poesie di Giuseppe Ungaretti presentate a Benito Mussolini con fregi di Francesco Gamba* (La Spezia: Ettore Serra, 1923)

——*Il sentimento del tempo* (Florence: Vallecchi, 1933)

——*Il dolore: 1937–46* (Milan: Mondadori, 1947)

——*La terra promessa: frammenti* (Milan: Mondadori, 1950)

——*Vita d'un uomo: tutte le poesie*, ed. by Leone Piccioni (Milan: Mondadori, 1969)

VILLA, EMILIO, GIULIA NICCOLAI, and LUCIANO CARUSO, *Foresta ultra naturam*, ed. by Paul Vangelisti, trans. by Ippolita Rostagno, Pasquale Verdicchio, and Paul Vangelisti (Los Angeles: Red Hill Press, 1989) [VANGELISTI 1989]

VIVANTE, ARTURO, ed., *Italian Poetry: An Anthology from the Beginning to the Present* (Wellfleet, MA: Delphinium Press, 1996) [VIVANTE 1996]

VITIELLO, JUSTIN, ed., *Italy's Ultramodern, Experimental Lyrics: Corpo 10* (New York & London: Peter Lang, 1992) [VITIELLO 1992]

WEAVER, WILLIAM, and ARCHIBALD COLQUHOUN, eds, *Italy 1963*, special issue of *The London Magazine*, 3.7 (1963)

WEAVER, WILLIAM, ed., *Open City: Seven Writers in Postwar Rome* (South Royalton, VT: Steerforth Press, 1999)

WEISSBORT, DANIEL, BRIAN SWANN, and RUTH FELDMAN, eds, 'Contemporary Italian Poetry', *Modern Poetry in Translation*, 26 (1975), 1–25 [WEISSBORT, FELDMAN, AND SWANN 1975]

WETHERBY, TERRY, ed., *New Poets, Women: An Anthology* (Milbrae, CA: Les Femmes Publishing, 1976)

WILLIAMSON, EDWARD, ed., 'Contemporary Italian Poetry', *Poetry*, 79.3 (1952), 159–81, and 79.4 (1952), 233–44 [WILLIAMSON 1951/1952]

ZANZOTTO, ANDREA, *Selected Poems of Andrea Zanzotto*, trans. by Ruth Feldman and Brian Swann (Princeton, NJ: Princeton Legacy Library, 1976)

——*In nessuna lingua in nessun luogo: le poesie in dialetto 1938–2009*, with an introduction by Giorgio Agamben and a preface by Stefano Dal Bianco (Macerata: Quodlibet, 2019)

Secondary Literature

ACETOSO, MATTIA. 'Renato Poggioli's Intellectual Project and the Psychology of Exile', in *Renato Poggioli: An Intellectual Biography*, ed. by Roberto Ludovico, Lino Pertile, and Massimo Riva (Florence: Olschki, 2013), pp. 125–43

ADORNO, THEODOR, *Prisms*, trans. by Samuel and Sherry Weber (Cambridge, MA: MIT Press, 1967)

AIELLO, LUCIA, JOU CHARNLEY, and MARIANGELA PALLADINO, eds, *Displaced Women: Multilingual Narratives of Migration in Europe* (Newcastle upon Tyne: Cambridge Scholars, 2014)

ALEXANDER, MICHAEL, 'Ezra Pound as Translator', *Translation and Literature*, 6 (1997), 23–30

ALFANO, BARBARA, *The Mirage of America in Contemporary Italian Literature and Film* (Toronto: University of Toronto Press, 2013)

ALLEN, BEVERLY, 'From One Closet to Another? Feminism, Literary Archaeology, and the Canon', in *Italian Women Writers from the Renaissance to the Present: Revising the Canon*, ed. by Maria Ornella Marotti (University Park: Pennsylvania State University Press, 1996), pp. 25–36

ALLEN, BEVERLY, and MARY J. RUSSO, eds, *Revisioning Italy: National Identity and Global Culture* (Minneapolis: University of Minnesota Press, 1997)

APPADURAI, ARJUN, *Modernity at Large: Cultural Dimensions of Globalization* (Minneapolis: University of Minnesota Press, 1996)

APTER, EMILY, *The Translation Zone: A New Comparative Literature* (Princeton, NJ: Princeton University Press, 2006)

APTER, RONNIE, *Digging for the Treasure: Translation after Pound* (New York: Peter Lang, 1984)

ARNALDI, MARTA, 'Transnational Melancholia: Depression and Exile in Italian Women's Poetry from the Early-modern to the Contemporary', in *Women in Transition: Crossing Boundaries, Crossing Borders*, ed. by Maria-José Blanco and Claire Williams (London: Routledge, 2021), pp. 133–48

ASOR ROSA, ALBERTO, *Un altro Novecento* (Florence: La Nuova Italia, 1999)

BACIGALUPO, MASSIMO, 'Il Novecento nelle antologie in lingua inglese', in *Visti da fuori: la poesia italiana oggi in Europa*, ed. by Damiano Sinfonico and Stefano Verdino, special issue of *Nuova Corrente*, 153 (2014), 71–77

BÄCKSTRÖM, PER, and BENEDIKT HJARTARSON, 'Rethinking the Topography of the International Avant-garde: Introduction', in *Decentring the Avant-garde*, ed. by Per Bäckström and Benedikt Hjartarson, Avant-garde Critical Studies 30 (Leiden: Brill, 2014), pp. 7–32

BARNHISEL, GREG, *James Laughlin, New Directions, and the Remaking of Ezra Pound* (Amherst: University of Massachusetts Press. 2005)

BAROLINI, HELEN, *Their Other Side: Six American Women and the Lure of Italy* (New York: Fordham University Press, 2006)

BAUDRILLARD, JEAN, *Amérique* (Paris: Grasset, 1986)

BAUMAN, ZYGMUNT, *Liquid Modernity* (Cambridge: Polity Press, 2000)

BARTHES, ROLAND, *Le degré zéro de l'écriture* (Paris: Seuil, 1953)

—— *Writing Degree Zero*, trans. by Annette Lavers (New York: Farrar Straus & Giroux, 1968)

—— 'La Mort de l'auteur', *Manteia*, 5 (1968), 12–17

—— *Image, Music, Text*, ed. and trans. by Stephen Heath (New York: Hill & Wang, 1977)

BEACH, CHRISTOPHER, *The Cambridge Introduction to Twentieth-Century American Poetry* (Cambridge: Cambridge University Press, 2003)

BEAN, HEIDI, and MIKE CHASAR, eds, *Poetry after Cultural Studies* (Iowa City: University of Iowa Press, 2011)

BENCIVENNI, MARCELLA, *Italian Immigrant Radical Culture: The Idealism of the Sovversivi in the United States, 1890–1940* (New York: New York University Press, 2011)

BENJAMIN, WALTER, 'The Task of the Translator' [1923], in *Illuminations*, ed. and with an introduction by Hannah Arendt (New York: Harcourt, Brace & World, 1968), pp. 69–82

BERCOVITCH, SACVAN, ed., *The Cambridge History of American Literature*, 8 vols (Cambridge: Cambridge University Press, 1994–2005)

BERGER, JOHN, *Ways of Seeing* (London: Penguin, 1972)

BERMAN, ANTOINE, *La Traduction et la lettre, ou l'auberge du lointain* (Paris: Seuil, 1991)

BERNSTEIN, MICHAEL ANDRÉ, *The Tale of the Tribe: Ezra Pound and the Modern Verse Epic* (Princeton, NJ: Princeton University Press, 1980)

BERTOLDO, ROBERTO, 'Intervista ad Alfredo De Palchi' (2012) <http://www.alfredodepalchi.com/interviste/int_de%20Palchi.html> [accessed 28 September 2018]

BERTOLDO, ROBERTO, BARBARA CARLE, and LUIGI FONTANELLA, eds, *Scritti sulla poesia di Alfredo De Palchi con inediti dell'autore* (Turin: Ebenon, 2000)

BHABHA, HOMI, *The Location of Culture* (London: Routledge, 1994)

BLAKESLEY, JACOB, ed., *Sociologies of Poetry Translation: Emerging Perspectives* (London: Bloomsbury Academic, 2018)

BLOOM, HAROLD, *The Western Canon: The Books and School of the Ages* (New York & London: Harcourt Brace, 1994)
BLUM SARTINI, CINZIA, *Rewriting the Journey in Contemporary Italian Literature: Figures of Subjectivity in Progress* (Toronto, Buffalo & London: University of Toronto Press, 2008)
BOHN, WILLARD, *The Other Futurism: Futurist Activity in Venice, Padua and Verona* (Toronto: University of Toronto Press, 2004)
BONAFFINI, LUIGI, 'Translating Dialect Literature', *World Literature Today*, 7 (1997), 279–88
BOND, EMMA, 'Towards a Trans-national Turn in Italian Studies?', *Italian Studies*, 69 (2014), 415–24
BONSAVER, GUIDO, ALESSANDRO CARLUCCI and MATTHEW REZA, eds, *Italy and the USA: Cultural Change Through Language and Narrative* (Oxford: Legenda, 2019)
BOTTA, ANNA, 'Renato Poggioli and the Byzantine Origins of Comparative Literature', in *Renato Poggioli: An Intellectual Biography*, ed. by Roberto Ludovico, Lino Pertile, and Massimo Riva (Florence: Olschki, 2013), pp. 145–61
BORGESE, GIUSEPPE ANTONIO, *Tempo di edificare* (Milan: Treves, 1923)
BOURGEOIS, LOUIS, 'The Scorpion's Dark Dance: An Interview with Alfredo De Palchi', *Rain Taxi*, 15 (2010) <http://www.alfredodepalchi.com/interviste/The%20Scorpion's%20 Dark%20Dance.pdf> [accessed 28 September 2018]
BRAZIEL, JANA EVANS, and ANITA MANNUR, eds, *Theorizing Diaspora: A Reader* (Oxford: Blackwell, 2003)
BREVINI, FRANCO, *Le parole perdute: dialetti e poesia nel nostro secolo* (Turin: Einaudi, 1990)
BROCK, GEOFFREY, 'Two Tunnels: A Note on Translation', in *The FSG Book of Twentieth-Century Italian Poetry*, ed. by Geoffrey Brock (New York: Farrar, Straus & Giroux, 2012), pp. xli–iii
BROOKS, VAN WYCK, *The Dream of Arcadia: American Writers and Artists in Italy, 1760–1915* (London: Dent, 1958)
BROWN, JOHN, 'Guiding the Commerce of Ideas', *Books Abroad*, 47.2 (1973), 307–11
CACIOPPO, MARINA, *'If the Sidewalks of These Streets Could Talk': Reinventing Italian-American Ethnicity. The Representation and Construction of Ethnic Identity in Italian-American Literature* (Turin: Otto, 2005)
CARREVETTA, PETER, 'The United States', in *Poets of the Italian Diaspora*, ed. by Luigi Bonaffini and Joseph Perricone (New York: Fordham University Press, 2014), pp. 1061–71.
CASANOVA, PASCALE, *The World Republic of Letters*, trans. by M. B. Debevoise (Cambridge, MA: Harvard University Press, 2004)
CASELLI, DANIELA, 'Value and Authority in Anthologies of Italian Poetry in English (1956–1992)', in *Twentieth-Century Poetic Translation: Literary Cultures in Italian and English*, ed. by Daniela Caselli and Daniela La Penna (London: Continuum, 2008), pp. 55–67
CHELSEA EDITIONS, 'Mission Statement' <http://www.chelseaeditionsbooks.org/About.htm> [accessed 28 September 2018]
CIXOUS, HÉLÈNE, *Le Rire de la Méduse et autres ironies* (Paris: Editions Galilée, 1975)
—— 'The Laugh of the Medusa', trans. by Paula Cohen and Keith Cohen, *Signs*, 4 (1976), 875–93
CLARO, ANDRÉS, 'Ezra Pound's Poetics of Translation: Principles, Performances, Implications' (unpublished doctoral thesis, University of Oxford, 2004–05)
CONLEY, TIM, *Joyce's Mistakes: Problems of Intention, Irony, and Interpretation* (Toronto: University of Toronto Press, 2003)
CONNELL, LIAM, and NICKY MARSH, eds, *Literature and Globalization: A Reader* (London & New York: Routledge, 2011)
CONTINI, GIANFRANCO, 'Saggio introduttivo', in Carlo Emilio Gadda, *La cognizione del dolore* (Turin: Einaudi, 1963), pp. 7–28

—— *Ultimi esercizî ed elzeviri* (Turin: Einaudi, 1989)
COTTINGTON, DAVID, *The Avant-garde: A Very Short Introduction* (Oxford: Oxford University Press, 2013)
CRIVELLI, TATIANA, 'L'eccezione che non fa la regola: riflessioni sul rapporto tra scrittura femminile e canone', in *Dentro/fuori, sopra/sotto: critica femminista e canone letterario negli studi di italianistica*, ed. by Alessia Ronchetti and Maria Serena Sapegno (Ravenna: Longo, 2007), pp. 39–52
CROCCO, CRISTINA, *La poesia italiana del Novecento: il canone e le interpretazioni* (Rome: Carocci, 2015)
—— 'La poesia italiana del Novecento: il canone e le interpretazioni' (2015) <http://www.leparoleelecose.it/?p=18439> [accessed 20 October 2020]
D'ELIA, ANTONIO, *La peregrinatio poetica di David Maria Turoldo* (Florence: Olschki, 2012)
DEAN, FRANCO, 'Pluralism and Postmodernism: The Histories and Geographies of Ethnic American Literature', in *The Cambridge Companion to Postmodern American Fiction*, ed. by Paula Geyh (New York: Cambridge University Press, 2017), pp. 112–30
DE MAN, PAUL, *Blindness and Insight: Essays in the Rhetoric of Contemporary Criticism* (London: Methuen, 1983)
DELEUZE, GILLES, and FÉLIX GUATTARI, *Kafka: pour une littérature mineure* (Paris: Minuit, 1975)
—— 'What is a Minor Literature?', trans. by Robert Brinkley, *Mississippi Review*, 11 (1982), 13–33
DELLA TERZA, DANTE, *Da Vienna a Baltimora: la diaspora degli intellettuali europei negli Stati Uniti d'America* (Rome: Editori Riuniti, 1987)
DERRIDA, JACQUES, *Marges de la philosophie* (Paris: Minuit, 1960)
DURANTE, FRANCESCO, 'Seven Points on Poetry of the Italian Diaspora', in *Poets of the Italian Diaspora*, ed. by Luigi Bonaffini and Joseph Perricone (New York: Fordham University Press, 2014), pp. xix–xxi
DURANTE, FRANCESCO, and OTHERS, eds, *Italoamericana: The Literature of the Great Migration, 1880–1943* (New York: Fordham University Press, 2014)
ELLIOTT, BRICE, DAVID GERBER, and SUZANNE SINKE, eds, *Letters Across Borders: The Epistolary Practices of International Migrants* (New York: Palgrave Macmillan, 2006)
ELLWOOD, DAVID, *The Shock of America: Europe and the Challenge of the Century* (Oxford: Oxford University Press, 2012)
EOYANG, EUGENE CHEN, *Two-way Mirrors: Cross-cultural Studies in Glocalization* (Lanham, MD: Lexington Books, 2007)
EVEN-ZOHAR, ITAMAR, 'Polysystem Studies', *Poetics Today*, 11 (1990), 1–268
FINZI, GILBERTO, *Poesia in Italia: Montale, Novissimi, postnovissimi, 1959–1978* (Milan: Mursia, 1979)
FISHMAN, JOSHUA, *The Rise and the Fall of the Ethnic Revival: Perspectives on Language and Ethnicity* (Berlin & New York: de Gruyter, 1985)
FLAJŠAR, JIŘÍ, and ZÉNÓ VERNYIK, eds, *Words into Pictures: E. E. Cummings' Art Across Borders* (Newcastle upon Tyne: Cambridge Scholars, 2007)
FONTANELLA, LUIGI, *Migrating Words: Italian Writers in the United States* (New York: Bordighera Press, 2012)
FRABOTTA, BIANCAMARIA, 'La viandanza', in *Scrittori, tendenze letterarie e conflitto delle poetiche in Italia*, ed. by Rocco Capozzi and Massimo Ciavolella (Ravenna: Longo, 1993), pp. 87–89
—— *La viandanza, 1982–1992* (Milan: Mondadori, 1995)
—— 'La viandanza femminile e la poesia', *Horizonte*, 1 (1996), 73–79
FREDMAN, STEPHEN, *A Concise Companion to Twentieth-Century American Poetry* (Malden, MA: Blackwell, 2005)

Frank, Armin Paul, 'Anthologies of Translation', in *Routledge Encyclopaedia of Translation Studies*, ed. by Mona Baker and Gabriela Saldanha (London & New York: Routledge, 1998), pp. 13–16

Gabbaccia, Donna, *Italy's Many Diasporas* (London: Routledge, 2000)

Games, Alison, *Migration and the Origins of the English Atlantic World* (Cambridge, MA: Harvard University Press, 1999)

Gansel, Mireille, *Translation as Transhumance*, trans. by Ros Schwartz, foreword by Lauren Elkin (London: Les Fugitives, 2017)

Gardini, Nicola, *I baroni: come e perché sono fuggito dall'università italiana* (Milan: Feltrinelli, 2009)

—— *Tradurre è un bacio* (Borgomanero: Ladolfi, 2015)

Gaudin, Colette, and others, eds, *Feminist Readings: French Texts/American Contexts*, special issue of *Yale French Studies*, 62 (1981)

Gilroy, Paul, *The Black Atlantic: Modernity and Double Consciousness* (Cambridge, MA: Harvard University Press, 1993)

Hainsworth, Peter, and David Robey, eds, *The Oxford Companion to Italian Literature* (Oxford: Oxford University Press, 2005)

Hallberg, Robert von, 'Avant-Gardes', in *The Cambridge History of American Literature*, ed. by Sacvan Bercovitch, 8 vols (Cambridge: Cambridge University Press, 1994–2005), viii, 83–122

Haller, Hermann, *Una lingua perduta e ritrovata: l'italiano degli italo-americani* (Florence: Nuova Italia, 1993)

—— 'Literature in Dialect and Dialect in Literature: A Sociolinguistic Perspective', in *Italian Dialect and Literature: From the Renaissance to the Present*, ed. by Emmanuela Tandello and Diego Zancani (London: Institute of Romance Studies, 1996), pp. 73–80

—— *The Other Italy: The Literary Canon in Dialect* (Toronto & Buffalo: University of Toronto Press, 1999) [Haller 1999]

—— 'Italian in New York', in *The Multilingual Apple: Languages in New York City*, ed. by Joshua Fishman and Ofelia García, 2nd edn (Berlin & New York: de Gruyter, 2002), pp. 119–42

Healey, Robin, *Twentieth-Century Italian Literature in English Translation: An Annotated Bibliography, 1929–2016* (Toronto: University of Toronto Press, 1998)

—— *Italian Literature since 1900 in English Translation: An Annotated Bibliography, 1929–1997* (Toronto: University of Toronto Press, 2019)

Heilbron, Johan, 'Le Système mondial des traductions', in *Les Contradictions de la globalisation éditoriale*, ed. by Gisèle Saphiro (Paris: Nouveau Monde, 2009), pp. 253–74

Hewitt, Nicholas, *The Culture of Reconstruction: European Literature, Thought and Film, 1945–50* (Basingstoke: Palgrave Macmillan, 1989)

Howarth, Peter, *The Cambridge Introduction to Modernist Poetry* (Cambridge: Cambridge University Press, 2012)

Inghillieri, Moira, *Translation and Migration* (London: Routledge, 2016)

Irigaray, Luce, *Ethique de la différence sexuelle* (Paris: Minuit, 1984)

—— *Speculum of the Other Woman*, trans. by Gillian C. Gill (Ithaca, NY: Cornell University Press, 1985)

—— *This Sex Which Is Not Mine*, trans. by Catherine Porter and Carolyn Burker (Ithaca, NY: Cornell University Press, 1985)

Jay, Paul, *Global Matters: The Transnational Turn in Literary Studies* (Ithaca, NY: Cornell University Press, 2010)

Jewell, Keala, *The Poiesis of History: Experimenting with Genre in Post-war Italy* (Ithaca, NY: Cornell University Press, 1992)

Katz, William, Linda Stenberg Katz, and Esther Crain, eds, *The Columbia Granger's Guide to Poetry Anthologies* (New York: Columbia University Press, 1994)

Katz, Daniel, *American Modernism's Expatriate Scene: The Labour of Translation* (Edinburgh: Edinburgh University Press, 2007)

Kendall, Tim, ed., *Poetry of the First World War: An Anthology* (Oxford: Oxford University Press, 2013)

Kenner, Hugh, *The Pound Era* (London: Faber & Faber, 1972)

Kenny, Kevin, *Diaspora: A Very Short Introduction* (Oxford: Oxford University Press, 2013)

Killinger, Charles, 'Renato Poggioli and Antifascism in the United States', in *Renato Poggioli: An Intellectual Biography*, ed. by Roberto Ludovico, Lino Pertile, and Massimo Riva (Florence: Olschki, 2013), pp. 39–57

Kittel, Harald, ed., *International Anthologies of Literature in Translation* (Berlin: Erich Schmidt Verlag, 1995)

Kołodziejczyk, Ewa, ed., *Open Cultural Studies: Migration and Translation* (2017) <https://www.degruyter.com/dg/page/migration-translation/open-cultural-studies-migration-and-translation> [accessed 28 September 2018]

Král, Françoise, *Critical Identities in Contemporary Anglophone Diasporic Literature* (Basingstoke: Palgrave Macmillan, 2009)

Kriegel, Joel, ed., *The Oxford Companion to International Relations* (Oxford: Oxford University Press, 2014) <https://www.oxfordreference.com/view/10.1093/acref/9780199738878.001.0001/acref-9780199738878> [accessed 20 July 2021]

Kristeva, Julia, 'Un nouveau type d'intellectuel: le dissident', *Tel Quel*, 74 (1977), 3–8

'Le Temps des femmes' in *33/34: Cahiers de Recherche de Sciences des Textes et Documents*, 5 (1979), 5–19

——'Women's Time', trans. by Alice Jardine and Harry Blake, *Signs*, 7 (1981), 13–35

——*Revolution in Poetic Language*, trans. by Margaret Wallet (New York: Columbia University Press, 1984)

——'A New Type of Intellectual: The Dissident', in *The Kristeva Reader*, ed. by Toril Moi (Oxford: Basil Blackwell, 1986), pp. 292–300

——'Why the United States?', in *The Kristeva Reader*, ed. by Toril Moi (Oxford: Basil Blackwell, 1986), pp. 272–91

——*Soleil noir: dépression et mélancholie* (Paris: Gallimard, 1987)

——*Etrangers à nous-mêmes* (Paris: Fayard, 1988)

——*Strangers to Ourselves*, trans. by Leon S. Roudiez (New York: Columbia University Press, 1991)

——*Contre la dépression nationale: entretien avec Philippe Petit* (Paris: Textuel, 1998)

Lazzaro-Weis, Carol, *From Margins to Mainstream: Feminism and Fictional Modes in Italian Women's Writing, 1968–1990* (Philadelphia: University of Pennsylvania Press, 1993)

Lefevere, André, *Translation, Rewriting, and the Manipulation of Literary Frame* (London: Routledge, 1992)

Lennon, Brian, *In Babel's Shadow: Multilingual Literatures, Monolingual States* (Minneapolis: University of Minnesota Press, 2010)

Lerer, Seth, *Tradition: A Feeling for the Literary Past* (Oxford: Oxford University Press, 2016)

Livorni, Ernesto, 'Renato Poggioli's *Theory of the Avant-garde* and its Legacy', in *Renato Poggioli: An Intellectual Biography*, ed. by Roberto Ludovico, Lino Pertile, and Massimo Riva (Florence: Olschki, 2013), pp. 179–96

Longfellow Institute, Harvard University, <http://www.fas.harvard.edu/~lowinus> [accessed 28 September 2018]

Luconi, Stefano, 'Italian Migration and Diasporic Approaches: Historical Phenomena and Scholarly Interpretations', in *The Cultures of Italian Migration: Diverse Trajectories and*

Discrete Perspectives, ed. by Graziella Parati and Anthony Julian Tamburri (Lanham, MD: Fairleigh Dickinson University Press, 2013), pp. 153–68

Ludovico, Roberto, 'Introduction', in *Renato Poggioli: An Intellectual Biography*, ed. by Roberto Ludovico, Lino Pertile, and Massimo Riva (Florence: Olschki, 2013), pp. ix–xvii

Luisetti, Federico, and Luca Somigli, eds, *A Century of Futurism, 1909–2009*, special issue of *Annali di Italianistica*, 27 (2009)

MacGowan, Christopher, *Twentieth-Century American Poetry* (Oxford: Blackwell Publishing, 2004)

Macrì, Oreste, *La teoria letteraria delle generazioni*, ed. by Anna Dolfi (Florence: F. Cesati, 1995)

Marazzi, Martino, *Little America: gli Stati Uniti e gli scrittori italiani del Novecento* (Milan: Marcos y Marcos, 1997)

——*A occhi aperti: letteratura dell'emigrazione e mito americano* (Milan: Franco Angeli, 2011)

——*Voices of Italian America: A History of Early Italian American Literature with a Critical Anthology*, trans. by Ann Goldstein (New York: Fordham University Press, 2012)

Marchione, Margherita, *The Fighting Nun: My Story* (New York: Cornwall Books, 2000)

——'Prezzolini mio maestro', in *Twentieth-Century Italian Poetry: A Bilingual Anthology*, ed. by Margherita Marchione, sketches by Filomena Puglisi (Rutherford, NJ: Farleigh Dickinson University Press, 1974), pp. 294–301

Matteo, Sante, 'Italian Roots in Global Soil', in *Poets of the Italian Diaspora: A Bilingual Anthology*, ed. by Luigi Bonaffini and Joseph Perricone (New York: Fordham University Press, 2014), pp. xi–xviii

Mazzoni, Guido, *Forma e solitudine* (Milan: Marcos y Marcos, 2002)

McAfee, Noëlle, *Julia Kristeva* (New York: Routledge, 2004)

McGuinness, Patrick, *Other People's Countries: A Journey into Memory* (London: Jonathan Cape, 2014)

MELUS, The Society for the Study of the Multi-ethnic Literature of the United States <http://www.melus.org/about/> [accessed 28 September 2018]

Merjian, Ara H., '"Howls from the Left": Pier Paolo Pasolini, Allen Ginsberg, and the Legacies of Beat America', in *Pier Paolo Pasolini, Framed and Unframed: A Thinker for the Twenty-first Century*, ed. by Luca Peretti and Karen T. Raizen (London: Bloomsbury Academic, 2018), pp. 37–62

Miłosz, Czesław, 'Notes on Exile', *Books Abroad*, 50 (1976), 282–84

Ming Xie, 'Pound as Translator', in *The Cambridge Companion to Ezra Pound*, ed. by Ira B. Nadel (Cambridge: Cambridge University Press, 1999), pp. 204–23

Moretti, Franco, *Graphs, Maps, Trees: Abstract Models for a Literary History* (London: Verso, 2005)

——*Distant Reading* (London: Verso, 2013)

Mottram, Eric, 'Conversation with Basil Bunting on the Occasion of his 75th Birthday, 1975', *Poetry Information*, 19 (1978), 3–10

Naaijkens, Ton, 'The World of World Poetry: Anthologies of Translated Poetry as a Subject of Study', *Neophilologus*, 90 (2006), 509–20

Nadel, Ira B., 'Introduction: Understanding Pound', in *The Cambridge Companion to Ezra Pound*, ed. by Ira B. Nadel (Cambridge: Cambridge University Press, 1999), pp. 1–21

Noland, Carrie, and Barrett Watten, eds, *Diasporic Avant-gardes: Experimental Poetics and Cultural Displacement* (Basingstoke: Palgrave Macmillan, 2011)

OED, <http://ezproxy-prd.bodleian.ox.ac.uk:2355> [accessed 28 September 2018]

Olson, Jonas, *Moral Error Theory: History, Critique, Defence* (Oxford: Oxford University Press, 2014)

Ostriker, Alicia Suskin, *Stealing the Language: The Emergence of Women's Poets in America* (Boston, MA: Beacon Press, 1986)

PARATI, GRAZIELLA, and ANTHONY JULIAN TAMBURRI, eds, *The Culture of Italian Migration: Diverse Trajectories and Discrete Perspectives* (Lanham, MD: Fairleigh Dickinson University Press, 2011)
PEARCE, ROY, *The Continuity of American Poetry* (Princeton, NJ: Princeton University Press, 1961)
PERLOFF, MARJORIE, *The Poetics of Indeterminacy: Rimbaud to Cage* (Princeton, NJ: Princeton University Press, 1981)
——*The Dance of the Intellect: Studies in the Poetry of the Pound Tradition* (Cambridge: Cambridge University Press, 1985)
——*The Futurist Moment: Avant-garde, Avant Guerre, and the Language of Rupture* (Chicago: University of Chicago Press, 1986)
——*Poetic License: Essays on Modernist and Postmodernist Lyric* (Evanston, IL: Northwestern University Press, 1990)
PICCHIONE, JOHN, *The New Avant-garde in Italy: Theoretical Debate and Poetic Practices* (Toronto: University of Toronto Press, 2004)
POGGIOLI, RENATO, 'Gli esiliati della cultura', *Solaria*, 1 (1933), 45–54
——'Italian Literature of Exile', *Decision*, 1.6 (1941), 40–43
——'Non programma ma premio', *Inventario*, 1 (1946a), 1–6 (repr. in *Il secolo dei manifesti: programmi delle riviste del Novecento*, ed. by Giuseppe Lupo and Giuseppe Langella (Turin: N. Aragno, 2006), pp. 340–47)
——'Letter to Italy', *Briarcliff Quarterly*, 11 (1946), 209–11
——'*Quaderno Gotico* by Mario Luzi' [review], *Books Abroad*, 22.2 (1948), 203
——'The Italian Success Story', in Renato Poggioli, *The Spirit of the Letter: Essays in European Literature* (Cambridge, MA: Harvard University Press, 1965), pp. 199–221
——*Teoria dell'arte d'avanguardia* (Bologna: Il mulino, 1962)
——*The Theory of the Avant-garde*, trans. by Gerald Fitzgerald (Cambridge, MA: Belknap Press of Harvard University Press, 1968)
——*The Spirit of the Letter: Essays on European Literature* (Cambridge, MA: Harvard University Press, 1965)
POLEZZI, LOREDANA, 'Translation and Migration', *Translation Studies*, 3 (2013), 345–68
POOVEY, MARY, 'Feminism and Deconstruction', *Feminist Studies*, 14 (1988), 51–65
POUND EZRA, *Ezra Pound: Translations*, ed. by Hugh Kenner (New York: New Directions, 1953)
——*Literary Essays of Ezra Pound*, ed. and with an introduction by T. S. Eliot (New York: New Directions, 1954)
PRATT, MARY LOUISE, 'Arts of the Contact Zone', *Profession*, (1991), 33–40
PREZZOLINI, GIUSEPPE, *Cristo e/o Machiavelli*, ed. by Beppe Benvenuto (Palermo: Sellerio, 2004)
——*Dio è un rischio*, with a preface by Giulio Andreotti (Florence: Vallecchi, 2004)
PYM, ANTONY, *Translation and Text Transfer: An Essay on the Principles of Cross-cultural Communication* (New York: Peter Lang, 1992)
RAMAZANI, JAHAN, *Poetry of Mourning: The Modern Elegy from Hardy to Heaney* (Chicago & London: University of Chicago Press, 1994)
——*A Transnational Poetics* (Chicago and London: University of Chicago Press, 2009)
RAMAZANI, JAHAN, RICHARD ELLMANN, and ROBERT O'CLAIR, eds, *The Norton Anthology of Modern and Contemporary Poetry*, 2 vols (New York & London: Norton, 2003)
RANISH, ROBERT, and STEFAN SORGNER, eds, *Post- and Transhumanism: An Introduction* (Frankfurt: Peter Lang, 2014)
RE, LUCIA, '(De)constructing the Canon: The Agon of the Anthologies in the Scene of Modern Italian Poetry', *MLR*, 87 (1992), 585–603

——'Amelia Rosselli: A Life of Poetry', in Amelia Rosselli, *War Variations*, trans. by Lucia Re and Paul Vangelisti (Los Angeles: Otis Books, 2016), pp. 5–26

——'Mythic Revisionism: Women Poets and Philosophers in Italy Today', in *Italian Women Writers from the Renaissance to the Present: Revising the Canon*, ed. by Maria Ornella Marotti (University Park: Pennsylvania State University Press, 1996), pp. 187–233

REYNOLDS, MATTHEW, *The Poetry of Translation: From Chaucer & Petrarch to Homer & Logue* (Oxford: Oxford University Press, 2011)

——*Likenesses: Translation, Illustration, Interpretation* (Oxford: Legenda, 2013)

——*Translation: A Very Short Introduction* (Oxford: Oxford University Press, 2016)

REYNOLDS, MATTHEW, ed., *Prismatic Translation* (Oxford: Legenda, 2019)

REYNOLDS, MATTHEW, MOHAMED-SALAH OMRI, and BEN MORGAN, eds, *Comparative Criticism: Histories and Methods*, special issue of *Comparative Critical Studies*, 12 (2015)

ROBERTSON, ROLAND, 'The Universalism-Particularism Issue', in *Literature and Globalization: A Reader*, ed. by Liam Connell and Nicky Marsh (London & New York: Routledge, 2011), pp. 24–26

RUSHDIE, SALMAN, *Imaginary Homelands: Essays and Criticism 1981–1991* (London: Granta Books/Penguin, 1991)

RUSSELL, RINALDINA, ed., *Feminist Encyclopaedia of Italian Literature* (Westport, CT: Greenwood Press, 1997)

SAID, EDWARD, *Beginnings: Intention and Method* (Baltimore, MD: Johns Hopkins University Press, 1975)

SALVAGNI, LORENZO, 'In the Garden of Letters: Marguerite Caetani and the International Literary Review *Botteghe Oscure*' (unpublished doctoral thesis, University of North Carolina at Chapel Hill, 2013)

SANTAEMILIA, JOSÉ, *Gender, Sex and Translation: The Manipulation of Identities* (Abingdon & New York: Routledge, 2014)

SARTARELLI, LINDA SUSMAN, 'Linguistic History of Italian Dialects in the United States', in *The Italian American Experience: An Encyclopaedia*, ed. by Salvatore LaGumina (New York: Garland, 2000), pp. 40–42

SAVIOLI, SILVIA, ed., *A 'Meeting of Minds': carteggio 1947–1950. Cesare Pavese, Renato Poggioli* (Alessandria: L'orso, 2010)

SCHIPPERS, BRIGIT, *Julia Kristeva and Feminist Thought* (Edinburgh: Edinburgh University Press, 2011)

SCHWARTZ, THOMAS ALAN, 'Marshall Plan', in *The Oxford Companion to International Relations*, ed. by Joel Krieger (Oxford: Oxford University Press, 2014) <https://www.oxfordreference.com/view/10.1093/acref/9780199738878.001.0001/acref-9780199738878> [accessed 20 July 2021]

SCIORRA, JOSEPH, 'Multivocality and Vernacular Architecture: The Our Lady of Mount Carmel Grotto in Roseband, Staten Island', in *Studies in Italian American Folklore*, ed. by Luisa Del Giudice (Logan: Utah State University Press, 1992), pp. 203–44

SEGRE, CESARE, *Lingua, stile e società* (Milan: Feltrinelli, 1974)

SEIDEL, MICHAEL, *Exile and the Narrative Imagination* (New Haven, CT: Yale University Press, 1986)

SIMON, SHERRY, *Gender in Translation: Cultural Identity and the Politics of Transmission* (London: Routledge, 1996)

SOLLORS, WERNER, *Beyond Ethnicity: Consent and Descent in American Culture* (New York: Oxford University Press, 1986)

——*The Invention of Ethnicity* (New York: Oxford University Press, 1988)

SOLLORS, WERNER, ed., *Multilingual America: Transnationalism, Ethnicity, and the Languages of American Literature* (New York & London: New York University Press, 1998)

Spatola, Maurizio, 'Marcello Angioni, *Analfabetica* (1982)', <http://www.archiviomaurizio spatola.com/prod/pdf_tamtam/T00121.pdf> [accessed 28 September 2018]

Sulis, Gigliola, 'Ridefinire il canone: i dialettali e le antologie poetiche del Novecento', *The Italianist*, 24.1 (2004), 77–106

Sullivan, John, *Ezra Pound and Sextus Propertius: A Study in Creative Translation* (London: Faber & Faber, 1965)

Tamburri, Anthony Julian, Paolo Giordano, and Fred Gardaphé, eds, *From the Margin: Writings in Italian Americana* (West Lafayette, IN: Purdue University Press, 1991)

Taylor, Joshua, *Futurism* (New York: Museum of Modern Art, 1961)

Tedeschi, John, Giorgio Caravale, and Stefania Pastore, eds, *Intellettuali in esilio: dall'Inquisizione romana al fascismo* (Rome: Storia e Letteratura, 2012)

Toury, Gideon, *Descriptive Translation Studies, and Beyond* (Amsterdam: Benjamin, 1995)

Valli, Stefania, *La rivista 'Botteghe Oscure' e Marguerite Caetani: la corrispondenza con gli autori italiani, 1948–1960* (Rome: L'Erma di Bretschneider, 1999)

Venuti, Lawrence, *The Translator's Invisibility: A History of Translation* (London: Routledge, 1995)

—— *The Scandals of Translation: Towards an Ethics of Difference* (London: Routledge, 1998)

Verdicchio, Pasquale, *Bound by Distance: Rethinking Nationalism Through the Italian Diaspora* (Madison: Farleigh Dickinson University Press, 1997)

Walker, Rebecca, 'Becoming the Third Wave', *Ms. Magazine*, 11 (1992), 39–41

Walters, Margaret, *Feminism: A Very Short Introduction* (Oxford: Oxford University Press, 2005)

Welle, John, 'Hermann Haller, The Hidden Italy' [review], *World Literature Today*, 62 (1998), 112

West, Rebecca, 'Who's In, Who's Out: A Feminist and "Queering" Perspective on Modern Italian Lyric Poetry Anthology Formation in Italy and the United States (1970–2005)', in *Dentro/fuori, sopra/sotto: critica femminista e canone letterario negli studi di italianistica*, ed. by Alessia Ronchetti and Maria Serena Sapegno (Ravenna: Longo, 2007), pp. 25–37

Wilson, Rita, and Leah Gerber, eds, *Creative Constraints: Translation as Authorship* (Clayton: Monash University Publishing, 2012)

Wind, Jerry, Stan Sthanunathan, and Rob Malcom, 'Great Advertising is Both Local and Global', *Harvard Business Review*, 29 March 2013 <https://hbr.org/2013/03/great-advertising-is-both-loca> [accessed 28 September 2018]

Woolf, Virginia, *Three Guineas* (Oxford: Blackwell, 1938)

Yao, Steven, *Translation and the Languages of Modernism: Gender, Politics, Language* (New York: Palgrave Macmillan, 2002)

Young, Robert, J. C., *Postcolonialism: A Very Short Introduction* (Oxford: Oxford University Press, 2003)

Zancan, Marina, *Il doppio itinerario della scrittura: la donna nella tradizione letteraria italiana* (Turin: Einaudi, 1998)

Zorat, Ambra, 'La poesia femminile italiana dagli anni settanta a oggi: percorsi di analisi testuale' (unpublished doctoral thesis, University Paris IV Sorbonne and the Università degli Studi di Trieste, 2008–09)

INDEX

Lightning Source UK Ltd.
Milton Keynes UK
UKHW012050121122
412052UK00004B/67

9 781781 886748